THE SARATOGA CAMPAIGN

The Saratoga Campaign

Uncovering an Embattled Landscape

WILLIAM A. GRISWOLD

DONALD W. LINEBAUGH

EDITORS

University Press of New England | Hanover and London

University Press of New England
www.upne.com
© 2016 University Press of New England
All rights reserved
Manufactured in the United States of America

Designed by April Leidig
Typeset in Caslon by Copperline Books Services

For permission to reproduce any of the material in this book,
contact Permissions, University Press of New England,
One Court Street, Suite 250, Lebanon NH 03766;
or visit www.upne.com

Library of Congress Cataloging-in-Publication Data
The Saratoga Campaign : uncovering an embattled landscape /
William A. Griswold and Donald W. Linebaugh, editors.
pages cm
Includes index.
ISBN 978-1-61168-896-2 (pbk.) — ISBN 978-1-61168-965-5 (ebook)
1. Saratoga Campaign, N.Y., 1777. 2. Saratoga National Historical Park
(N.Y.) — Antiquities. 3. Military archaeology — New York (State) —
Saratoga National Historical Park. 4. United States — History —
Revolution, 1775–1783 — Antiquities. I. Griswold, William A., editor,
author. II. Linebaugh, Donald W., editor, author.
E241.S2S268 2016
973.3'13 — dc23   2015036865

5 4 3 2 1

Contents

vii Acknowledgments

ix Introduction
Donald W. Linebaugh and William A. Griswold

CHAPTER ONE
1 The Coming Revolutionary War Battles at Saratoga
John Luzader

CHAPTER TWO
39 The Tactics of the Battles of Saratoga
Eric H. Schnitzer

CHAPTER THREE
81 The British Fortifications
Dean R. Snow

CHAPTER FOUR
105 The River Overlook Fortifications on Bemis Heights
William A. Griswold

CHAPTER FIVE
127 The American Fortifications
David R. Starbuck

CHAPTER SIX
145 The Retreat to Victory Woods
Matthew Kirk and Justin DiVirgilio

CHAPTER SEVEN
163 The Surrender and Aftermath of the Battles
Scott Stull, Michael Rogers, and Len Tantillo

CHAPTER EIGHT
179 The Schuyler House
David R. Starbuck

CHAPTER NINE

195 The Saratoga Battles in Fifty Artifacts
Christine Valosin

CHAPTER TEN

229 Commemorating and Preserving an Embattled Landscape
Donald W. Linebaugh

259 About the Contributors

263 Index

Acknowledgments

THE EDITORS WOULD LIKE to thank many individuals at the Saratoga National Historical Park for unconditional support toward the production of this work, especially retired Superintendent Joe Finan, without whose support this project would not have been possible. Others at the Park, including Chris Martin, chief of natural and cultural resources; Bill Valosin, park ranger; Eric Schnitzer, historian; Chris Valosin, curator; Gina Johnson, chief of interpretation; and Leslie Green, administrative officer, went above and beyond the call of duty to make this project possible. Publication of this book was funded in part by the Saratoga National Historical Park, Northeast Region Archaeology Program, National Park Service, and the University of Maryland School of Architecture, Planning, and Preservation.

Introduction

DONALD W. LINEBAUGH AND WILLIAM A. GRISWOLD

THE REVOLUTIONARY WAR battlefield near Saratoga, New York, has long been of interest to scholars, tourists, and the general public because of its military and political importance as a major turning point in the conflict. However, the relatively brief nature of the battle and ephemeral remains of the fortifications left few visible reminders of the hard-fought American victory. A landscape that was cultivated and farmed at the time of the battle quickly returned to agricultural uses when troops moved on to other engagements. As farming again took hold in this area, the earthen military features and surface evidence of the battles rapidly disappeared under the plow. Thus, it would be left to historians and archaeologists in later centuries to rediscover the physical layout and spatial organization of the battle lines and camps of the opposing British and American forces. What follows is the story of those investigations.

Starting in the nineteenth century, historians extensively documented British General John Burgoyne's campaign down the Hudson to crush the rebellion that was taking place within the former colonies. These scholars also deftly chronicled his ultimate defeat at Saratoga by General Horatio Gates and the American army. Because of the victory at Saratoga, France entered the war on the side of the Americans and ultimately aided their quest for independence. Given its military and political significance, the victory at Saratoga garnered considerable public interest.

By the early nineteenth century, the Revolutionary War battlefields and fortifications of the 1777 northern campaign, including Saratoga and Fort Ticonderoga, were becoming part of the increasingly popular "fashionable" or "northern" tour.[1] This route took visitors up the Hudson River to see the forts of the lower Hudson, between New York harbor and the river's confluence with the Mohawk River near Troy, New York; stopped in the fashionable resort of Saratoga Springs; and then traveled to the battlegrounds of Saratoga and Ticonderoga. However, unlike the picturesque ruins of Fort Ticonderoga to the north, the Saratoga battlefield had largely reverted to a landscape of farming by the 1830s. Visitors' reports from the 1820s indicate that the battlefield features, the camps, redoubts, and so on, were still visible but rapidly vanishing.[2] One traveler reported that "the plough has strove with invidious zeal, to destroy even these few remaining evidences of revolutionary heroism. Each succeeding year, the agriculturist turns afresh the sod of the weather-beaten breastworks."[3] With surface evidence fading, the only remaining indications of the battles were the plowed-up artifacts of war—bones, bullets, and cannonballs. However, even these relics proved finite as treasure hunters scoured the land.[4] It was reported in 1824 that "'some foolish mortals have dug holes' in the various redoubts, 'hoping to get treasure which they hope was buried' there."[5]

In a comment that applied equally well to the Saratoga battlefield, a travel writer reported in 1834 that the ruins of the nearby French and Indian War Fort William Henry "still exist as a monument of deeds long past; but those ruins are rapidly mouldering to decay, and soon traditions and History alone will be able to point to the spot, where they once stood."[6] While traditions and history were the only options available in the early nineteenth century for understanding the stories of sites like Fort William Henry and Saratoga, the relics and treasures spoken of by early visitors belie the potential for another approach—archaeology.

The present volume picks up on this suggestion, drawing on a multidisciplinary approach to examine the battles that took place at Saratoga, one that integrates not only traditional historical narratives, but also information derived from the now more than seventy years of archaeological and geophysical projects conducted at the park.[7] Thus, the stories in this volume expand, complement, and challenge the historical narratives of the battles.

As visitors began to descend on Saratoga in the 1820s, historical archaeology was nonexistent and archaeological inquiry into the prehistoric peoples of the Americas and the classical civilizations of the Mediterranean was still largely antiquarian and speculative in nature.[8] It was not until well into the second half of the nineteenth century that archaeology developed into a scholarly discipline, and yet another hundred years until historical archaeology was recognized as a legitimate subdiscipline. In fact, the formal organization of the discipline dates to the 1968 founding of the Society for Historical Archaeology. Although a scholarly and professional practice was long in coming, there were numerous early forays into historical archaeology, some of particular interest in terms of Saratoga and other Revolutionary War battlefields in New York and the region.[9]

During the early twentieth century, the use of historical archaeology was embraced by two remarkable amateur archaeologists from New York, William F. Calver and Reginald Pelham Bolton. Archaeologist Jacob Gruber writes that "amateurs like Calver and Bolton . . . so pushed their own enthusiasms that they can be said to have invented an historical archaeology" at a time when the academy had yet to embrace it.[10] Working on important military and domestic sites around New York City, these gentleman scholars demonstrated the value of archaeological research at historic sites, and their work went beyond simple collection and classification of artifacts to emphasize chronology and interpretation.[11] As noted previously for Saratoga, in a period when public exploration of farmland to collect ancient artifacts had reached faddist proportions, Calver, Bolton, and their Field Exploration Committee joined "the products of their controlled excavations with the documents of history in order to expand both the knowledge and the understanding of the human activity."[12] Of particular relevance to the Saratoga battlefield, Calver and Bolton's Field Exploration Committee rediscovered and excavated several Revolutionary War encampments in the Hudson highlands section of the Hudson River, north of New York City, that were part of the broader 1777 northern campaign.[13]

While of great interest in terms of offering an early example of the use of archaeology at military sites, particularly Revolutionary War battlefields, Calver and Bolton's work was a short aberration in the overall history of the discipline. Beyond the "treasure hunting" and collection of relics during much of the nineteenth and early twentieth centuries, it was not until the 1940s that archaeology was formally employed at the Saratoga battlefield. The work at Saratoga, while ultimately directed at obtaining information for interpretation at the new park and for the eventual reconstruction of structures that stood on the battlefield, was quite modern in many ways, examining the redoubts, battle lines, and camps across the embattled landscape.

In the early 1940s, archaeologist Robert W. Ehrich conducted the first professional archaeological excavations at the Saratoga battlefield. Working with Civilian Conservation Corps laborers in 1940 and 1941, Ehrich led an archaeological reconnaissance designed to "locate and assess any archaeological remains associated with the battle within the proposed boundary of the Park."[14] Ehrich also designed the survey to "assess the feasibility of a more comprehensive archeology program," and to provide data that would allow the restoration or reconstruction of battlefield features.[15] Ehrich and his staff investigated five areas within the park: American lines, west flank; American lines, east flank; British lines, east flank; Balcarres Redoubt; and Breymann Redoubt.[16]

At the American lines, west flank, Ehrich identified sections of what he recognized as a fortification ditch, postholes, and a possible artillery emplacement; artifacts included nails, animal bones, a brass buckle, brass button, and fragments of an iron vessel, all of which could have dated to military activities in the area.[17] In the area of the American lines, east flank, Ehrich's crew identified a zigzag stretch of a fortification ditch and a crescent-shaped ditch that he thought might be a "lunette outwork."[18]

Working at the British lines, east flank, Ehrich's excavations identified a long east-west-trending ditch filled with rich organic matter; this feature was thought to be a remnant of a detached fortification shown on Wilkinson's 1777 map. Artifacts from this area included nails and unidentified iron fragments, along with Native American projectile points and flakes that reflected the area's previous inhabitants.[19]

Excavations in the area of Balcarres Redoubt revealed "the locations of the eastern and western walls of the southern half of the Redoubt."[20] Ehrich also identified a "double burial within both the eastern and western ditches" along with a possible artillery emplacement. These excavations yielded many Revolutionary-period military artifacts, including bullets, canister, uniform hardware, and clay tobacco pipe fragments.[21]

Working around the Arnold monument (in its original location), Ehrich sought out evidence for the Breymann Redoubt. His work identified "vestiges of Revolutionary War–period fortifications"; two refilled pits, possibly a hearth and refuse pit; and an artillery emplacement.[22] Testing in this area produced likely Revolutionary War–period artifacts including bullets, canister shot, musket parts, and uniform hardware.

Although Ehrich's excavation work at Saratoga ended with his service in World War II, he went on to create an ambitious proposal for an ongoing archaeology program at the park.[23] In addition to further identifying and investigating battlefield features, Ehrich wrote that the work should help to "complement, contradict, or comment on the documentary evidence, and contribute to knowledge of such specialized fields as military history and 18th-century technology."[24]

John Cotter, one of the founding fathers of historical archaeology, also worked extensively at Saratoga in the late 1950s and 1960s. Over the course of several decades, while regional archaeologist for the National Park Service (NPS), Cotter conducted excavations within the park at the Neilson house, Freeman's farm, the Schuyler house, and in various areas along the tour road. This work is recorded in many reports available at the park and documents numerous forays into the evolving and developing subdiscipline of historical archaeology.[25]

Working at Fort Necessity in western Pennsylvania, pioneering historical archaeologist J. C. "Pinky" Harrington was also breaking new ground in terms of military archaeology during this period with his detailed excavations at this important French and Indian War site.[26] Harrington, often called the father of historical archaeology, had a background in both architecture and archaeology, a combination of skills that he put to good use excavating at Jamestown, Virginia, in the 1930s. Like Ehrich, Harrington's work as an NPS archaeologist was informed by thorough documentary research and his excavations sought to answer some specific questions about the fort's location, construction, and place in the military campaign. His thorough understanding of the documents and meticulous excavation techniques allowed Harrington to sort out and answer these questions as part of the bicentennial celebration for the fort in 1954. Harrington's investigations resulted in a new reconstruction of the fort, one grounded in clear physical evidence recovered through archaeology, and that firmly established the value of archaeology for examining military sites.

The stories told in the chapters that follow build on the excellent work of Ehrich and Cotter at Saratoga, and the clear precedents set by Harrington at Jamestown, Fort Necessity, and several other military sites. In a similar fashion to the work of the early Saratoga archaeologists, the stories in this volume languished in obscure technical reports on bookshelves or in file cabinets at Saratoga National Historical Park (NHP). Available only to scholars and park managers, these documents were created specifically to support park projects or programs designed to both protect and interpret the area's historical resources, work that drew on the expertise of historians, curators, and archaeologists. It is indeed fortuitous that a few of the individuals who wrote so much of this unpublished material were willing to contribute to the present volume and help bring research on the site dating back over half a century to a broader audience.

While the focus of this book is on the Saratoga battles, the area contains a vast number of archaeological sites, both prehistoric and historic, that represent occupation of the region before the battles at Saratoga. Mankind has been exploiting the vast resources of the area for thousands of years. Indeed, there are dozens of precontact, contact, and pre–Revolutionary War period sites within the Schuylerville-Stillwater corridor. In fact, there is so much prehistory and pre–Revolutionary War history in this area that a complete discussion must await a separate volume. Although the present volume focuses exclusively on the Revolutionary War battles at Saratoga, to fully appreciate the lead-up to and outcome of the battles, as well as the subsequent memorialization and commemoration activities, it is necessary to briefly consider the environmental setting and prewar history and landscape of this section of the Hudson River corridor.

The Setting

Although scholars do not generally view the local environment as the sole causal factor in deciding wars or shaping past cultures, the outcome of the Saratoga battles demonstrates the immense importance that topography and landscape can play in military engagements and other cultural exchanges. In fact, the landscape has emerged as an important scale of analysis for a variety of disciplines including archaeology, history, and military studies. As discussed in the following, the landscape and environment of the Saratoga region were utilized in different ways by various groups in the past. Prior to contact with the Europeans, Native Americans found the area to be rich in resources. Likewise, European settlers also discovered a rich landscape for exploitation. During the war, the British army extracted large quantities of natural resources over a short

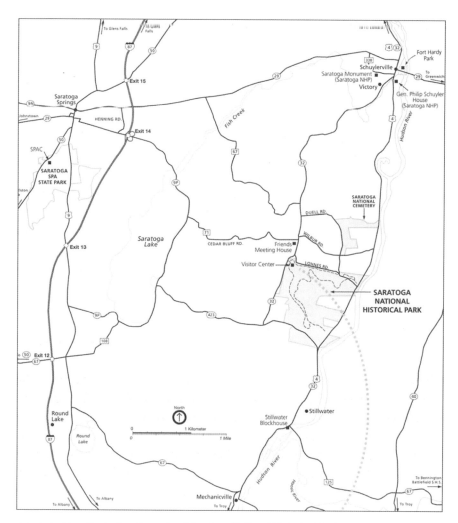

FIGURE I.1. Map illustrating the units of Saratoga National Historical Park. Courtesy of Saratoga National Historical Park.

period of time, quickly exhausting the land's resource potential. Similarly, the topographic advantages of the area along a major transportation corridor resulted in multiple conflicts over territory, resources, and political power across many centuries. As a result, varying expressions of people's former use of the environment are still evident on and below the surface. By combining the historical and archaeological records it is possible to more fully explore how the broader landscape helped to shape the American military victory at Saratoga.

The long-contested landscape that now forms Saratoga National Historical Park consists of four separate properties, the Schuyler house, Saratoga monument, and Victory Woods tracts and the large battlefield tract, stretching south from Schuylerville to Stillwater, New York (figure I.1). Saratoga National Historical Park was first authorized in 1927 as a New York State historic preserve on its sesquicentennial, and became part of the National Park Service in 1938. Located along the west bank of the Hudson River about forty-five miles north of Albany, New York, and fifteen miles east of Saratoga Springs, the park area provided the ideal setting for the battles of 1777, particularly in terms of topography and hydrology, as it did for the many conflicts that came before.

The Hudson River and high bluffs along its west bank at and north of Bemis Heights are the defining physiographic features in the park.[27] Flowing through the glaciated Allegheny plateau physiographic region, the Hudson cuts a "steep-sided valley whose high bluff tops would have been desirable places to its Native American [and later European] residents," providing well-drained settlement areas with access to both upland and riverine environments and access to a major north-south transportation route.[28] A series of glaciated ridges run parallel to the river and these ridges are dissected by ravines running west to east into the Hudson; several tributaries flow into the Hudson including Fish Creek at Schuylerville and Kroma Kill, Mill Creek, American's Creek, and Great Falls Creek near Stillwater. The narrow floodplain on the west bank between the bluffs and river and the steeply sloped ground on the eastern bank offered a restricted passage with clear military advantages. From high on the bluffs, the road running along the narrow floodplain and the river itself were easily guarded and movement along the river corridor could be restricted.

The geology of the region includes two formation types: bedrock deposits and unconsolidated deposits overlaying bedrock. While bedrock is exposed in some areas, particularly stream valleys, most of the area is overlain by several hundred feet of unconsolidated deposits that are glacial in origin.[29] The retreat of the Laurentian glacier from the area about 10,000 years ago left these unconsolidated deposits. The western portion of the park has unsorted glacial debris or till, often covered by gravel and sand deposits of glacial outwash. Gravel and sand deposits, averaging twenty-five feet in thickness, extend east to the bluffs overlooking the river. Along the river, recent alluvium has built up on the floodplain.[30]

The soils in the park area are quite variable with glacial deposits in the westernmost section of the park, clays and sands running up to the bluffs along the Hudson, and alluvium on the floodplain. Overall, the upland soils are fairly well drained and, although "considered to possess fair to poor agricultural potential," this area was being profitably cultivated by the mid-eighteenth century.[31] Portions of the upland area, part of the glacial Lake Albany plain, have sandy soils, while other sections contain clay and clayey loam soils.[32] The alluvial soils on the river floodplain are rich and well suited to farming; they have been cultivated by both Native Americans and European settlers for at least a thousand years.[33]

The flora of the park region was directly tied to climatic change as the glaciers retreated. Spruce forests developed across much of the area and by approximately 9,000 years ago were replaced by pine-dominated forests. Pine forests gradually became mixed with hardwoods and have developed to give us the present predominantly hardwood configuration. The upper Hudson, the section of the river north of its confluence with the Mohawk River, has been characterized by a northern hardwood forest, dominated by beech, birch, and sugar maple, for the past several centuries. Human influence began to significantly alter the landscape sometime before the seventeenth century when Native peoples began to burn and clear forest tracts for planting crops. Disease and depopulation due to interaction with Europeans left many cleared fields abandoned by the time of European settlement of the area. Forest clearing to create farms for agricultural use intensified with expanding European settlement, and by the mid-eighteenth century, farms dotted the region; much of the area, however, remained forested. By far, the biggest push in land clearance for agriculture came in the nineteenth century. So much so, that by 1877, the centennial year of the battles, more than 90 percent of the region was cleared.[34]

The fauna of the region was diverse and included a range of large- and medium-sized mammals, including deer, elk, black bear, and moose, and smaller mammals such as raccoon, beaver, otter, fox, and squirrels. Birds such as turkeys, ducks, hawks, and egrets also inhabited the area along with small reptiles like turtles and snakes. Finally, the Hudson and its tributaries were home to both freshwater and anadromous (seasonally migrating) fish including trout, bass, pickerel, pike, shad, herring, striped bass, and Atlantic salmon. Thus, the region was rich with food sources for Native occupants of the region as well as later European settlers.[35]

Prehistory

Although the Saratoga region is known first and foremost as the site of a major Revolutionary War battle, it has been occupied by humans for thousands of years. The area along the western bank of the Hudson contained narrow, well-drained, sandy floodplain terraces, particularly near the confluence of Fish Creek at Schuylerville, which provided ideal locations for fishing and settlement. Furthermore, natural springs in the area provided dependable sources of freshwater in the form of ponds and lakes. Although there is no evidence that Native Americans established long-term settlements along this portion of the Hudson, archaeological investigations suggest that the region was visited repeatedly by many different peoples.[36]

While fish runs in the Hudson provided an excellent source of food for pre-contact people during the spring, at other times of the year additional resources, including a variety of plants and animals for use as food as well as clothing, were likely sought in the adjacent upland environments. The archaeological evidence for the region points to numerous short-term encampments or logistical forays along the river as people moved about in their seasonal rounds.

While evidence of Paleo-Indian (12,000–9000 BP [before the present]) and Early Archaic (9000–3000 BP) occupations has been found up and down the Hudson, none of these sites are located in the immediate vicinity of the Saratoga battlefield.[37] Although earlier Native Americans lived and hunted in the upper Hudson River valley, sustained and growing populations did not become common until about 8,000 years ago.[38] Given the scant material evidence from this time period, it is likely that small groups of Native Americans periodically used the battlefield area as part of a much larger landscape from which to hunt and gather resources.

During the Late Archaic period (6000–3000 BP), more frequent visits were made to this portion of the Hudson, so the archaeology is "characterized by an increase in both the number of sites and the diversity of site locations."[39] Archaeologist Eric Johnson suggests an intensification of subsistence activities during this period, such as the "increasing use of shellfish and nuts, the construction of fishweirs, the use of controlled burning . . . and experimentation with the cultivation of indigenous plants."[40]

Archaeologist Robert Funk has reported that Woodland (3000 BP–AD 1600) materials are most commonly found along the main rivers of the Hudson drainage and are rarely found in the uplands.[41] Johnson notes that settlement patterns "reflect small, mobile residential units subsisting by hunting, gathering, and fishing" with some cultivation of indigenous plants (but not maize).[42] Settlement patterns suggest increasing permanence or sedentism in the Middle and Late Woodland.[43]

By the sixteenth century, the upper Hudson Valley was home to the Mahican (Mohican) Indians.[44] Prior to European contact, Mahican settlements consisted of small dispersed sites created by "foragers and fishermen who lived by an ecological sense of time" following "a well-established pattern of seasonal movement." Most settlements contained only a few dwellings and no large villages have been found to date.[45] Direct contact with European explorers in the upper Hudson Valley did not occur until the early seventeenth century.

In 1609, Henry Hudson explored the upper Hudson River, reporting on the region's Mahican people and describing their villages.[46] With a population estimated at about 5,000 at contact, the Mahicans are known to have inhabited villages near present-day Castleton, at Fort Orange, and near the confluence of the Mohawk and Hudson.[47] The closest known Mahican site to the Saratoga battlefields was located along Fish Creek.[48]

With the establishment of European settlement at Fort Orange (later Albany) in the 1620s and the beginning of trade with local Indians, hostilities increased between the Mahicans and the Mohawks, a Haudenosaunee or Iroquois people to the west.⁴⁹ In what was likely a continuing contest for control of this section of the upper Hudson River valley, the Mahicans "abandoned their lands on the west side of the Hudson, including, presumably, their settlement on Fish Creek" in 1628. It appears that the Mohawk soon began to use this territory for spring fishing.⁵⁰

Initial European Settlement

The area of the 1777 Saratoga battles was known as rich in resources by the earliest European explorers of the region, and, as witnessed during the contact period, was already a contested area because of its abundant resources and strategic location. Initial Dutch settlement, lasting from approximately 1624 to 1664, was characterized by scattered farmsteads and trading posts.⁵¹ Although the English took control of this embattled landscape in 1664, they did not earnestly settle the area until the early 1700s. In 1683, the land in the vicinity of what would become Schuylerville was part of a large land transaction known as the Saratoga Patent. A small group of investors led by Pieter Philip Schuyler purchased land in the vicinity of the present-day Schuyler house from a group of Native Americans that included Mohawk and Mahicans.⁵² The Schuyler family guided the development and settlement of this area over the next hundred years, especially as its strategic location became apparent to English colonial officials facing repeated French Canadian incursions. This strategic significance is evidenced by the multiple fortifications erected in the area to defend against attacks from the north.

To help protect the fledging settlement against the French and their Indian allies during King William's War (1689–97), the commissioners in Albany directed funds for the construction of a blockhouse, likely little more than a fortified house, near Fish Creek on the farm of Bartel Vrooman. Fort Vrooman, as it came to be known, was left to rot after settlers found the area too unsafe for habitation. In 1702, the Schuyler family attempted to increase settlement of the area by constructing a brick farmhouse, gristmill, and, later, a sawmill.⁵³ Another fortification was then raised on the east side of the Hudson River across from the Fish Creek during Queen Anne's War in 1709.⁵⁴

By 1721, with a new threat emerging from French Canada, Philip Livingston, another major patent holder, directed the construction of a larger fort, perhaps near the site of Fort Vrooman. Known as Fort Saratoga, the outpost was attacked and burned by the French in reprisal for the English capture of Louisburg in November 1745. In all, thirty settlers were killed and one hundred more captured during a raid known as the Saratoga Massacre. Subsequently rebuilt and renamed Fort Clinton, the fort continued to serve as an important English outpost against French incursions, although numerous settlers were killed and taken prisoner by the French. As a result of political infighting, the governor of the colony ordered the fort to be abandoned and burned in 1747.[55]

In 1757, Fort Hardy was built just east of the present village of Schuylerville on the flats below the area later named Victory Woods. A map of the fort and its environs depicts the Schuyler sawmill just below the hill of Victory Woods.[56] The map suggests the land may have been timbered for the mills, despite the fact the mill was not operational during the construction of the fort.[57] The Schuyler family increased their landholding in 1768 by purchasing over 4,000 acres along Fish Creek from the heirs of Robert Livingston.[58] Within the next few years, the British decommissioned Fort Hardy and dismantled the building, although apparently much of the defensive earthworks were still extant during the Revolutionary War.[59] As later explained by General Philip Schuyler, the family leased much of their holdings to tenants; their farmland likely included all of the fertile lands along Fish Creek and the Hudson.[60]

By the summer of 1777, the battlefield area was made up of small farms of about 100 to 150 acres each, leased from lot holders of the Saratoga Patent. Most of the farms had been occupied for less than fifteen years due to the hostility of the region. In general, Europeans settled the valleys along the Hudson River earlier than the upland areas around Saratoga because the river, trail, and road networks afforded an easy means of transportation. Early maps illustrate that there were dwellings and outbuildings scattered along the river lowlands from Half Moon (modern-day Waterford) north to the larger settlement at Saratoga (modern-day Schuylerville). By the 1760s, settlement of farms had been extended from the river flats areas to the upland areas of the Saratoga Patent between Stillwater and Saratoga. At the time of the battles in 1777, about 35 percent of the area that would make up the battlefield was cleared land in agriculture.[61]

The Battles of Saratoga

In the chapters that follow, contributors literally and figuratively sift through the September 19 and October 7, 1777, battles of Saratoga, drawing on their unique disciplinary perspectives. The story they tell by combining these multiple streams of evidence provides a deeper, more meaningful account of the battles than previously available. While history provides the backbone of the story, the multidisciplinary approach of archaeology, geophysics, and object studies enhances and expands the narrative, grounding it in the physical landscape.

Former Saratoga NHP historian John Luzader sets the stage for the Saratoga battles in chapter 1. Based on his extensive research and publications, including his book *Saratoga* (2008, 2010), the chapter brings together decades of study and historical investigation and contextualizes the political and military situation leading up to the battles. The stories of both the British and American sides are uncovered and retold by Luzader, as is the march to Saratoga by Burgoyne and his army.

Current Saratoga NHP historian Eric Schnitzer picks up the historical narrative in chapter 2 with a detailed tactical account of the battles. Whereas Luzader unpacks the broad political and military situation leading up to the engagements at Saratoga, Schnitzer focuses on the tactics and strategy of the individual battles. Schnitzer's nuanced understanding of the tactics of both the British and American soldiers comes from years of study, reconstructing the many twists and turns of both the September 19, 1777, Battle of Freeman's Farm and the October 7, 1777, Battle of Bemis Heights. The Battles of Saratoga were a closer and more equal fight than the outcome would suggest. Schnitzer analyzes the battle tactics and assesses the strengths and weaknesses of each side during the battles at Freeman's farm and on Bemis Heights.

The next six chapters connect the historical narratives of Luzader and Schnitzer to the battlefield landscape through geophysical and archaeological research and historical reconstruction. Chapter 3, written by archaeologist Dean Snow, is based on Snow's groundbreaking research in the park in the 1970s. Although discoveries by Snow were made in many areas of the park, his most impressive results came from the work on the British fortifications at both the Balcarres and Breymann Redoubts. Excavations at these sites uncovered not only evidence of the redoubts and their construction, including their shape, function, and strategic placement, but also information on the soldiers (and civilians) defending them.

Snow's work utilized aerial photo interpretation, magnetometry, and soil coring, cutting-edge archaeological methods in the 1970s. Snow and his colleagues at Pennsylvania State University are still conducting technically advanced research at the park, now involving the analysis of LiDAR data sets. LiDAR, or light detection and ranging, is a sophisticated method of measuring distance by light pulses to closely map landscape and archaeological features.

In chapter 4, archaeologist William Griswold further explores the American fortifications on Bemis Heights based on recent geophysical investigation of the River Overlook. Griswold uses archaeological, geophysical, and historical information to examine how the American fortifications were designed and built by the legendary Polish-born military engineer Thaddeus Kosciuszko. Building on Snow's earlier research and new geophysical and soil-coring results for the South Redan, the southernmost of the River Overlook fortifications, Griswold argues that the entire River Overlook was fortified by the Americans, supporting historical accounts that the physical and military bottleneck along the river made southward passage by Burgoyne untenable. This heavily fortified corridor ultimately left only the route to the west across the heights as a viable passage for

British troops. The largely sandy deposits on top of the River Overlook meant that Kosciuszko could quickly construct large, effective fortifications.

In chapter 5, archaeologist David Starbuck shares his discoveries at the American headquarters and hospital sites. Based on the results of archaeological field schools conducted through Rensselaer Polytechnic Institute in the 1980s, Starbuck presents the major finds associated with extensive trench excavation in the area of the American headquarters. While few military discoveries were made, foundations were uncovered that Starbuck has identified as the American headquarters and the American hospital buildings.

Almost a decade ago, extensive research was undertaken in Victory Woods, in Schuylerville (Old Saratoga) before the parcel was opened to the public as part of the park. This was the area to which Burgoyne and his troops retreated following the Saratoga battles. In chapter 6, archaeologists Matthew Kirk and Justin DiVirgilio discuss their excavation of and discoveries on this parcel and present results of a geophysical investigation of the property. Not only were features associated with the Revolutionary War and Burgoyne's retreat identified, but a large assemblage of Native American artifacts and features was also found.

Chapter 7 presents research on the Field of Grounded Arms, the area where the surrender of the British army actually took place. The field lay adjacent to the site of Fort Hardy, the French and Indian War supply fort discussed previously. Buried beneath a public park and ball field, the location and dimensions of both the Field of Grounded Arms and Fort Hardy became mired in uncertainty. Both locations have now been identified by archaeologists Scott Stull and Michael Rogers using a combination of archaeological and geophysical techniques, documentary evidence, historic maps, and landscape analysis. By establishing the layout of the fort during the French and Indian War, the authors determined the location of the Field of Grounded Arms based on documentary evidence, as the actual grounding of the weapons left no archaeological signature. The archaeological and documentary remains of Fort Hardy and of the field have been expertly rendered in three-dimensional displays by landscape reconstruction artist Len Tantillo, bridging the all-important gap between discovery and public dissemination of the information.

One of the most important cultural and archaeological resources in the park is the Schuyler house. Home to General Philip Schuyler, the first commander of the Northern army and one of the wealthiest landholders in the region, the dwelling is located in Schuylerville (Old Saratoga), south of Fish Creek. In chapter 8, David Starbuck discusses his archaeological campaigns on the Schuyler property. The general's grand estate was the setting for at least twenty buildings, including sawmills and a sizeable mansion house. Schuyler's fields of grain were cut down by Burgoyne's soldiers, his buildings were vandalized, and then the British burned down the house, mills, and outbuildings. The house that currently stands on the property is a "new" house built soon after the surrender of the British in October 1777, but is actually the third dwelling house on the property.

The Schuyler property was acquired by the National Park Service in 1950, and numerous archaeological excavations have been conducted by John Cotter, Edward Larrabee, and other Park Service researchers. Archaeological field schools, directed by Starbuck, were conducted on the property in the 1980s. Starbuck concisely summarizes what is currently known about the house and property through the numerous archaeological excavations.

Chapter 9 presents a unique view of Saratoga through a curatorial lens. Saratoga NHP currently manages the data from more than twenty-five different archaeology projects from the park's battlefield and Old Saratoga units. In fact, excluding archival collections, more than 90 percent of the museum collections at Saratoga NHP are archaeological in nature. Saratoga NHP curator Christine Valosin takes the reader on a tour of the collections housed at the park, rendering the history of the battles in fifty objects. Beginning with the archaeological collections made from the various farms that constituted the battlefield (Neilson, Freeman, and Taylor sites), Valosin continues with an examination of the collections at the Schuyler house. In addition to the collections made on the various farms, Valosin presents material evidence from both the British and American fortifications and encampments. As discussed in the final chapter, the collection of battlefield artifacts and memorabilia began soon after the conflict ended, and has continued to the present. Some extraordinary information comes from genealogical research and provenance of the items that have come into the collection through donations.

Finally, in chapter 10, archaeologist and historian Donald Linebaugh examines the early national curiosity about the battle and its later recognition, memorialization, and commemoration, activities that began shortly after the battle ended and were spurred on with the passing of the Revolutionary generation. Linebaugh traces visits to the site by early tourists to the Hudson River valley, examines the movement to commemorate the site and erect a monument, explores the various celebrations of major battle anniversaries, and presents the formation of the state and subsequent national park. In so doing, he looks at the important connections between archaeology and commemoration in terms of the physical and tangible marking of the battle sites.

This collection gathers and presents the most up-to-date information that we have about the battles at Saratoga from work conducted at the park during the past half century. Previous studies of the battles have drawn almost exclusively from historical documents to portray the battles. Seeking to infuse new understanding to a contested landscape, the authors draw on multiple disciplines and new data to deepen our knowledge of and appreciation for the battles at Saratoga.

NOTES

1. Dona Brown, *Inventing New England: Regional Tourism in the Nineteenth Century* (Washington, DC: Smithsonian Institution Press, 1995), 23.

2. Thomas A. Chambers, *Memories of War: Visiting Battlefields and Bonefields in the Early American Republic* (Ithaca, NY: Cornell University Press, 2012), 47–48.

3. "General Hoyt's Visit to the Battle Ground in 1825," in *Visits to the Saratoga Battle Grounds, 1780–1880*, ed. William L. Stone (Albany, NY: Munsell, 1895), 190, 196, and 199.

4. Chambers, *Memories of War*, 48.

5. "Diary of a Scot," quoted in Chambers, *Memories of War*, 48.

6. "Journey through NY State and Upper and Lower Canada, 1834," 219–22, New-York Historical Society (hereafter N-YHS).

7. Geophysics is an academic discipline that uses various scientific instruments to sense anomalies below the surface of the earth. Archaeologists use a selected group of these instruments to find archaeological features.

8. See Gordon R. Willey and Jeremy A. Sabloff, *History of American Archaeology* (London: Thames and Hudson, 1974).

9. See Donald W. Linebaugh, *The Man Who Found Thoreau: Roland W. Robbins and the Rise of Historical Archaeology in America* (Hanover, NH: University Press of New England, 2005).

10. Jacob W. Gruber, "Artifacts Are History: Calver and Bolton in New York," in *The Scope of Historical Archaeology: Essays in Honor of John L. Cotter*, ed. David G. Orr and Daniel G. Crozier, 13–27 (Philadelphia: Temple University, Laboratory of Anthropology, 1984), 18.

11. Ibid., 17.

12. Ibid., 19. The Field Exploration Committee, formed by Bolton and Calver and members of the New-York Historical Society, was among the first organizations engaged in research in historical archaeology.

13. William Louis Calver and Reginald Pelham Bolton, *History Written with Pick and Shovel: Military Buttons, Belt-Plates, Badges and Other Relics Excavated from Colonial, Revolutionary, and War of 1812 Camp Sites by the Field Exploration Committee of the New-York Historical Society*, 1950, N-YHS.

14. Eric Johnson, *Archaeological Overview and Assessment of the Saratoga National Historical Park New York* (Lowell, MA: National Park Service, New England System Support Office, 1997), 32.

15. Ibid.
16. Ibid.
17. Ibid., 33.
18. Ibid., 34.
19. Ibid.
20. Ibid., 35.
21. Ibid.
22. Ibid., 36.
23. Ibid.

24. Ibid.

25. Ibid., 38–58.

26. J. C. Harrington, *New Light on Washington's Fort Necessity: A Report on the Archeological Explorations at Fort Necessity National Battlefield Site* (Richmond, VA: Eastern National Park and Monument Association, Pennsylvania, 1957).

27. The editors have chosen to use the spelling *Bemis* throughout the volume to be consistent with current usage on maps and NPS signage. Some historical documents suggest the eighteenth-century spelling was *Bemus*.

28. Johnson, *Archaeological Overview and Assessment*, 7.

29. Ibid., 7.

30. Ibid., 8.

31. Ibid.

32. W. Broad, *Soil Survey of Greene County, New York* (Washington, DC: United States Department of Agriculture, Soil Conservation Service, in cooperation with Cornell University Agricultural Experiment Station, Catskill, NY, 1993).

33. Johnson, *Archaeological Overview and Assessment*, 8–10.

34. Ibid., 10.

35. Ibid., 10–11.

36. Robert E. Funk, *Recent Contributions to Hudson Valley Prehistory*, New York State Museum, Memoir 22 (Albany: University of the State of New York, State Education Department, 1976), 27. Funk conducted extensive excavations and analysis of Native American sites within the Hudson River valley during the 1970s.

37. Dean R. Snow, *The Archaeology of New England* (New York: Academic Press, 1980), 4; Johnson, *Archaeological Overview and Assessment*, 12, 19.

38. R. L. Aston, "Evidence of Paleo-Indian and Early Archaic Occupation in Washington County, New York," *The Bulletin: Journal of the New York State Archaeological Association* 107 (1994): 20–24; R. E. Funk and J. Walsh, "Evidence of Late-Paleo-Indian Occupation at Saratoga Lake, New York," *The Bulletin: Journal of the New York State Archaeological Association* 96 (1988): 1–4; M. A. Levine. "New Evidence for Postglacial Occupations in the Upper Hudson Valley," *The Bulletin: Journal of the New York State Archaeological Association* 98 (1989): 5–12.

39. Johnson, *Archaeological Overview and Assessment*, 16.

40. Ibid. For example, a site at the confluence of Fish Creek and the Hudson River, dating from the Late Archaic to early Middle Woodland, contains midden deposits typical of a repeatedly used location for spring anadromous (spring-spawning) fishing; H. J. Brumbach, "Anadromous Fish and Fishing: A Synthesis of Data from the Hudson River Drainage," *Man in the Northeast* 32 (1986): 35–66.

41. Funk, *Recent Contribution to Hudson Valley Prehistory*, 278.

42. Johnson, *Archaeological Overview and Assessment*, 18.

43. H. J. Brumbach and S. J. Bender, "Winney's Rift: A Late Woodland Village Site in the Upper Hudson River Valley," *The Bulletin: Journal of the New York State Archaeological Association* 92 (1986): 1–8. Several archaeological sites along Fish Creek contain evidence of increased occupation during both cold and warm seasons; Johnson, *Archaeological Overview and Assessment*, 18.

44. Robert S. Grunet, *Historic Contact: Indian Peoples and Colonists in Today's Northeastern United States in the Sixteenth through Eighteenth Centuries* (Norman: University of Oklahoma Press, 1995), 164.

45. James W. Bradley, *Before Albany: An Archeology of Native-Dutch Relations in the Capital Region, 1600–1664*, New York State Museum Bulletin 509 (Albany: State University of New York, State Education Department, 2007), 8–9.

46. Johnson, *Archaeological Overview and Assessment*, 19.

47. Snow, *Archaeology of New England*.

48. Johnson, *Archaeological Overview and Assessment*, 19.

49. Ibid., 19.

50. Ibid.

51. Ibid., 20.

52. T. Holmes and L. Smith-Holmes, *Saratoga: America's Battlefield* (Charleston, SC: The History Press, 2012), 20.

53. Holmes and Smith-Holmes, *Saratoga*, 21; C. L. Stevens, L. White, W. A. Griswold, and M. C. Brown, *Cultural Landscape Report and Archaeological Assessment for Victory Woods, Saratoga National Historical Park, Saratoga, New York* (Boston: US Department of the Interior, National Park Service, 2007), 39.

54. Holmes and Smith-Holmes, *Saratoga*, 15–17.

55. Ibid.

56. Stevens et al., *Cultural Landscape Report and Archaeological Assessment*, 39.

57. Ibid., 31.

58. Ibid., 32.

59. Ibid., 31.

60. R. M. Ketchum, *Saratoga: Turning Point of America's Revolutionary War* (New York: Henry Holt, 1997), 23.

61. Stephen Olausen, Kristen Heitert, Laura Kline, and Carey Jones, *National Register of Historic Places Nomination Form* (Saratoga, NY: Saratoga National Historical Park, 2011), 5.

THE SARATOGA CAMPAIGN

CHAPTER ONE | JOHN LUZADER

The Coming Revolutionary War Battles at Saratoga

GEOGRAPHY DICTATED the Champlain-Hudson corridor's strategic primacy, and its importance was not limited to the water route between Montreal and New York City. Approximately fifteen miles east of Montreal is the junction of the corridor's northern segment, the Richelieu River with the St. Lawrence; the Richelieu is also Lake Champlain's outlet. Thus, an army operating from the St. Lawrence could ascend the river, cross the lake from north to south and emerge within less than twenty miles of the Hudson River at Fort Edward. From Fort Edward it is just forty miles to the old Dutch town of Albany, near where the Mohawk River, gateway to Iroquois country, joins the Hudson. To reach New York City from Albany is a trip of another 156 miles. Informed men on both sides of the Atlantic recognized the importance of the Champlain-Hudson corridor for accomplishing the strategic isolation of New England. Cutting off New England, known to the English as the "cradle of sedition," would allow England to stamp out the colonial revolt. Strategic isolation neither implied nor required physically sealing the region from all contacts with the middle and southern provinces, an obvious impossibility. What the strategists in Whitehall intended was severing access for the large rebel armies and their supplies, to keep them from threatening the rear of British forces operating in the American interior. As historian Piers Mackesy explains: "British control of the Hudson would have been disastrous. Permanent control of the whole length of the river was unnecessary, for if the British held the Highlands they could use the waterway beyond at any time, and cut the last link in Washington's lateral communications. His supplies and reinforcements would have been strangled with decisive effect."[1]

The British View

The Champlain-Hudson corridor's importance was central to both the doomed American invasion of Canada in 1775 and British General Sir Guy Carleton's aborted 1776 invasion of the American northern frontier. After abandoning the invasion, Sir Guy gave his subordinate General John Burgoyne a memorandum to deliver to Lord George Germain, secretary of state for the American colonies and the member of Lord North's cabinet responsible for directing the American war.[2] Burgoyne was returning to England to attend Parliament and tend to the deaths of his wife and father-in-law, arriving in London the night of December 9, 1776. That memorandum contained general proposals and requisitions for a renewed northern offensive, and Carleton recommended Burgoyne to Lord Germain as a source of firsthand information. However, Lord Germain had already received a plan from the ranking British general in America, General Sir William Howe, that not only preceded but fundamentally affected plans for a renewed northern offensive.

On November 30, 1776, while General Washington's demoralized men retreated across New Jersey, Sir William Howe, recently knighted for his victory on Long Island, composed two letters to Lord Germain. The first reported the details of the recent Westchester fighting and Fort Lee's capture. The second notified the colonial minister that he intended quartering a force in "East Jersey," and that he expected Washington to establish a defensive line on either the Delaware or Raritan River to protect Philadelphia. More important to later events at Saratoga, Howe proposed a plan for a 1777 campaign. He had learned that Sir Guy Carleton had aborted his advance down the Champlain-Hudson corridor, but expected him to renew that drive in the spring and projected reaching Albany in September 1777, a reasonable estimation.

Howe offered a plan he believed might "finish the War in one year by an extensive and vigorous Exertion of His Majesty's arms." He intended to continue operations against New England with two simultaneous offensives: one moving from Rhode Island against Boston, and another moving from New York City up the Hudson to rendezvous with Carleton's anticipated advance from Canada. He also proposed a third campaign moving against Washington in New Jersey to exploit American fears for Philadelphia. He "proposed to attack [Philadelphia] in the Autumn, as well as Virginia, provided the success of the other operations will admit of an adequate force to be sent against that province." Howe's initial proposal required 35,000 men and ten additional ships of the line to guarantee success against the 50,000 men the Continental Congress had resolved to raise.[3] Providing 35,000 rank-and-file soldiers would require hiring 15,000 men from Russia or a German state.

Sir William's second letter to the secretary of state reflected a significant strategic assumption that only the hope for French help kept the rebellion alive. If, he reasoned, the threat of that support were neutralized and the force he proposed was "sent out, it would strike such Terror through the Country, that no Resistance would be made to the Progress of His Majesty's Arms in the Provinces of New England, New York, the Jerseys & Pennsylvania, after the junction of Northern and Southern Armies." Howe's ultimate objective continued to be recovery of territory rather that the destruction of the rebel army. Like Henry Clinton and unlike Lords Cornwallis and Germain, Howe believed that victory ultimately required expansion of the area of imperial control, meaning that he sought to retake only so much territory as he expected to be able to occupy. The royal army's presence, he argued, would enable the loyal majority to declare itself, organize loyalist corps, and assume an expanding participation in restoring imperial authority.[4] Britain's senior commander in the thirteen colonies expected to be victorious by moving with overwhelming power through centers of rebellion, "relying upon overawing the disaffected, animating the loyal, and demonstrating to the wavering the futility of resistance, rather than upon hard and costly fighting against an elusive and resilient adversary."[5]

Sir William's correspondence reached Germain on December 30, 1776, and the Cabinet began discussing the letters on January 10, 1777. Like most Britons, the ministers expected an early victory in America, and the general's first letter endorsed that optimism, setting the tone for responding to the second. Because the general's strategic proposals for 1777 did nothing to dispel the prevailing euphoric view of a short conflict, Lord North's colleagues approved them. However, his projection of manpower requirements made them uneasy, and Germain's letter to Howe of January 14 reflected that disquiet.

A compulsion for reassurance produced a body of correspondence marked by wishful thinking, ambiguity, and flawed interpretation of critical information. The Cabinet members persuaded themselves that a reinforcement of 15,000 troops would increase Howe's strength to about 42,000 men, more than the 35,000 he said he needed. A failure to analyze returns from the field provided the ministers with what seemed like a good basis for believing that a 7,000-man reinforcement would bring Howe's strength to nearly 34,000 troops.[6]

Howe's goal of recovering only as much territory as he could effectively occupy, and thus his estimate of the needed reinforcements, presupposed garrisoning occupation troops in the regained regions. In brief, the strategy for defeating the rebellious colonists required a continuing expansion of military reconquest until all the colonies were restored to the British Empire. This implied that with tactical success, more men would be required to occupy the regained territory and, simultaneously, continue campaigning against areas still in rebellion.

Whitehall delayed official comment on Sir William's strategic plans until after Lord North's ministers learned more about the American situation at year's end. Lord Germain informed Howe that judgment was suspended until "His Majesty . . . shall have an Opportunity of taking into consultation the whole State of this Momentous Affair."[7]

While the government in London struggled to develop a strategy, the situation in America changed. On December 20, ten days before his November 30 letters reached London, Howe sent Germain a new plan for 1777, responding to a dramatically different situation. As discussed in more detail below, Howe's army had pursued Washington across New Jersey to the Delaware-Pennsylvania line, making the American capital at Philadelphia enticingly vulnerable; the rebellion seemed to be stumbling toward collapse. People were daily forswearing their treasonous acts and seeking pardons that would restore their allegiance with Great Britain. Those persisting in their disloyalty were finding it increasingly difficult to maintain the revolt's momentum.[8]

Both British and American strategists knew that Pennsylvania and its neighbors were critically important to the success of their causes. The region was politically and economically mature, consisting of a relatively well-informed, prosperous citizenry that included a larger proportion of men of liberal views than any other region. Philadelphia was America's major port, a lively cultural and financial center, the empire's third-largest city, and since the autumn of 1774, the Revolution's political capital.

Pennsylvanians and their neighbors were less militantly hostile to imperial policies than Virginians and New Englanders. Their diversified economy was less vulnerable to parliamentary measures, and many people sensed that they profited from membership in the empire. Recalling the painful nature of breaking imperial ties, William Livingston reported that residents of the Middle Colonies "had themselves suffered little, if at all, under imperial rule. . . . Under it they had prospered and multiplied." Colonists living in the pluralistic middle of British North America already enjoyed, to an important degree, the kind of economic and political society that other Americans aspired to, and it had become a reality without a revolution. In spite of articulate and reasoned opposition, an effective majority favoring resistance to imperial rule developed with difficulty.[9]

Because Howe believed that American reverses in New York and New Jersey enhanced opposition to rebellion, he reasoned that threatening Philadelphia would force an elusive Washington to stand and give battle, bringing British victory within his grasp. Howe wrote:

> [T]he opinion of the people being much changed in Pennsylvania, and their minds in general, from the progress of the army, disposed to peace, in which Sentiment they would be confirmed by our getting possession of

Philadelphia, I am from this consideration fully persuaded the Principal Army should act offensively on that side where the enemy's strength will certainly be collected.[10]

Changing the order of priorities required delaying the New England offensive until after reinforcements arrived from Europe, so "that there might be a corps to act offensively on the lower part of Hudson's River to cover Jersey and facilitate in some degree the approach of the Canada army."[11] The 3,000 men committed to that effort could do little to support action on the northern frontier, but Howe did not expect that it would be needed before September, by which time events in America and reinforcements from Europe would have enhanced British capabilities. Sir William's December 20 letter departed from assumptions upon which British strategy had been founded since 1775. Instead of concentrating power against New England, he proposed letting the army from Canada force its way southward, while he overran the middle states, captured Philadelphia, and ended organized rebellion.[12]

Before the Cabinet had received *either* of the general's proposed plans, events in New Jersey took a dramatic turn that destroyed the optimism on which Howe predicated those plans, forcing him to reorder his priorities. With desperation-inspired audacity, George Washington attacked and captured most of Howe's German troops at Trenton during the morning of December 26, defeated General Lord Cornwallis's rear guard at Princeton on January 3, and pulled off a superbly executed retreat to the hills around Morristown. Washington's army, emerging from near dissolution, survived and retook West Jersey.[13]

Ignorant of the events that made Washington's triumphs at Trenton and Princeton immortal in military history, Germain wrote to Howe on January 14, 1777, that he could view 1776 with justifiable satisfaction. His efforts to date had raised, equipped, and transported large armies to North America. Canada was securely British, Manhattan and Long Island were reclaimed, and, so far as he knew, New Jersey and Rhode Island were safe. The rebellion seemed ready to collapse and Britain close to winning. Ironically, Great Britain was actually closer to winning the war in America than it ever would be again.

Failure to end the war during 1776 exposed the empire to perils that only strategic victory in 1777 could dispel. Britain's commitment of so much of its military resources to North America was a bold, calculated gamble taken in the face of France's hostility. In the presence of that danger, ending the war before Britain's European neighbors could intervene was critical. That the rebellion was almost crushed was not good enough; its decisive defeat had to be accomplished quickly because French conduct during 1776 made it clear that European peace depended upon an early British victory. France had inched toward war throughout the summer, looking for an opportunity to recover interests and power lost during the Seven Years' War. Achieving those ends depended on events in America. Would Albion and its rebellious children reconcile? Could the rebels continue their fight? When Howe succeeded on Manhattan, seemingly answering the second question in the negative, France retreated from internationalizing the war, yet England still needed an early, unequivocal victory to make that withdrawal permanent.

Washington's New Jersey victories were the war's most important turning point. Coming after an unbroken series of defeats, the victories revived the languishing rebellion and dismayed loyalists who had anticipated an early end to the conflict, which would have confirmed their decision to remain loyal to the empire. With Washington's victories, the value of Continental currency recovered and military morale, which had approached near collapse, rebounded immediately. As a result, recruiting parties enrolled new companies in Virginia, Pennsylvania, and Delaware. Observant Europeans, especially in France, began to believe that the rebellion, which after American reverses on Long Island and Manhattan had appeared to be doomed, might be worth encouraging and exploiting.[14]

The effect of the phoenix-like American recovery on Sir William Howe was immediate and profound, dooming his and his brother Admiral Lord Richard Howe's peace efforts. The weaknesses in their pacification-grounded strategies now stood exposed. Sir William, who on December 20 confidently predicated his plans for the next campaign on exploiting American longings for peace, eleven days later predicted that achieving victory would require another major campaign.[15]

By mid-January, intensifying pessimism led Howe to the unwelcome conclusion that he did not "now see a prospect for terminating the war but by a general action and I am aware of the difficulties in our way to obtain it, as the Enemy moves with so much more celerity than we can. . . ." A "general action" was needed to engage Washington's revived army and would require substantial reinforcements. Twenty thousand additional troops would not be excessive, but he could make do with 15,000; the larger number would enable him to advance against Pennsylvania by both land and water. The main force could operate through New Jersey, while the balance of his men would ascend the Delaware River. The larger number would also enable Howe to post a sufficient force in Rhode Island to raid New England.[16]

General Howe anticipated that any plan for 1777 would include renewing aggressive action in the Champlain-Hudson corridor. As noted previously, Sir Guy Carleton sent a brief draft of just such a plan by way of John Burgoyne when the latter returned to London in December 1776. In his memorandum, Sir Guy requested a 4,000-man augmentation, part of which he intended to use to increase his regiments' strength by one hundred men each, enabling him to detach "a large Corps . . . to operate upon the Mohawk River" and, possibly, to "penetrate to [the] Connecticut River." His main force would cross Lake Champlain southward to retake Fort Ticonderoga, join with the Mohawk column, and set up a base from which to attack Massachusetts and Connecticut.[17] He clearly intended to carry out this strategy without help from troops stationed in the lower Hudson.[18] Carleton's memorandum consisted of a few short sentences on a single sheet of paper, little more than a first draft that he asked Burgoyne to enlarge upon. The latter did so during his homeward voyage in a sixteen-page paper titled "Memorandum & Observations relative to the Service in Canada."[19]

On another note, a very disgruntled General Henry Clinton returned to London from North America, not with a plan for 1777, but with aspirations for a new command. Clinton was currently serving under Howe in the New York area. He was the son of former royal governor of New York and kinsman of the Duke of Newcastle. General Henry Clinton returned to London with two objectives. The first was to secure redress for an affront that he believed the colonial minister had published in the *Gazette* concerning Clinton's conduct during the recent Carolina expedition. A second and even more cherished objective for Clinton was a command that would release him from serving under Sir William Howe. By the end of 1776, Clinton knew that he disliked Howe, with whose strategy and tactics he had fundamentally disagreed during the New York City campaign. As previously noted, Howe focused on taking territory with a minimum of risk to troops, a strategy precluding an early decision at arms. Clinton, by contrast, favored aggressive tactics that included concentrating troops to attack and destroy the enemy's army. The only time that Howe had accepted Clinton's proposed strategy, and then reluctantly, was during the fight for Long Island, when he led the main assault around Washington's left wing. This was an aggressive, enveloping assault that carried the British behind the American center and produced arguably the most brilliant imperial success of the war. Henry Clinton wanted no more duty under a commander who gave him the most onerous tasks, rejected his advice, and squandered the fruits of his performance.[20]

The political climate in England seemed to favor Clinton. The Cabinet blamed Howe for the state of affairs resulting from Washington's stunning recovery at Trenton and Princeton. The opposition would have grist for its mill if conditions on the battlefront became common knowledge, and Clinton had it in his power to embarrass the North administration by raising questions about Howe's management of the recent campaign. Refraining from doing this, Clinton's public statements were prudent and his letter to the *Public Advertiser* minimized Washington's achievements and represented prospects for a British victory as being better than they appeared to be.[21]

Clinton was, indeed, in a strong position to command the next northern invasion, as he was Burgoyne's senior and enjoyed the King's favor. In fact, on February 24, four days before Burgoyne's arrival at Whitehall, George III informed

Lord North that he intended to propose Clinton for the northern command and Burgoyne for his replacement as Howe's second.[22] While the post seemed his for the asking, Clinton did not ask.

The ministry eventually offered Clinton the Canadian military command, demoting Carleton to civil governor. It was an attractive offer to a man who longed for an independent command; however, out of regard for Carleton, he rejected it.[23] He thus faced two unattractive alternatives: resignation or return to service under Howe. The King would not consent to his retirement. In the end, receipt of the Order of the Bath sweetened the deal for Clinton, returning the newly invested knight to Howe's staff with a dormant commission to succeed Sir William should he resign or become incapacitated. With that, Clinton's enthusiasm for publicizing interesting dispatches relating to the failed Carolina campaign waned.[24]

In the meantime, John Burgoyne submitted a detailed memorandum to the colonial secretary, "Thoughts for Conducting the War from the Side of Canada," that offered alternative proposals for realizing the objectives of Carleton's 1776 campaign.[25] He introduced no strategic novelties, but offered proposals for continuing the strategy that had informed imperial planning since 1775.

The first objective of Burgoyne's new campaign would be securing the navigation of Lake Champlain, the failure of which had doomed Carleton's 1776 campaign. Reoccupying the abandoned fort at Crown Point would provide the base of operations for retaking Fort Ticonderoga in early summer, which would "become a more proper place for arms than Crown Point." Possession of Fort Ticonderoga, the "Gibraltar of the North," would secure control of the lake. Subsequent decisions depended upon two important factors: actions taken by the Americans and "the general plan concerted at home." If the general plan provided for Sir William Howe's committing his entire force to a Hudson River offensive and Burgoyne's mission was to "effect a junction with that force," he proposed advancing south to Albany via Lake George.[26] Because he assumed that the Americans would appreciate that lake's military significance, he expected them "to be in force upon the lake." If they remained there in force, he would need to leave "a chain of posts as the army advanced to secure communication with Canada," constituting a serious strain on his limited manpower. He was realistic enough to suggest an alternative to aggressive land operations by proposing that his army have the capacity for advancing by water, obviously profiting from Carleton's experiences at Valcour Island the previous year.

A possible alternative strategy would entail operating directly against New England by joining along the Connecticut River with corps from Rhode Island. Should that junction be effected, "it would not be too sanguine an expectation that all New England provinces will be reduced by their operation." He also suggested that a secondary offensive along the Lake Ontario–Mohawk River corridor would provide "a diversion to facilitate every proposed operation."

More radical was the suggestion that if the force committed to invading the northern frontier was too small

> for proceeding upon the above ideas with a fair prospect of success, the alternative remains of embarking the army at Quebec, in order to effect a junction with General Howe by the sea, or be employed separately to cooperate with the main designs, by such means as should be within their strength upon other parts of the Continent. . . . This last measure ought not be thought of, but upon positive conviction of necessity.[27]

Only a strategic situation much more desperate than that existing could justify invoking this alternative. While he was a congenital optimist, Burgoyne was not so irresponsible as to be oblivious to potential problems.

The "Thoughts" did not anticipate physically isolating New England with a cordon of forts from Canada to New York City, an objective exceeding the British army's capabilities. Tactical success along that frontier might strategically quarantine the rebellion's birthplace, but that would be a by-product of the campaign's real purpose, making a powerful force in America's interior available to General Howe to execute whatever plan the ministry in Whitehall eventually adopted.

Once Fort Ticonderoga was again secured, the general plan would identify objectives and define tactics in a document prescribing how Burgoyne and Howe would cooperate to achieve a common objective. The closest Burgoyne came to articulating a strategic purpose was when he wrote that the basic assumption of his proposals was that the expedition's only purpose was joining Howe, or "after cooperating so far as to get possession of Albany and open communication with New York to remain upon Hudson's River, and thereby enable that general to act with his whole force to the southward." Burgoyne intended to act in concert with Sir William, but he did not anticipate the specific objectives, leaving that decision to the King and Cabinet.

Burgoyne's native optimism did not blind him to the problems that both the Champlain-Hudson environment and American forces might pose. He expected the enemy to invest heavily in defending Fort Ticonderoga, whose works could accommodate 12,000 men; post a flotilla on Lake George; and block the country's primitive roads by felling trees, destroying bridges, and constructing fortifications; his service in America had demonstrated to him American skill in the last. Expecting nature and the enemy to conspire against his success, Burgoyne proposed a force of at least 8,000 regulars, 2,000 Canadians, 1,000 Indians, a corps of watermen, and a powerful train of artillery.

King George III took very seriously his prerogative of captain-general. Relying on the professional assistance of General Lord Jeffrey Amherst and Adjutant General Edward Harvey, he responded to Burgoyne's proposals in "Remarks on the Conduct of the War from Canada." That he gave the matter close personal attention is reflected in the detailed, handwritten comments made about the proposals' contents. The king assigned the campaign its purpose when he wrote that "the force from Canada must join [Howe] at Albany," underlining his words.[28]

While the King had given the army in Canada its mission, the question remained as to who would command that army when it renewed Britain's northern campaign. Sir Henry Clinton briefly seemed the likely choice, as he clearly wanted the assignment, was Burgoyne's senior, enjoyed the King's favor, and had powerful friends. But Lord North's ministry preferred Burgoyne and on March 1, Burgoyne received command of forces to invade New York from Canada.[29]

George III had assigned the Canada army its mission, and the Cabinet had named its commander. But the ministers had yet to develop a plan for how Britain's commanders in America would engage their adversaries. Even before the King penned his "Remarks," he began drafting a strategic mandate that responded to Howe's optimistic December 20 letter and to Burgoyne's royally endorsed "Thoughts." Before he could complete his draft, however, he received Sir William's pessimistic correspondence, reflecting Howe's reaction to the changed strategic situation produced by Trenton and Princeton.

The colonial minister was unable to reconcile the inherent contradictions in the general's plans in terms of assumptions, strategic goals, and resources. In a state of helplessness, he took refuge in ambiguity, informing General Howe that the King was delaying a response to his plan and that he was

> now commanded to acquaint you that the King entirely approves your proposed Deviation from the Plan which you formerly suggested being of the Opinion that Reasons which have induced to recommend this Change in your Operations are solid and decisive.[30]

The King had reduced Burgoyne's projected alternatives to a single royal mandate to join with Howe at Albany, and it remained for the ministry and generals to execute it. Critical to the plan's implementation was commissioning a commander to lead the army from Canada. That man would have to guide his army to Albany and once there would become Sir William's ranking subordinate.

Conflicting strategic priorities complicated the Cabinet's general plan for 1777. General Howe believed that concentrating on the Middle Colonies, capturing the American capital, and limiting territorial acquisition to what could be governed was essential to victory. The King persisted in viewing New England as the rebellion's center, having a healthy respect for Yankee intellectual, military, and maritime potential. Lord Germain transmitted George III's recommendation that the Howe brothers remember to take operations against New England into "serious consideration, so far as Plan will permit," but he was more than just the King's mouthpiece. He was the man most involved in developing and articulating the plan for 1777, helping form the Crown's perceptions, and authoring the general plan "concerted at home."

Although the colonial secretary brought to his task devotion to duty, tenacity, and intelligence, he confronted realities more powerful than the resources available. He and his colleagues were poorly informed, being dependent upon Carleton, Burgoyne, Howe, and lesser men for flawed, out-of-date intelligence. And they were captives of personal dynamics of which they were, at best, dimly aware.

On March 26, the day General Burgoyne attended the royal noon levee and received oral instructions, Lord Germain composed orders for General Carleton telling him that

> it was his Majesty's pleasure that you should return to Quebec, and take with you such parts of your army . . . that you should detach General Burgoyne, or such other officer as you think most proper, with the remainder of the troops, and direct the officer so detached to proceed with all possible expedition to join General Howe, and put himself under his command.[31]

He concluded by noting that he would "write to Sir William Howe by the first packet, but you will never the less endeavour to give the earliest intelligence of this measure."[32]

General Howe never received that message from the colonial secretary. When Germain stopped at his office on his way to Kent, he learned that his aides had not completed preparing a copy of the order to Howe. With his carriage standing in the street, he refused to wait. His deputy proposed informing Howe by sending him a copy of Burgoyne's instructions. The order to Howe was completed while Germain was en route to Kent, but, lacking a signature, it was filed and never sent. Thus, Howe never received orders to send troops northward to Albany to rendezvous with Burgoyne.[33]

Howe thus felt free to act based on Germain's May 18 letter, which notified him that the King approved of his plan to take Philadelphia, "trusting, however, that whatever you meditate, will be executed in time for you to cooperate with the army ordered to proceed from Canada."[34] Like other eighteenth-century Europeans, Lord George found the scope of North American geography perplexing. He apparently anticipated that Sir William could make a rapid expedition to Philadelphia, easily occupy it, devote a few days to organizing a loyal government, and return to New York in time to undertake whatever action was required to cooperate with Burgoyne's forces' advancing south to meet him at

Albany. So confident was Germain that Howe could return to New York City in time to cooperate with Burgoyne, or that he would leave a force adequate for that purpose in the city, he neither issued clear orders to Howe nor informed Burgoyne of Sir William's intent.

Confident of Howe's judgment, Germain contented himself that the general would not permit the Philadelphia campaign to jeopardize Burgoyne's success. Germain's May 18 letter to Howe did not reach the general until August 16, too late to influence events because by then Howe was on his way to Philadelphia, and Burgoyne was advancing down the Champlain-Hudson corridor.[35]

As noted previously, John Burgoyne attended the March 26 royal noon levee, where he had an audience with the King, who gave him oral instructions. That same day, Germain wrote Carleton a letter that contained the only written orders pertaining to Burgoyne's new command. Burgoyne left London for Plymouth on March 27, and from there sent a brief note to Howe advising him of the contents of his oral instructions and boarded HMS *Apollo*. He reached Quebec on May 6, six days later went to Montreal, and assumed his new command at St. Jean on June 13.[36]

As of June 30, Burgoyne's command included some 4,000 British soldiers and almost 3,200 Germans. In total, 8,177 regulars crossed the frontier to invade New York. By July 1, fifteen regulars and 886 auxiliaries brought the grand total to 9,078 men.[37] In addition to the regulars, two French Canadian companies and an unknown number of Indians brigaded with Brigadier Simon Fraser's Advanced Corps; two provincial battalions were assigned "out of the line." According to a letter Burgoyne wrote from Montreal to the adjutant general and acting commander-in-chief Edward Harvey on May 19, 1777, his campaign began under very favorable circumstances.[38] The invading army included British regiments rich in battle honor and tradition. Likewise, the German regiments had officers and men who had experienced combat and earned reputations during the Seven Years' War. The field and company-grade officers were as competent as any who served in North America, including a remarkable number who survived to become generals in the British army.

The American Story

Professional limitations, aggravated by personal and regional animosities, marred American planning and, until late August 1777, affected tactical performance. Intelligence collection and analysis was poor, and generals and politicians shared an ignorance of what Burgoyne would do. Commander-in-Chief Washington believed that the enemy force was too weak to fight its way down the Champlain-Hudson corridor to Albany. He and a majority of members of the Continental Congress expected the army from Canada to move by sea to join General Howe at New York City. Working from his Albany mansion or his rural estate at the village of Saratoga (modern Schuylerville, New York), General Philip Schuyler, commander of the American Northern Department, expected Burgoyne to reverse Jeffrey Amherst's 1760 route by ascending the St. Lawrence, crossing Lake Ontario, and descending the Mohawk River to Albany.[39]

Horatio Gates, onetime Royal Army major, first Continental army adjutant general, and, in 1777, Schuyler's subordinate and rival, predicted that Burgoyne would "make the entire Conquest of the State of New York the first and main Object of the ensuing Campaign." He sent his analysis to Continental Congress President John Hancock, asking him to bring it to the delegates' attention.[40] Gates bolstered his analysis by citing the history of French and British colonial campaigns, the military ramifications of New York's geography, the potentials inherent in the large number of loyalists living in New York, and the importance of pro-British Indians. He observed that the Americans were too weak on the Hudson and Mohawk to repel the invasion; he feared that Washington would be drawn into New Jersey and caught between Burgoyne and Howe in a strategic vise. Gates also worried that British success on the lower Hudson would afford them access to the Atlantic, creating a Montreal-to-New York City axis. Gates demonstrated an accurate knowledge of strategic realities and the ability to interpret them logically.[41]

By mid-June, when Scots-born Arthur St. Clair, a former British officer and veteran of the Seven Years' War, assumed command of Fort Ticonderoga, Burgoyne's army was a few miles north of Crown Point on the Bouquet River, and the department and post commanders knew that Gates's analysis was prophetic.[42] Thus, June 12, the day he arrived at his new post, was not a happy one for Arthur St. Clair. Because its garrison had burned the abatis for firewood, the fortifications were weaker than when the Americans had seized the fort. In addition, stores were low, the pontoon bridge overlooking Mount Independence was unfinished, and the garrison numbered only 2,089 infantry and 238 gunners, too few to man the extensive works. On June 13, St. Clair reported to Schuyler that the fort and its garrison "are very ill prepared."[43]

The Americans had options, but all of them presented a challenge to moral courage and wisdom. Because there were too few troops to man the works on both sides of the lake, Schuyler and James Wilkinson, deputy adjutant general, considered evacuating the artillery and all but 1,500 men to Fort George. However, the adjutant general argued that an evacuation could not be done without prior congressional authority.[44]

Abandoning Fort Ticonderoga, the "Gibraltar of the North," in which both Americans and British invested excessive uncritical significance, was politically unthinkable. More unthinkable would be condemning its garrison to the fate

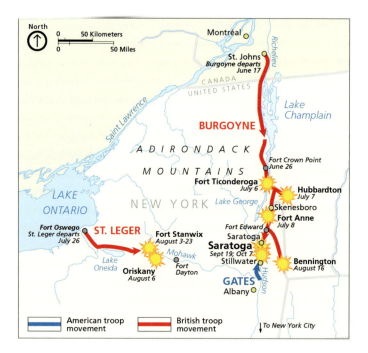

FIGURE 1.1. Map illustrating encounters connected with the British invasion of 1777. Courtesy of Saratoga National Historical Park.

of a "forlorn hope," sacrificed to an exaggerated sense of the post's importance. Only about 700 Continentals manning a few decrepit posts, functioning as stockaded depots, stood between Fort Ticonderoga and Albany. If the current garrison could not repel a British attack, they had to retire immediately, while retreat was possible.[45]

Schuyler convened a council, consisting of St. Clair and Brigadier Generals Enoch Poor, John Paterson, and Alexis de Fermoy, to consider the situation at Ticonderoga. On June 20 the council arrived unanimously at ten conclusions. Although they could not defend the entire works, they would hold the fort and Mount Independence as long as possible. However, if, as was probable, they would have to evacuate one, they would concentrate on retaining the mount. They would also try to strengthen obstructions between the lower and upper Champlain, even though doing so would require six weeks. If they could not hold Independence, everyone would retreat southward, using bateaux being collected and held in readiness. The Council concluded with a resolution to ask Commander-in-Chief Washington for reinforcements, knowing full well that he could not dispatch them from New Jersey in time to save Ticonderoga.[46]

Having provided for a doomed defense, and expecting the chorus of condemnation that would follow news that Ticonderoga had fallen, General Schuyler departed on June 22 to do what he could to hasten supplies and plead with Washington for reinforcements. St. Clair was left to conduct the best defense possible.

Burgoyne expected retaking Fort Ticonderoga to be a heroic undertaking. He attached great symbolic and strategic importance to its possession, as it blocked the route to his objective, Albany, and to the American interior (figure 1.1). His nation had fought France for the fort during the final war for an American empire. Its loss to Ethan Allen and the "Green Mountain Boys" was a serious blow to imperial pride and a potential nemesis to any commander aspiring to redeem British fortunes on the northern frontier. Restoring it to the British Empire would make "Gentleman Johnny" and his men heroes.[47]

Because he assumed that the Americans would be in "great force" defending Ticonderoga, Burgoyne provided his army with an especially large artillery train of 138 guns that included eighty field pieces, twelve howitzers, and forty-six mortars under the command of Major Griffith Williams, Royal Artillery, and Captain Georg Pausch of the Hesse-Hanau Artillery.[48]

At Ticonderoga, St. Clair had 2,089 infantrymen and 238 gunners present, one-fourth of the minimum needed to man the more than 2,000 yards of outer defense lines and fort proper. Shortages of arms, clothing, and food sapped morale and combat readiness.[49] Preserving those men to form a nucleus for future resistance was imperative to the larger cause.

The Fighting Begins

Operations against Fort Ticonderoga began on July 2, 1777, when a detachment of the Advanced Guard, supported by loyalists and Indians, approached American-entrenched sawmills at Mount Hope. The works' garrison set fire to the mills and withdrew to "old French lines," entrenchments that extended across much of the promontory northwest of the masonry fort. General Simon Fraser remained at Mount Hope covering the area between the fort and the portage to Lake George, while Indians and British rangers engaged defenders of the American outworks.

St. Clair hoped against logic that the enemy would try to retake Fort Ticonderoga by massed frontal assault, and early on July 2 he interpreted General William Phillips's men firing upon the fort from a distance of less than one hundred yards as a prelude to such an attack. St. Clair ordered his men to remain under cover and not to respond until ordered to fire.

Emboldened by the lack of return fire, a British soldier crawled toward the American lines. James Wilkinson, whose craving for fame competed with Benedict Arnold's, ordered a sergeant to shoot the lone British soldier and, obediently, the sergeant fired. Assuming that his shot was a signal to open fire, the entire American line leaped to their collective feet and poured successive volleys in the enemy's direction, enthusiastically supported by gunners. When their officers finally restored order, the foe had withdrawn a distance of about 300 yards, leaving the sergeant's target lying dead. In a disappointing demonstration of marksmanship, the Americans fired at least 3,000 musket balls and eight cannons at a 500-man line from a range of one hundred yards, killing only one man and wounding two.[50]

Burgoyne, who had moved his headquarters from the flagship *Royal George* to high ground behind Fraser's Advanced Corps where dismounted German dragoons provided security, ordered engineer Lieutenant William Twiss to reconnoiter Mount Defiance.[51] A light infantry detail occupied the position during the night, resulting in the mounting of light twenty-four-pounders and medium twelve-pounders on it during the next day.[52]

Because the distance from Mount Defiance's crest to the masonry fort was about 1,700 yards, exceeding the 1,200-yard range of Burgoyne's heaviest guns, the guns mounted there did not seriously threaten the fort. But they could, as the general recorded, "command the bridge and communications" and oversee "the exact situation of the vessels, nor could the enemy, during the day, make any material movement or preparation, without being discovered."[53] Guns on Mount Defiance could bombard the extensive American lines surrounding the masonry fort and Mount Independence and, more important, effectively interdict the Ticonderoga garrison's escape route.[54]

With few options left, St. Clair and his men evacuated Ticonderoga during the early-morning hours of July 6. Colonel Pierce Long and about 400 men took supplies south to Skenesborough (modern-day Whitehall, New York) by boat. Meanwhile, St. Clair marched the rest of his men along a primitive trace toward Hubbardton in present-day Vermont. From there he intended to move on to Castle Town (now Castleton, Vermont), then west to Skenesborough to meet Colonel Long's flotilla. While Fraser's Advanced Corps and part of General von Riedesel's Germans pursued St. Clair by land, Burgoyne garrisoned Ticonderoga and set out to chase Long's flotilla.[55]

Reaching the small hamlet of Hubbardton that evening, St. Clair left Colonel Seth Warner and 150 of his "Green Mountain Boys" and the 2nd New Hampshire Regiment with orders to bring up the rear guard, Colonel Ebenezer Francis's 11th Massachusetts Regiment. Warner, endowed with a plethora of courage and a paucity of disciplined prudence, disobeyed orders and decided to spend the night where he was. During the next day, he and his men fought and lost one of the fiercest battles of the war.

At Castle Town, St. Clair heard the sounds of battle. Riedesel's Germans sang hymns as they advanced at Hubbardton, but St. Clair had no hymn-singing professional soldiers to dispatch to the battle. What he did have were two militia regiments who had dropped out of line and encamped two miles closer to Hubbardton. However, those regiments refused to go to their comrades' support and hastily rejoined the same main column they abandoned the day before. As he tried to organize a relief force, St. Clair learned of Warner's defeat. That settled the matter and Ticonderoga's veterans continued their withdrawal.[56]

Colonel Long's flotilla, retreating from Ticonderoga, reached Skenesborough on July 6, closely pursued by Burgoyne's main force. Long quickly decided that the place could not be defended and set fire to what was flammable, including most supplies, and set out for Fort Anne, about eleven miles south on Wood Creek. Burgoyne entered Skenesborough the same day, and sent Lieutenant Colonel John Hill with part of the 9th Regiment in pursuit. The abominable condition of the road slowed Hill, and he did not reach his position, about a mile from the fort, until the evening of July 8. Here, a rather farcical story unfolded.[57]

Apparently, an American appeared during the morning of July 9, claiming to be a deserter, and told Hill that 1,000 men defended Fort Anne. Because he had only 190 men with him, the colonel sent to Burgoyne for reinforcements. Emboldened by a 400-man reinforcement, Long attacked Hill about 10:30 in the morning of July 8. During a confused engagement, the men of both forces heard an Indian-like "war whoop," and the Americans aborted their attack. But there were no actual Indians, just a lone Englishman, Captain John Money, who was trying to lead an Indian party to his regiment's support. The warriors, having no enthusiasm for involvement in a pitched battle, left the captain to strike ahead without them. When he reached the scene of combat, he sounded what he hoped would resemble a battle cry. Low on ammunition and taking council of prudence, the Americans set fire to the fort and beat a hasty retreat to Fort Edward.

Burgoyne almost caught up with the Americans at Fort Edward on July 30, and captured the recently abandoned fort, marking his campaign's high point. Every advance he and his men made after securing Fort Edward proved illusory and resulted in the failure of the general's plan for "conducting the War from the Side of Canada." For example, on August 16, New Hampshire Militia Brigadier General John Stark and Colonel Seth Warner's Green Mountain Regiment decisively defeated German Lieutenant Colonel Baum's foraging expedition on the Walloomsac River in the Battle of Bennington.[58]

Even more devastating than Baum's defeat at Bennington was the collapse of the British invasion of the Mohawk Valley. American Colonels Peter Gansevoort and Marinus Willett and their Fort Schuyler [Fort Stanwix] garrison doomed British Brigadier Barry St. Leger's conquest of the Mohawk by repulsing his siege of their rebuilt colonial fort on the site of modern Rome, New York.[59] Thus, St. Leger would not join Burgoyne at the confluence of the Hudson and Mohawk Rivers to move on to Albany.

Arriving at the dilapidated Fort Edward meant that Burgoyne's army had reached the Hudson River, succeeding where Carleton had failed in 1776. The campaign's initial stage, passing Lakes Champlain and George, was accomplished. But the march to Albany lay ahead, and Burgoyne knew that he faced daunting tests during his expedition's next phase. The impressive distances he and his army covered had lengthened and rendered vulnerable their communications with Canada and compounded supply problems. And he had yet to engage his foe in decisive battle. But Burgoyne and his commanders were professional soldiers who knew that as long as the Northern Department's military capability survived, his strategic objective remained unaccomplished.

On August 14, the army moved to colonial Fort Miller, and Burgoyne set up headquarters in William Duer's country house.[60] The general now had to choose between two routes to Albany. One lay along the Hudson's east bank, and the other along its west. In favor of the west-bank route were the facts that Albany was on that side, the river was wider and deeper, and the west river road offered closer access to the town. Fatefully, the Northern Department's main army was also on that side, in a position and strength about which the British commander was poorly informed.

Burgoyne chose the western road, and on August 13 his British regiments, followed by the Germans, crossed the river to the village of Saratoga (modern-day Schuylerville). In three columns, they began their three-day advance to Swords's house, near the mouth of the Krummach Kill, less than three miles north of American fortifications on Bemis Heights.[61]

The Northern Department's main army had retreated to the Hudson-Mohawk junction, and on August 19 its new commanding general, former British Major Horatio Gates, joined it.[62] Gates's appointment ended a months-long competition for, at that point, the dubious honor of redeeming American fortunes on the Champlain-Hudson frontier, competition marked by personal, regional, and professional animosities.

Intrigue marred the Continental Congress's process for choosing Gates, but intrigue often accompanies power struggles. Ultimately, the American Revolution was a struggle for power, where it would reside and who would exercise it. Horatio Gates had spent his life as a soldier and brought to the Northern Department the professional talents required for victory. Philip Schuyler, loser in the contest for command, deserved well from the country he served, but was not a skilled strategist or tactician. He also suffered from hypochondria, never personally led men in battle, and was not an inspiring figure whose talents and resources could win battles when victory depended on a decisive battle with an enemy led and manned by professional soldiers. Furthermore, he would have to take to the field with citizen soldiers, only some of whom were veterans of the last war for empire or had previous service in the Continental army.

The approximately 4,000 men present at the main American camps nine miles north of Albany were organized into four brigades commanded by Brigadier Generals John Paterson, John Glover, John Nixon, and Ebenezer Learned.

Learned's brigade, however, was on detached service with Major General Benedict Arnold's Mohawk reinforcements, and units not assigned to the brigades included about 300 artillerymen and eighty artificers. There were also departmental troops in the Mohawk Valley under the command of Colonel Goose Van Schaick of the 1st New York Regiment and east of the Hudson with Major General Benjamin Lincoln, the Northern Department's second-ranking general officer.[63] Most of the men at the main camp were Continentals and overwhelmingly New Englanders: eleven of the fourteen regiments were from Massachusetts, and three were from New Hampshire. The Northern Department's preponderance of New Englanders had been an embarrassment to the New Yorker Schuyler.

The Northern Department's army soon received important reinforcements with the help of George Clinton, who had defeated General Schuyler to become New York's first elected governor. Within three weeks of assuming his command, Gates issued orders creating two new regiments of 500 men each from Albany County militia. The most important addition arrived on August 30, when Colonel Daniel Morgan's Rifle Regiment, composed of 500 sharpshooters from Virginia, Maryland, and Pennsylvania, arrived.[64] Because reloading a rifle was much slower than doing so with the smooth-bore musket, riflemen were vulnerable to both musket fire and bayonet attack. Gates dealt with that problem by brigading the sharpshooters with Dearborn's light infantry, who were armed with muskets.[65]

Administrative detail, especially logistical in nature, consumed Gates's time. His experience as a staff officer and as the Continental army's first adjutant general was useful, as were the services of General Schuyler, whose most valuable asset was his logistical skill.[66] Another favorable factor was that Gates enjoyed being able to function with interior lines of communication and supply. By the first week of September, Gates commanded a stronger, better-supplied army with higher morale than was ever available to his predecessor.

Soon after arriving at Van Schaick's Islands in the Hudson, Gates received valuable intelligence from George Measam that had been collected from a garrulous Hanoverian who deserted from the British 53rd Regiment at Fort Edward. The deserter reported that Burgoyne commanded some 4,000 men at Fort Edward: six British regiments, totaling 300 men each, and five German regiments, totaling 2,200 men. Indians and loyalists numbered between 400 and 500.[67] His reported regimental strengths were inaccurate, but the information provided a generally accurate description of the invading force.

Gates now had to develop a new plan to block Burgoyne's drive to reach Albany and prevent him from joining up with Sir William Howe. He knew that his foe could not remain at Fort Miller and must soon retreat to Ticonderoga or drive on to Albany. He could not winter anywhere between those two locations, and having spent a northern winter at the former, it was not a tempting alternative. For several reasons, Albany was the better alternative in that the lower Hudson provided communication with Britain's base at New York City, thus, possessing Albany would make resources much more accessible and in larger quantity than would control of the remote Ticonderoga. Finally, bringing his army to Albany and making it available to Sir William for his next campaign was the expedition's royally mandated purpose. Withdrawing to Ticonderoga would therefore be tantamount to admitting defeat without having engaged the Americans in decisive combat. That was exactly what Guy Carleton had done in 1776, and Burgoyne would not repeat it in 1777.[68]

The Battles of Saratoga

Understanding the events occurring during the month between September 18, 1777, and Burgoyne's capitulation requires a consideration of Generals Burgoyne's and Gates's strategic and tactical objectives. The latter had a deceptively simple goal: block the enemy's southward advance. The longer he could do that, the more likely would be Burgoyne's failure, because he had to reach his objective, Albany, before winter. Burgoyne's army could not survive on the northern Hudson without shelter and supplies, whereas Gates had access to stores in Albany and New England, and could remain in the field indefinitely. Bemis Heights was the last good defensive position in that field for Gates, and he was determined to use it to thwart his foe.[69]

Burgoyne faced a situation that every commander tries to avoid: being forced to act on his opponent's terms. He had two unattractive options: he could continue on the Albany Road and try to force his way through American batteries on the river bluffs and flats; or he could attack Gates in his fortified camp on Bemis Heights. While retreat was a third option, Burgoyne did not consider it. The American militia operating east of the Hudson under Benjamin Lincoln, John Stark, and John Brown were positioned to stage ambushes that would make the route north a death march; Gates could pursue the British with more ease and safety than they could retreat. The sixty-five miles to Fort Ticonderoga would have been a nightmare, and wintering there was not an inviting prospect.[70]

The first alternative offered little or no promise of success. The British might overcome the river batteries, but fortifications on the bluffs were secure, and a column marching broadside to them could not survive the attempt to negotiate the narrow pass between the heights and the river. Thus, the British commander resorted to the only potentially viable option: attempting to lure or drive the Americans off Bemis Heights.

Burgoyne's tactical solution to his strategic problem was to commit three columns to an assault on Gates's fortified camp, the extent and strength of which

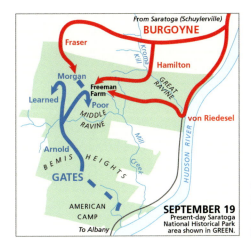

FIGURE 1.2. Graphic illustrating the fighting between American and British forces on September 19, 1777. Courtesy of Saratoga National Historical Park.

he was fundamentally ignorant (figure 1.2). To that end, he committed Brigadier Simon Fraser's Advanced Corps, plus most of the loyalists and Indians and Breymann's German 530-man corps. The center column consisted of 1,700 men of the British line under Brigadier James Hamilton. Burgoyne and his headquarters accompanied the central column, potentially putting him on the firing line and compromising his control of the action. The left 1,600-man column, commanded by General von Riedesel, remained, for the time being, on the Albany Road to exploit any favorable move relaxing American interdiction of the road by Gates's right wing. General William Phillips followed with artificers, leaving the artillery park, hospital, and baggage.[71] The British objective was to threaten the American left so effectively as to force or entice the Americans off Bemis Heights.[72]

Fraser's and Breymann's corps marched along a road running westward to a point three miles from the river, and then turned southward toward the American west wing. Hamilton followed a short distance behind and turned left onto a road that led to a point north of John Freeman's farm. Riedesel and Phillips, whose units made up the largest of the three columns, moved southward along the Albany Road. When the columns reached their assigned positions, a signal gun coordinated a simultaneous advance against Bemis Heights.[73]

Learning of the enemy's moves, Gates ordered Colonel Daniel Morgan's corps of riflemen and light infantry to reconnoiter the woods and fields north of the American lines. Major General Benedict Arnold's entire division soon followed. At about noon, members of Morgan's corps fired upon and killed or wounded most of Hamilton's Advanced Guard in the Freeman farm clearing. Morgan's men rushed forward to pursue the survivors but were outflanked and scattered by some of Fraser's men. Morgan soon rallied his men and they and

Enoch Poor's brigade bore the brunt of the day's fight.[74] For more than three hours the fighting surged across the weed-grown, stump-studded farm.

Although often characterized as such, it was not a battle between professional soldiers and raw backwoodsmen. Most of the Americans were veteran Continentals, many of whom were in their third year of service, and they deployed, attacked, retreated, and rallied again in a disciplined, soldierly manner. British regiments performed in a manner consistent with the honorable traditions of their service, counterattacking repeatedly against increasingly heavy odds. Burgoyne often exposed himself to enemy fire, paying a price for sharing the private soldier's perspective.[75]

In the light of the opposing commanders' objectives, the Americans, while losing the battle, had the advantage. The British possessed the battlefield, but the Americans continued to occupy Bemis Heights and block movement to Albany; the British also suffered twice as many causalities.[76]

During the next sixteen days, soldiers of the two armies faced each other under arms and toiled to strengthen their positions. The Europeans constructed a strong line of field fortifications extending in a shallow arc from the bluff north of Kroma Kill's ravine to the Freeman farm, where they raised the "Light Infantry Redoubt" (now called the Balcarres Redoubt), their strongest post. Almost a fourth of a mile north of that fortification, Germans and loyalists erected a log outpost, the "Breymann Redoubt," covering their right wing. Simultaneously, the Americans extended and improved their lines, collected supplies, and absorbed militia reinforcements, enhancing their already powerful strategic position.[77]

As the Americans' strategic position improved, a potential for disaster simmered on Bemis Heights, when, three days after the battle, a sordid quarrel flared between Gates and Benedict Arnold. Earlier relations had been cordial, as Gates had saved Arnold's career when, in 1776, he refused the Hazen court-martial order to arrest Arnold and dissolved the court. A subsequent conflict between Gates and Arnold over accounting irregularities led to Arnold's resigning on July 11, 1777. Washington later requested Arnold's assignment to command the Northern Department's militia, and after asking Congress to suspend his resignation, Arnold and Benjamin Lincoln joined Schuyler during July.[78]

General Gates reported to President John Hancock concerning the Freeman farm fight that "the General good Behaviour of the Troops on this important Occasion cannot be surpassed by the most veteran Army, to discriminate in praise of the Officers would be Injustice, as they all deserve the Honor & Applause of Congress."[79] Someone untruthfully told Arnold that Gates referred in the report to Arnold's division as a "detachment of the Army" and that its language insulted Arnold. The informer was probably Richard Varick, who as deputy muster master general had access to headquarters. His letters to General Schuyler testify to knowledge of staff affairs to which he was privy. For instance, in a September 21 letter to Schuyler, Varick bragged about stealing a copy of Colonel John Brown's report to General Lincoln reporting events at Ticonderoga.[80] Varick and Henry Brockholst Livingston were devoted to Schuyler and detested his successor. After Gates became department commander, Varick continued serving as deputy muster master general and Livingston as one of Arnold's aides-de-camp. They wrote almost daily to their patron, always in derogatory language of Gates; Arnold encouraged them and preserved their correspondence.[81]

Benedict Arnold would not tolerate a perceived insult and confronted his commander in headquarters during the evening of September 22. Livingston described the confrontation to General Schuyler as being one in which "matters were altercated in a very high Strain."[82] According to James Wilkinson, Gates responded to his subordinate by questioning whether, in light of his suspended resignation, he had a legitimate rank to command except the one he had at the northern commander's discretion. Arnold responded with "high words and gross language; and Arnold demanded a pass to go to Philadelphia."[83] Gates surprised him by not pleading with him to stay, replying that "General Lincoln would be here in a day or two, that he should have no Occasion for him; and would give him a pass to go to Philadelphia whenever he chose it."[84] Arnold had bluffed and Gates called his bluff. Both men knew the kind of welcome the former would receive from Commander-in-Chief Washington, who detested any hint of insubordination. Arnold did not intend to join Washington, but expected Gates to keep him in the north by apologizing and writing a report that would mention Arnold by name. Horatio Gates's weaknesses did not include moral cowardice.

Rejoining the troops on Bemis Heights as second in command, Benjamin Lincoln outranked Arnold, and Gates made him commander of the right wing, assuming the left wing under his personal direction. Arnold remained in camp without a command, a potential source of trouble. Remarkably, surviving documents contain no references to the rupture; and Gates never mentioned it in his correspondence or personal papers.[85]

During the seventeen days following the Freeman farm fight, more than 6,000 militiamen from Massachusetts, Connecticut, New Hampshire, and New York arrived at Bemis Heights, bringing the troop number to slightly more than 12,000. The Americans extended and strengthened their fortifications until they formed a solid front from water batteries near Bemus's tavern to John Neilson's farm and from there southwestward. Brigadier John Glover reported that "[w]e are making every necessary preparation to receive them by felling trees & and abiteeing [sic] between the North [Hudson] River & Saratoga Lake about 6 miles distance."[86]

Although the American fortified camp was a reasoned defensive strategy,

Burgoyne's offensive plans demanded relentless pressure imposed by a mobile force that would give the enemy no time for marshaling defensive resources. But occupation of Freeman's farm and its environs forced Burgoyne to prepare defensive fieldworks. He had another important reason for securing his position: he was counting on help from General Sir Henry Clinton in New York City and needed security while establishing contact with him. The defensive fieldworks raised by his men reflected mastery of the required technology and Burgoyne's respect for his American foe.[87]

With its many streams and ravines, the terrain gave the British an important advantage. Their engineers improved their position by erecting a series of small outworks along the northern crests of the southern-facing ravines. As these ravines turn southward, the ravine system forms a plateau, most of which belonged to farmer Jeremiah Taylor. Burgoyne's troops dug a strong line of entrenchments along the plateau's axis to a point on the hill above the river, where a series of redoubts extended north and south along bluffs above the Albany Road and covering the artillery park, hospital, and bateaus. The southernmost of the three hilltop fortifications north of the Kroma Kill came to be called the Great Redoubt; outposts north of the kill's ravine protected the rear.

The main purpose of both armies' defenses was to repel attacks from the west. The British were more vulnerable because, unlike their foe, they had no strong natural position in their western sector comparable to the crest of Bemis Heights and the ridges between there and Lake Saratoga. To counter that serious disadvantage, Burgoyne's soldiers erected two redoubts: the Light Infantry Redoubt [Balcarres] on Freeman's farm and a smaller German post on the McBride property [Breymann]. To protect the interval between those redoubts, Canadian troops stockaded two cabins that stood on the road between the farms.

The Light Infantry Redoubt's twofold purpose was to defend the interval between the ravine systems and cover the head of the southern ravine where it originates in a couple of small rivulets south and west of Freeman's farm. Hauptmann Georg Pausch wrote: "The Army immediately began to fortify on the fields where the battle was fought. General Fraser's corps encamped behind a great redoubt [Balcarres], built of timbers and earth. Its length must have been at least One hundred fifty chains [a conservative estimate]. The walls in some places were six feet high. Eight cannon, four light six-pounders, two light three-pounders, and two five and a half inch howitzers were mounted in embrasures."[88] Northwest and within sight of the light infantry post, Oberstlieutenant Heinrich Breymann's Brunswick grenadiers built a smaller, critically important redoubt "both for the protection of the right flank of Fraser's division and for the defense of a road leading from this point to the rear of the army."[89] Pausch described it, noting that a "fortification of trees was built *en potence*. Its front occupied seven hundred fifty feet and stood seven feet high with musket ports."

He added that the camp lay behind it in an angle, "protected by a breastwork of trees."[90] Two of Pausch's light six-pounders were detached from his artillery company to further augment Breymann's defenses.[91]

While his soldiers fortified their positions, scouted, and skirmished with American patrols, General Burgoyne waited for the tentative promise contained in a coded message he received before dawn on September 21. Written by Sir Henry Clinton ten days earlier, it read when decoded:

> You know my good will and are not ignorant of my poverty. If you think two thousand men can assist you effectually, I will push at [Fort] Montgomery in about ten days, but ever jealous of my flanks. If they [the Americans] move in force on either of them, Must return to save this important post [New York City] I expect reinforcements every day. Let me know what you wish.[92]

Only a desperate commander could extract hope from Clinton's message, and John Burgoyne was desperate. Clinton wanted Burgoyne's approval for action he wanted to undertake but dared not act without the latter's specific request, because it would pose risk to New York City. Even if reinforcements did arrive shortly, Clinton could not leave for the Hudson Highlands for about ten days, meaning that no troops would depart before September 22; if the Americans threatened his flanks, he would return to defend the city. Burgoyne's forlorn belief that 2,000 men were coming to Albany reflected his true despair. At least, he reasoned, raising fortifications would buy time.

Desperation also led Burgoyne, normally solicitous of his soldiers' well-being, to mislead them in a general order for October 3: "There is reason to be assured, that other powerful Armies are actually in cooperation with the Troops."[93] In reality, he and his men were strategically isolated; Clinton was in New York City, and the Americans had severed the Canadian supply line. To make matters worse, time favored the Americans as disparities between forces increased, and cool autumn nights and fall rains foretold winter's approach. Nor could he transfer to Clinton responsibility for taking Albany. Burgoyne knew that he could not postpone the decision to act aggressively by either attacking Bemis Heights or aborting the campaign and trying to escape northward.

When Burgoyne, Riedesel, and Fraser met on October 4, they knew that the American right wing was impregnable and that frontal attack of the enemy camp could only fail and result in the slaughter of their men. In desperation, the commander proposed an enveloping move around Gates's left flank, followed by an attack on his rear. To that end, he would commit his entire force, minus an 800-man camp guard. It would be highly dangerous because it would separate most of the army from the river and all sources of supply for at least three days. Riedesel urged withdrawing to Fort Edward "as soon as possible, especially on account of the only slight possibility of the early arrival of General Clinton."[94]

At another council convened on October 5, Riedesel proposed retreat to the Battenkill to await more explicit intelligence from Clinton. While Fraser concurred and Phillips withheld comment, Burgoyne categorically rejected the idea of a retreat. Adopting the German's proposal would certainly have worsened the Royal Army's situation. General Lincoln had deployed militia opposite the village of Saratoga immediately downstream of the Battenkill, and John Stark's Bennington victors and the Green Mountain Boys were in position to effectively counter every effort to cross to the Hudson's east bank. Gates and his numerically superior army would have pursued a heavily burdened, retreating foe, making their withdrawal deadly. If Burgoyne survived to cross the river to the Battenkill and take a defensive position, no fortifications existed comparable to those at or near Freeman's farm. Ultimately, only removing the Americans from Bemis Heights could save Burgoyne and his army.

> Imprecision marked the British commander's communication of his objective, leading to different interpretations of whether he launched a "reconnaissance in force" or an attempt to possess a site from which to attack Bemis Heights from the west. An October 20 letter to Lord Germain compounds the confusion, noting that: It was judged advisable to make a movement to the enemy's left, not only to discover whether there were any possible means of forcing passage should it should be necessary to advance or of dislodging him for the convenience of retreat, but also to cover a forage of the army which was in greatest distress on account of the scarcity.[95]

That letter lends credence to the "reconnaissance in force" interpretation. But the General's "Narrative" of the campaign argues for the other: "But confidant I am upon minute examination of the ground since, that had the other idea been pursued, I should in a few hours have gained a position, that in spite of the enemy's numbers, would have put them in my power."[96] General von Riedesel wrote his sovereign that "it was decided on the 7th of October to undertake a reconnaissance against the left wing of the enemy, and if it was found invulnerable to consider retreat."[97]

The composition of the force committed to the move is an important clue to its purpose. In officers and men, it included 1,700 of the best troops, representing slightly more than 22 percent of Burgoyne's 7,183-man force. Committing the best soldiers makes it likely that the purpose was more than a reconnaissance of the American left wing or a cover for foraging. A better clue to its purpose was deployment of ten pieces of artillery that included six six-pounders, two twelve-pounders, and two eight-inch howitzers, the last being especially useful against entrenchments, arguing strongly that Burgoyne intended to attack Gates's left wing.

FIGURE 1.3. Graphic illustrating the fighting between American and British forces on October 7, 1777. Courtesy of Saratoga National Historical Park.

At about noon on October 7, Generals Burgoyne, Phillips, Riedesel, and Fraser led their men out of camp, marching them south along the Quaker Springs Road through the abandoned Marshall farm, a fringe of woods and into the open fields of the Barber farm, driving out Americans posted in the house (figure 1.3). The British light infantry and 24th Regiment moved westward along a road, across a wheat field, through more woods, and into a smaller field. The column's objective was a low north-south ridge 800 yards west of the angle formed by the American fortification on Neilson's farm. Its possession would enable British artillery to deliver enfilade fire, supporting an attack on Gates's left and rear. If successful, the move would position Burgoyne to follow up on the eighth with an attack "with his entire army." If such an attack was not feasible, Burgoyne would, on the eleventh, retreat to the Battenkill.[98] Lieutenant William Digby of the 53rd Regiment's grenadier company explained that the general gambled that his October 7 probe could gain and hold an advanced enfilading position in preparation for a flank assault, yet leaving the strong American right wing free to attack a vulnerable British fortified camp and Burgoyne's left flank.[99] Doing that was taking council of desperation because, waiting until the second week of October, the only chance Burgoyne had of avoiding defeat was for Gates to lose his nerve and make a disastrous blunder. Hope was a poor substitute for strategy.

After moving into the small field, the light infantry deployed at the base of a slope while the 24th Regiment assumed its post along the farm road to the light infantry's left. The Germans were to the 24th's left along the road crossing the Barber wheat field, and the grenadiers deployed to their left, with their own left in adjacent woods. Detachments from Hamilton's four regiments were left of the grenadiers, extending northward toward Freeman's farm. The British main line thus extended from the field west of the Barber farm to the Freeman farm's southern fringe. The front was mostly open, but the British grenadiers and the 24th rested in the woods and a hill overlooked the light infantry. Woods and hill made those units very vulnerable to a flank attack.

A better than two-to-one numerical advantage along with tactical and strategic advantages favored the Americans, such that only a miracle could wrest victory from them. As he had on September 19, Burgoyne tried again to entice or drive Gates off Bemis Heights. Brave British and German soldiers would burnish their regiments' reputations, but could not work the miracle that would open the way to Albany. Phillips's signal guns alerted Gates, and he ordered the lines manned about one o'clock. His anticipation that the "old gamester" Burgoyne would try another throw of fortune's dice was fulfilled. His men were ready at their alarm posts.

From an outpost south of the Barber farm, Deputy Adjutant General Wilkinson observed the enemy moves and interpreted them as covering a foraging expedition. Wilkinson recalled that "they are foraging and endeavoring to reconnoiter your left; and I think, Sir, offer you battle . . . their front is open, and their flanks rest in the woods, under cover of which they may be attacked, their right is skirted by a lofty height, I would indulge them." Gates responded, "Well then, order Morgan to begin the game."[100] Wilkinson delivered the order to Morgan, who was in front of the American entrenchments. The colonel proposed a circuitous approach that would bring him onto an elevation right of the enemy flank as soon as other troops fired on the British left wing.

Gates accepted Morgan's proposal and ordered General Enoch Poor to attack the British front and left flank while General Ebenezer Learned deployed his brigade against the British 24th Regiment and German units between Burgoyne's right flank and the British grenadiers.[101] Delayed by their circuitous march, Morgan's corps did not attack Fraser's 24th Regiment and light infantry until about 4:00 p.m., at which time the 1st, 2nd, and 3rd New Hampshire Continentals from Poor's brigade came onto line opposite the British grenadiers, who were supported by two six-pounders.[102] The rest of Poor's regiments faced drafts from the British 9th, 21st, and 62nd Regiments and Alexander Fraser's Rangers and Pennsylvania Provincials.[103]

The main American attack, which began between 3:30 and 4:00 p.m., was classically simple. Poor's brigade struck the left where the British grenadiers and units from Hamilton's division stood. Morgan's corps hit the enemy right, composed of the British light infantry and the 24th. Learned's target was the Germans in the center of Burgoyne's line. One of Morgan's riflemen soon contributed to success by fatally wounding Brigadier Simon Fraser as he tried to rally his outnumbered men. Poor's brigade overwhelmed the grenadiers and struck the dwindling ranks of the British left, forcing them into retreat toward the Light Infantry Redoubt.[104] Learned's six regiments, supported by one of Jonathan Warner's Massachusetts regiments, attacked the Germans, who, with flanks exposed, repulsed them. A renewed assault forced Riedesel's badly damaged regiments to join the general retreat to the cover of fortifications on Freeman's farm.[105] Burgoyne's men suffered more than 400 casualties and lost all their field pieces. At least 8,000 Americans were by now on the field, although not all participated in the fighting.

Sometime after Learned's brigade attacked the British center, Benedict Arnold dashed onto the field and joined the brigade. Excluded from command by his threat to leave the Northern Department, he would not tolerate his former division dominating the battle without him. As soon as the Germans withdrew, he, perhaps with some of Learned's men, joined elements of Poor's brigade, who were driving the enemy through the woods and across the fields of the Marshall and Freeman farms, overrunning a small outpost on "Bloody Knoll," and massing in front of the Light Infantry (Balcarres) Redoubt. That massive fortification, the strongest of British positions, measured more than 500 yards long, with walls, in some parts, six feet high, four exterior sally ports, eight interior entries from the British camp, and eight cannons. It now sheltered more than 1,000 men who had retreated from the main line of resistance, plus seven battalion companies of the Regiment von Riedesel, bringing the number in the works to at least 1,500.[106]

Arnold led approximately 3,400 men, unsupported by artillery, against that force. Prudence dictated that they pin down the redoubt's defenders with a heavy, steady fire and await a flanking maneuver around the enemy right, which was defended by numerically weak Germans.[107] Prudence was not Arnold's salient attribute, and he led Poor's and Paterson's exposed, unsupported soldiers in a series of futile and costly attacks.[108] But 3,000 brave Americans could not overcome the 1,500 desperate Europeans defending the post. The Americans charged repeatedly, only to become entangled in a maze of felled trees fronting the fort's base. However one judges Arnold's role in the attack, most Americans who died on October 7 fell before the Light Infantry Redoubt.

General Learned's turning of Burgoyne's right wing by taking the timber fortification manned by 200 Germans under Oberslieutenant Heinrich Christoph Breymann became the key to American victory. Captain Benjamin Warren of the 7th Massachusetts wrote this terse description of the attack:

> We marched to the right of Col. Morgan's riflemen to the lines within ten rods of a strange fort, fought them boldly for better than half an hour when they gave way, left the fort and fled. Our people marched in and took possession of their cannon and 600 tents, standing with baggage etc. The fire was very hot on both sides.[109]

As men of Learned's and Nixon's brigades stormed the post, Arnold left the troops facing the Light Infantry Redoubt, rode between the fire of both armies, joined men entering the Germans' rear, and fell wounded in the leg, an event memorialized by the famous "Boot Monument" (see chapter 10).[110]

Lieutenant Colonel von Specht led a failed effort to recover the fallen post. Under the cover of darkness, Burgoyne withdrew to the river, where his army remained on October 8 covered by fortifications overlooking the artillery park, the bridge of boats to the eastern shore, the encampment, and the hospital.

The Retreat and Surrender

The Europeans spent October 8 under artillery and sniper fire, preparing to retreat.[111] At day's end, Burgoyne and senior officers escorted the body of Simon Fraser, who died that morning, to the redoubt, where Chaplain Edward Brudenel read the Church of England's Burial Office. American gunners, not aware of the nature of the event, tried valiantly to disrupt it.[112] Immediately after the burial service, the defeated army began a muddy march to the village of Saratoga (Schuylerville).[113]

Even before the fight of October 7, Gates prepared to deny his foe an escape by posting militia east of the Hudson and north of Saratoga. John Stark and his Bennington veterans, who had left the Hudson the day before the Freeman farm fight, captured Fort Edward's small garrison and came southward to Stark's Knob just north of Saratoga village. Two thousand New Hampshire militiamen, commanded by Brigadier General Jacob Bailey, constructed an entrenched camp on high ground north of Fort Edward, while 1,300 Berkshire County militiamen, commanded by Brigadier General John Fellows, entrenched the "Heights of Saratoga," east of the river.[114]

The defeated Europeans reached Saratoga village during the evening of October 9 in a state of advanced exhaustion. They had been under arms for three days, fought an aggressive battle, and marched through cold rain along a road that had become a sodden ditch. They went into camp without shelter because as Schüler von Senden noted in his *Tagebuch* (diary), "We burnt our tents and all other ballast, as the troops cannot carry them any longer."[115] The rain stopped during the night, followed by a heavy frost. In spite of fatigue, hunger, cold, and stony ground, the men prepared breastworks that made their position a strong one.[116]

The head of the pursuing American column reached the Fishkill, opposite their foe, in the late morning of the tenth, and when their comrades arrived, they, too, prepared entrenchments. For a week, the two armies were locked in an eventful siege while commanders negotiated, and events south of Albany seemed to sustain the besieged commander's hopes to avert complete and ultimate defeat.

By October 3, Sir Henry Clinton had moved upriver from New York City with 3,000 men and by the eighth had broken through the Hudson Highlands. Sir Henry, in a letter that fell into American hands, wrote: "*Nous y Voici* and now nothing between us but Gates."[117] After reaching the village of Fishkill, he embarked 2,000 infantry under Major General John Vaughan to sail as far upstream as safe and come to Burgoyne's relief. Receiving regular reports of Vaughan's progress, Gates could not be certain of British intentions; during the evening of the thirteenth, he received word that Burgoyne wished to negotiate a cease-fire. The American promptly replied that he would receive a field officer at ten o'clock on the fourteenth.[118] Burgoyne sent Lieutenant Colonel Robert Kingston, his adjutant general and interim military secretary, who was met by Colonel James Wilkinson, who blindfolded and escorted him about a mile south of the Fishkill on the Albany Road to Gates's headquarters, located southeast of the colonial Dutch Church.

After polite preliminaries and then less polite discussion of an exchange concerning Lady Harriet Ackland, the burning of General Schuyler's country home, and prisoner exchange, Kingston presented the letter that Burgoyne had prepared with the approval of a council of war on the thirteenth. General Gates pulled a paper from his pocket and presented it to the colonel, saying: "There Sir, are the terms upon which General Burgoyne must surrender." This was such a violation of protocol that Kingston declined to deliver it, asking that it be transmitted by an American officer, which Gates refused to do. The American general not only flouted protocol, his terms were tantamount to demanding unconditional surrender.[119]

After Kingston returned with Gates's draft, Burgoyne convened his council and prepared his response. Responding to Gates's description of his foe's strategic situation as being so dire that their only option was unconditional surrender, the British replied that "while they have arms in their hands," they rejected the idea of an unconditional surrender. Gates's sixth article was especially offensive. It provided that once the articles were signed, Burgoyne's troops would form in their encampment, "where they will be ordered to ground their arms, and may thereupon be marched to the river side, to be passed over on their way toward Bennington," becoming prisoners of war. The implications were both symbolic and substantive. No British army had been so humiliated since the English civil war. Burgoyne's response reflected that reality: "If General Gates does not recede from the 6th article, the treaty ends at once. . . . This army will to a man proceed to any act of desperation rather than submit to this article. . . . The cessation of arms ends this evening."[120]

The fortunes of war gave Gates overwhelming authority. He had thwarted British strategic objectives and imposed an undeniable tactical defeat. He had under his personal command an almost three-to-one numerical advantage over his opponent, whom he surrounded, whose supplies were reduced to four days' rations, whose munitions were exhausted, whose men were physically and emotionally exhausted, and whose hope for relief had vanished.[121]

There was, however, a small cloud on Gates's southern horizon. Burgoyne had known since receiving Clinton's message on October 6 that while some of his troops would advance toward Albany, Sir Henry would neither take responsibility for the future of the men at Saratoga nor undertake a breakthrough to rescue them.[122] But Gates did not know the limitations of Clinton's objectives nor how they affected his own situation, and he was sufficiently distracted to want to terminate negotiations as early as possible; hence, the protracted bargaining between an unimperious victor and very opportunistic suitor. General Burgoyne sought to mitigate the severity of conditions attending his inevitable capitulation. To that end, he offered counterproposals. The first addressed a significant symbol of the professional soldier's honor: "The troops to march out of their camp with the honours of war, and the artillery of their entrenchments." Gates generously acceded and directed that they march to "the verge of the river, where the old fort [Fort Hardy] stood, where their arms must be left." Burgoyne's men had certainly earned the respect being accorded them. Gates agreed to the free passage of the army to a port "from whence its men would be transported to Great Britain upon the condition of not serving again in North America during the war," but he specified Boston as the port of embarkation. Other concessions included the securing of personal property from search, guarantee that officers would not be separated from their men, inclusion of noncombatants in the treaty, permitting Canadians to return home, and permitting three officers to take dispatches to General Howe. Finally, Gates dictated that "the capitulation to be finished by 2 o'clock this day. And the troops march from their encampment at five, and be in readiness to march towards Boston tomorrow morning."[123] Burgoyne accepted the terms, but with another caveat: "We have, Sir unguardedly called that a treaty of capitulation, which the army means only as a treaty of convention."[124] Gates did not believe that semantics were important, except to salve his foe's pride, and agreed, hoping that doing so would end the negotiation.

That hope, however, was premature. A loyalist came into camp during the night and reported that Clinton had advanced to Esopus nearly a week prior. Not aware that Vaughan had stopped south of Albany, the British commander convened another council and asked his commanders two questions: could he honorably break the convention, and if the unconfirmed information the loyalist brought were true, did it improve their situation? They answered both in the negative.[125] In spite of his generals' vote, Burgoyne continued to delay and wrote a letter to Gates accusing him of detaching troops southward, reducing the numerical superiority that had brought him to the negotiating table, and requesting permission to detail two officers to determine American numbers. Gates rejected the proposal; he expected Burgoyne to ratify or dissolve the treaty, and that required an immediate and final response. After another council of war, the defeated general signed the "Convention of Saratoga" on the sixteenth, acknowledging defeat and delivering up his army.[126]

The formal surrender took place on October 17, 1777. At the appointed hour, the British and German generals and their staffs rode between American soldiers drawn up on both sides of the road leading from their camp to Gates's headquarters. Meanwhile, north of the Fishkill, near the remains of colonial Fort Hardy, the men who had faithfully and courageously fought against great odds for Britain's empire laid down their guns, some with grim dignity, others with unashamed grief and resentment. Then, they too crossed the creek's ford and marched between silent files of victorious Americans. In their presence, John Burgoyne tendered his sword to Horatio Gates, who returned it. The men of the convention army marched into captivity, first near Boston and then to points as distant as Albemarle County, Virginia.[127]

American victory at Saratoga radically changed the Revolution's strategic dynamics. British historian Piers Mackesy writes that

> in round figures the British loss at Saratoga was not large. But it would be difficult to replace, and more serious still was the proof of what the perceptive had long suspected: that the American with its armed population might be beyond the power of Britain to reconquer with any force which she could raise and sustain in America. The grand design of 1775 lay in ruins.[128]

He summarized the changes Saratoga wrought vis-à-vis Britain and its rebellious offspring: The first and most obvious was eliminating a well-trained and experienced army, a severe loss to a manpower-short power. Also lost were thirty-seven cannons left at Fort Ticonderoga and Fort George and another thirty-six in the artillery train committed at Freeman's farm and Bemis Heights. Along with those were muskets, German jäger rifles, gunflints, powder, and cannonballs. A second was the defeat of the strategy that had informed imperial strategy in 1776 and 1777, a strategy that was geopolitically sound and with a capacity for taking advantage of American weaknesses. George III and his ministers had to develop new strategies with fewer options and resources at their command. They did, however, profit from learning that attacking the rebels where they could capitalize on their assets produced failure.

Victory in the Champlain-Hudson corridor changed the Revolution from a civil war into an international conflict, making it beyond Britain's power to prevail. France had emerged from the Seven Years' War without its empire and reduced to a cipher in international politics. Before the ink was dry on the treaty ending that war, its leaders were devoting its resources to taking revenge on

England. The American rebellion gave opportunity to fish in Britain's troubled waters, and since mid-1776, French money and arms had increasingly helped sustain that rebellion.[129]

While working to sustain the American rebellion, France itself inched toward war, influenced by the Revolution's varying fortunes. When the Americans seemed to be making their declaration of independence a reality, the French ventured a little closer to the brink. Washington's defeats on the lower Hudson and in Manhattan caused them to draw back. Although encouraged by Washington's brilliant recovery at Trenton and Princeton, British possession of Philadelphia and rumors of peace overtures made intrusion into the Anglo-colonial family fight less attractive.

All this changed when news of Burgoyne's surrender reached Paris on December 3, 1777. Fevered invocation of national interest replaced watchful waiting. On February 6, 1778, American and French diplomats signed two treaties that bound what was traditionally an absolute monarchy and a peoples' rebellion to a common cause. Louis XVI received the Continental Congress's commissioners at Versailles on March 20, transforming a civil war into an international conflict, a momentous diplomatic revolution.[130]

NOTES

1. Piers Mackesy, *The War for America* (Cambridge, MA: Harvard University Press, 1964), 143–44.
2. Sir William Howe to Lord George Germain, 30 November 1776, Public Records Office, London (hereafter PRO), CO 5/83, 609–15.
3. John F. Luzader, *Saratoga: A Military History of the Decisive Campaign of the American Revolution* (New York: Savas Beatie, 2008), 8.
4. Ira Gruber, *The Howe Brothers and the American Revolution* (Chapel Hill: University of North Carolina Press, 1972), 156–57, 179, 194, 199–200.
5. Luzader, *Saratoga*, 3.
6. Ibid., 4.
7. Germain to Howe, 14 January 1777, PRO, 5/94, 1–12.
8. Luzader, *Saratoga*, 5.
9. John A. Neuenschwander, *The Middle Colonies at the Coming of the American Revolution* (Port Washington, NY: Kennikat Press, 1973), 29–30; William Livingston, *A Memoir of the Life of William Livingston*, ed. Theodore Sedgwick (New York: J. and J. Harper, 1833), 29.
10. Howe to Germain, 20 December 1776, PRO, 5/74.
11. Ibid.
12. Luzader, *Saratoga*, 6.
13. Ibid.
14. Don Higginbotham, *The War of American Independence: Military Attitudes, Policies, and Practice* (New York: Macmillan, 1971), 170–71.
15. Mackesy, *War for America*, 92, 98, 112, 116–18, 125, 150–51; Sir John Fortescue, *History of the British Army*. 13 vols. (London: Macmillan, 1899–1902) 3:201; Luzader, *Saratoga*, 6.

16. Howe to Germain, 20 January 1777, PRO, CO 5/196, 41–50.

17. "Memorandum of General Carleton relative to the next campaign communicated to Lt. Genl. Burgoyne to be laid before Government," PRO, 42/35, 449.

18. Luzader, *Saratoga*, 9.

19. "Memorandum & Observations relative to the Service in Canada submitted to Lord George Germain," PRO, CO 43/36, 11–27.

20. William B. Willcox, *Portrait of a General: Sir Henry Clinton in the War of Independence* (New York: Alfred A. Knopf, 1964), 121–31.

21. Willcox, *Portrait of a General*, 131.

22. George III, King of Great Britain, and J. W. Fortescue, *The Correspondence of King George the Third from 1760 to December 1783: Printed from the Original Papers in the Royal Archives at Windsor Castle*, no. 1964, George III to Lord North, 24 February 1777 (London: Macmillan, 1927–28).

23. Willcox, *Portrait of a General*, 335–36.

24. Ibid.

25. PRO, CO 42/36, 37, ff; Germain Papers, William L. Clements Library, Ann Arbor, MI (hereafter Germain Papers); John Burgoyne, *State of the Expedition from Canada* (London: Printed for J. Almon, 1780), appendix III.

26. Burgoyne emphasized that his "Thoughts" responded to the "supposition that it be the *sole* purpose of the Canada army to effect a junction with General Howe, or after co-operating so far as to get possession of Albany and open communication with New York to remain upon Hudson's River, and thereby enable that general to act with his whole force to the southward" in conformity with Sir William's November 30 plan.

27. PRO, CO 42/36, 37, ff; Germain Papers; Burgoyne, *State of the Expedition*, appendix III.

28. Fortescue, *Correspondence of King George*, no. 1996, "Remark on Conduct of the War from Canada"; British Museum, additional manuscript 738, 186.

29. Luzader, *Saratoga*, 21; James Lunt, *Burgoyne of Saratoga* (New York: Harcourt Brace Jovanovich, 1975), 124.

30. Germain to Howe, 3 March 1777, PRO, CO 5/94, 215.

31. PRO, CO 42/36; PRO, CO 30/55, Carleton Papers, no. 462.

32. Ibid.

33. Luzader, *Saratoga*, 25.

34. Germain to Howe, 18 May 1777, PRO, CO 5/94, 33840.

35. Luzader, *Saratoga*, 25.

36. Ibid., 33.

37. Burgoyne, *State of the Expedition*, 3 and appendices XII–XVIII; "Extract of a Letter from Lord George Germain to General Carleton, dated Whitehall, 26th March 1777," Germain Papers; Carleton to Burgoyne, 10 June 1777, PRO, 42/36; Gerald Howson, *Burgoyne of Saratoga: A Biography* (New York: Times Books, 1979), 151; Lunt, *Burgoyne of Saratoga*, 138.

38. Burgoyne, *State of the Expedition*, appendix, "Extract of a Letter to General Harvey, Montreal, May 19, 1777."

39. Luzader, *Saratoga*, 49.

40. General Gates to President John Hancock, 11 May 1777, *Papers of the Continental Congress, 1774–1789*, National Archives, Washington, DC.

41. Hoffman Nickerson, *The Turning Point of the Revolution; or, Burgoyne in America* (Boston: Houghton Mifflin, 1928), 138.

42. Ibid., 123.

43. Arthur St. Clair to Schuyler, 13 January 1777, Philip Schuyler Papers, New York Public Library (hereafter Schuyler Papers).

44. James Wilkinson, *Memoirs of My Own Times*, 3 vols. (Philadelphia: Abraham Small, 1816), 1:173.

45. Nickerson, *Turning Point of the Revolution*, 138–39.

46. Wilkinson, *Memoirs*, 1:174–76.

47. Luzader, *Saratoga*, 52.

48. Howson, *Burgoyne of Saratoga*, 157; James Murray Hadden, *Hadden's Journal and Orderly Books: A Journal Kept in Canada and upon Burgoyne's Campaign in 1776 and 1777* (Albany: J. Munsell's Sons, 1884), lxxiv–lxxix.

49. John F. Luzader, *Decision on the Hudson: The Battles of Saratoga* (Fort Washington, PA: Eastern National, 2002), 20–22; St. Clair to Schuyler, 13 June 1777, Schuyler Papers.

50. Luzader, *Saratoga*, 53.

51. E. B. O'Callaghan, ed., *Orderly Book of Lieut. Gen. John Burgoyne from His Entry into the State of New York until His Surrender at Saratoga, 16th Oct., 1777. From the Original Manuscripts Deposited at Washington's Head Quarters, Newburgh Head Quarters* (Albany, NY: J. Munsell, 1860), hereafter cited as *Burgoyne's Orderly Book*, 26–27, General Order, 4 July 1777.

52. Hadden, *Journal and Orderly Book*, 54, 84–85.

53. Ibid., 54; Burgoyne, *State of the Expedition*, appendix VII, "Journal of the late principal Proceedings of the Army," xxiv.

54. Luzader, *Saratoga*, 55–59.

55. Ibid., 55–59, ff.

56. Ibid., 65–67.

57. Wilkinson, *Memoirs*, 1:215; Roger Lamb, *An Original and Authentic Journal of Occurrences during the Late American War from Its Commencement to the Year 1785* (Dublin, 1809), 142; Hadden, *Journal and Orderly Book*, 227; Burgoyne, *State of the Expedition*, "Journal of the Proceedings of the Army."

58. Luzader, *Saratoga*, 93, 113; Riedesel Urkunden, Wolfenbuettel, Militargeschlicter, "Journal des Feldzugs" and "Report to Herzog on the Bennington Fight," Burgoyne to Germain, 20 August 1777, Germain Papers; Baronin von Riedesel, *Berufs=Reise*.

59. Luzader, *Saratoga*, 115–40; Marinus Willett, "Narrative," New York Public Library; Germain to Carleton, 26 March 1777 and 27 August 1777, Germain Papers; "Colonel [Daniel] Claus Account of the Battle of Oriskany and Defeat of St. Leger's Expedition," New York State Library, Albany.

60. Hadden, *Journal and Orderly Book*, 117, General Order, 17 August 1777.

61. Luzader, *Saratoga*, 92.

62. On August 4, by a vote of eleven states to one, the Continental Congress conferred the northern command to former British Major Horatio Gates; *Journals of the Continental Congress* (Washington, DC: Library of Congress, 1907), 8:604.

63. Luzader, *Saratoga*, 185; Gates to Washington, August 22, 1777, New-York Historical Society, Horatio Gates Papers, 5:170 (hereafter Gates Papers).

64. Luzader, *Saratoga*, 189.

65. Don Higginbotham, *Daniel Morgan: Revolutionary Rifleman* (Chapel Hill: University of North Carolina Press, 1961), 57.

66. Luzader, *Saratoga*, 199.

67. Measam to Gates, "Private Intelligence," Gates Papers.

68. Luzader, *Saratoga*, 201.

69. Ibid., 205; Nickerson, *Turning Point of the Revolution*, 284.

70. Luzader, *Saratoga*, 205; Nickerson, *Turning Point of the Revolution*, 284, 291; Paul David Nelson, *General Horatio Gates: A Biography* (Baton Rouge: Louisiana State University Press, 1976), 113.

71. Luzader, *Saratoga*, 229–30; Niedersacchisches, Wolfenenbuttel, German, Briefschaften und Akten des Generaillieutenants Fredrich Adolf von Riedesel Freiherr zu Eisenbach, Riedesel to the Duke of Braunscheig, hereafter cited as Riedesel, Briefe 21 October; Burgoyne, *State of the Expedition*, appendix xiv, lxxxv; James Phinney Baxter, ed., *The British Invasion from the North: The Campaigns of General Carleton and Burgoyne from Canada, 1776–77. With the Journal of Lieut. William Digby of the 53d or Shropshire Regiment of Foot* (Albany, NY: J. Munsell's Sons, 1887), 271–72, hereafter Digby, *Journal*.

72. Luzader, *Saratoga*, 229–30.

73. Ibid.

74. Ibid., 234–35.

75. Ibid.

76. Ibid., 246.

77. Digby, *Journal*, entry for 20 September 1777, 274; Luzader, *Saratoga*, 249–55.

78. Luzader, *Saratoga*, 257–71; Gates to Hancock, 20 September 1777, Arnold to Gates, 22 September 1777, Gates to Arnold, 23 September 1777, Gates to Hancock, 23 September 1777, Arnold to Gates, 23 September 1777, all in Gates Papers; Varick to Schuyler, 17 September 1777, Varick to Schuyler, 19 September 1777, 22 September 1777, 24 September 1777, Livingston to Schuyler, 23 September 1777, all in Schuyler Papers.

79. Gates to President John Hancock, 20 September 1777, Gates Papers.

80. Varick to Schuyler, 21 September 1777, Schuyler Papers.

81. Varick to Schuyler, 21 September 1777, Livingston to Schuyler, 23 September 1777, all in Schuyler Papers; Luzader, *Saratoga*, 258–63.

82. Livingston to Schuyler, 23 September 1777, Schuyler Papers.

83. Wilkinson, *Memoirs*, 1:254.

84. Gates to Arnold, 23 September 1777, Gates to Hancock, 23 September 1777, Arnold to Gates, 23 September 1777, all in Gates Papers; Varick to Schuyler, 22 September 1777, Livingston to Schuyler, 23 September 1777, all in Schuyler Papers.

85. Luzader, *Saratoga*, 271.

86. Ibid., 247–49, 259.

87. *Burgoyne's Orderly Book*, General Order, 29 June 1777.

88. *Tagebuch Pausch*, 20 September and 8 October 1777, Hessisches Staatsarchiv, Cassel, Germany. Freiherr von Riedesel's Feldzug [Campaign] confirms that description.

89. Max von Eelking, *Memoirs and Letters and Journals, or Major General Ridesel, during his Residence in America*, trans. William L. Stone (Albany, NY: J. Munsell, 1868), 1:151–52.

90. Pausch to Bauermeister, 26 November 1777, Hessisches Staatsarchiv, Marburg, Germany.

91. Georg Pausch, *Georg Pausch's Journal and Reports of the Campaign in America*, trans. Bruce E. Burgoyne (Bowie, MD: Heritage Books, 1996), 79.

92. Clinton to Burgoyne, 11 September 1777, Sir Henry Clinton Papers, William L. Clements Library, University of Michigan, Ann Arbor.

93. *Burgoyne's Orderly Book*, General Orders, 3 October 1777.

94. Luzader, *Saratoga*, 276.

95. Burgoyne, *State of the Expedition*, lxxxix.

96. Ibid.

97. Riedesel, Briefe Urkunden, 21 October.

98. Luzader, *Saratoga*, 279.

99. Digby, *Journal*, 286.

100. Wilkinson, *Memoirs*, 1:267–68.

101. Ibid., 1:269.

102. Ibid., 1:273.

103. Ibid.

104. Luzader, *Saratoga*, 284–85.

105. Ibid., 285.

106. Niedersachschisches, Staatsarchiv Wolfenbuttel, Germany, Militgeschichter Nachlass.

107. Luzader, *Saratoga*, 286; Burgoyne, *State of the Expedition*, appendix xxci; Wilkinson, *Memoirs*, 1:271–74.

108. Luzader, *Saratoga*, 287.

109. Ibid.

110. Ibid., 293–94.

111. Digby, *Journal*, 291–92.

112. Ibid., 292–93; Riedesel, *Berufs = Reise*, 172; Burgoyne, *State of the Expedition*,73.

113. Luzader, *Saratoga*, 297–98.

114. Gates to Bayley, 24 October 1777, Gates Papers; Wilkinson, *Memoirs*, 1:280.

115. Von Senden, Johann Ernst Schüler, *Schueler von Senden Diary*, trans. Hans Mayer (D, Morristown NHP, 1960), 67.

116. Luzader, *Saratoga*, 298–300, 306–7.

117. Clinton to Burgoyne, 6 October 1777, Clinton Papers.

118. Burgoyne to Gates and Gates to Burgoyne, 13 October 1777, Gates Papers.

119. Wilkinson, *Memoirs*, 1:311; Burgoyne, *State of the Expedition*, "Major-General Gates's Proposals; together with Lieutenant-General Burgoyne's Answers," appendix ciii.

120. Burgoyne, *State of the Expedition*, appendix xv, "Minutes of a Council of War, holden on the Heights of Saratoga, Oct. 12," "Minutes and Proceedings of a Council of War consisting of all the general Officers and Field Officers, and Captains commanding Corps, on the Heights of Saratoga, October 13," "Major Kingston delivered the following Message to Major-General Gates, October 14," "Major-General Gates's Proposals; together with Lieutenant-General Burgoyne's Answers."

121. Luzader, *Saratoga*, 323–24.

122. Clinton to Burgoyne, 6 October 1777, Clinton Papers.

123. Negotiation documents, box 8, Gates Papers.

124. Ibid.

125. Riedesel Urkunden, "Briefschaften und Akten."

126. Negotiation Documents, box 8, Gates Papers.

127. Luzader, *Saratoga*, 334–36.

128. Mackesy, *War for America*, 141.

129. Luzader, *Saratoga*, 348–49.

130. Samuel Flagg Bemis, *The Diplomacy of the American Revolution* (Bloomington: Indiana University Press, 1957), 16, 60; Mackesy, *War for America*, 157, 182–84; B. F. Stevens, *Facsimiles of Manuscripts in European Archives Relating to America, 1773–1783*, number 1310, *Journals of the Continental Congress*, 17 and 24 September 1777, 30 December 1777; David Hunter Miller, *Treaties and Other International Acts of the United States of America*, 8 vols. (Washington, DC: U.S. Government Printing Office, 1921–48), 2:35–40.

CHAPTER TWO | ERIC H. SCHNITZER

The Tactics of the Battles of Saratoga

Introduction

Like so many other battles of the American War for Independence, the Battles of Saratoga conjure popular images of brilliant, polished, scarlet-coated veteran British soldiers, marching in close-packed, rigid, linear formations on rugged paths through a densely wooded forest. In this scenario, drummers and fifers vigorously play European marches while officers, arrogant and lazy, ride on horseback. Unbeknownst to the King's men, local colonial minutemen, armed with rifles, creep cautiously through the woods, keeping watchful eyes on their unsuspecting foes; they are spread out, independent, and, although untrained in warfare, they know the local landscape. Upon a general's order, or on their own initiative, they begin to shoot their victims, beginning with the officers. Depending on the version of this fictional narrative, the redcoats either react with mindless precision drill or dither in fear. Either way, the hapless British, incapable of entering the woods, remain on the path and the only survivors are those who surrender.

Revolutionary War battle narratives like this one have been, and continue to be, perpetuated in popular media like novels and movies, and even in historical documentaries and nonfiction studies. While some of the elements contained in these scenarios have a basis in fact, general combat situations had little in common with these popular notions. Long before the Battles of Saratoga, the British adapted their combat style to be more effective, including new tactical flexibility for "treeing" (fighting in wooded terrain). Fighting alongside the British component of the army from Canada were "Hessians," soldiers from the duchy of Braunschweig and the country of Hessen-Hanau, who also modified their tactical doctrine to fight more effectively, using trees and buildings for cover. Their formations included riflemen, something that British forces are generally not popularly recognized as having during the war. Supplementing these formidable European troops were a host of American loyalists, French Canadians, and First Nations warriors, the majority of whom continually operated at the army's front and became, or already were, adept at the guerrilla warfare tactics that proved highly effective throughout the first half of the Northern Campaign of 1777.

The great majority of soldiers serving in the Northern Department of the Army of the United States in 1777, either in the congressionally authorized Continental army or individual state militias, were hardly crafty woods fighters. In fact, these soldiers were instructed with the same drill manual as the British. Nor were these soldiers completely inexperienced; most had served in at least one battle or campaign and therefore had more wartime service than most of their European adversaries. "Southern" riflemen drafted from the main Continental army and Oneida, Tuscarora, and Stockbridge warriors came to augment an army otherwise devoid of riflemen and American Indian allies.

Thus, the Battles of Saratoga were more equal fights than generally realized. Both sides dealt with advantages and disadvantages in their respective tactical formations, weapons and equipment technologies, command and control capacities, and personnel composition. These, as well as the natural landscape, numerical superiority, initiative, and logistical considerations, were all significant factors affecting the ways in which the Battles of Saratoga were fought.

This chapter presents a chronological narrative of the Battles of Saratoga, fought in upstate New York on September 19 and October 7, 1777.[1] Particular emphasis is given to the strategic, tactical, and personnel realities facing both armies. After each battle narrative, the results are assessed, including analyses of casualties and use of landscape; effectiveness of the combatants, commanders, and weapons; and the all-important strategic implications.

Burgoyne's Strategy: September 19, 1777

By the time Lieutenant-General John Burgoyne was positioned to bring battle against the American troops entrenched at Bemis Heights, his strategic advantages were few. He led a disparate force of about 8,500 soldiers, sailors, Indians, civil army employees, and followers.[2] Because he was advancing through unfriendly territory, everything needed for his army's sustenance and support, including hospital supplies, food, baggage, ammunition, and all manner of other war matériel, had to be transported with it. Since it was impossible for large ships to portage between Lakes Champlain and George and the headwaters of the Hudson, scows and bateaux were used to move most of the army's vital supplies, while carts on the River Road carried the remainder. Because the logistics of this phase of the campaign relied on the river and its paralleling road, Burgoyne was bound to them both, making certain that a large portion of his army was in constant contact with this valley-bound lifeline. If the infantry did not support his watercraft, then the vital supplies they carried could easily be captured or destroyed. Because Burgoyne could not afford to abandon the Hudson River or the River Road during his advance south, this simple logistical challenge informed every strategic decision he made.

Encamped at Thomas Swords's house, three miles north of the American forces dug in at Bemis Heights, Burgoyne, who was aware of the enemy's position, was presented with two fundamental choices. First, he could move his army in a column along the River Road, funnel his way past the Great Vly (a large swamp), and make a frontal attack on the American defensive lines on the river flats and the Bemis Heights bluffs. Second, he could direct most of his troops to attack the Americans in their fortified camp on the high ground west of the bluffs where, theoretically, the Americans were more vulnerable. The first alternative offered little hope for success. While Burgoyne may have been able to drive the Americans out of the river defenses, assuming that he could bring enough troops past the swamp unmolested, the fortifications on the bluffs were insurmountable and attacking them directly was not a viable option. Since offensive action was necessary in order to proceed, that left the only other alternative: take the high ground west of the fortified American camp, strike at their camp's flank from those heights, roll up the entire American line, and open the way to Albany. Although Burgoyne had only one viable option, he may have been emboldened by his previous success with this same basic strategy at Forts Ticonderoga and Independence.

On the morning of September 19, Burgoyne's army broke camp at Swords's house and went into "marching order"; that is, soldiers stuffed knapsacks with their worldly possessions and spare ammunition and slung them over their shoulders, along with tin water flasks and haversacks heavy with three days' rations. Tents for officers and men alike were dismantled and piled onto baggage carts. The general hospital's massive tents and supplies were likewise loaded, the ammunition carts were stockpiled, and artillery was limbered and hitched to teams of horses.[3] Watercraft on the river were weighed down with tons of provisions and spare artillery, gunpowder, and shot. Companies, battalions, and brigades were formed, and because they were expecting to march into combat that day, bayonets were fixed and every soldier had one hundred rounds of prepared ammunition.

Brigadier-General Simon Fraser's advanced corps, including First Nations allies, French Canadians, and American loyalists, composed the right column of about 2,400 men. Lieutenant Colonel Heinrich Breymann's German reserve corps of 530 men formed behind them. These two corps had the combatant elite of the army, ready to provide the most skilled and powerful punch against the Americans. The center column, which Burgoyne himself accompanied,

FIGURE 2.1. Private, Grenadier Company, 20th Regiment of Foot, 1777. Grenadiers were the elite of the British army, being composed of some of the most experienced and tallest soldiers. Unlike many of their American counterparts, British soldiers were not drafted but joined the army voluntarily. This private soldier is dressed in marching order, with tin water flask, haversack (carrying multiple days' rations), and knapsack (carrying personal belongings and spare ammunition). This equipment would be piled on the ground upon entering a battle situation. Burgoyne's grenadiers did not wear their famous, tall bearskin caps in 1777, but rather used caps cut from wool felt hats. Painting by Don Troiani. www.historicalimagebank.com.

consisted of 1,700 regular British troops commanded by Brigadier-General James Hamilton. The left column was drawn from slightly more than 1,600 Germans under Major General Friedrich Riedesel. Major-General William Phillips, who brought up the civil military employees, the park of artillery (uncommitted reserve artillery), general hospital, army baggage, and followers, traveled behind Riedesel with nearly 1,000 additional people. The boats, manned by sailors of the Royal Navy and American loyalists, floated down the river beside the 290-man British 47th Regiment. The 590-man Hessen-Hanau Regiment Erbprinz was left behind at Swords's house as the army's rear guard.

Fraser's and Breymann's troops marched in a column along a road leading into the wooded hills west of Swords's house, then picked up a road to the south. Hamilton's center column followed Fraser's for a short distance and turned south on the first road, which led into the Great Ravine. The left column, composed of

FIGURE 2.2. Private, Leibcompany, Light Infantry Battalion von Bärner, 1777. Referred to as "foreign Mercenaries" in the Declaration of Independence, most German officers and soldiers were instead part of existing corps leased by the British government from various German princes. Any men enlisted in order to meet the quota of soldiers agreed to in the British-Braunschweig treaty were volunteers. Despite being a light infantry battalion, soldiers in this corps wore cocked hats, long coats, and swords, similar to common German musketeers. Of this unit's five companies, one was a jägercompany, in which the men were uniformed differently and armed with rifles and sword-length bayonets. Painting by Don Troiani. www.historicalimagebank.com.

Riedesel's and Phillips's forces, was the largest of the three and marched slowly south along the River Road. When the three columns reached their preassigned positions, a signal gun from Hamilton's brigade coordinated a simultaneous movement toward the unseen American camp (figures 2.1 and 2.2).

Gates's Strategy: September 19, 1777

By September 19, Major General Horatio Gates, commander of the Northern Department of the Army of the United States, enjoyed a great many strategic advantages. His army was composed of numbers nearly equal to those of Burgoyne's, an advantage to any army intending to use fortifications for defense. While Burgoyne's lines of communication to the north were severed once his army crossed the Hudson River in mid-September, Gates had the advantage of operating in nearly every direction, save immediately north, unmolested and supported by a substantial majority of the civilian population. Another advantage was the strength of the area's natural landscape made stronger by manmade fortifications. Bemis Heights, the ground where Gates chose to make his stand, was a line of high bluffs overlooking the river valley. At this one place, the Hudson River made an unusual bend to the west and edged very close to the Bemis Heights bluffs. Here, the River Road, which any army marching to Albany had to take, was squeezed in between the river and the bluffs. Strong fortifications were built in the valley and upon the bluffs, made insurmountable by a ring of abatis.[4] About a half mile north of the valley defenses was the Great Vly, a huge swamp, which blocked all approaches in the valley save the road itself. West of the bluffs, the rising high ground was fronted by a series of noncontiguous ravines and ended at a large hill known as the Summit. The American forces encamped in the valley, on the bluffs and rising high ground, and on the Summit, covering a front more than one mile in length. A well-supplied train of artillery, consisting of twenty-two cannons, was positioned throughout the lines in order to rake British forces if they approached.

Although some of Gates's Continental regiments had taken a beating earlier in the year at various battles and skirmishes against enemy troops, most were fresh and had not fought in battle during the present campaign.[5] Because "the people in the Northern Army seem so intimidated by the Indians," Washington ordered Colonel Daniel Morgan and his elite 400-man Detached Rifle Battalion north to join Gates's army in order to fight Burgoyne's First Nations allies "in their own way."[6] Joining the riflemen was a newly formed 300-man light infantry battalion commanded by Major Henry Dearborn, composed of "the most able, active, spirited Men," handpicked from Gates's New England Continental army regiments.[7] While Morgan's riflemen could shoot much further and with more accuracy than any soldier armed with a smoothbore musket, their rifles were slower to load and could not mount bayonets. Dearborn's agile light infantrymen, armed with smoothbore muskets and bayonets, were intended to work in concert with the riflemen for mutual offensive and defensive support. Together, the two battalions were called "Morgan's corps."

Gates's strategy for the impending battle was simple: allow the British to approach the defenses, attack, and spend themselves in an attempt to break through the lines. He felt his army was secure behind its fortifications, a defensive strategy the American army employed regularly in the early years of the war, such as in the Battle of Bunker Hill. Although Bunker Hill was a tactical loss for the Americans, it was only so because American troops were greatly outnumbered and many ran out of ammunition. At Bemis Heights, Gates's army was in danger of neither situation (figures 2.3 and 2.4).

FIGURE 2.3. Private, Colonel Thomas Marshall's (10th Massachusetts) Regiment, 1777. All fifteen Massachusetts Continental army regiments were present with Gates's army, including Marshall's regiment, which was raised in the winter of 1776 to 1777. As in other Continental army corps, most soldiers of this unit were a mix of volunteers and draftees forced to serve by the government for enlistment terms of three years or the indefinite duration of the war. Even enslaved men were sometimes forced to serve in place of their drafted owners. Dress in Gates's army varied considerably between regiments and sometimes within regiments. While not all soldiers had uniform coats, the most common colors issued were blue, green, and brown. Painting by Don Troiani. www.historicalimagebank.com.

The Battle of Freeman's Farm, September 19, 1777

British preparations to attack were by no means kept secret. American officers observed their decamping process, and the cannon firing that coordinated the advance of the three columns gave the Americans fair warning. Learning of the British movements, Major General Benedict Arnold, Gates's de facto second in command, convinced the American commander to send Morgan's corps forward to "observe their Direction, and harrass [sic] their advance" north of the camp.[8] Morgan's quick-moving troops were well suited for making initial contact with the enemy north of camp. The ground was a maze of farm clearings enclosed within a labyrinth of wooden-rail fences and dotted with dwellings

FIGURE 2.4. American Militiaman, 1775–1783. Most militia serving with Gates's army at Saratoga were from New England, not New York. Officers and soldiers were called up by their respective state governments for short-term, finite service, the quotas being filled with a mix of volunteers and draftees. Many drafted men opted to escape militia service by paying fines, finding volunteer replacements, or forcing enslaved men to serve in their stead. Militia laws required that militiamen supply their own arms and accoutrements, but as not everyone was able to fulfill this obligation, the government provided the balance. Dress varied greatly, since the officers and soldiers alike wore their own clothing. Painting by Don Troiani. www.historicalimagebank.com.

and outbuildings. Innumerable roads and paths cut though these farms and the woods that separated them, and the topography was crossed by numerous creeks and ravines. At about noon, Morgan's corps rushed toward Freeman's farm, located about 1¼ miles north of the American camp, near where British advance sentries of the center column were exchanging shots with American sentries already stationed there.

Freeman's farm was an oblong, boot-shaped clearing with its "leg" running east to west and its "foot" stretching south (figure 2.5). Along the southern side of the "leg," a very deep wood-covered branch of the Middle Ravine skirted the farm's primary cultivated field. This field was flat, measuring about 800 by 400 yards,

FIGURE 2.5. 3ᵈ & 4ᵗʰ Position 19ᵗʰ Septʳ 1777 (detail). This map, oriented with north on the bottom, depicts Freeman's farm during various phases of action, including the arrival of German forces toward the end of the fighting; note how the Continental army rifle battalion, anchoring the American's right in the woods, was outflanked by blue-coated German musketeers arriving from the river valley. American Continentals and British infantry are depicted in the open field and woods of Freeman's farm. To the right, west of Freeman's farm, lay Marshall's farm, where the 24th Regiment deployed and entered the woods between the farm fields in order to fight Dearborn's light infantry. Drawn by William Cumberland Wilkinson, ca. 1778. Library of Congress, G3803.S353 1777.W5 Faden 69a.

with over one half of the cultivation devoted to wheat and rye. To the north, the entire farm clearing was bordered by the wooded northern branch of the same creek, described as a "large gutter," which ran east until turning south, wrapped around the eastern side of the clearing, and eventually joined the deeper ravine on its southern side.[9] The western side of Freeman's clearing consisted of elevated ground primarily formed by a few large hills that played decisive roles in the ensuing battle. Freeman's house and barn were situated on top of the northernmost hill (the house situated north of the barn), and a log outbuilding stood on the southernmost height. Fences bound the entire perimeter, beyond which were primeval woods. A mix of girdled and healthy trees dotted the uncultivated portions of Freeman's clearing, most heavily on the southernmost elevation.[10] A dirt road extended from the east through the flat, cultivated field and in between the two large hills, where it wrapped around the northern hill on its western flank, and went into the woods on the northern end of the farm over the "large gutter" by way of a small bridge.[11]

About twenty-five yards within the woods west of Freeman's clearing sat a commanding hill that dominated the forest surrounding it. Continuing west a couple hundred yards, these woods opened upon Micajah Marshall's farm, a roughly triangular clearing measuring 400 yards across at its greatest width. As with Freeman's property, it was also flat, partially cultivated, and fenced. The Marshall farm contained two structures flanking opposite sides of the Quaker Springs Road, which ran in a north-south direction through the clearing.[12]

At about 12:45 p.m., the British center column's one-hundred-man picket led by Major Gordon Forbes moved in extended formation across the wooded "gutter" and advanced into the open field on the northern side of the clearing.[13] Their purpose was to flush out American sentries posted at the farm who had been holding up the center column's sentinels since about noon. Forbes and his men entered the field and maneuvered up the low rising hill toward the fences and house, behind and within which the American sentries were firing. At that moment, the front of Morgan's rifle battalion arrived to support the outnumbered sentries. Forbes's men opened fire on the advance party of riflemen, but with little effect, and Morgan's riflemen stepped up the pace to close the gap. A further exchange of fire and overwhelming numbers resulted in Forbes and his men falling back to the safety of the woods from where they came. The riflemen, moving as a column a distance ahead of Dearborn's light infantry, sought to take tactical advantage of the developing situation, and pursued the retreating redcoats. But the advancing riflemen overextended themselves and were outflanked by British light infantry reinforcements sent from Fraser's advanced corps. This unexpected strike scattered the rifle battalion and caused it and the sentinels to withdraw to the south.[14]

Hamilton's main body remained in line on the wooded road north of the "gutter" and farm, and upon hearing the ever-increasing sound of fire coming from that direction, was ordered to prepare for a potential enemy attack. A crashing noise in the woods along the British front suggested that the enemy was approaching, and some redcoats opened fire without orders. Sadly, the soldiers crashing through the woods were the remnants of Forbes's pickets and thus, the first shots fired in the Battle of Freeman's Farm by the main body of British soldiers were upon their own men.[15]

After the scattered retreat of the riflemen and sentinels, Dearborn positioned his corps of light infantry about 275 yards southwest of Freeman's house on the commanding rise of ground in the nearby woods. Upon reaching their destination, Dearborn formed his men into line and, using the trees as cover, waited for the inevitable sight of British troops pouring out onto the field. Meanwhile, the riflemen, scattered into disparate groups and detachments from the initial shock of being outflanked, were in the process of being reformed by Morgan in the woods about a half mile south of the farm.[16]

After this poor start to the battle, one of the British light six-pounders from the center column fired through the woods at Freeman's house in order to clear out any Americans still hiding there. The cannonball passed through the building. No Americans were present, having already evacuated the farmhouse. The four British battalions composing the center column, the 9th, 21st, 62nd, and 20th Regiments (from right to left), moved south through the woods and onto Freeman's farm; there, they formed parallel to the clearing's tree line, their battle formation facing south. Teams of horses pulling the four limbered light six-pounders likewise negotiated the "gutter" and forest and spilled out onto the open field.[17]

Burgoyne ordered the 9th Regiment to leave the field and take possession of two cabins flanking the road from where the center column had just come. This was done in order to solidify lines of passage and communication with the advanced corps. The American's corps of light infantry, posted on the wooded eminence about 275 yards away, took a position that had the potential to drive a wedge between the center column and the advanced corps.[18] Following standard operating procedure, the men of the three British regiments piled heavy knapsacks with blankets, haversacks, tin water flasks, and kettles behind them, which unburdened them for the fight to come.[19]

During the interval between two and three o'clock, by which time the British line was formed on Freeman's farm and Dearborn's light infantry was waiting on the wooded height, the British took the initiative and advanced. The 21st Regiment, commanded by Major George Forster, and 62nd Regiment, commanded by Lieutenant-Colonel John Anstruther, marched forth, the officers directing their advancing battalions obliquely across the field in a southwesterly direction, targeting the wooded hill topped by Dearborn's men. It was at this time that Colonel Joseph Cilley's 1st New Hampshire Battalion, dispatched by Arnold to support Morgan's corps, arrived to reinforce the American position. By the time Cilley's men formed, the British regiments had advanced about halfway across the field, passing John Freeman's house and barn. As the British passed the buildings, Cilley attacked. Although the New Hampshire men sustained the attack as best they could, after about twenty minutes of firing and receiving a high number of casualties, Cilley ordered his battalion to withdraw back to camp. Dearborn attempted to assist Cilley but was too late. While Cilley and his battalion were retiring through the woods, they were met by Colonel Alexander Scammell leading the 3rd New Hampshire Battalion, sent by Arnold as reinforcement for Morgan's corps and Cilley. Cilley turned his men around and, with Scammell's troops, returned to the field of battle.[20]

With the return of Cilley's battalion and the addition of Scammell's, the battle was "renewed, with great Warmth and Violence."[21] Arnold moved between the camp and the field of battle in order to keep abreast of its progress, and through his observations of the fighting and the reports coming in from the field, decided to send additional forces. As such, Cilley and Scammell were quickly joined by Colonel Thaddeus Cook's battalion of Connecticut militia, later followed by Brigadier General Enoch Poor and the remainder of his brigade, the 2nd New Hampshire Battalion, 2nd and 4th New York Regiments, and Colonel Jonathan Latimer's battalion of Connecticut militia. American regiments filled the woods on the south and southwestern sides of the farm, using the perimeter fences and tree lines for cover, and when they were exposed on the field, the girdled trees afforded them some protection. As the battle wore on, Morgan's rifle battalion, reformed after some delay, took position behind a series of deep wooded ravines on the right of the American line. The ravines afforded not only a prime defense for the American's right flank, but specifically for Morgan's slower-loading rifles. Dearborn's light infantrymen defended the main line's left flank, within the band of woods between Freeman's and Marshall's farms.[22]

Unlike the American line of battle, the British line was noncontiguous. The 62nd and 21st Regiments, each supported with two light six-pounders, bore the brunt of fire from the New Hampshire line and Cook's militia. The Americans concentrated their fire on the front of these regiments and extended their line so as to outflank the 62nd Regiment. In turn, the 62nd refused its left wing grand division in order to avoid becoming enveloped.[23] Four additional "heavy guns" eventually arrived from the River Road and were placed on the northern side of Freeman's farm. These heavy field pieces, able to fire larger-sized round or case shot with greater force and at longer distances, were essential for preventing American troops from taking better advantage of their superior numbers.[24] Fraser sent his German light infantry and jäger to Hamilton's support in order to help cover the left and rear of the 62nd Regiment.[25] The 62nd Regiment inflicted enough casualties on Cook's militia that they were forced to retreat from the field. Arnold ordered up Continental army reinforcements, drawn from the picket of Learned's brigade, to replace Cook's beaten battalion.[26]

Ordered into the woods, the 62nd Regiment's initial attacks appeared successful, since the "rebels fled at every charge deeper still into the woods," but upon returning to their initial position on the open field, the redcoats were "slowly followed, and those who had been the most forward in the pursuit [of the Americans] were the first to fall."[27] Following one of their unsuccessful attacks in the woods against New Hampshire Continentals and Connecticut militia, the 62nd Regiment quit the southernmost height, abandoned the two light six-pounders, and retreated north through the clearing. The American pursuit was followed by a British rally and the British once again advanced.

The 20th Regiment of Foot, located to the left of the 62nd Regiment, was sent "into the wood on the left of the corn field" to force back the well-positioned riflemen anchoring the American's right flank. But the British were unsuccessful in part due to a deeply cut ravine preventing them from making contact with the riflemen in the woods.[28]

Throughout the battle, it became clear that the four British light six-pounders were increasingly becoming a focal point of the defensive and offensive tactics of both sides. At every opportunity the Americans advanced in an attempt to capture the British guns left behind in the field during the ebb and flow of the battle, only to be stymied in their attempts. Thus, the concentration of fire on Royal Regiment of Artillery personnel was high. At one point, a pair of guns were captured by the American riflemen, but "not knowing how to manage it they lost it again."[29] During another action in the battle, captured artillery was lost again "only for the want of horses to draw them off."[30]

As Fraser's advanced corps proceeded south, British and German battalions and subdivisions were positioned to secure buildings and passages at key points. The bulk of the advanced corps marched into the Marshall farm clearing and the adjacent woods bordering Freeman's farm. American troops in the woods prevented a further advance and Fraser's forward elements were turned back. Similarly, the American line pressed forward through the woods, but their advance was checked by the equally protected line of the British advanced corps. Fraser's own 24th Regiment was posted in the Marshall farm clearing itself.[31]

As the battle wore on, Dearborn's light infantry guarded the main American line's left flank, in the woods between the Marshall and Freeman farms. His men were "constantly opposed to a body of British light infantry [the 24th Regiment] destined to turn the left of our main line."[32] The American light infantry's preoccupation with checking the 24th Regiment prevented their exploiting the weakness of Hamilton's center column, which was vulnerable due to its singular focus on Poor's brigade and Morgan's riflemen. In the woods, Dearborn's men were so secure that they forced five subdivisions of the 24th Regiment out of the woods and back into the Marshall farm clearing. Not taking this beating lightly, the 24th repositioned and filed into the woods north of their initial point of attack, allowing them to strike at the Americans in "their own manner from behind Trees."[33]

For over three hours the battle swept back and forth across Freeman's farm. In the woods to the west, Fraser's column remained engaged with Learned's brigade, which was ordered to support Poor and prevent him from being outflanked. Riedesel's column on the River Road remained at a relative standstill because the Americans had destroyed every bridge between Kroma Kill, which meandered through the Great Ravine before emptying into the Hudson River, and Bemis Heights.

Soon after marching off that morning, Burgoyne's left column came to a halt at the mouth of Kroma Kill and the junction of the Great Ravine. The Americans previously destroyed the bridge crossing Kroma Kill and it took more than half the day to rebuild it. During this delay, Riedesel moved his German battalions to advantageous positions throughout the area. Cannons covered the flats in the floodplain, and the small squadron of Braunschweig dragoons rode southward to reconnoiter. The bridge was eventually completed, but because of the swampy ground near the outlet of the Great Ravine, other minor bridges and footways had to be repaired before the column could continue. After completing these tasks, the column advanced only 500 yards until encountering the ruins of another major bridge. Once again, repairs were begun and Riedesel posted his men advantageously, leapfrogging advance forces southward toward yet another substantial creek and a third destroyed bridge site. Even as the gunfire in the vicinity of Freeman's farm was growing louder, no orders were received to come to the center column's support. In the absence of clear direction from Burgoyne, Riedesel continued to very cautiously position his troops at advantageous points in the floodplain and on the bluffs in order to repel any attack the Americans might make against them. Of primary importance was the defense of "everything that had to do with the sustenance of the army" for which Riedesel's men were entrusted.[34]

Late in the day, an officer finally brought orders for Riedesel to strengthen his positions in the floodplain for defense, and "fall on the enemy's right flank at Freeman's Farm with all the troops he possibly could spare."[35] The baron immediately took personal command of his own regiment, two companies of the Regiment von Rhetz, and two of Captain Georg Päusch's light six-pounders, and proceeded toward Freeman's farm. The forces remaining on the floodplain, now commanded by Brigadier Johann Specht, continued work on repairing the second bridge.

Riedesel's men reached the ravine bordering the eastern side of Freeman's farm at dusk. From this vantage point, they could observe the clearing ahead of them, including the dead and wounded of both armies mingled together. They further observed:

> The enemy were stationed at the corner of a wood, and were covered on their right flank by a deep swampy ravine, whose steep banks covered with bushes had moreover been made quite insurmountable by means of an abatis. There was an open space in front of this corner of the wood, in which the English Regiments had formed into line. The possession of this open piece of ground, on which Freemann's [sic] Habitation was situated, was the apple of discord during the whole of the day, and was now occupied by the

one party now by the other. . . . There was nothing but dense forests round the place where the English Brigade had formed into line.[36]

The German general immediately sent his two von Rhetz companies over the bridge that crossed the ravine that separated them from Freeman's farm clearing. There, they struck the American's right flank, which was then advancing from the safety of the tree line. Päusch's cannons were sent over the bridge too, and dragged across the Freeman's farm clearing along the road to the hills on the other side of the field where the entire British line was being pushed back. With great difficulty, Päusch's guns were moved up a hill overlooking the battleground and, so reinforced, the British rallied. The Regiment von Riedesel and the von Rhetz companies received orders to "force their way through the ravine [on the southern side of the farm] no matter what it cost."[37] The 21st Regiment was repositioned to this quarter, where they "rushed into the wood together with us [Germans] in a terrific hurrah."[38] This surprise attack made by strong numbers of fresh troops against the Americans was overwhelming, and the American line "retreated safely" under the cover of darkness.[39]

Tactical and Strategic Assessment of the Battle of Freeman's Farm

While the Americans withdrew and lost the battle on tactical grounds, they gained an important strategic victory by preventing the British from breaking through their lines of defense. More important, the British got nowhere near the American lines of defense during the course of the battle and instead expended their efforts on what resulted in a pyrrhic victory.

Over 300 officers and soldiers of the Army of the United States were killed or severely wounded and a further twenty-three captured by the British. The highest casualties were borne by regiments in Poor's brigade, especially the 1st New Hampshire Battalion (over fifty casualties) and Cook's battalion of Connecticut militia (over fifty casualties). The officer corps suffered a surprisingly high number of casualties in the battle too, with twenty-seven killed or mortally or severely wounded. Of those killed or mortally wounded, two held the rank of lieutenant colonel. In addition, two captains and one lieutenant were captured.[40] Arnold, who generally managed the battle from afar but was positioned to view it on occasion, was alarmed at the high number of officer deaths, observing that "two [sic] many officers, that Zeal & Spirit push'd on" led from "the front of their companies" instead of taking up their "proper stations" in the rear.[41]

Perhaps the greatest tactical disappointment of the battle was the failure of Morgan's corps to act as intended—that is, as a single, cohesive, body. This is not surprising, since its two battalions were newly formed, served together for less than one week, and had no combined-arms training.[42] Instead, the riflemen were scattered soon after the battle started because the light infantry was unable to arrive in time to support, resulting in the rifle battalion being placed out of commission for some time. As the battle progressed, both battalions were well placed on opposite ends of the line of battle in order to defend the flanks of Poor's brigade, with Dearborn's light infantry on the left and Morgan's riflemen anchoring the right. But the unintended result was that Morgan's riflemen had to rely solely on the natural landscape for their defense (the ravines, woods, and abatis) rather than the bayonet-armed light infantry. With the arrival of Riedesel's Germans at dusk, the outflanked riflemen had no choice but to retreat.

Although Washington ordered that men serving in the rifle battalion be "none but such as are known to be perfectly skilled in the use of these guns [rifles], and who are known to be active and orderly in their behaviour," their actual prowess in the use of rifles is questionable. Most were drafted from musket-armed regiments and had to transition to army-issue rifles that were not their own.[43] Given that the rifle battalion numbered about 400 officers and soldiers and were engaged for most of the battle, one might expect that they should have been capable of shooting down every British soldier in the field that day (given their numbers and time engaged).

This is not to say that the battalions, fighting independently, did not fight brilliantly; in the end, both were judiciously placed, and they inflicted over three times the number of casualties they received. Although exaggerating, Gates had reason to claim that the "Glory of the action . . . was entirely owing to the Valor of the Rifle Regiment & Corps of Light Infantry" under Morgan's command.[44] However, it is obvious that the first combined-arms corps experiment was a failure, since at no point in the battle did the riflemen and light infantry serve together. Twice in the battle, at the beginning and at the end, when the riflemen were in need of protection against outflanking British forces, the light infantry was not positioned to help.

Despite the stereotype of being a ragtag band of ill-equipped citizen soldiers, American troops were well armed, with many Continental regiments and even some militia outfitted with surplus French muskets and bayonets issued to them earlier that summer.[45] State militia laws mandated that every militia soldier own his own "gun" and a bladed weapon, and thus militia soldiers were also adequately armed.[46] However, despite being well armed, one shortcoming of Continental and militia equipment alike was the inability of their cartridge pouches to carry substantial amounts of ammunition.[47] Thus, American soldiers went into battle with significantly less ammunition than did their enemies.[48]

There were few engagements in the war in which American troops chose their positions better than at Saratoga, making excellent use of the forests and wood lines, hills, and ravines. These natural defenses, strengthened by field-improvised fortifications, provided cover to the American forces for much of the battle. While often used, albeit not always successfully, by American troops during the first years of the war, this tactic was applied brilliantly at Freeman's farm.[49] Another factor accounting for their success is that most of the American troops committed to combat were experienced veterans, as a great number had seen prior service in 1775, 1776, and/or earlier in 1777. They were not the green, untested, and untried citizen soldiers commonly associated with American combatants, but instead, they "behaved like veterans."[50]

On a strategic level, the battle was a success due to Arnold's aggressive strategy. By sending one battalion after another to the field of combat, he was able to close tactical weak points in the American line as needed. His gradual but consistent commitment of fresh battalions throughout the day made it impossible for the British to formulate a cohesive offensive strategy, which completely stymied Burgoyne's advance toward the American camp. The Battle of Freeman's Farm was a strategic success for the American army because of Arnold's initiative and measured deployment of his division's battalions.

Gates has long been blamed for supposedly denying Arnold reinforcements during the course of the battle. An assessment of Gates's decision must include his personal experience with Arnold with regard to the October 1776 Battle of Valcour Island on Lake Champlain. Gates gave Arnold command of a newly constructed fleet of vessels for the defense of Lake Champlain and Forts Ticonderoga and Mount Independence, where Gates commanded. In the subsequent battle initiated by Arnold, over fifty miles north of the forts, the Americans suffered nearly 200 casualties and lost almost every vessel. The British, having incurred about forty casualties and the loss of only a few small gunboats, were unable to besiege the forts due to the lateness of the season and returned to Canada.[51] Gates may have learned a valuable lesson: Arnold's battlefield tenacity could result in his taking too many risks and losing nearly everything. After Valcour Island, the two commanders did not work together again until Saratoga, and so this lesson may have been foremost on Gates's mind. As it was, Arnold was not prevented from committing half the army in order to combat nearly two-thirds of Burgoyne's.[52]

Although the British "won" the Battle of Freeman's Farm, it was a tactical, not a strategic, victory; the British position afterward was strategically weaker than it was that morning. Burgoyne suffered a great number of casualties and completely lost the initiative, advancing only one mile south and gaining control of strategically irrelevant farm fields and woods located only a little closer to the American defensive lines.

British casualties included about 550 officers and soldiers killed or severely wounded and a further forty-one captured by the Americans. The brunt of casualties were suffered by the regiments of Hamilton's brigade, particularly the

62nd Regiment (over 160 casualties) and the 20th Regiment (over 115 casualties). Perhaps surprisingly, no officer above the rank of captain was killed or mortally wounded, and the Americans were able to take only a few low-ranking officers into captivity.[53] While the British officer corps suffered more casualties than that of the Americans, thirty-four killed or mortally or severely wounded, the number was not that much greater, and it was the Americans who lost officers of much higher rank.

For the British, a major tactical disappointment of the battle was the general failure of the Royal Regiment of Artillery to effectively combat the American forces. While the Americans had no artillery at Freeman's farm, the British employed four light six-pounders through the entirety of combat and, later on, four additional "heavy guns" brought up from the river valley. These guns should have been well positioned to rake American troops and cause them to suffer higher casualties, but as one American officer remarked, "not a shot from their field pieces took effect, except among the limbs of trees."[54] One reason for the general ineffectiveness of British artillery fire was certainly the terrain. Another reason was that the guns were employed primarily as a defensive device, used to prevent Americans from pouring onto the field of battle in overwhelming numbers, rather than as an offensive one. Given the realities of the ravine-cut, wooded terrain, and a low force concentration of British troops at Freeman's farm (compared to the Americans), this was probably unavoidable.

Burgoyne's British and German regiments were well armed, the British infantry carrying both the older long and the newer short land pattern muskets, and non-jäger Germans using their own Prussian-like Germanic smoothbore muskets. A significant advantage enjoyed by the British forces over the Americans was their high-capacity cartridge pouches. Each British and German soldier was issued one hundred rounds of ammunition before the battle, and the army was therefore better equipped to sustain itself in a prolonged engagement.[55]

A myriad of reasons can be attributed to the British victory in the battle, as well as their general inability to smash through the American lines. During the majority of the fighting, American regiments overwhelmed the British, creating a force concentration that the British were unable to overcome until the very end, when substantial German reinforcements arrived. Even the center column's reserve unit, the 9th Regiment, was not brought into action. Burgoyne's choice to avoid committing reserves may be reflective of an arrogance and obstinacy that led him to continually underestimate his adversary, both strategically and tactically, throughout the Saratoga Campaign of 1777.

That the timely arrival of Riedesel's Germans saved the victory for Burgoyne is no doubt accurate. But the manner of tactical support the Germans lent is unusual; Braunschweig musketeers, inexperienced in "treeing," were sent into the woods and successfully outflanked American riflemen. The Germans would have been incapable of performing such an action before the August 16 Battle of Bennington, in which the Germans learned a hard lesson about the realities of fighting American troops often using the cover of woods. Recognizing this, Riedesel ordered his men to modify their tactical doctrine and "seek trees or other cover behind which they can hide, and run from behind one tree to another" so as to better "attack and dislodge the enemy in a wood without great loss." This concept was no doubt fresh in the minds of his men when the baron ordered them to deploy in the woods against the American right.[56]

Following the battle, Burgoyne admonished his redcoats for firing their weapons with "impetuosity and uncertain aim . . . and the mistake they are still under, in preferring it to the Bayonette [sic]."[57] This was perhaps not surprising, since the regiments were primarily composed of subalterns and soldiers who were green, inexperienced, and had never before experienced combat.[58] In addition, hundreds of British redcoats were actually recently recruited Germans, most of whom were likewise untested in battle.[59] Furthermore, this was the first battle of the war in which Burgoyne, Phillips, Hamilton, and most British regimental commanders at Freeman's farm personally commanded troops in combat, and their lack of strategic coordination and tactical experience was perhaps evident.[60] By comparison, Arnold, Poor, and the Continental and militia battalion commanders in the battle all had some, often significant, previous combat experience. In the end, British advantages in the battle were a better-trained force, cartridge pouches with greater carrying capacities and more ammunition, and, most certainly, the timely infantry and artillery reinforcement led by Riedesel.

The Defensive Interval

Following the Battle of Freeman's Farm, it was the general belief that combat would commence on the following day, and Gates made preparations for an expected attack. Burgoyne, however, decided to rest his army and allow commanders of those regiments depleted by casualties to reorganize their ranks, particularly among the young subalterns. On September 21, when it was again assumed battle was forthcoming, fate intervened. Burgoyne received a secret message from Lieutenant-General Sir Henry Clinton, commander of British forces in the city of New York, in which he promised to send 2,000 troops from the city and "make a push at" Fort Montgomery in the Hudson Highlands, proposing that such an attack might assist Burgoyne "effectually."[61] Burgoyne replied positively and from that point on rested his further hopes for success on Clinton's supposed Hudson Highlands diversion. This striking change in strategy suggests that Burgoyne understood the real danger he faced after the Battle of Freeman's Farm.

During the next two weeks, Burgoyne's men built an intricate system of fortifications protecting their encampments and supplies, stretching west from the Hudson River about one and a half miles. This defensive network was anchored on its southwestern corner by Balcarres Redoubt, which was garrisoned by the British light infantry battalion commanded by Major Alexander Lindsay, Sixth Earl of Balcarres, and further protected by the rest of Fraser's advanced corps.[62] Northwest of the Balcarres Redoubt was Breymann Redoubt, a fortified complex protecting the camp of Breymann's reserve corps.[63]

Ironically, the forthcoming battle would show that although these two fortifications were considered to be some of the most secure, the very flaw was in their disarticulation. The Balcarres Redoubt, shaped in the form of an elongated, oblong rectangle, with its broadside facing west, was built upon the hills where some of the heaviest fighting occurred during the Battle of Freeman's Farm. Four pieces of artillery were placed on the southern end of the redoubt, facing the direction of a potential American attack. The fortification was constructed "of both logs and earth, but much of it is on such shallow soil that much reliance is put on trees and little entrenching is done."[64] Freeman's house and barn were incorporated in the fortress, and the farm's perimeter fences were dismantled. The redoubt had two flanking satellite outposts, one placed on the hill to which Dearborn's light infantry initially withdrew during the battle, while the other was located fifty yards northwest of the redoubt on a smaller hill.

Burgoyne's two French Canadian companies were posted in log cabins that lay in the low ground of a "small vale" northwest of the Balcarres Redoubt.[65] The spaces around each of the cabins were fortified with logs and earth. Although seemingly unimportant, these small cabins were some of the most essential defensive points in Burgoyne's entire army, as they plugged the gap between the advanced corps and reserve corps encampments and guarded the road that ran into the Great Ravine behind Burgoyne's entire defensive network.

The Breymann Redoubt, consisting of three parts, was built on elevated ground north of the cabins. The main defense was a one-hundred-yard-long zigzag wall built of logs that faced northwest. About eighty yards north of this wall was another, separate, perpendicular defensive line facing northeast. This second zigzag wall was about eighty-five yards long and located on the edge of a bluff overlooking a steep ravine. The third fortification was a small, enclosed square-shaped outpost built on a hilltop about eighty yards north of the main one-hundred-yard, zigzag wall. The hilltop itself was higher in elevation than the main fortification wall, creating a substantial blind spot directly in front of Breymann Redoubt. Two light six-pounders were positioned near the main zigzag wall's center in order to cover the short, hill-protected approach from the front.

As defensive design strategy goes, Breymann's fortified camp was curiously built. Although naturally protected to the north by the deep ravine, its southeastern rear, where the camp of the garrison lay, was open. The eighty-yard gap between the two fortification walls was a decisive weakness, as was the nearby hill in front of the primary wall.[66]

Together, the Balcarres Redoubt, the cabins, and Breymann Redoubt collectively protected Burgoyne's army's entire right flank. These defenses were consciously designed to be "complementary" to one another during defensive action, despite the fact that the Balcarres Redoubt and Breymann's fortifications were located about 470 yards apart. The defense of this substantial gap was left to one hundred disaffected French Canadian militia draftees garrisoning the two small cabins.[67]

British Plans for a Reconnaissance-in-Force

After two weeks of waiting since receiving Clinton's note that promised a diversion in the Highlands, Burgoyne was running out of time. Not only was there no further communication from Clinton, there was no additional intelligence regarding his movements. Further complicating the situation, Burgoyne's scouts watching Bemis Heights from the eastern side of the river reported that American defenses were being strengthened and that Gates's army was growing in number. The increasing frequency and boldness of American patrols attacking Burgoyne's sentinels and pickets in the valley and along the front of the main British and German camp defenses was consistent with these observations.

Burgoyne decided in early October that he could no longer wait for Clinton's promised diversion. Plagued by severe supply shortages and desertions, and faced with the onset of cold weather, he knew he had to act soon. After a few days of conferring with Phillips, Riedesel, and Fraser, Burgoyne decided that sending a reconnaissance-in-force to probe the American left flank while, at the same time, foraging for much-needed food was the best of the various options discussed. The plan was that if the British found the American left wing at the summit vulnerable, Burgoyne would launch an all-out attack on the following day. If an attack was not feasible, he planned to wait until October 11 and, in the absence of any other favorable developments, withdraw north about ten miles to the Batten Kill.

The reconnaissance force was formed on the morning of October 7. Numbering about 1,500 officers and men drafted from most corps of the army, the force set off with ten pieces of artillery in the direction of the American's left flank. Captain Alexander Fraser's British rangers, one hundred loyalists, Indian warriors, and half the Canadian militia—over 200 men in all—were sent through the woods to the southwest in advance of the reconnaissance force in order to divert the Americans by gaining their rear near the summit.

A majority of the main reconnaissance force was drawn from the Balcarres Redoubt (about 700), Breymann's fortified camp (about 300), and the Canadian cabins (about 50) garrisons. Because the reconnaissance force set off from the army's right wing, it was deemed safe to sap these garrisons rather than take more personnel from the defenses of Burgoyne's main camp. This decision was probably conceived due to the incessant skirmishing occurring daily across the fronts of the valley and main camp defenses.[68]

The British Advance and American Response: October 7, 1777

At about 11:00 a.m., Generals Burgoyne, Phillips, Riedesel, and Fraser led the reconnaissance force out of camp, moving generally southwest toward the American left. Similar to the movements of the army on September 19, the reconnaissance force advanced in three columns along roads in the woods and across fields until spilling out onto two adjacent farm clearings about one mile from the Summit.[69]

The easternmost of these farm clearings measured about 350 by 250 yards, and was enclosed by fences on its eastern, western, and northern sides, but apparently not on its southern edge (figure 2.6). While the main road continued south toward the Summit, another road intersected it from the west, through the southern end of the field. Just north of the road near the center of the field was high ground topped by a building that German authors referred to as "Weisser House."[70] The yard surrounding these two buildings was also enclosed by a fence on all sides except the south, and more fences flanked much of the road. A deep, wood-covered ravine defined the eastern boundary of the field. As with other farms in this region, a wall of high trees enclosed the entire clearing, and wheat grew in the field.[71]

The perpendicular road that ran east to west bent to the southwest in the shape of a hollow arch. Described as "a damned difficult pathway," it crossed the wheat field, ran through about 250 yards of forest cover, and then entered another farm field.[72] This second clearing was completely surrounded by fencing and behind that was more woods. The oblong clearing measured about 250 by 550 yards, running north to south at its widest point. Two buildings were located near the center of the field, where the road terminated. The most noticeable feature here was immediately west of the clearing, a long, wooded height that offered a commanding view of the field below. Any force that occupied the hill would have a decided tactical advantage over an enemy in the clearing below.

The superior numbers of Gates's army allowed them to have advance sentinels and pickets located much closer to the British forces than the British forces could get to the Americans. Gates's advance sentries happened to be located in the Weisser house, keeping a ready eye on the road and woods for any signs of British activity. In the early afternoon, the advancing British columns were

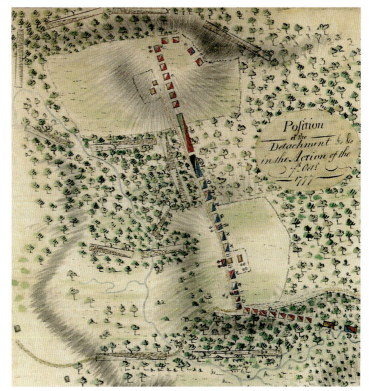

FIGURE 2.6. Position of the Detachment &c &c in the Action of the 7th Oct' 1777 (detail). This map, oriented with north to the right, shows Burgoyne's deployment of forces on the two adjacent wheat fields on October 7. As with other British maps depicting the various actions of the Battles of Saratoga, this one marks American troops as generic, speckled blocks. Although showing all American forces simultaneously rather than in the chronological order of their deployment, the artist accurately depicted the strong flanking attacks developed by Morgan and Poor, both of whom made brilliant use of the natural landscape. Drawn by William Cumberland Wilkinson, ca. 1778. Library of Congress, G3803.S353 1777.W5 Faden 69a.

spotted, and the Americans quickly withdrew so that headquarters could be informed immediately.[73]

As the three columns entered the adjacent fields, Braunschweig jäger were ordered forward to reconnoiter the ground to the south. The British light infantry detachment established a position on the western clearing at the base of the wooded hill. The 24th Regiment formed next to them on the crooked road in the woods between the fields. The Braunschweig and Hessen-Hanau musketeers from the German line were posted in the eastern clearing, next to the 24th Regiment. The Braunschweig grenadier detachment formed the central defense of the open field on the crooked road flanking the house. To their left, the detachment of British grenadiers formed a roughly L-shaped line; the short segment formed on the crooked road, facing south, while the rest of the battalion wound back to the rear through the woods, facing generally east. In order to deter American forces from attacking, cannons were placed in pairs at key points along the line. Burgoyne's small probing force was thus thinly spread over a very large area, and "took up . . . positions in such a manner according to the nature of the ground, [so] that our small force could not be discovered by the enemy."[74]

THE TACTICS OF THE BATTLES OF SARATOGA | 61

Officers climbed on the roof of the Weisser house in an attempt to observe the American's left-wing defenses at the Summit, but the tall trees surrounding the field obstructed any view of the American position.

Although the primary objective of Burgoyne's probing force to reconnoiter the American left was temporarily thwarted, a secondary goal could be readily achieved as both farms had wheat available for the taking. This was not a complete surprise, since British scouts previously observed that wheat was to be had in this area. The army, however, was never previously able to access it due to American dominance of the area. Burgoyne's isolated army, with its finite food supply, was increasingly reliant upon local crops for the sustenance of men, women, children, and animals alike. As bread and flour rations were cut by one-third only days earlier, the discovery of so much wheat appeared to be a godsend. Word was sent back to the camp at Freeman's farm to bring up carts in order to collect the grain. As this promised to take some time, the soldiers were ordered to sit in position and rest. The reconnaissance force was therefore temporarily repurposed to provide cover for a large foraging party.

By this time, Burgoyne's movements were hardly secretive, and the American sentinels reported their observations of the enemy advance. Gates dispatched his deputy adjutant general, Lieutenant Colonel James Wilkinson, to assess the situation. Wilkinson returned, reporting that the British were "foraging, and endeavouring to reconnoiter" Gates's left. Wilkinson also suggested that the British, whom he assumed were offering battle, were located on indefensible ground.[75] Although the British were not looking for a fight, their aggressive entry into that quarter, the large number of troops, and their significant artillery strength suggested otherwise.

Gates directed Morgan to make an immediate and decisive attack upon the British right flank. Morgan, who inquired of Wilkinson about the position of the British probing force, proposed to "make a circuit with his corps by our left, and under cover of the wood to gain the height on the right of the enemy," and from there "commence his attack."[76] Gates approved, and further ordered Poor to assault the British left flank. Poor's men would strike the British grenadier detachment from the ravine by taking advantage of the cover provided by the woods. While Morgan's corps advanced toward the hill, Poor's brigade marched north along the main road that led to the eastern farm clearing. It was planned that these strong flanking assaults, taking complete advantage of the natural landscape, would commence simultaneously.

The Battle of Bemis Heights: October 7, 1777

At approximately 3:00 p.m., jäger scouring the woods in front of the British reported that a significant American force was forming nearby. To deter the

FIGURE 2.7. Brigadier General Enoch Poor (1736–1780). Although only appointed a brigadier general in February 1777, Enoch Poor was entrusted with commanding the largest, most active brigade in Gates's army. This portrait, the only known likeness of Poor, was drawn by Colonel Thaddeus Kosciusko during the war. Drawn by Thaddeus Kosciusko, ca. 1777. New Hampshire Historical Society.

Americans from advancing toward the reconnaissance force, the two medium twelve-pounders were fired blindly into the woods in the direction the enemy was reported to be. Although the cannons were repeatedly reloaded and fired, the Germans noted that the Americans "did not take any notice of them, and it looked as though they wanted to form themselves into line against us, although it was not the most favorable spot to attack us."[77] However, the American commanders judged the situation differently.

American skirmishers engaged the probing force's jäger and sentinels in the woods near Mill Creek, south of the farm. Just past four o'clock, Poor's men "drew up along the skirts of the wood behind trees" and made an overwhelming attack against the British grenadier battalion.[78] Poor's brigade, consisting of seven regiments and numbering over 2,500 officers and men, was so overwhelming that it "enabled them in a few minutes to extend the attack along the front of the Germans"[79] (figure 2.7). After making an initial stand, some of the German troops panicked and "retired, or more correctly said, ran from their positions, into the bushes" north of the field.[80]

Morgan's corps attacked the British right shortly after Poor's assault began on the British left. Having gained the wooded height, Morgan's riflemen and light infantry rushed the British light infantry with full force. Morgan's corps, numbering nearly 700 officers and soldiers, was overwhelming, moving through the woods behind the British in an attempt to envelop them. Informed of this development, Burgoyne ordered the British light infantry and the 24th Regiment to reposition in order to prevent the Americans from cutting off a line of retreat.[81] The withdrawal of the British light infantry and 24th Regiment cleared the way to the eastern wheat field and Morgan's corps took advantage of this opening, pressing the attack against the greatly outnumbered detachment of the Hessen-Hanau Regiment Erbprinz.

As American troops pressed hard on the flanks of Burgoyne's line, Learned's brigade arrived and attacked the British forces directly along their front. Päusch took the initiative to reposition his exposed light six-pounders and placed them behind an earthen fortification built in front of the Weisser house, where the medium twelve-pounders were located. After repeatedly firing his artillery toward the nearby American line, Päusch, whose position was becoming untenable due to the probing force's faltering defense, decided that retreat was in order. He directed his men to abandon the cannons and encouraged them to save themselves by fleeing into the woods.[82]

By about 5:00 p.m., the surviving, uncaptured elements of the British reconnaissance force was fully withdrawn from the wheat fields and spilled out onto the nearest clearing to the northeast, the Marshall farm, which had played a peripheral part in the Battle of Freeman's Farm. While some officers and soldiers were fleeing for their lives, Fraser took command of the rear guard, hoping to make a stand and cover the rest of the retreating reconnaissance force, thereby providing time for the garrisons to prepare for probable attack. Poor's brigade and Morgan's corps pressed forth, and after a short firefight in the Marshall farm field, "Gen'l Fraser received a mortal wound, and the fire of our Troops instantly compelled the Enemy [British] to retire to his works, after losing two more 6 pounders that were on his left."[83]

By about 5:30 p.m., Burgoyne's probing force sustained a significant number of casualties and lost substantial equipment and weaponry. His faltering troops fell back in confusion to the Balcarres Redoubt, the strongest and closest of all British fortifications. Poor's brigade pressed after the retreating British, through the woods and into Freeman's farm, where they were "entirely exposed, or partially sheltered by trees, stumps, or hollows, at various distances not exceeding 120 yards" from the walls of the massive fortification.[84] Poor's Continentals and militia attacked, conquered the two small flanking fortifications and advanced upon the wall of the redoubt itself. However, Poor ordered his men to fall back when he "observed a body of [enemy] troops, moving in the rear, which he presumed was a reinforcement" for the British garrison.[85]

In the meantime, Morgan's corps moved north through the Marshall farm, its adjoining woods, and into the field where Breymann Redoubt was located. Most of the riflemen and light infantry skirted the field and arrived safely behind the steep-banked hill located directly in front of Breymann Redoubt. There, behind the hill, they were protected from cannon and musketry fire from the nearby German garrison. Approximately 50 percent of Breymann's reserve corps had joined the reconnaissance force earlier in the day but none returned, as all survivors of the probing force were ordered to seek cover in the Balcarres Redoubt. This left a little more than 200 German grenadiers, light infantrymen, artillerymen, and American loyalists to defend Breymann's camp. Because American troops controlled the entire area right up to the walls of the Balcarres Redoubt and Breymann's defenses, their respective garrisons were prevented from assisting each other. With the Balcarres Redoubt's northernmost flanking outpost captured, the only remaining defenses left in the vale between Fraser's and Breymann's camps were the two cabins garrisoned by French Canadians, who were also at reduced strength. They were quickly overrun by Learned's brigade, which moved onto the field from the direction of the Marshall farm, bypassing the Balcarres Redoubt altogether.

The eventual assault on Breymann Redoubt was overwhelming and decisive due to the great number of American troops, the weakness of the garrison, and the vulnerabilities inherent in the overall design of the defensive works. As Continental army and militia battalions gathered to the front and left of the fortifications, the attack began. Lieutenant Colonel Richard Butler, second in command of the rifle battalion, observed that during this "storm of their works, Genl Arnold was the first who Enterd, one Major [Joseph] Morris with about 12 of the Rifle men follow^d him on the Rear of their . . . flank while I led up the Rest of the Riflemen in front." The officers and soldiers making the frontal attack "entered rapidly; some through the sally port [the eighty-yard gap between the log walls], some through the embrasures [the openings in the wall for the artillery], and others by climbing over the breast work, which was formed of small timbers, seven or eight feet high."[86] This coordinated attack caused the entire German and loyalist garrison to retreat through the camp and into the woods. Breymann was killed, perhaps by his own men, and the left leg of "the Gallant Major General Arnold" was "fractured by a Musket Ball."[87] With the collapse of the reserve corps' defenses, their entire camp was exposed and captured, but due to the "extreme darkness of the night, the fatigue of the men, and the disorder incident to undisciplined troops after so desultory an action," the Americans were unable to take further advantage of the victory.[88]

Tactical and Strategic Assessment of the Battle of Bemis Heights

For American forces, the Battle of Bemis Heights was a brilliant success in every measureable way. What began as an attempt to stop the perceived threat of attack on Gates's camp's left wing ended with the complete capture of Burgoyne's right-wing defenses—defenses that protected access to the road behind which lay the entire British camp. If Burgoyne's position was difficult before, it was now untenable.

American casualties were fewer than those suffered in the Battle of Freeman's Farm, with about 150 officers and soldiers killed, severely wounded, or captured. The reduced casualty numbers may have been the result of American forces not only taking full advantage of the natural landscape but also striking in overwhelming numbers at decisive points against a poorly positioned and underprepared enemy.

This battle demonstrated the advantages of Morgan's rifle and light infantry battalions operating together, as originally intended. Unlike the first battle where the two battalions fought independently and without cooperation, they worked in concert and generally coordinated their movements in the second. Their joint attack on the British light infantry and assault along the front of Breymann's fortifications proved decisive.

The battle demonstrated that Gates's overall strategy—allowing British forces to initiate events and then react to those movements—was successful. The all-out attack authorized by Gates on October 7 was different from his more conservative strategy of September 19 because the situations were quite different. On September 19, Burgoyne's entire army, which at the time outnumbered Gates's, was advancing to attack. If Gates had committed too many troops to combat and those troops failed, his defensive lines would have been exposed to attack. And, as there was little precedent to demonstrate that an unfortified American army would likely defeat a British army on the field of battle, Gates's decision to hold back half of the army was a sound one. But on October 7, a relatively small portion of the enemy's army, unable to receive reinforcements, sat in open fields surrounded by commanding ground. It is not surprising that Gates, whose army numbered about 12,500 officers and soldiers that day, should have felt confident about ordering an attack.

Unlike the Battle of Freeman's Farm, Arnold's role in the Battle of Bemis Heights was, while audacious, relatively insignificant. By October 1, Arnold's relationship with Gates was so badly marred that Arnold was being "treated Only as a Cypher in the Army, never consulted; or acquainted with one occurrence in the Army." Arnold further accused the commanding general of coordinating plans with "officers some of Inferior Rank to me who have had little experience in Military matters."[89] Thus, when the brigades of Arnold's division were ordered to the field on October 7, Gates had this done directly through the army's deputy adjutant general, circumventing the established chain of command and Arnold's authority. The series of events that led to their relationship deteriorating are myriad and complex.

With the arrival of Major General Benjamin Lincoln, Washington's appointment as second in command of the Northern Department, Gates believed that

Arnold's time serving as a "volunteer" to fill in the command gap was at an end. For his part, Arnold was enraged that Gates either neglected, or outright refused, to support him in his attempt to have his rank of major general backdated, despite his oft-expressed patriotic "Zeal for the Cause of my Country."[90] By October 7, Arnold found himself without a patron, without leave to participate in the fight, and without the prospect of further promotion, and so decided to join the battle, perhaps to once again demonstrate his courage and worthiness for promotion. Although Arnold's presence must have encouraged men on the field, the decisive attacks that developed against the British throughout the day were already under way when he joined them.[91] Despite the obvious discord between these two generals, its ill effects did not negatively affect the outcome of the battle.

If Burgoyne still had any hopes of reaching Albany on the morning of October 7, either through Clinton's Hudson Highlands diversion or from observations made during the course of reconnoitering, those hopes were completely gone by that evening. Burgoyne, who arrogantly claimed at the commencement of the campaign that "this army must not retreat," was now forced to look north for his army's wholesale withdrawal.[92]

British casualties were heavy, with about 450 officers and soldiers killed or severely wounded and an additional 180 captured. Unlike the first battle, Burgoyne lost a high number of command and staff officers; not only were Fraser and Breymann dead, but many other senior officers were taken captive in the field.[93] American troops were also able to capture a significant quantity of artillery, shot, and artillery stores both on the field and in Breymann's camp.[94] Burgoyne was unable to recover from so many losses in personnel and equipment.

Nearly every one of Burgoyne's plans, from the troops selected for the reconnaissance and the ground chosen for defense, to the concept of the mission itself, was flawed. Small detachments of soldiers were drafted from various units across Burgoyne's army in order to leave the defensive lines garrisoned. The 1,500 officers and soldiers selected from so many disparate units to serve in the probing force resulted in an awkward and inefficient tactical formation, one that had never fought together in such a configuration before that day. Ironically, because the reconnaissance force was moving in a generally southwest direction, the advanced corps and reserve corps were called upon to provide the greatest proportion of men. It was wrongfully assumed that their defenses—that is, the Balcarres and Breymann Redoubts—were the least likely to be attacked because any such assault made by American troops would have to break through the probing force first. Although Burgoyne saw this as an unlikely scenario, that is exactly what happened.

Another reason the British lost so decisively is because of the poor defensive positions they took up both in the field and in camp. Burgoyne had time to array his probing force in the best advantage according to the lay of the land on the adjacent wheat fields, yet his 1,500 troops were too few to cover the expansive landscape, resulting in a disparate arrangement of the line. Even more surprising is the poor positioning of the line's flanks, the left being at the edge of a wooded ravine and the right commanded by a wooded height. But where the army in the field failed, the fortified camp of the reserve corps fared worse. Its defenses were so ill conceived that it would have been shocking if the Americans failed to take the position. As it was, the American command was able to formulate decisive attacks based upon sound observations of the natural and cultural landscape, something the British were unable to do.

Finally, the very concept of Burgoyne's reconnaissance-in-force raises many questions. It was hardly a last-minute decision, as the army's most senior generals conferred for days beforehand regarding what to do. In the end, both the plan and decision to adopt it was Burgoyne's. In their assessments, historians have commonly confused Burgoyne's intentions that day by assuming that he set out with a plan to attack the American defenses or at the very least threaten the American position and force their evacuation. But the prebattle record of the plan fixed upon by Burgoyne shows that he only intended to reconnoiter the American left and, if the opportunity developed, forage for food. The probing force's large number of men and artillery were only meant to deter an American attack against them and nothing more. As in the Battle of Freeman's Farm, Burgoyne grossly underestimated the resolve, strength, tenacity, and strategic and tactical skills of the American command, its officers, and soldiers.[95]

Retreat, Pursuit, and Surrender

Immediately following the Battle of Bemis Heights, Burgoyne consolidated his army on the high ground surrounding the floodplain; retreat began in the evening of the following day. Due to inclement weather, multiple stops, missed opportunities, and battle-weary leadership, the British forces took up positions in and around the small village of Saratoga. Gates's army, in conjunction with cooperating militia troops acting to the north and east, inevitably surrounded Burgoyne, forcing him to sign the Convention of Saratoga on October 16, 1777.

NOTES

1. The Battles of Saratoga were fought in what was then Stillwater District, Albany County. Today, the battlefield is located within the town of Stillwater, Saratoga County. The Village of Saratoga was incorporated as the Village of Schuylerville in 1831, after which the Village of Saratoga ceased to exist.

2. By September 19, Burgoyne's army included about 3,800 British infantry and artillerymen; 2,800 Braunschweig and Hessen-Hanau infantry, cavalry, and artillerymen; 700

loyalist American volunteers, 110 French Canadian militia draftees; 150 Seven Nations of Canada warriors and Fort Hunter Mohawk warriors and family refugees; 150 Royal Navy sailors; hundreds of army department staff and support personnel; and hundreds of followers, including officer and soldier families, local loyalist refugees, and sutlers. See Charles Snell, *A Report on the Strength of the British Army under the Command of Lieutenant-General John Burgoyne, July 1 to October 17, 1777, and on the Organization of the British Army on September 19 and October 7, 1777*, document (D), Saratoga National Historical Park (NHP), February 28, 1951. Also see Eric Schnitzer, *Organization of the Army from Canada Commanded by Lieutenant-General John Burgoyne—September 19 to October 7, 1777* (D, Saratoga NHP, January 2013). Snell's study is sound for determining unit numbers; Schnitzer's study is preferred for determining army organization.

3. Most of Burgoyne's artillery was mounted on two-wheeled traveling carriages, which in order to be moved had to be limbered. Limbers were two-wheeled carriages that, when attached to traveling carriages, allowed draft animals to pull both efficiently.

4. An abatis was formed by felling trees, the branches of which were turned in the enemy's direction.

5. By September 19, Gates's army included about 6,900 Continental infantry, cavalry, and artillerymen (primarily from Massachusetts, New Hampshire, New York, Virginia, Pennsylvania, Connecticut, and Canada), 1,300 militia infantry and cavalrymen (from Connecticut and New York), over one dozen Stockbridge Mohican, Munsee, and Wappinger warriors, hundreds of army department staff and support personnel, and hundreds of followers, including soldier families and sutlers. See Charles Snell, *A Report on the Organization and Numbers of Gates' Army, September 19, October 7, and October 17, 1777, Including an Appendix with Regimental Data and Notes* (D, Saratoga NHP, February 1, 1951). Also see Eric Schnitzer, *Organization of the Army of the United States under the Command of Major General Horatio Gates at Bemus Heights 19 September 1777* (D, Saratoga NHP, January 2013). Snell's study is sound for determining unit numbers; Schnitzer's study is preferred for determining army organization.

6. General George Washington to Major General Israel Putnam, August 16, 1777, George Washington, *The Writings of George Washington from the Original Manuscript Sources, 1745–1799*, vol. 9, ed. John Clement Fitzpatrick (Washington, DC: US Government Printing Office, 1939), 70–71.

7. Unlike other Continental army infantry battalions in 1777, Dearborn's light infantry corps consisted of five subdivisions, not eight, and as such was commanded by a major (Dearborn). Although originally including draftees from the 2nd and 4th New York Regiments, they were soon after removed from the battalion for reasons unknown. See Eric Schnitzer, *A Review of the Organization of the Corps of Light Infantry, Northern Department, August–November 1777* (D, Saratoga NHP, October 2009).

8. Major General Horatio Gates to President of Congress John Hancock, September 22, 1777, New-York Historical Society, Horatio Gates Papers, 5:718. Arnold was only de facto because Benjamin Lincoln, who was senior to Arnold, was not present with the army at Bemis Heights until after the battle. Lincoln assumed command of the army's right wing on September 25.

9. James Murray Hadden, *Hadden's Journal and Orderly Books: A Journal Kept in Canada and upon Burgoyne's Campaign in 1776 and 1777*, ed. Horatio Rogers (Boston: Gregg Press, 1972), 164. Hadden was a second lieutenant in Captain William Borthwick's company, 3rd Battalion, Royal Regiment of Artillery.

10. A girdled tree is one in which a ring of bark is removed around the tree's circumference

for the purpose of killing it. That the farm had a number of girdled trees suggests that the Freemans were in the process of clearing additional land.

11. British-generated, scaled mapping of Freeman's farm was thorough. See William Cumberland Wilkinson, *The Encampment & Position of the Army under His Exc*^{y}*. L*^{t}*. G*^{l}*: Burgoyne, at Swords*^{s} *and Freeman's Farms on Hudsons River near Stillwater 1777*, pen-and-ink and watercolor on paper, ca. 1778, Library of Congress, Geography and Map Division: LC Maps of North America, 1750–1789, 1182. Wilkinson was a lieutenant in the 62nd Regiment and appointed to act as an assistant engineer shortly before the Battle of Freeman's Farm. Wilkinson's manuscript maps were used by William Faden as the basis for creating the printed versions subsequently published in Burgoyne's apologia, *A State of the Expedition from Canada*, in 1780. Also see *Plan of the Position of the Army under the Command of Lieut*^{t} *Gen*^{l} *Burgoyne near Still Water, in which it encamped on y*^{e} *20th Sept*^{r} *1777*, pen-and-ink and watercolor on paper, ca. 1778, British Library, R.U.S.I. Collection. Also see Hadden, *Hadden's Journal*, 164–65, for his manuscript map of the Battle of Freeman's Farm.

12. This farm was previously identified as the "George Coulter" farm, after the property's previous lessee, in popular histories of the battles such as Charles Neilson's *An Original, Compiled and Corrected Account of Burgoyne's Campaign, and the Memorable Battles of Bemus's Heights, Sept. 19, and Oct. 7, 1777, from the most Authentic Sources of Information; including many Interesting Incidents Connected with the Same.* (Albany, NY: J. Munsell, 1844). However, Philip Schuyler's estate records demonstrate Micajah Marshall assumed the freehold lease on the property in 1771 following Coulter's death. *Estate of Philip Schuyler, Dec[eased]*, Chancery Decree, MS, New York State archives, Department of State Docket 35, 312–15. Property lessee information was provided to Saratoga NHP by Leslie B. Potter, attorney-at-law.

13. This picket was composed of officers and men drafted from each of Hamilton's four British infantry regiments; that is, the 9th, 20th, 21st, and 62nd. Forbes was major of the 9th Regiment of Foot.

14. The effectiveness of this outflanking movement is notable, considering that two companies of British light infantry, numbering about 120 officers and men, were able to scatter the 400-man rifle battalion. Despite their tactical error, the rifleman suffered few casualties on September 19 (six rank and file killed, nine rank and file severely wounded, and one officer captured). See *A Return of the Kill*^{d} *&c of the Division under the Command of Maj*^{r} *Gen*^{l} *Arnold between Stillwater & Saratoga Sep*^{r} *19th 1777*, MS, New York Public Library, Thomas Addis Emmett Papers. Also see James Wilkinson, *Memoirs of My Own Times*, vol. 1 (Philadelphia: Abraham Small, 1816), 237–38. Wilkinson was a lieutenant colonel and deputy adjutant general of the Northern Department. Also see Thomas Anburey, *Travels though the Interior Parts of America. In a Series of Letters*, vol. 1 (London: William Lane, 1789), 411. Anburey was an ensign in the 24th Regiment of Foot. Also see Henry Dearborn, *Revolutionary War Journal of Henry Dearborn, 1775–1783*, ed. Lloyd A. Brown and Howard H. Peckham (Chicago: Caxton Club, 1939), 105. Also see Samuel Armstrong, "From Saratoga to Valley Forge: The Diary of Lt. Samuel Armstrong," ed. Joseph Lee Boyle, *Pennsylvania Magazine of History and Biography* (July 1997): 245–46. Armstrong was ensign of Captain John Burnam's company, Colonel Michael Jackson's (8th Massachusetts) regiment, appointed to the light infantry corps.

15. Hadden, *Hadden's Journal*, 163. A probable explanation for this undisciplined firing is given in the "Tactical and Strategic Assessment of the Battle of Freeman's Farm" section.

16. Dearborn, *Revolutionary War Journal*, 106. Also see Wilkinson, *Memoirs*, 237–38. Wilkinson's account includes an elaborate narrative in which he found all three rifle battalion field officers (Colonel Daniel Morgan, Lieutenant Colonel Richard Butler, and Major Joseph Morris) scattered after the initial engagement. Only Morgan was found trying to

reform his men (during which time Morgan "burst into tears"); Butler, with three men, was "tree'd" and ready to receive a further attack of the enemy; Morris was alone and focused on recounting his near escape. If true, the apparent mix of apathy and shock displayed by these men may help explain the otherwise surprising delay in getting the battalion, described as "broken and scattered in all directions," back into action.

17. Hadden, *Hadden's Journal*, 164.

18. Initial orders were for the 9th Regiment to defend these cabins "to the last extremity." However, during the forthcoming battle, the regiment was relieved and ordered back to their original position on the wooded road north of Freeman's farm in order to "form a corps-de-reserve" for the center column, a reserve that was never employed. The totality of casualties suffered by the 9th Regiment's battalion companies in the battle was sixteen officers and men killed, captured, and wounded, which resulted from the picket skirmish. Ironically, the 9th Regiment was the sole battalion of the center column that had prior combat experience in this campaign (the July 8 Battle of Fort Anne, New York). See John Burgoyne, *A State of the Expedition from Canada, as Laid before the House of Commons by Lieutenant-General Burgoyne, and Verified by Evidence, with a Collection of Authentic Documents, and an Addition of Many Circumstances Which Were Prevented from Appearing before the House by Prorogation of Parliament* (London: J. Almon, 1780), 82. Also see Anton Adolph du Roi (atrib.), *The Specht Journal*, trans. Helga Doblin, ed. Mary C. Lynn (Westport, CT: Greenwood Press, 1995), 136. Du Roi was second lieutenant of Major Carl Friedrich von Ehrenkrook's company, Braunschweig Musketeer Regiment Specht.

19. The exact timing of when this was done in relation to the events of the battle is not clear, but it was early in the engagement. Standard operating procedure called for British soldiers in marching order entering combat to pile knapsacks, haversacks, tin water flasks, and all other camp equipage behind them by subdivision so as to operate at maximum efficiency. See Thomas Simes, *The Regulator; or, Instructions to Form the Officer, and Complete the Soldier, upon Fixed Principles* (London: William Richardson, 1780), 164. Henry Hallowell later remembered that his battalion "broke their ranks and went to Plundering," for which they were admonished by their commander that if the like happened again, they would be executed. See Henry Hallowell, *Lynn in the Revolution*, pt. 1, ed. Howard Kendall Sanderson (Boston: W. B. Clarke, 1909), 164. Hallowell was a private in Captain Ebenezer Winship's company, Colonel Rufus Putnam's (5th Massachusetts) regiment.

20. Hadden, *Hadden's Journal*, 164–66. Also see Dearborn, *Revolutionary War Journal*, 106. Also see Frederic Kidder, *History of the First New Hampshire Regiment in the War of the Revolution* (Albany, NY: Joel Munsell, 1868), 34. The journalist, Thomas Blake, was the ensign of Captain John House's company, 1st New Hampshire Battalion. Also see Colonel Alexander Scammell to Dr. Samuel Scammell, September 21, 1777, New York State Library, Phelps-Gorham Papers, item 6013. Scammell commanded the 3rd New Hampshire Battalion.

21. Gates to Hancock, September 22, 1777, New-York Historical Society, Horatio Gates Papers, 5:718.

22. Ibid. Also see Oliver Boardman, "Journal of Oliver Boardman of Middletown 1777 Burgoyne's Surrender," *Collections of the Connecticut Historical Society* 7 (1899): 225. Boardman was a private in Captain Joseph Blague's company, Colonel Thaddeus Cook's battalion of Connecticut militia. Also see Dearborn, *Revolutionary War Journal*, 106. Also see Lieutenant Colonel Richard Butler to Colonel James Wilson, January 22, 1778, Historical Society of Pennsylvania, Gratz Collection, case 4, box 11. Butler was lieutenant colonel of the 1st Pennsylvania Regiment serving as second in command of Morgan's rifle battalion. Also see Lieutenant Colonel Richard Varick to Major General Philip Schuyler, September 19,

1777, New York Public Library, Papers of General Philip Schuyler 1710–1805. Varick was the Northern Department's deputy muster master general and a supernumerary aide-de-camp to Arnold. Also see Major General Benedict Arnold to Gates, October 1, 1777, New-York Historical Society, Horatio Gates Papers, 5:726.

23. When a military formation refused a flank, the personnel of the flank being refused were moved back from the standard, linear alignment and placed at an angle with the line. In this case, the 62nd Regiment turned its left wing grand division (two companies, accounting for 25 percent of the battalion's personnel) back by as much as ninety degrees, so as to be placed perpendicular with the remaining three grand divisions of the regiment. This maneuver allowed the regiment to better defend itself on two fronts against superior enemy numbers.

24. Although Burgoyne sent orders for these cannons to be brought up from the Park of Artillery early in the action (at 2:00 p.m.), Royal Artillery personnel were forced to make a circuitous route and retrace their steps back to Swords's house and follow the system of roads taken by Hamilton's column in order to arrive safely. Although the specific types of guns brought up from the River Road is unrecorded, they must have been four medium twelve-pounders or two light twenty-four-pounders and two medium twelve-pounders. Friedrich Christian Cleve, *Journal of the Brunswick Troops in North America under the Orders of Major-General von Riedesel*, trans. "in England," HZ 302–HZ 304, Hessian Documents of the American Revolution, 1776–1783, Morristown NHP, Lidgerwood Collection, fiche 180–193. Cleve was a lieutenant and second adjutant to Riedesel. Inventories of Burgoyne's ordnance stores included round shot (for cannons), case shot (for cannons, howitzers, and mortars), and shells (for howitzers and mortars) only; Burgoyne's army had neither grape nor tin-case (canister) shot available for use. National Archives and Records Administration, *Numbered Record Books Concerning Military Operations and Service, Pay and Settlement of Accounts, and Supplies in the War Department Collection of Revolutionary War Records*, vol. 129, roll 39.

25. The only riflemen in Burgoyne's army were Braunschweig jäger ("hunters"), numbering about fifty officers and soldiers by the time of the Battles of Saratoga. They formed the second company of the Braunschweig light infantry battalion commanded by Major Ferdinand Albrecht von Bärner. Because von Bärner was severely wounded during the second phase of the Battle of Bennington and incapacitated, the battalion was commanded by its jägercompany captain, Maximillian Schottelius.

26. A picket was a large guard posted before an army, placed in order to give notice of an approaching enemy.

27. The 62nd Regiment "charged four times with the 'national weapon'" in this manner during the battle, a sight "grievous to behold" because the "contest was unequal," resulting in significant British casualties. John Money, *A Letter to the Right Honorable William Windham, on the Partial Re-Organization of the British Army* (London: T. Egerton and Carpenter, 1799), 16–17. Money was a captain in the 9th Regiment and the deputy quartermaster general of Burgoyne's army.

28. Hadden, *Hadden's Journal*, 164–66.

29. Varick to Schuyler, September 19, 1777, New York Public Library, Papers of General Philip Schuyler 1710–1805.

30. Frank Moore, *Diary of the American Revolution: From Newspapers and Original Documents*, vol. 1 (New York: Charles Scribner, 1860), 497. Moore attributes the letter fragment, dated September 20, to Brigadier General Enoch Poor.

31. Wilkinson, *Encampment & Position of the Army*.

32. Henry Dearborn, "A Narrative of the Saratoga Campaign—Major General Henry

Dearborn, 1815," *Bulletin of the Fort Ticonderoga Museum* 1, no. 5 (January 1929): 6. Although written nearly forty years after the events, Dearborn's sound recollections were used by Wilkinson while compiling research materials for his 1816 *Memoirs*.

33. Joshua Pell Jr., "Diary of Joshua Pell, Junior, an officer of the British Army in America 1776–1777, part 2," *Magazine of American History* 2, no. 2 (February 1878): 109. Pell was a volunteer in the 24th Regiment of Foot. His account confirms execution of British training for "treeing"; that is, fighting from behind trees. For further elaboration, see Matthew H. Spring, *With Zeal and with Bayonets Only: The British Army on Campaign in North America, 1775–1783* (Norman: University of Oklahoma Press, 2010). This work is a publication of Spring's doctoral dissertation regarding British army tactics employed throughout the American War for Independence.

34. Cleve, *Journal of the Brunswick Troops in North America*, HZ 304.

35. Ibid., HZ 304–HZ 305.

36. Ibid., HZ 305–HZ 306.

37. Ibid., HZ 307–HZ 308.

38. Ibid., HZ 308. Also see Wilkinson, *Encampment & Position of the Army*, third and fourth position overlay.

39. Varick to Schuyler, September 19, 1777, New York Public Library, Papers of General Philip Schuyler 1710–1805. Varick blamed the American withdrawal on a *"want of ammunition."*

40. Lieutenant Colonel Winborn Adams (2nd New Hampshire Battalion) was killed and Lieutenant Colonel Andrew Colburn (3rd New Hampshire Battalion) was mortally wounded (he died the following day). Captains Van Swearingen (rifle battalion) and Jason Wait (1st New Hampshire Battalion), and First Lieutenant John Moore (1st New Hampshire Battalion) were captured; *Names of the Officers Killed, Wounded, Missing*, September 21, 1777, MS, New York Public Library, Thomas Addis Emmett Papers. Initial casualty returns list Swearingen as killed, but he was instead captured unscathed. See Anburey, *Travels*, 411–12. Also see *A List of Prisoners taken in the Action on the 19th Sep^{br} 1777*, New-York Historical Society, Horatio Gates Papers, 18:973.

41. *Orderly book of Capt [sic] Thaddeus Cook of Wallingford Connecticut*, MS, American Antiquarian Society, octavo volume no. 12. Arnold's divisional order was dated September 20, 1777. Also see *Names of the Officers Killed, Wounded, Missing*, September 21, 1777, MS, New York Public Library, Thomas Addis Emmett Papers.

42. Dearborn, *Revolutionary War Journal*, 104–5. Also see Armstrong, "From Saratoga to Valley Forge," 244–45. Also see Butler to Wilson, January 22, 1778, Historical Society of Pennsylvania, Gratz Collection, case 4, box 11. Also see Schnitzer, *Review of the Organization of the Corps of Light Infantry*. Also see Tucker F. Hentz, "Unit History of the Maryland and Virginia Rifle Regiment (1776–1781): Insights from the Service Record of Capt. Adamson Tannehill," *Virginia Historical Society* (2007), accessed August 26, 2012, http://www.vahistorical.org/research/tann.pdf. Tannehill was a first lieutenant in Captain Gabriel Long's company, Colonel Daniel Morgan's Detached Rifle Battalion.

43. Officers and men of Morgan's rifle battalion were primarily drafted from the 5th, 6th, 7th, 8th, 9th, and 11th Virginia Regiments and the 1st, 5th, 8th, and 12th Pennsylvania Battalions. Upon being drafted, Washington saw to their arming in general orders dated June 13, 1777, stating that "such rifles as belong to the States, in the different brigades, to be immediately exchanged with Col. Morgan for muskets," adding that if "a sufficient number of rifles (public property) can not be procured, the Brigadiers are requested to assist Col. Morgan, either by exchanging, or purchasing those that are private property." See

George Washington, *The Writings of George Washington from the Original Manuscript Sources, 1745–1799*, vol. 8, ed. John Clement Fitzpatrick (Washington, DC: US Government Printing Office, 1933), 246. Washington's description regarding wanting men with rifle proficiency, activity, and orderly behavior was posted in June 1, 1777, general orders. See Washington, *Writings of George Washington*, 8:156. Also see Eric Schnitzer, *Officers on Morgan's Rifle Battalion Pay Lists, 1777* (D, Saratoga NHP, October 2009).

44. Gates to Jeremiah Powell, September 29, 1777, New-York Historical Society, Horatio Gates Papers, 5:772.

45. The April 20, 1777, arrival of *L'Amphitrite* at Portsmouth, New Hampshire, laden with thousands of stands of French arms, hundreds of thousands of bullets and flints, thousands of pounds of gunpowder, and other war matériel, proved a boon for the Army of the United States. Although most of the small arms—the French fusil models 1763, 1766, and modified 1766—were deemed unusable or in need of repair, thousands of serviceable pieces were issued to arms-deficient Continental regiments in the Northern Department and subsequently used in the Battles of Saratoga. See "*L'Amphitrite*," American War for Independence—at Sea: The Continental Navy, accessed June 3, 2013, http://www.awiatsea.com/Conn.html. Also see Brian N. Morton and Donald C. Spinelli, *Beaumarchais and the American Revolution* (Lanham, MD: Lexington Books, 2003). For information regarding the poor condition of most arms shipped on *L'Amphitrite*, see Robert F. Smith, "'A Veritable . . . Arsenal' of Manufacturing: Government Management of Weapons Production in the American Revolution" (PhD diss., Lehigh University, Department of History, 2008). Examples of extant pieces delivered to Portsmouth in 1777 can be seen in Don Troiani and James L. Kochan, *Don Troiani's Soldiers of the American Revolution* (Mechanicsburg, PA: Stackpole Books, 2007), 167. Also see Michael R. Carroll, *New Hampshire Marked French Revolutionary War Muskets* (Potomac, MD: privately printed, 2009).

46. Examples include 1775 New York militia law, which demanded that every militia soldier own "a good musket . . . & Bayonet Sword or Tomahawk" and a variety of supplemental ammunition and supporting implements. A 1775 Massachusetts militia law ordered that every soldier have similar, excepting the bayonet was mandatory. Failure to abide by these regulations could be met with fines, and soldiers who were unable to provide for themselves were supplied by public stores. See Berthold Fernow, ed., *Documents Relating to the Colonial History of the State of New York*, vol. 15 (Albany, NY: Weed, Parsons, 1887), 30. Also see *Acts and Resolves, Public and Private, of the Province of the Massachusetts Bay*, vol. 5 (Boston: Wright and Potter, 1886), 448.

47. Cartridge pouches and boxes used by Americans throughout the war varied considerably. Pouch carrying capacities, particularly during the first years of the war, generally varied between fifteen and twenty-three rounds, significantly less than those worn by pouch-carrying British troops. See Troiani and Kochan, *Don Troiani's Soldiers*, 96–145.

48. Cartridge distribution in Gates's army apparently varied. On September 15, Poor ordered his brigade's regimental commanders to issue "flints and Ammunition at least to Thirty Rounds a man." However, Ambrose Collins stated that he was issued only "24 cartridges." In general orders covering the entire army, Gates expected that "every man Will be Ready for action Compleat [sic] with 30 Rounds" on October 9. See *Orderly book of Cap[t] [sic] Thaddeus Cook*. Also see Rev. Augustine George Hibbard, *History of the Town of Goshen, Connecticut, with Genealogies and Biographies* (Hartford, CT: Case, Lockwood, and Brainard, 1897), 145. Collins was a sergeant in Captain Tarball Whitney's company, Colonel Thaddeus Cook's battalion of Connecticut militia.

49. An example of categorical failure in relying on this strategy is the 1776 Long Island–Manhattan campaign. Following the 1775 Battle of Bunker Hill, British army tactical doctrine changed in order to decisively counter the American's common reliance upon natural and man-made defenses during combat. For further discussion, see Spring, *With Zeal.*

50. Varick to Schuyler, September 19, 1777, New York Public Library, Papers of General Philip Schuyler 1710–1805.

51. Although the Battle of Valcour Island was a tactical disaster for American forces, historians traditionally credit Arnold for delaying the British invasion from Canada for a year, some even suggesting that the battle "may well have saved the American Revolution." This is false, however, because the battle and retreat/pursuit action lasted less than three days, a time frame that delayed no British offensive operations. Alternatively, historians credit Arnold for delaying the British invasion due to his fleet-building operations at Skenesborough (present-day Whitehall, New York), suggesting that the British were forced to react in kind by committing inordinate time, resources, and energy into the construction of their own fleet at St. John's, Canada. This was only coincidental, however, as the British had no vessels on Lake Champlain and were forced to build a fleet from scratch simply to transport the thousands of troops destined for the invasion. That they built a substantial armed fleet was simply reflective of their knowledge that the Americans had controlled the lake since the beginning of the war and would have to be combated. Further, there is no evidence suggesting the British fleet was built in reaction to the American's shipbuilding program at Skenesborough or that the invasion was called off, even in part, due to the Battle of Valcour Island. Notably, American forces controlled Lake Champlain since the beginning of the war due to Arnold's aggressive strategy and capture of British shipping at St. John's in May 1775. Mark M. Boatner, "Valcour Island," in *Encyclopedia of the American Revolution* (New York: Van Rees Press, 1969), 1136.

52. Varick to Schuyler, September 22, 1777, New York Public Library, Papers of General Philip Schuyler 1710–1805. Evidence that Gates denied Arnold reinforcements appears here, in which Varick reported to his patron that, after being informed that the 3rd New Hampshire Battalion was marching to the field of battle, Gates "declared no more should go" because he would "not suffer the Camp to be Exposed." However, the 3rd New Hampshire Battalion was only the second reinforcement Arnold sent to support Morgan's Corps, and it was subsequently followed by no less than nine full battalions. Either Varick misremembered, lied, Gates's instructions were not appropriately relayed to Arnold, Gates changed his mind, or Arnold outright disobeyed orders.

53. Ensign Louis Joseph, Chevalier D'anterroches (62nd Regiment), Ensign Levinge Cosby Phillips (62nd Regiment), and Maurice Spillard (an assistant commissary officer) were captured; Phillips was also mortally wounded (he died September 21). The only British-forces captains killed or mortally wounded were Thomas Jones (4th Battalion, Royal Regiment of Artillery) and David Monin (Montréal District militia). For biographies of 62nd Regiment officers, see "Officers of the 62nd Regiment of Foot during the Period of the Northern Campaign of 1777," http://www.62ndRegiment.org/officers.htm, accessed July 20, 2013. Also see du Roi, *Specht Journal,* 136–37.

54. A transcript of this unattributed letter, dated September 20, 1777, is in Saratoga NHP files. Its author was probably a staff officer.

55. Standing general orders "to remain in force during the whole campaign" for British and German infantryman to carry one hundred cartridges was issued on June 28 and reiterated on July 10. Edmund B. O'Callaghan, ed., *Orderly Book of Lieut. Gen. John Burgoyne* (Albany,

NY: J. Munsell, 1860), 12–13, 36. British regimental general reviews, purchase warrants, and extant examples demonstrate that the 9th and 62nd Regiments were recently issued the newer 1769 short land pattern muskets while the 21st, 24th and 47th Regiments carried the older 1756 long land pattern muskets (issuing warrants show the 20th had a mix of both). Despite what their parent battalions may have been issued, light infantry companies received short land service pattern muskets; Royal Regiment of Artillery other ranks carried lightweight pattern carbines (Royal Regiment of Artillery sergeants and corporals of the Canada army having replaced their halberds with firearms in 1776). See Erik Goldstein and Stuart Mowbray, *The Brown Bess* (Woonsocket, RI: Mowbray, 2010). Regimental general reviews are located in the War Office (WO) papers, class 27, in the National Archives, Kew, UK. Issuing warrants are recorded in De Witt Bailey, *Small Arms of the British Forces in America 1664–1815* (Woonsocket, RI: Mowbray, 2009). During the American War for Independence, there was no universal British army cartridge pouch. Instead, pouches were purchased by individual regimental commanders and, depending upon the pattern, usually had twenty-six-, twenty-nine-, or thirty-six-round capacities. Documenting a specific pouch pattern for any regiment at any given time is nearly impossible; however, in 1777 the 62nd Regiment's battalion companies were carrying "reversing block" pouches able to carry thirty-six cartridges each. See Troiani, *Don Troiani's Soldiers*, 22, 30. Any remaining balance of cartridges issued that would not fit in the pouches (and eighteen-round supplemental boxes, which most battalions left in Canada) was to be "carefully packed up by men in paper or linen, & put in the top of the knapsack." Frank C. Deering, ed., *Orderly Book Burgoyne's Campaign of 1777 Ticonderoga to Saratoga 47th Regiment of British Foot* (Saco, ME: privately printed, 1932), 33. Study of American War for Independence German arms and cartridge pouches is currently minimal, but for references, see Troiani, *Don Troiani's Soldiers*, 61–80. Also see George C. Neumann, *Battle Weapons of the American Revolution* (Texarcana, TX: Scurlock, 1998), 114–19.

56. *Orderly Book of the Braunschweig Corps in North America*, trans. Virginia Rinaldy, 56–57. Hessian Documents of the American Revolution, 1776–1783, Morristown NHP, Lidgerwood Collection, fiche 214–227. The baron's order, which reiterated that "if the enemy is on a plain, we must take pains to close in on him and, without firing, fall on the enemy with lowered bayonets," was dated August 26.

57. O'Callaghan, *Orderly Book of Lieut. Gen. John Burgoyne*, 116.

58. Subalterns were commissioned officers ranked below captain-lieutenant, such as ensigns, second lieutenants, and first lieutenants. In any army, subalterns were usually teenagers and men in their twenties.

59. For a study of the common British soldier experience in the American War for Independence, see Don Hagist, *British Soldiers, American War* (Yardley, PA: Westholme, 2012). This volume also contains nine British soldier narratives, of which three were from men who served in Burgoyne's army in 1777. Further adding to the number of inexperienced men, additional companies for Burgoyne's British regiments, with hundreds of new recruits, arrived on September 3, 1777, and were immediately integrated with their parent battalions. See O'Callaghan, *Orderly Book of Lieut. Gen. John Burgoyne*, 91–94. Until recently, the advent of British army "von Scheither" volunteers recruited in Germany has been wholly overlooked. Surprisingly, in the Battle of Freeman's Farm, nearly 25 percent of the 62nd Regiment's battalion rank and file was composed of new, non-English-speaking German recruits. See Eric Schnitzer, "'The Men in general very tolerable; much better than could have been expected,' or, 'a good deal of useless stuff': 106 German Recruits for the 62nd Regiment of Foot," *The Hessians: Journal of the Johannes Schwalm Historical Association* 14 (2011): 78–83.

60. This was the first battle in which Brigadier-General James Hamilton commanded a brigade and the first time Lieutenant-Colonels John Lind (20th Regiment) and John Anstruther (62nd Regiment), and Majors George Forster (21st Regiment) and William Agnew (24th Regiment), commanded regiments in battle (although Forster, when a captain, commanded a small body of mixed British forces in a series of May 1776 engagements known as the Battle of the Cedars). Major Alexander, Earl Balcarres (British light infantry battalion) and Major John Acland (British grenadier battalion) had little combat command experience prior to 1777.

61. Hoffman Nickerson, *The Turning Point of the Revolution*, vol. 2 (Boston: Houghton Mifflin, 1928), 320.

62. The name "Balcarres Redoubt" is the twentieth-century name for a fortification the British formally called the "Light Infantry Redoubt."

63. The name "Breymann Redoubt" is the twentieth-century name for a fortification complex British forces commonly referred to as "Breymann's Entrenchment" and "Breymann's fortified camp." Because it was not a proper redoubt, it was never referred to as such.

64. Feldprediger (chaplain) Johann August Milius to Father Heinrich Milius, September 29, 1777, trans. John Luzader, Niedersächsisches Staatsarchiv Wolfenbüttel. Milius was feldprediger of the Braunschweig Musketeer Regiment von Riedesel.

65. Adjutant Heinrich Wilhelm Uhlig to a "Respected Friend," November 23, 1777, trans. John Luzader, Niedersächsisches Staatsarchiv Wolfenbüttel. These were the same two cabins occupied by the 9th Regiment during much of the Battle of Freeman's Farm. Uhlig was the adjutant of the reserve corps.

66. Uhlig to a "Respected friend," October 2, 1777, trans. John Luzader, Niedersächsisches Staatsarchiv Wolfenbüttel. Although Uhlig ignorantly proclaimed that the reserve corps was "in a strong position that the rebels dare not attack," he added that he did not trust the French Canadian cabin defenders, as "they are poor in discipline and no faith can be placed in them."

67. Uhlig to a "Respected Friend," November 23, 1777, trans. John Luzader, Niedersächsisches Staatsarchiv Wolfenbüttel.

68. Major General Friedrich Adolph Riedesel, Freiherr (Baron) zu Eisenbach, to Carl, Herzog (Duke) von Braunschweig und Lüneburg, und Fürsten (Prince) von Braunschweig-Wolfenbüttel, October 21, 1777, trans. Julie K. Snell, Niedersächsisches Staatsarchiv Wolfenbüttel. Also see Lieutenant-General John Burgoyne to Secretary of State for American Colonies Lord George Germain, October 20, 1777, Henry B. Dawson, *Battles of the United States, by Sea and Land: Embracing Those of the Revolutionary and Indian Wars, the War of 1812, and the Mexican War; with Important and Official Documents*, vol. 1 (New York: Johnson, Fry, 1858), 305.

69. Traditionally, these adjacent farm fields have been associated with the Barber family and the place name "Barber Wheat field." However, records show the Barber brothers, Simeon and Joshua, did not lease these farms until 1782. Currently, it is unknown who lived on the property in 1777. The land composed farm number 5 in Great Lott 16 of the Saratoga Patent, owned by Philip Schuyler. *Estate of Philip Schuyler, Dec[eased]*, 312. Property lessee information is provided to Saratoga NHP by Leslie B. Potter, attorney-at-law.

70. The meaning of "Weisser House" is unknown and made difficult due to differences in phraseology used by contemporary writers. Variations include "the Weisser House," "Weisser's House," "the Weiss House," and "a house in a clearing called Weissers House." These could refer to a white-colored house, a family surnamed White or Weisser, or something altogether different. It is notable that the German word for wheat, *weizen*, is too similar

to *Weisser* to discount as coincidental, particularly as the house stood in a wheat field. See du Roi, *Specht Journal*, 90. Also see Cleve, *Journal of the Brunswick Troops in North America*, HZ 335. Also see *Excerpt from a Military Memoir Concerning the American Campaign in the Year 1777*, October 18, 1777, trans. Helga Doblin, D, Saratoga NHP, n.d., 5. Also see Johann Friedrich Specht et al., *Major General Riedesel's justification piece concerning the events of the Campaign of 1777 in America*, October 18, 1777, D, Saratoga NHP, n.d., 7.

71. Wilkinson, *Encampment & Position of the Army*. Also see *Plan of the Position of the Army*.

72. Georg Päusch, *Georg Pausch's Journal and Reports of the Campaign in America*, trans. Bruce E. Burgoyne (Bowie, MD: Heritage Books, 1996), 87. Päusch was captain of the Hessen-Hanau Princely Corps of Artillery.

73. Cleve, *Journal of the Brunswick Troops in North America*, HZ 335.

74. Ibid.

75. Wilkinson, *Memoirs*, 267–68.

76. Ibid. This wooded height is called "Morgan Hill" today.

77. Cleve, *Journal of the Brunswick Troops in North America*, HZ 335.

78. Burgoyne, *State of the Expedition*, 92. This comes from the testimony before the House of Commons given by Thomas Blomefield. Blomefield was captain-lieutenant of Captain Elis Walker's company, 3rd Battalion, Royal Regiment of Artillery, commander of the center division of the park of artillery, and major of brigade to the Royal Regiment of Artillery.

79. Burgoyne to Germain, October 20, 1777, in Dawson, *Battles of the United States*, 305.

80. Päusch, *Georg Pausch's Journal*, 86.

81. Burgoyne to Germain, October 20, 1777, in Dawson, *Battles of the United States*, 305.

82. Päusch, *Georg Pausch's Journal*, 88.

83. Dearborn, "A Narrative of the Saratoga Campaign," 8. Most nineteenth-century anecdotes give credit to Timothy Murphy for having shot Fraser. When Fraser was mortally wounded, he was commanding the rear guard covering the retreating British reconnaissance force and therefore his wounding did not herald the chaotic retreat from the field of battle. Thus, had he survived unscathed, the battle would have turned out little different. Murphy was a private soldier in Captain Hawkins Boon's company, Colonel Daniel Morgan's Detached Rifle Battalion.

84. Wilkinson, *Memoirs*, 271.

85. Henry Alexander Scammell Dearborn, *The Life of Major General Henry Dearborn*, vol. 2, ch. 4, MS, Maine Historical Society, Brinley Place, 1822, 36.

86. Dearborn, *Life of Major General Henry Dearborn*, 37.

87. Although it cannot be corroborated, German scuttlebutt claimed that "Breymann was killed by his own grenadiers after he had killed four of them." See Friedrich Julius von Papet, *Canada during the American Revolutionary War: Lieutenant Friedrich Julius von Papet's Journal of the Sea Voyage to North America and the Campaign Conducted There, 15 May 1776 to 10 October 1783*, trans. Bruce E. Burgoyne (Bowie, MD: Heritage Books, 1998), 78. Von Papet was first lieutenant of Captain Conrad Anton Alers's company, Braunschweig Musketeer Regiment von Rhetz. Although he was not present with Burgoyne's army (he remained in Canada), this intelligence was received from a fellow German officer and recorded in his journal on October 24. For Arnold, see Gates to Hancock, October 12, 1777, New-York Historical Society, Horatio Gates Papers, 5:1052.

88. Wilkinson, *Memoirs*, 272.

89. Arnold to Gates, October 1, 1777, New-York Historical Society, Horatio Gates Papers, 5:826.

90. Ibid. The date of Arnold's appointment to the rank of major general was a contentious

issue. Originally passed over for promotion to that rank on February 19, 1777, he was commissioned a major general on May 2. Various efforts, and even a congressional vote, to backdate his commission to February 19 failed. After Burgoyne's surrender and Arnold's merit again brought to the attention of Congress, in late November it ordered that Arnold's rank be regulated by the commander in chief; Washington did so by backdating Arnold's commission to February 17, 1777.

91. Some Americans even blamed Arnold for meddling with the attack's progress, not helping it. In the opinion of Philip Van Cortlandt, Arnold's orders to Poor to "bring his men into better order as we were pursuing" the British retreating into the Balcarres Redoubt during the battle "arrested our progress and prevented our taken [sic]" the fort. He further opined that Poor's men would otherwise have "Intered [sic] it almost as soon as the British" had Arnold not interfered. Van Cortlandt was colonel of the 2nd New York Regiment. Philip Van Cortlandt, *The Revolutionary War Memoir and Selected Correspondence of Philip Van Cortlandt*, ed. Jacob Judd (Tarrytown, NY: Sleepy Hollow Restorations, 1976), 48.

92. This was posted in general orders to the army on June 30. O'Callaghan, *Orderly Book of Lieut. Gen. John Burgoyne*, 17.

93. Among these were Burgoyne's principle aide-de-camp (Lieutenant and Captain Sir Francis Clarke, baronet, who was also mortally wounded), commander of British artillery (Captain and Major Griffith Williams), deputy quartermaster general (Captain John Money), and commander of the British grenadier battalion (Major John Acland). Also, during a bizarre nighttime attempt to retake Breymann's camp after the battle, the senior field officer of the Braunschweig musketeer Regiment von Riedesel (Lieutenant-Colonel Ernst von Speth) was captured.

94. The Army of the United States captured two medium twelve-pounders, six light six-pounders, hundreds of rounds of round and case shot, two ammunition wagons, five tumbrels, over fifty port fires, one barrel of powder, and more. See National Archives and Records Administration, *Numbered Record Books Concerning Military Operations and Service, Pay and Settlement of Accounts, and Supplies in the War Department Collection of Revolutionary War Records*, vol. 129, roll 39.

95. Because of the reconnaissance-in-force's secrecy of purpose (including among the British force's own officer corps), and the American command's ignorance of Burgoyne's intentions, historians have long confused the point of Burgoyne's movements on October 7. However, Burgoyne's plan was not ambiguous and is well documented. See Eric Schnitzer, *What's His Motivation: Analyzing the Purpose of Burgoyne's 7 October 1777 Reconnaissance Force* (D, Saratoga NHP, October 2009).

CHAPTER THREE | DEAN R. SNOW

The British Fortifications

As demonstrated at Saratoga, historical archaeology provides information that is often not available from documents. The identities of many of the major players in the Saratoga battles are known, the maps they made show the locations and forms of major fortifications, and documents they wrote describe the engagements that produced archaeologically discoverable evidence. Because historical archaeologists already know much about what to expect at sites like the Saratoga Battlefield, their excavations can often be strategically and precisely targeted. As such, they can contribute to our understanding of specific events, adding detail and nuance to the story drawn from the documents. There is also the possibility of encountering something that is completely unexpected, something that can force a rethinking of the current narrative. As is presented in the following, the British fortifications at Saratoga provide an excellent example of both the confirmation and the deepening of history already known and the archaeological discovery of history that would have otherwise remained hidden.

The Documentary Record for the British Fortifications at Saratoga

The books of eminent historians, such as Richard Ketchum and John Luzader, have done much to illuminate the history of the battles at Saratoga writ large.[1] Military historians such as Douglas Cubbison, Charles Snell, and Eric Schnitzer have further clarified the details of those same events.[2] While more can still be wrung out of the surviving documentary sources, it seems unlikely that there will be major changes in our understandings of the events that unfolded in what is now Saratoga County in 1777. Certain persistent errors and myths about the battle, for example, the notion that Timothy Murphy shot Simon Fraser, may be corrected, even while the basic outline of the battlefield history is little altered.[3]

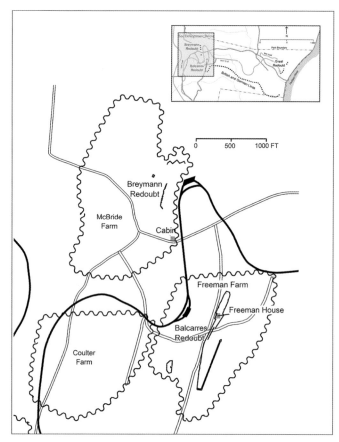

FIGURE 3.1. Northern portion of the Saratoga Battlefield showing the main British fortification areas. Note park boundary and the modern tour road (*gray*); other roads date to 1777. The enlarged area illustrates western British and German fortifications as established on September 20, 1777, showing farm clearings and roads. The modern park tour road (*black*) provides context. Map drafted by the author.

Thus, what has characterized the efforts of archaeologists working on the battlefield is the clarification of events that remain unclear based solely on documents, and discovery of unexpected details and stories that enhance our knowledge.

Construction of the British fortifications in the northern portion of the Saratoga National Historical Park was begun on September 21, 1777, following the Battle of Freeman's Farm two days earlier (figure 3.1). Although documentary sources such as reports, letters, and postbattle narratives mention these construction activities, they tend to be brief and unillustrated. As a result, it would be almost impossible to say much about the fortifications if these were our only sources. We know from documentary sources—for example, narratives by Ebenezer Wild, Georg Päusch, Henry Dearborn, Roger Lamb, John Burgoyne, and James Wilkinson—that British and German soldiers began building fortifications on the bluffs overlooking the Hudson Valley, and we know from those same sources which units were assigned to these tasks.[4] However, the sources tell us little or nothing at all about locations, layouts, or the details of construction.

Consequently, the most important documents for archaeologists working on the British fortifications on the battlefield are the set of maps made by Lieutenant William C. Wilkinson, a British engineer from the 62nd Regiment of Foot at the time of the battles.[5] Wilkinson drew detailed albeit imprecise maps of the British and German positions at the Saratoga Battlefield between September 19 and October 7, 1777. Sadly, we do not have anything equivalent for the American positions. While Snell was able to locate and hand copy a sketch map of the American lines made by Rufus Putnam in 1777 or later, the location of the original is unknown and the quality of the map does not approach that of Wilkinson's.[6]

Charles Snell also produced a historical base map of the Saratoga Battlefield to illustrate the situation on October 7, 1777. Produced as part of the master plan for Saratoga National Historical Park, the map was based on both the documents mentioned previously and archaeological research carried out by Robert Ehrich in 1941.[7]

Although Wilkinson was able to provide a general picture of the British fortifications on October 7, 1777, he lacked both sufficient time and adequate surveying equipment. The result is that features, such as the three principal redoubts (Breymann, Balcarres, and Great), are each rendered individually rather well, but their positions relative to each other on the larger landscape of the battlefield are much less precise.

Cartographic specialists at The Pennsylvania State University recently assisted the National Park Service in rectifying the Wilkinson maps to modern landscape features and coordinate systems. Using LiDAR (light detection and ranging) satellite imagery from 2011, they corrected much of the imprecision found on the originals. The results of this work allow us to more accurately depict the locations of the British and German units between the Battle of Freeman's Farm on September 19 and the Battle of Bemis Heights on October 7, 1777.[8]

The Balcarres Redoubt

The British and German regiments under Burgoyne dug in following the September 19, 1777, Battle of Freeman's Farm. Their defensive line mirrored in a very general way that of the Americans on Bemis Heights to the south. The Freeman farmhouse became the apex of the British line, much as Neilson's house and barn did on the American line. Trees were felled and their branches sharpened to form an abatis. Trenches were dug at various points along the line that stretched eastward from Freeman's farm to the bluffs overlooking the Hudson. The line angled sharply from Freeman's farm to the northwest to protect the British right from a possible American flanking attack (see figure 3.1). The apex at Freeman's farm was made especially strong with entrenchments, log and earthen walls, and emplacements for eight of the ten artillery pieces from Walker's company of Royal Artillery.

The Balcarres Redoubt was manned by the British light infantry battalion from soon after September 19 to October 7, 1777. The battalion was made up of light infantry companies detached from ten infantry regiments and put under the command of Major Alexander Lindsay, the earl of Balcarres, whose title became associated with the fortification.

Curiously, according to both the Wilkinson maps and archaeological research, the Balcarres Redoubt was not confined to the natural ridge on which Freeman's farmhouse was situated, but extended another 700 feet south across the flat field that had been the killing ground during the September battle. Four cannons were placed at the southern end of this long extension, which was separated from the more defendable northern portion of the redoubt by a farm road and low wet ground. The result was a nearly 1,200-foot-long redoubt, two-thirds of which was a vulnerable salient, or section of the fortification that jutted out, forming the southern protrusion that is visible in figure 3.1. At the narrow southern end of the Freeman farm clearing, the gun crews and light infantry assigned to defend the redoubt were vulnerable to sniper attacks from the woods on three sides. Thus, at first glance, the placement of the Balcarres Redoubt salient appears counterintuitive, perhaps even recklessly illogical.

The logic of the Balcarres salient was more strategic than tactical. This was the ground that Hamilton's brigade, in particular the 62nd Regiment of Foot, had advanced across six times during the fighting on September 19. Five times the Americans had pushed them back to the north side of Freeman's farm, and they might well have done so a sixth time had darkness not fallen. Burgoyne claimed a technical victory, but only because his army held the disputed ground at the end of the day. Thus, the Balcarres salient appears to have been created out of concern for morale and broader strategic goals to hold that ground in the days following the Battle of Freeman's Farm. It is possible, perhaps likely, that the British thought that if attacked, the four cannons positioned at the vulnerable southern end of the Balcarres Redoubt could have been pulled back quickly. The British light infantry battalion was camped in and around the redoubt. It was the unit best suited to defend the salient and effect its prompt evacuation if that became necessary because it was composed of light mobile troops.

Archaeological Research at the Balcarres Redoubt

Robert Ehrich conducted archaeological excavations on the Balcarres Redoubt in 1941, as part of the transfer of the battlefield from state to federal control. As would be the case for the 1972 excavations, his initial focus was on testing the accuracy of Wilkinson's depiction of the Balcarres salient. His approach was to excavate four long, roughly east-west trenches at intervals across the redoubt

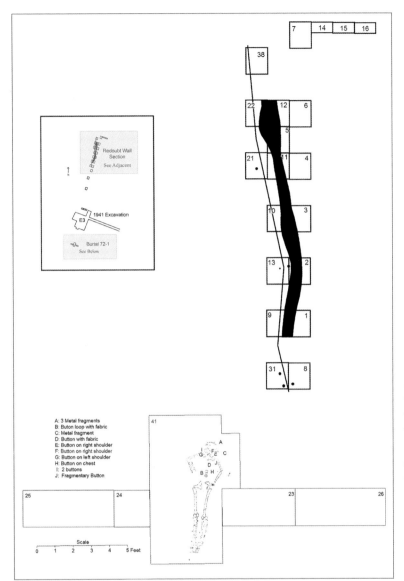

FIGURE 3.2. Locator map and detail of 1972 excavations showing a portion of the Balcarres Redoubt foot trench and a line running along the projected top of the parapet just to the west. Post molds (•) mark places where vertical posts reinforced the parapet. The illustration at the bottom is burial 72-1, uncovered in 1972. Maps drafted by the author.

in order to intercept and map the British fortification walls. The four trenches excavated in 1941 were not laid out on a common grid, so the directions of their axes differ. Ehrich's trenches and units that I excavated in 1972 were compiled into a single map by Hartgen Associates. Figure 3.2 is derived from that compilation. In three of the four 1941 trenches, they were widened at their western ends when Ehrich discovered important archaeological features. Unfortunately, Ehrich's field records appear to be incomplete and the locations of the artifacts and human remains he recovered are unknown.[9]

Research teams from the University at Albany conducted major archaeological investigations on the battlefield from 1972 to 1978. While archaeologists typically work on sites that contain dense concentrations of artifacts and features deposited over long time periods, the Saratoga Battlefield required techniques that could productively investigate archaeological remains that were both very thin and very widespread.[10] Although aerial photography had been used productively by John Cotter prior to 1972, it had not been integrated into a research plan that also included techniques other than excavation. The 1972 research design required that new aerial coverage be flown at low altitude. This work allowed for the production of detailed maps with close contour intervals (two feet). Furthermore, stereo pairs of aerial photos could be used by researchers to detect very subtle topographic variations. This technique revealed probable 1777 fortifications even in areas that had been repeatedly plowed for the past two centuries.

The 1972 investigations also made use of magnetometer survey and soil sampling. Magnetometers detect subtle variations in the earth's magnetic field that can indicate the presence of hearths or disturbances resulting from the digging of trenches and the construction of earthen walls, even where these features were later reduced by farming and natural processes. Magnetometer technology was in its infancy in 1972, and all readings had to be recorded manually; computer software to manage conversion of large numbers of readings to two-dimensional map images did not yet exist. The prototype magnetometer produced an audio tone that depended upon operator interpretation rather than the numeric digital output now available on commercial magnetometers. Consequently, the magnetometer was primarily used to run repeated transects across and perpendicular to suspected 1777 entrenchments, depending on the operators to detect anomalies by way of subtle audio tone changes that signaled archaeological features.

Soil samplers were used to probe along the same transects as a means to confirm suspected subsurface features. Quick and minimally invasive, hollow metal soil probes were pushed into the ground in order to extract an intact core of soil, providing a view of the soil column. Unfortunately, they were difficult to use in the hard clayey soils that cloak much of the battlefield. Nevertheless, soil sampling provided further confirmation of features first detected by the magnetometer or by analysis of stereo pairs of aerial photographs.

Test excavation, an expensive and inherently destructive application of traditional archaeological techniques, was reserved for clarifying evidence collected by noninvasive means, or where the payoff in new information was judged to be high. The units excavated in 1972 were laid out on a grid anchored to a baseline running along the natural ridge on which the Freeman farmstead and the 1777 Balcarres Redoubt were constructed.[11] As a result, our nominally east-west trenches were designed to cross fortification lines at or close to right angles.

The 1972 fieldwork resulted in the confirmation and fine-tuning of the location and size of the Balcarres Redoubt. Ehrich's 1941 observations were largely confirmed and additional details were added. Excavations identified the foot trench of the redoubt along with post molds found in association with the trench. This relationship between embankment and trench was unexpected. Standard earthen fortifications of the sixteenth, seventeenth, and eighteenth centuries featured robust parapets and external ditches; for example, the kind of structure found at Fort Raleigh in North Carolina (1585–86).[12] However, structures like Fort Raleigh were intended to be relatively small and permanent, circumstances that justified the heavy labor investment required to dig dry-moat ditches and build high parapets. Thus, in retrospect it should not have been a surprise to find that the Balcarres Redoubt was more simply constructed. The Balcarres Redoubt was much bigger than Fort Raleigh and it was not intended to last for more than a few weeks at most.

Another trench, east of a line running along what we infer was the crest of the parapet (figure 3.2), was apparently excavated as a foot trench to give soldiers additional cover; no exterior dry moat was identified. Soldiers of the British light infantry battalion posted here between the two battles dug the trench and threw the soil to the western side for cover. This made the natural exterior slope steeper, while at the same time providing good cover for soldiers who might be called upon to fire westward from within the redoubt. Large post molds were identified here, occasionally with large river cobbles that were apparently hauled to the site and used to stabilize vertical posts that were part of the parapet. Additional logs were apparently laid horizontally as added protection before the earth from the foot trench was thrown up on them. Curiously, the foot trench was not found in the two units excavated at the southern end of the area shown in figure 3.2. However, post molds were found in these units, suggesting that there was a sally port, or opening, located in this part of the Balcarres Redoubt wall.

Burials in the Balcarres Redoubt

The 1941 excavations by Ehrich uncovered four burials in the widened excavation area at the western end of trench E1. Burials 14-1 and 14-4 lie together in the left central part of the trench. Two more burials, 14-2 and 14-3, were uncovered about twenty feet east of the first two. All four burials had associated brass buttons, and burial 14-3 had nine associated pewter buttons. This implies that all four were probably the remains of British Royal Artillery soldiers, who we know wore uniforms with brass buttons.[13] American soldiers and militiamen were generally clothed in hunting clothes, lacking uniforms at Saratoga.[14] Moreover, dead soldiers were typically stripped of their clothing by burial parties or scavengers following the American army before they were buried. Some wounded and unconscious soldiers even regained consciousness to find themselves stripped and lying naked in the cold at Saratoga.[15] These circumstances suggest that the burials found by Ehrich at the southern end of the Balcarres Redoubt were British soldiers that had not been accessible to the scavengers. Moreover, they were enlisted men, because officers were typically accorded single burial by British burial parties while enlisted men were often placed in common graves as were those interred in burials 14-1 and 14-4 and 14-2 and 14-3.[16]

Burial 14-1 also contained case shot, which the British artillery used on September 19; the American artillery was not in action at Freeman's farm that day. It is not likely that the artillerymen would have fired into the backs of their own infantry, or that the case shot would have lodged in the soldier's body if they had. Thus, the case shot associated with burial 14-1 was probably an accidental inclusion of battlefield debris made by the burial party.

It is possible that the four burials found in 1941 were casualties of the October 7 Battle of Bemis Heights, when the light infantry battalion defending the Balcarres Redoubt was supplemented by men retreating from the action on the wheat field. However, British forces retreated from the Balcarres Redoubt to the vicinity of the Great Redoubt overlooking the Hudson River during the night following the battle, and it is unlikely that many of the British dead received burial at that time. American burial parties operating during the days following the second battle were probably preceded by scavengers who would have stripped the British dead. All of this argues for the likelihood that all four of these burials were of British casualties in the September 19 battle.

A single burial (72-1) was uncovered during the 1972 excavations in a unit that had been excavated to explore the redoubt foot trench and wall south of the area examined by Ehrich (E3) (figure 3.2). When the burial was encountered, a new larger excavation unit (41) was laid out over the feature to provide finer excavation control (figure 3.2). The buried individual proved to be lying face down in the trench with the head oriented northward. There were several pieces of shot, a mixture of buckshot and slightly smaller swan shot, associated with the lower legs. This individual's face had been destroyed by shot and there were pellets inside the cranium and associated with the right arm. The use of shot is not unexpected, as the Americans, Continentals and militia alike, were reported to be loading their muskets with both a ball and two to four buckshot on October 7, when they assaulted the Balcarres Redoubt.[17]

Various considerations, some of them erroneous, led us to initially conclude that this burial was that of an American militiaman. The face was missing because of trauma at the time of death, and the pelvis was not well preserved, which made the assignment of sex difficult. The stature of the individual was small, such that in life this person would not have stood more than about five feet two inches. Just as striking was the advanced age of the individual, which at the time could be estimated only as probably greater than sixty years.[18]

Burial 72-1 was encountered before the trench and wall features shown in figure 3.2 could be defined and evaluated. Because we were at the time expecting to find an earthen parapet wall and an external ditch, we initially concluded that the burial was that of a person who had fallen and had been buried outside the wall when the Americans assaulted and tried to take the Balcarres Redoubt. Consequently, the initial working hypothesis was that the individual had been buried in an external ditch after the battle. This added weight to our initial inference that the burial was that of an American man, albeit an unusually small and elderly man.

The excavation revealed that the body had been covered by small logs before being covered with earth, and there was no evidence that the body had been stripped of clothing. The buttons and fabric found around the torso indicated that the body was clothed at the time of burial. This was not consistent with the many other burials of American soldiers who had been stripped after dying on the battlefield. While the body appeared not to have been stripped, the pewter buttons with iron wire shanks supported our inference that this was the body of an American rather than a British or German soldier.

At the time of the excavation we also did not yet know that American soldiers were commonly loading their muskets with both ball and shot in 1777. Richard Patterson later pointed this out.[19] Furthermore, although we initially inferred that the burial had been placed outside the redoubt wall, reexamination in light of the excavations just to the north (figure 3.2) made it seem more probable that the burial had been put into the foot trench just inside the wall. A more detailed analysis of the burial was completed in 1986 at the request of the National Park Service.[20] The osteological findings remained a bit ambiguous because the burial was clearly that of a battle casualty that we had long assumed to be male. However, the low to no cranial muscle relief, the lack of brow ridges, the small mastoids, the small occipital condyles, and the small size of the skull overall all indicated it was female. In addition, the sciatic notches and the lightness of the bone in the pelvis also indicated that this was a female. The evidence eventually forced us to favor the interpretation of skeleton 72-1 as female. Finally, a more thorough review of the documentary evidence also supported the inference that the burial could have been a female casualty.

Documentary records indicate that in addition to the wives and children of some of the British and German officers, there were many women with Burgoyne's army. In fact, at least 215 women traveled with the British troops and another eighty-two with the Germans.[21] Historians are increasingly recognizing the vital roles played by women on both sides in the campaigns of the American Revolution.[22] One of the British women could easily have been assisting her husband and other men in the Balcarres Redoubt during the fighting of October 7. Thus, it now seems much more likely that burial 72-1 was that of a

British woman who was in late middle age when she died during the fighting on October 7, 1777.

Given the number of burials discovered during limited archaeological excavations, it is possible to roughly estimate the total number of burials in the area of the redoubt. The Balcarres Redoubt has a total area of approximately 151,600 square feet. Ehrich excavated approximately 8,200 square feet in 1941.[23] The University at Albany crew excavated 1,221.5 square feet of the Balcarres Redoubt in 1972. Taken together, the two Balcarres Redoubt excavations totaled about 9,400 square feet, or about 6 percent of the total area of the redoubt. Thus, the sample of five burials found in the 1941 and 1972 excavations suggests that a total of roughly eighty burials should be expected for the area within and immediately around the Balcarres Redoubt were it to be totally excavated.

The southern half of the Balcarres Redoubt was in the middle of the killing ground that the armies fought over on September 19, 1777. Burgoyne lost about 600 killed, wounded, and missing that day, while the Americans lost 319 killed, wounded, and captured.[24] An unknown fraction of the immediate fatalities were buried the next day, near where they had fallen. The fraction of those casualties who later died of their wounds would have been buried elsewhere, mainly in the vicinities of the American and British hospitals. The projected number of approximately eighty burials in or immediately around the Balcarres Redoubt is reasonable in this context.

On October 7, the Americans lost 150 killed and wounded while Burgoyne's army lost about 630 killed, wounded, and captured.[25] Some of those killed that day fell in or around the Balcarres Redoubt, but it is likely that most of those found buried in the Balcarres Redoubt were soldiers who died on September 19, and that the bulk of those who died on October 7 were buried elsewhere.

The Northern Portion of the Balcarres Redoubt

The northern part of the Balcarres Redoubt is on the ridge previously occupied by the Freeman farmstead. The archaeology of this area was made difficult by the thinness of the soil covering the shale bedrock of the ridge. The Wilkinson maps show Freeman's house, or perhaps the barn, incorporated into the western wall of the Balcarres Redoubt. However, the thinness of the soil and the high concentration of nineteenth-century metal debris made it difficult for crews to find unambiguous archaeological evidence of 1777 features. Only thin and unconvincing traces of a foot trench and redoubt walls could be detected in this section.

An intensive, high-resolution metal detector survey of the northern portion of the redoubt might turn up better evidence of the Freeman farm structures, but the effort would be difficult and expensive. There is so much metal debris from

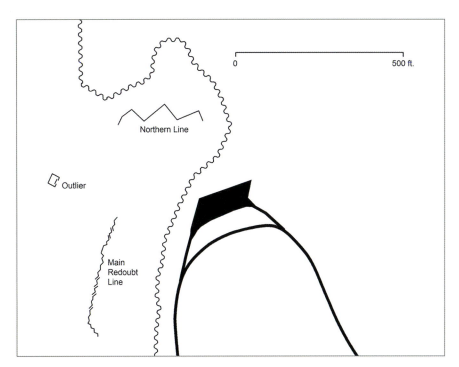

FIGURE 3.3. Components of the Breymann Redoubt as currently interpreted. Tour stop 7 and tour road shown for context. Map drafted by the author.

pre- and postbattle farming activities in this area that metal evidence from the 1777 battles, including bullets, buttons, gun parts, buckles, and cutlery, continues to be obscured by the nonbattle materials.[26]

Archaeological Research at the Breymann Redoubt

The 1972 field program also explored the Breymann Redoubt using low-level aerial photography, soil samplers, magnetometry, and test trenching. Wilkinson's 1777 maps indicated that the Breymann Redoubt remains were probably in three segments: a long main fortification line, a shorter fortification to the north that covered a deep ravine on the right flank, and a small outlier on a hilltop to the northwest (figure 3.3). Experience had shown that Wilkinson was generally accurate in the depiction of individual sets of fortifications of this kind even when he made errors fixing their locations relative to other sets of fortifications at larger scale.

When Wilkinson's drawing of the Breymann Redoubt components was considered in light of the highly detailed contour map that had been produced from

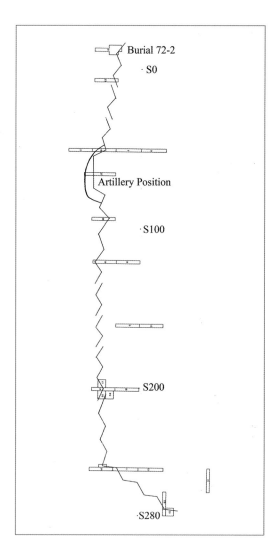

FIGURE 3.4. The zigzag rail and log fence line that made up the main fortification line of the Breymann Redoubt. Points prefixed with "S" (for south) show scale in feet on the grid baseline, which runs 16.5° east of true north. Map drafted by the author.

the low-level aerial photography, it was immediately clear that the long main fortification line of the redoubt was probably where it is now interpreted to be, rather than 300 feet west, where park signage interpreted it in 1972. Archaeological investigation was designed to test this new interpretation (figure 3.4).

The location of the main fortification line was also discussed in the documentary record. Around 4:00 p.m. on October 7, Lieutenant Colonel John Brooks approached the Balcarres Redoubt with the 8th Massachusetts Continental regiment. Benedict Arnold suggested they immediately attack the Balcarres Redoubt frontally, but Brooks could see that such an attack would be futile. Brooks determined from scouting reports that the Breymann Redoubt appeared to be vulnerable from the west, and Arnold and Brooks both agreed that an attack might succeed there. Units of Brooks's and men from other Massachusetts units of Learned's and Nixon's brigades set off in that direction, leaving Arnold to continue his effort to rally American soldiers in front of the Balcarres Redoubt.[27]

The Massachusetts men moved northwestward through the cover of woods so that they came up behind a hill that shielded them from fire coming from the main line of the Breymann Redoubt. The outlier that was positioned on that hill was quickly abandoned by German troops, who fell back a hundred yards across the boggy ground that separated it from the main line.[28]

Off to their right, between the Breymann and Balcarres Redoubts, was a huge four-hundred-yard gap in the line of the British right flank (see figure 3.1). The area was protected by a unit of Canadians stationed in a small log house and barn, structures later referred to as the "Canadian cabins." Some of the Massachusetts men attacked toward the south end of the Breymann Redoubt and these structures. The Canadians fled, leaving the left flank of the Breymann Redoubt uncovered. At almost the same moment, Benedict Arnold appeared, having galloped between the firing lines of the units still contesting for the Balcarres Redoubt. He charged past the buildings vacated by the Canadians toward the exposed rear of the redoubt, picking up other Americans along the way.[29]

Other Massachusetts men were ordered to charge from their position below the hillcrest west of the Breymann Redoubt. Dearborn's light infantry fell in behind Arnold, along with men from several other Continental regiments. Arnold was wounded at this point in the attack. The details provided in the documentary sources can only be accommodated by an interpretation of the Breymann Redoubt that positions it where it is currently located in that there would be no hillcrest to conceal the men of the Massachusetts regiments if it were located elsewhere.[30]

The location of the main line of the Breymann Redoubt was confirmed by the 1972 exploratory trenches (figure 3.4). As at the Balcarres Redoubt, trenching was preceded by detailed aerial photography, soil sampling, and magnetometer transects. The excavations revealed post molds but no evidence of trenching or earthen parapet construction. This is consistent with the Wilkinson map and other contemporary descriptions that indicate that the main line of the Breymann Redoubt was built much like a worm fence. Such a fence could have been constructed of logs and rails with few vertical posts and no trenching. It was not surprising that archaeological evidence was mostly limited to post molds.

A probable artillery position was detected based on a layer of sandy clay on top of the natural A horizon topsoil (see figure 3.4). This deposit was traced in an arcing line using soil sample probing. The deposit thinned and faded to the east of the presumed fortification lines (see figure 3.4, on right), too gradually to be effectively mapped. This was most likely the position of the two cannons that were assigned to the redoubt on October 7, 1777.

The post molds found along the ridge were not evenly spaced or at a standard distance from the baseline of the archaeological grid. However, when the zigzag pattern of the main fortification line shown by Wilkinson's map was superimposed over the post molds, the fit was close (figure 3.4). The excavations at the south end of the main line revealed what was inferred to be the angle in the line as depicted by Wilkinson, providing a lock on the north-south placement of the main line. Finally, our exploratory transects also encountered traces of the zigzag fortification line along the top of the bluff north of the main fortification line. The three components of the Breymann Redoubt—the main fortification line, the right flank fortification, and the small outlier on a hilltop to the northwest—are shown in figure 3.3 as currently interpreted. A modern tour road provides access to the famous Arnold boot monument, which was located near the outlier in 1972. The monument is now located more appropriately near the southern end of the main redoubt line, where Arnold was wounded.

Robert Ehrich excavated in the vicinity of the outlier in 1941, apparently to test the possibility that the main fortification line was located there. His sketches show remains that correspond to what should be expected for the square outlier, but not what should be expected for the main fortification line. It is no longer possible to determine precisely where the 1941 test excavations were carried out, so it is not possible to incorporate Ehrich's sketches into later mapping. Both Wilkinson's map and Ehrich's sketches suggest that the outwork was about twenty-five feet square.[31]

Burial in the Breymann Redoubt

Burial 72-2 was discovered in the exploratory trench at the north end of the main fortification line of the Breymann Redoubt (figures 3.4 and 3.5). This burial was much easier to assess than was the Balcarres Redoubt burial 72-1. In this case, the burial pit was very shallow and basin shaped. The skull and the feet had been buried so close to the surface that they disappeared sometime during the following two centuries. Because the redoubt had been built with only a small amount of digging, the grave was probably the result of hasty work by an American burial party on October 8, 1777, as opposed to an interment in a trench feature that was already open. There was no fighting in this sector on September 19, so it is reasonably certain that this individual died in the second battle on October 7.

The individual in this case was clearly a male, probably around thirty years old at the time of his death. Plowing and other farming practices that followed the battles probably account for the missing skull (although the mandible survived) and lower legs. These disturbances probably also account for the postmortem fractures and missing bone fragments of the arms, which had been left raised above the head by the burial party.[32]

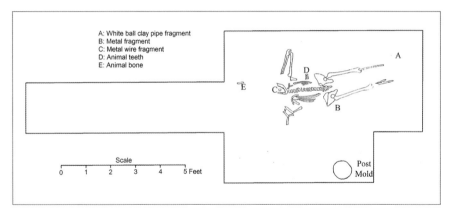

FIGURE 3.5. Burial 72-2, uncovered at the north end of the main fortification line of the Breymann Redoubt in 1972. Drafted by the author.

Burial 72-2 was associated with a few animal bones and discarded artifacts, but nothing to indicate that the man had been clothed when he was buried. Continental troops stayed in the redoubt through the night of October 7, and those men were probably responsible for burying the dead around it the following day. The dead soldier might have been a Loyalist, many of whom were posted at the Breymann Redoubt on October 7, or one of the German soldiers under Breymann's command. Alternatively, he might have been one of the handful of American men that fell there.

The Canadian Positions

Both of the cabin structures had seen use on the evening of September 19 as shelters for British wounded. Most of the wounded were taken to the British hospital tents along the Hudson River the following day. The buildings and the huge gap in the British and German line around them were manned by a few dozen Canadians on October 7.[33] These men retreated quickly around 4:00 p.m. that day when the Americans assaulted the Balcarres Redoubt and began to threaten the Breymann Redoubt. Their disappearance left the rear of the Breymann Redoubt open to attack, and it was by this route that Benedict Arnold and the men following him stormed into it.

Because they were small and insubstantial buildings, the locations of the two structures have been very difficult to determine. Close examination of low-level aerial photographs in 1972 revealed a rectangular pattern on a low knoll where Wilkinson's map suggested we might find the remains of one of the structures. The aerial photographs were taken in March 1972, just as a recent dusting of snow was melting off the otherwise barren landscape. Snow remained only in low areas and in other places where, for one reason or another, melting had been retarded. The north side of the knoll was still dusted with snow, but it had melted in a rectangular pattern on one portion of the slope, despite the apparent absence of significant earth ridging. The snow had not melted inside the rectangle, but only around its borders.

The aerial photos also revealed traces of the 1777 east-west road that crossed this sector just south of the rectangular anomaly. This relationship between the structure and road matches that shown on the Wilkinson map. Based on these clues, excavations were undertaken at the site of the presumed structure. The soil proved to be very clayey and hard and archaeological traces were all very near the surface; rain interfered with excavation and documentation. The only remains recovered were a few post molds, fragments of burned wood, and some soil stains. No artifacts were recovered and there were no traces of foundation walls. Despite the paucity of evidence, it seems likely that this was the location of one of the two structures where Canadians were posted.

The aerial photo evidence suggests that the structure measured about eighteen by twenty feet. The Wilkinson map indicates that it was probably fortified by a pentagonal wall made of rails and logs. If the single charred log found east of the rectangular anomaly was part of that wall, a diameter of no more than fifty feet is suggested for the pentagon. The Park Service posts outlining the site of this structure are as accurately placed as is currently possible. No trace of the second cabin or barn structure has been found. It is possible that it was covered or destroyed by later farming or road construction.

Archaeological Research at the Great Redoubt

Excavations in 1973 included exploration of the Great Redoubt, which most historians define as being comprised of three fortifications built by British and German troops on bluffs overlooking the Hudson River in what is now the northeast corner of the Saratoga National Historical Park. Testing carried out on the floodplain also resulted in the location of the foundation and cellar hole of the Taylor house, probably the structure in which Brigadier-General Simon Fraser died early on October 8, 1777.

One of Wilkinson's maps shows the British and German positions on and around the Great Redoubt on October 8, 1777. The relevant map's cartouche partly covers the representation of the bridge of boats Burgoyne's troops constructed across the Hudson starting on September 21, 1777. By October 8, the British light infantry battalion had left their previous camp at Freeman's farm and had taken up a position, west of the bridge of boats on the bluff just south of the ravine where the modern entrance road is located. North of the same ravine is the largest of three fortifications that comprise the Great Redoubt. Although the term *Great Redoubt* has sometimes been used to reference just this fortification, at other times it refers to all three of the fortifications on this bluff and the next two bluffs to the north. Only the latter usage is consistent with both the archaeological evidence and primary documentary sources. Wilkinson shows four pieces of artillery in the largest fortification. The next bluff northward has a fortification with two of them, and still farther north, the third and smallest fortification has no artillery. After the battle of October 7, the von Riedesel and von Rhetz infantry regiments were assigned to the largest fortification while the von Specht and Hanau Regiments were in and around the two-gun fortification on the next bluff north. Three British infantry regiments were on the northernmost of the three bluffs. Other British, German, and irregular units of Burgoyne's army were scattered around the three fortifications. The hospital and artillery park were both located on the river floodplain below the three bluffs. Three structures are shown at the foot of the northern bluff by Wilkinson, along with indication that the 9th Regiment of Foot was camped there. The three structures are interpreted to be the site of the Taylor house and two of its associated farm buildings.

After the National Park Service established the park in 1948, it built the tour road that is still used. Stop 9 on the tour road is on the southernmost of the three fortified bluffs, the location of the largest fortification, which contained four artillery pieces on October 8, 1777. This structure was designated "The Great Redoubt" at that time, and signage then indicated that this was where Simon Fraser had been buried.

Archaeologist Galen Ritchie wrote a brief report on his 1958 test excavations on the bluff at stop 9.[34] He found little of interest, but he did note that engineers planning and constructing the Champlain Canal along the river floodplain in 1817 had used the Fraser burial site as a datum point. Their maps appeared to indicate that Fraser had been buried on the central bluff. To this evidence can also be added a sketch made by Benson Lossing from a canal boat in the 1840s (figure 3.6). It also shows the burial site with a curving fence that tracks both the route of the 1777 funeral procession and the modern Fraser Burial Trail.[35]

Ritchie dug an exploratory trench on the central bluff, traces of which were visible when the University at Albany team returned to this area in 1973. New analysis of the canal engineers' maps using high-resolution contour maps, a transit, and low-level aerial photographs showed that Ritchie had been correct. Excavations on the top of the bluff revealed a grave, which Ritchie's test trench had missed by only a few feet. Figure 3.6 shows the grave outline, which was predictably precise and regular except for the right side. The disturbances on the right side prepared excavators for the possibility that the grave had been violated, possibly within hours of Fraser's interment.

There can be little doubt that Fraser was mortally wounded on the afternoon

FIGURE 3.6. Grave of Simon Fraser, uncovered in 1973. The grave was rectangular, two feet by six feet in size, initially dug to a depth of three feet. Later disturbance by looters widened the grave to approximately three feet. The inset at the top right of the photograph illustrates the central bluff of the Great Redoubt on which Simon Fraser was buried, facing west. Sketched by Benson Lossing around 1848. The fence follows the path taken by the funeral party in 1777 and the modern footpath. Photo by Dean Snow; inset from Benson J. Lossing, *The Pictorial Field-Book of the Revolution* (Rutland, VT: Charles E. Tuttle, 1972).

of October 7, 1777, and that he was buried in the grave found in the Great Redoubt in 1973. However, questions remain regarding the identity of the man who shot him. A nineteenth-century New York historian, Jeptha Simms, promoted the idea that Fraser had been shot by Timothy Murphy, one of Morgan's riflemen and later a resident of the Schoharie Valley. Murphy owned an unusual double-barreled rifle, and his descendants were happy to take credit for the shot once Simms began promoting it early in 1845.[36]

Timothy Murphy was among Daniel Morgan's men, as he had been on September 19. One source says that Morgan specifically urged Murphy to target Fraser.[37] The story seemed to gain credence from a comment made by Fraser himself, who said after he had been wounded that he had seen the man who shot him up in a tree.[38] Firing from a tree would have been typical of Morgan's riflemen.

One source says that before Fraser was hit, two shots grazed his horse and nearly hit him.[39] It was probably then that Fraser looked right and saw one or more riflemen in the trees. Fraser's aides tried to persuade him to retire to a safer location, but he refused. The fatal shot hit him soon after that. Fraser slumped and would have fallen from his horse had his aides not steadied him. It is unlikely that Fraser looked to see who had shot him after he was shot.

In 1895, William Stone republished the eyewitness account that Ebenezer Mattoon published in 1835, which reported that an anonymous elderly militiaman (probably from Albany County) shot Fraser with a hunting gun. Although he published the account, Stone himself did not accept the story, mainly on the grounds of Fraser's own statement saying that he had seen the man who had shot him.[40] The claim made by Simms a half century earlier was already established in Revolutionary lore and Stone was not inclined to challenge it.

Mattoon's eyewitness account is quite specific. Fraser was shot in his left side from a distance of twelve rods (198 feet). Fraser was probably facing the American attackers at the moment he was shot; Mattoon and the old soldier were ahead of Fraser and to his left. Morgan's riflemen were much farther off and on Fraser's right. The shot that wounded Fraser came from his left. Mattoon reports his conversation with the old militiaman immediately after the shot was taken, and their immediate conclusion was that it was Fraser who had been hit. Modern historians tend to doubt that Murphy shot Fraser.[41]

Fraser's grave was explored in 1973 in the hopes of finding the ball that had lodged near his spine and determine whether it was a musket or a rifle ball. We also hoped to find skeletal evidence of the direction from which the shot had come. However, the grave was empty, and any hope that we might find the ball that mortally wounded Fraser, or bone trauma that might indicate the direction from which it came, had to be abandoned.[42]

There is no evidence to support later rumors that Fraser's family came to the United States after the war in order to repatriate Fraser's remains. Informal inquiries with the Fraser family in Scotland have produced denials that any such effort was ever made. Although he has been condemned as a plagiarist in recent years, English soldier and journalist Thomas Anburey's report that he discovered Fraser's grave to have been violated by American treasure hunters before the defeated British army camped there again on October 17, 1777, now has the ring of truth.[43]

Researchers scoured the bluff top for additional graves in 1973 but found none. Like Ritchie, we also failed to find any clear evidence of fortifications. However, the existence of the single grave precisely where it was predicted to be by the 1817 and 1819 engineering maps and by Lossing's and Lane's sketches, as well as several campfire hearths, is good evidence that the bluff tops were not significantly eroded or modified before the area came under National Park Service protection. There is no basis on which to argue that erosion or soil removal in the nineteenth century destroyed the Great Redoubt fortifications and the Fraser interment. The best inference is that the fortifications shown by Wilkinson and Lane on these bluffs were made of rails and logs laid horizontally like those at the Breymann Redoubt. Earthworks like those constructed at the Balcarres Redoubt appear not to have been built at this location. Finally, the best inference is that the Fraser grave has been discovered, but that Fraser's remains were removed by persons unknown prior to October 17, 1777.[44]

The Taylor House Test Excavations

Examination of aerial photographs of the river floodplain below the bluffs of the Great Redoubt and east of the 1818 Champlain Canal revealed a depression that looked like the remains of an old cellar hole. The feature was located where the Wilkinson map showed the Taylor farmstead, suggesting that excavation could yield important information. After clearing of a dense growth of pioneer trees and shrubs, the depression was as visible to the casual observer as it was on the aerial photos. Two narrow crossing exploratory trenches were dug across the depression, and the cellar walls were revealed at four points. More important, an abundance of artifacts dating from 1760 to 1820 were recovered and these support the hypothesis that this is probably the site of the Taylor house. We know from documents that the house was moved to a location closer to the river later in the nineteenth century. This makes the discovery of undisturbed archaeological deposits from the original house site even more valuable because they are unlikely to be confused by later deposits. The matter may be confused by the possibility that there was once more than one Taylor house in the farmstead, but only one cellar hole was apparent to archaeologists.

Conclusions

Archaeological investigation of the British fortifications and surrounding features has provided not just supplementary information to the documentary record, but also information that has corrected things we erroneously thought we knew. Contrary to our expectations in 1972, British soldiers at the Balcarres Redoubt did not dig dry-moat ditches on the outsides of the redoubt walls but rather dug foot trenches on their interiors. Soldiers at the Breymann and Great Redoubts dug no trenches at all, but rather constructed cribworks of horizontally laid rails and logs.

The Balcarres Redoubt salient was real, at first glance inexplicable but understandable in light of overall British strategy. Although the salient at the south end of the redoubt was perhaps not wise militarily, it was most likely deemed necessary so that Burgoyne's army could claim victory in the September 19, 1777, Battle of Freeman's Farm by virtue of holding the ground that had been fought over that afternoon.

The Breymann Redoubt was built a hundred yards east of where one reading of the documents concluded it had been built, and where in 1972 the main section of the redoubt was thought to have been located. Research showed that the redoubt belonged where it is marked today. The famous boot monument to Benedict Arnold was also relocated after 1972 to a more appropriate location as a result of the research.

British women, or at least one of them, sometimes fought and died at their husbands' sides. Documentary sources indicate that there were women with both armies, and discovery of the remains of one elderly female battle casualty in the Balcarres Redoubt demonstrates that they were not necessarily passive participants. Other sources cited here have also argued for a more significant set of roles played by women in the American Revolution. They provided critically important support to supplement what commissaries provided. But they were also sometimes more directly engaged, as the female battle casualty found at the Balcarres Redoubt attests. Anburey also describes finding three dead American fighters on the day of the Battle of Bemis Heights, all three of them left unburied since the previous battle. One of them was a woman, her hands still clutching cartridges.[45]

The grave of Simon Fraser was found where documentary sources consistently indicate it should be in the Great Redoubt. One source indicates that the grave was disturbed by persons unknown prior to October 17, 1777. Archaeological excavation confirmed that the grave was empty. Although this has precluded archaeological confirmation of the details of Fraser's fatal wound, a reassessment of the documentary evidence has led modern historians to conclude that he was shot by an anonymous American militiaman, not by Timothy Murphy as previously thought. The Taylor house, probably where Fraser died on the morning of October 8, 1777, has been located and its place in the context of the other features of the British camp around the Great Redoubt is accurately interpreted for visitors.

It is rare for such an extensive set of eighteenth-century battlefield fortifications to be preserved in a well-protected park setting. It is still rarer for them to be of such importance to world history. Nine days after retreating northward from these lines, an entire British army surrendered for the first time in history. In retrospect, the events that played out in and around the British fortifications on the Saratoga Battlefield arguably tipped the likelihood of American independence from uncertain to inevitable.

NOTES

1. Richard M. Ketchum, *Saratoga, Turning Point of America's Revolutionary War* (New York: Henry Holt, 1997); John R. Luzader, *Saratoga: A Military History of the Decisive Campaign of the American Revolution* (New York: Savas Beatie, 2010).

2. Douglas R. Cubbison, *Burgoyne and the Saratoga Campaign: His Papers* (Norman, OK: Arthur H. Clark, 2012); Charles W. Snell, "Historical Base Map, Part of the Master Plan," Saratoga National Historical Park (NHP), National Park Service (NPS), 1950; Snell, "A Report on the American Fortified Camp at Bemis Heights, September 12 to October 8, 1777," Saratoga NHP, NPS, 1950; Snell, "A Report on the Organization and Numbers of Gates' Army, September 19, October 7, and October 17, 1777, including an Appendix with Regimental Data and Notes," Saratoga NHP, NPS, 1951; Snell, "A Report on the Strength of the British Army under Lieutenant-General John Burgoyne, July 1 to October 17, 1777, and on the Organization of the British Army on September 19 and October 7, 1777," Saratoga NHP, NPS, 1951. Eric Schnitzer's online "Tables of Organization," available at http://saratoganygenweb.com/Sarato.htm, is an invaluable resource.

3. Hugh T. Harrington, "The Myth of Rifleman Timothy Murphy," *Journal of the American Revolution* (March 2013), available at http://allthingsliberty.com/2013/03/the-myth-of-rifleman-timothy-murphy-and-the-power-of-the-written-word/.

4. Ebenezer Wild, "Journal of Ebenezer Wild," *Proceedings of the Massachusetts Historical Society* 1 (1890): 78–160; Georg Päusch, *Journal of Captain Päusch, Chief of the Hanau Artillery during the Burgoyne Campaign*, trans. William L. Stone (Albany, NY: Joel Munsell's Sons, 1886); Henry Dearborn, "A Narrative of the Saratoga Campaign," *Bulletin of the Fort Ticonderoga Museum* 1 (1929): 2–12; Roger Lamb, *Memoir of His Own Life* (Dublin: J. Jones, 1811); John Burgoyne, "Return of Lieutenant General Burgoyne's troops killed, wounded, prisoners, and missing in the actions of September 19 and October 7, 1777," in *MacKenzie Papers*, Wiliam L. Clements Library, University of Michigan, Ann Arbor; James Wilkinson, *Memoirs of My Own Times*, 3 vols. (Philadelphia: Abraham Small, 1816).

5. William C. Wilkinson, "Plan of the Position of the Army under the command of Lieut. Gen. Burgoyne near Stillwater, 1777," 5 vols., Library of Congress, Washington, DC, G3803. S3S3 1777.W. William Faden engraved and published lithographs of Wilkinson's maps in London titled "Plan of the Encampment and Position of the Army under His Excellency General Burgoyne at Braemus Heights on Hudson's River near Stillwater," London, William Faden, 1780.

6. Snell, "Report on the American Fortified Camp at Bemis Heights," Saratoga NHP, NPS, 1950.

7. Snell, "Historical Base Map, Part of the Master Plan," Saratoga NHP, NPS, 1950; "Saratoga National Historical Park Documentation for Historic Base Map," Saratoga NHP, NPS, 1951; Robert W. Ehrich, "Proposed Archeological Program for the SNHP," NPS, 1941; Ehrich, "Progress Report on the Archeological Program of Saratoga National Historical Park," NPS, 1941.

8. George Chaplin, "LiDAR Imagery for the Saratoga Battlefield," The Pennsylvania State University, 2012; George Chaplin and Dean R. Snow, "Metadata for Saratoga Geo-Referencing," The Pennsylvania State University, 2012. We were also able to produce rectified versions of Wilkinson's maps of unit positions during the courses of both battles, but those are not relevant here.

9. Ehrich, "Proposed Archeological Program; Ehrich, "Progress Report on the Archeological Program."

10. It was also the case that the crew and the budget were both small and time was short.

11. Magnetic declination was 13.5° west of true north in 1972. We set the baseline on the Balcarres Redoubt 30° east of magnetic north, meaning that the baseline laid 16.5° east of true north.

12. Jean C. Harrington, *Search for the Cittie of Ralegh: Archaeological Excavations at Fort Raleigh,* Archeological Research Series 6 (Washington, DC: NPS, 1962); Paul Ive, *The Practice of Fortification* (St. Clair Shores, MI: Gregg, 1972); Lewis Lochée, *Elements of Field Fortification* (London: Lewis Lochée, 1783).

13. Timothy J. Reese, *Uniforms of the American Revolution 1775–1783,* vol. 1, *American and British Forces,* compact disc (Greencastle, PA: Timothy J. Reese, 2006).

14. John Glover, "A Memoir of Gen. John Glover of Marblehead," *Historical Collections of the Essex Institute* 5 (1863): 97–130.

15. David E. Alexander, "Diary of Captain Benjamin Warren on Battlefield of Saratoga," *Journal of American History* 3 (1909): 212–13; Enos Hitchcock, *Diary of Enos Hitchcock, D.D., a Chaplain in the Revolutionary Army,* publication of the Rhode Island Historical Society 28, Rhode Island Historical Society, Providence (1900), 153; Charles Neilson, *An Original, Compiled and Corrected Account of Burgoyne's Campaign,* Kennikat American Bicentennial Series (Port Washington, NY: Kennikat Press, 1970), 180–81.

16. Lamb, *Memoir of His Own Life,* 192.

17. Neilson, *Original, Compiled and Corrected Account of Burgoyne's Campaign,* 165; Michael Stephenson, *Patriot Battles: How the War of Independence Was Fought* (New York: HarperCollins, 2007).

18. Dean R. Snow, "Report on the Archaeological Identification of the Balcarres and Breymann Redoubts, Saratoga National Historical Park," NPS, 1972, 17.

19. Richard Patterson, "Historical Comments on Skeletal Remains Discovered in 1972," NPS, 1985.

20. Dean R. Snow and Richard G. Wilkinson, "Archaeological and Osteological Analysis of Two Human Skeletons from Saratoga National Historical Park," NPS, 1986.

21. Stephenson, *Patriot Battles,* 181.

22. Walter Blumenthal, *Women Camp Followers of the American Revolution* (Philadelphia: G. S. MacManus, 1952); Robert M. Dunkerly, *Women of the Revolution* (Charleston, SC: History Press, 2007); Robert M. Dunkerly, "8 Fast Facts about Camp Followers," *Journal of the American Revolution* (2014); Don N. Hagist, "The Women of the British Army in America," available at http://www.revwar75.com/library/hagist/britwomen.htm.

23. The exact area is uncertain because his sketches are not complete.

24. Luzader, *Saratoga,* 393.

25. Ibid., 396.

26. We made some use of metal detector survey in the 1970s but this proved to be problematic because we did not yet have GPS and electronic surveying equipment to swiftly and accurately plot finds, portable computers to catalog them, adequate curation facilities to store them, or adequate protocols to maintain an accurate chain of custody. The need to meet these requirements persists. Although current technology solves the field requirements, adequate curation facilities have yet to be built to accommodate the large volume of artifacts such a project would generate. Moreover, the labor costs of implementation would be high. But if those costs could be covered, a long-term program of metal artifact recovery could tell much more than we now know about the redoubt and other parts of the battlefield.

27. Isaac Arnold, *The Life of Benedict Arnold: His Patriotism and His Treason* (Chicago: Jansen, McClurg, 1880), 199; Ebenezer Mattoon, Letter to Philip Schuyler, October 7, 1835, published in the *Saratoga Sentinel,* November 10, 1835, and reprinted as "Visit of General Ebenezer

Mattoon in 1835," in *Visits to the Saratoga Battle-Grounds, 1780–1880*, ed. W. L. Stone (Albany, NY: Joel Munsell's Sons, 1895), 247; Philip Van Cortlandt, "Autobiography of Philip Van Cortlandt, Brigadier-General in the Continental Army," *Magazine of American History* 2 (1878): 287.

28. Neilson, *Original, Compiled and Corrected Account of Burgoyne's Campaign*, 176; Wilkinson, *Memoirs of My Own Times*, 271–72; Rufus Putnam, *The Memoirs of Rufus Putnam* (New York: Houghton, Mifflin, 1903), 67–68.

29. Neilson, *Original, Compiled and Corrected Account of Burgoyne's Campaign*, 176–77; James Thatcher, *A Military Journal during the American Revolutionary War* (Boston: Cottons and Barnard, 1827), 101.

30. John Brooks, Colonel Brooks, and Captain Bancroft, *Proceedings of the Massachusetts Historical Society* 3 (1858): 271–77; Dearborn, "Narrative of the Saratoga Campaign," 8–9; Mattoon, "Visit of General Ebenezer Mattoon in 1835," 247; Stephenson, *Patriot Battles*, 227.

31. Snow, "Report on the Archaeological Identification of the Balcarres and Breymann Redoubts," 24–25.

32. Snow and Wilkinson, "Archaeological and Osteological Analysis of Two Human Skeletons," 33–38.

33. Snell, "Report on the Strength of the British Army," Saratoga NHP, NPS, 1951, 15.

34. Galen B. Ritchie, "Report of Excavations at Saratoga National Historical Park, Stillwater, N.Y., in Search of the Great Redoubt and the grave of Brigadier General Simon Fraser, July 1–31, 1958," NPS, 1958.

35. Benson J. Lossing, *The Pictorial Field-Book of the Revolution* (Rutland, VT: Charles E. Tuttle, 1972).

36. Jeptha Simms, *History of Schoharie County and Border Wars of New York* (Albany: Munsell and Tanner, 1845), 389.

37. Letter from Daniel Morgan, November 28, 1781, *Virginia Historical Register and Literary Companion* 6 (1853): 209–11.

38. Thomas Anburey, *Travels through the Interior Parts of America* (London: William Lane, 1789), 440.

39. Samuel Woodruff, "Samuel Woodruff's Visit to the Battle Ground in 1827," in *Visits to the Saratoga Battle-Grounds, 1780–1880*, ed. W. L. Stone (Albany: Joel Munsell's Sons, 1895), 212–34.

40. Mattoon, "Visit of General Ebenezer Mattoon," 245–46.

41. Harrington's "Myth of Rifleman Timothy Murphy" should suffice to put the myth to rest, but it will undoubtedly persist in many popular publications.

42. Dean R. Snow, "Report on the Archaeological Investigations of the American Line, the Great Redoubt, and the Taylor House, Saratoga National Historical Park," NPS, 1974. There may have been two Taylor houses, but this was almost certainly one of them.

43. Anburey's 1789 *Travels through the Interior Parts of America* has been shown by Thomas Bell to contain sections lifted from other sources without attribution. Although plagiarism is taken seriously today, in the eighteenth century it was an accepted practice to borrow accounts from others who shared a common experience. Anburey was a plagiarist, but not necessarily a liar.

44. A print of "The West Bank of the Hudson River . . ." was published by William Lane in London in 1789 (National Archives identifier: 532894); engraved by Barlow. This is often said to have been taken from a sketch by Francis Clerke, an aide to Burgoyne who was mortally wounded on October 7, 1777. The print depicts the Fraser funeral procession, which could not have been witnessed by Clerke, but he could have made the lost original to which the procession was later added by the lithographer.

45. Anburey, *Travels through the Interior Parts of America*, 437.

CHAPTER FOUR | WILLIAM A. GRISWOLD

The River Overlook Fortifications on Bemis Heights

AMERICAN GENERAL Horatio Gates clearly recognized that the location of the fortifications at Saratoga played a large role in the American victory over the British. Brushing off Dr. Benjamin Rush's 1778 praise for his victory at Saratoga, Gates responded, "Let us be honest. In war, as in medicine, natural causes not under our control, do much. In the present case, the great tacticians of the campaign were hills and forests, which a young Polish Engineer was skilful enough to select for my encampment."[1] Bemis Heights proved to be a brilliant choice to erect fortifications to withstand the British advance toward Albany. This chapter explores the River Overlook fortifications on Bemis Heights designed by Thaddeus Kosciuszko, the young Polish military engineer referred to by Gates. This piece of ground was clearly chosen by Kosciuszko to mount the primary line of defense against the advancing British army because of its strategic topographic advantages. While primary emphasis will be placed on the results of a geophysical survey (2010) conducted on the site commonly assumed to be the location of the South Redan,[2] other fortification elements associated with the American positions are also discussed in this chapter.

The Kosciuszko Influence

The story of the Bemis Heights fortifications really begins with the arrival of Polish-born military engineer Thaddeus Kosciuszko to America. Born in Poland in 1746, Kosciuszko began his military education at the Royal Knight School in Warsaw, where he studied fort construction, topography, mapmaking, trigonometry, drawing, and engineering.[3] The Polish Civil War (Bar Confederation 1768–72) soon caused Kosciuszko to seek a more stable country in which to continue his education, and he found this stability in France. Arriving in Paris in 1769, Kosciuszko and his friend Captain Joseph Orlowski entered the Royal Academy of Painting and Sculpture but privately sought out tutoring from professors at the École Militaire and the military engineering academy at Mézières; as foreigners they could not officially enroll in classes at these institutions.[4] From these professors, Kosciuszko added the military strategies of Marshal Sébastien le Prestre de Vauban and the philosophy of Montesquieu, Voltaire, Jean-Jacques Rousseau, and François Quesnay to his basic military education.[5] After visiting Holland, England, Switzerland, Saxony, and Rome, Kosciuszko returned to Poland in 1774.[6]

Spurned in love after his return to Poland, unable to buy a military commission, and armed with his studies in philosophy, Kosciuszko left Poland for greener pastures. His options, however, were not well thought out and he seems to have arrived in America by happenstance as much as by planning.[7] Once in America, he met Benjamin Franklin, who was about to travel to Paris. Franklin interrogated the young engineer, trying to get a true sense of his convictions, because many ill-qualified adventurers were arriving in America in search of military commissions.[8]

As historian Alex Storozynski explains in *The Peasant Prince*:

> [T]he seventy-year-old Franklin rose to his feet and said, "I am convinced of your clear and noble intentions." With that he leaned over and kissed the thirty-year-old volunteer on the forehead before saying, "But you have to admit, young man, that it was pretty unwise to travel two thousand miles without any commitments or connections?"
>
> Franklin then asked Kosciuszko exactly what type of test it was that he would like to take. The Pole responded, "Engineering, military architecture, etc."
>
> The elder statesman laughed at the idea that a new nation of farmers and merchants would have such expertise. Quite amused, Franklin said, "Who would proctor such an exam when there is no one here who is even familiar with those subjects? However, we do have a person who knows a little about geometry. We can have him give you a geometry exam."
>
> When Kosciuszko did well on the exam, Franklin personally recommended the Pole to Congress. On August 30, 1776, Kosciuszko went to the Pennsylvania State House (later renamed Independence Hall) to present his military credentials to Congress and the Board of War.
>
> Franklin headed the Pennsylvania Committee of Safety, which was in charge of preventing the British navy from sailing into the Delaware River's shipping channels. Worried about a possible attack on Philadelphia, Franklin hired Kosciuszko as his chief engineer and put him to work designing the fortifications.[9]

Following the construction of defenses for Philadelphia, Kosciuszko went to New Jersey, where he designed Fort Mercer. Evidently, General Horatio Gates befriended Kosciuszko when in the Philadelphia area and Kosciuszko accompanied the general to Albany when Gates took command of the Northern army in the spring of 1777.[10]

Once reassigned to the Northern army, Kosciuszko went to Ticonderoga, where he found the defenses quite inadequate but was powerless to change them. In June 1777, he returned to Ticonderoga with orders from Gates to fortify the hills around the fort, specifically Mount Defiance. His efforts were hampered by Colonel Jeduthan Baldwin, the site's chief engineer, who disagreed with Kosciuszko's plans;[11] many questioned Baldwin's competence in his position.[12] Leadership of the Northern army jockeyed back and forth between Generals Schuyler and Gates, and after the fall of Ticonderoga, Kosciuszko was assigned a different task by General Schuyler, then in command of the Northern army.

Schuyler gave Kosciuszko command of hundreds of soldiers who were instructed to block the way of the British advance. These fatigue parties cut down trees to block roads, destroyed bridges, and flooded streams, roads, and trails in an attempt to stall the British movement south.[13] Kosciuszko's men achieved the goal of slowing the advance, as it took British troops twenty days to advance twenty-two miles.[14]

Having achieved the respect of some of his commanders, Kosciuszko was tapped to aid in the selection of a spot to counter the British advance. He was reported to have ridden to the spot where Colonel Morgan Lewis had been positioning the troops and pointed out the problems with the chosen location, arguing that it was indefensible.[15] Lewis was hesitant to challenge Gates's selection (command of the Northern army had now returned to Gates) of the position, but after Gates discussed the objections with Kosciuszko, he ordered Kosciuszko to ride north and determine a spot to make a stand. Kosciuszko selected Bemis Heights, named after Jotham Bemus, a spot about fifteen miles southeast of present-day Saratoga Springs.[16]

At the time that the war arrived in his backyard, Bemus was operating a tavern along the River Road from Albany to Lake George and points north.[17] According to historian John Luzader, Bemus was by all accounts a respectable citizen who simply did not agree with the colonists' cause.[18] The selection of Bemis Heights offered certain tactical advantages to the Americans. Here Gates and the American army could watch over and control the road to Albany, British General John Burgoyne's intended pathway.[19]

The remainder of this chapter concentrates primarily on the fortifications overlooking the Hudson (River Overlook fortifications) and only secondarily discusses the fortifications extending from the River Overlook to the west toward the Neilson house or those extending to the east, culminating at the Hudson River.

FIGURE 4.1. A current view from Bemis Heights in the area of Reeve and Snow's 1974 work. Note the commanding view (looking northeast) of the floodplain, river, and the River Road from this position. Photo by the author.

The Selection of Bemis Heights

Bemis Heights was topographically ideal for defense (figure 4.1). To the east of the escarpment, the Hudson River curved west, transforming the broad floodplain into a narrow restricted passage that contained the River Road. This restriction would force an advancing army to move through what could best be described as a bottleneck. To the west of and adjacent to the restricted floodplain and the north-south River Road rose the heights, a plateau more than a hundred feet above the floodplain. The ascent to the heights was very steep and abrupt, creating a natural barrier to attack. The ridge at the top provided a commanding overlook of the floodplain below. The area west of the Bemis Heights ridge was heavily wooded and broken only by an occasional farm, and the area to the north contained deep ravines and Mill Creek.

Kosciuszko supplemented the topographical relief of the heights with extensive fortifications; work on these fortifications began on September 12, 1777.[20] Fortifications were not restricted to the River Overlook, as breastworks, ditches, and abatis (downed trees grouped together with sharpened branches pointed toward the enemy) continued from the heights all the way down to the river.

Likewise, fortifications continued from the River Overlook west to the American headquarters at the Woodworth farm. This heavily fortified area formed a massive barrier to the advancing British army.

Historian W. J. Wood has described the configuration of the American troops on the Heights, noting that

> Horatio Gates's forces were deployed about a center with two wings. The center, under Brigadier General Ebenezer Learned, was made up of Learned's own brigade of Continentals plus Colonel Livingston's New York regiment and the Massachusetts Continental regiments of Colonels Bailey, Jackson, and Wesson. The right wing, heavy in artillery, was composed of Continentals under Brigadier Generals Glover and Patterson, together with those of Colonel Nixon. This wing's positions dominated the ground sloping down to the river; it remained under Gates's own command.[21]
>
> The left wing, under Major General Benedict Arnold, included the New Hampshire Continental regiments of Colonels Cilley, Hale, and Scammel. Next there were New Yorkers under Colonels Van Cortlandt and Livingston, then Connecticut militia under Colonels Lattimer and Cook. Last, but certainly not least, was Colonel Daniel Morgan's corps of riflemen and Major Henry Dearborn's light infantry.[22]

If Burgoyne's army had attempted an advance along the river, road, or floodplain, they would have been exposed to artillery from the heights as well as fire from the floodplain fortifications on the American right flank. Kosciuszko had fortified the heights and the river so successfully that Burgoyne was forced to take a western approach toward the American army's left flank. No coordinated advance was ever attempted along the heavily fortified river corridor.

Primary Sources of Information on the River Overlook Fortifications

National Park Service (NPS) historians have analyzed the fortifications on Bemis Heights, collecting primary and secondary accounts of the development of these fortifications, including sketches and drawings of the fortifications.[23] The historical accounts contain descriptions by American, British, and German soldiers as well as descriptions from travelers who later visited the site, many accompanied by guides who had fought in the battles. The sources that are cited in these reviews include both primary and secondary accounts of the fortifications. Rather than repeat the work of these historians, this section focuses on providing information on the location, construction, and appearance of the River Overlook fortifications drawing on the more descriptive historical accounts available.[24]

The earliest account of the fortifications on the heights comes from Colonel Richard Varick. The Varick map, as it has come to be known, was illustrated in a letter sent to General Philip Schuyler on September 12, 1777, and records American troop positions on the heights before the entrenching began. The map is very schematic in its depictions of both natural and cultural features, at times using straight lines to illustrate what we know were complex landforms. Varick recorded a series of important features including the two primary roads in close proximity to the heights, the River Road and the road to Saratoga Lake; the Hudson River (North River), the Bemus Tavern, the Neilson House and the crest of the ridge are also illustrated.

Several days later, on September 16, 1777, Varick sent Schuyler another letter describing some of the earthworks on the heights. Evidently, this letter also contained a map but unfortunately only the letter has survived. Varick notes in this letter:

> You will also observe the Breast Work with a Ditch from the River to the Hill. . . . We have a picket on Very high Ground which commands our Camp except where Morgan lies, however the Trees fallen between that Ground & our Camp will prevent A Coup de Main from that Quarters. . . . I am informed we have small works on all the Hills worth contending for in our Front.[25]

Varick sent another note to Schuyler the following day, September 17, 1777, providing additional details:

> I wrote you last Eveng. inclosing a plan of our Works & Situation of our Camp. Since which a Strong Work is thrown up along the Verge of the Hill back of Bemus's House—Another small one just back of his Barn and a third on a small height North of the Second to Retard the Enemy's Attack.[26]

The story behind a second map that documents the fortifications, drawn by Colonel Rufus Putnam, is less clear. The Putnam map that scholars are currently using is a hand-traced copy from a copy believed to have been created by NPS historian Charles Snell in the 1950s; the location of the original is unknown. Although Snell is said to have traced the original, it is more likely that he worked from a copy of the original.[27]

Quite detailed for a sketch map, the Putnam map records both American and British positions along with a host of other features (figure 4.2). Natural features depicted on the map include the Hudson River, Mill Creek and other water-drainage features, the fortifications on Bemis Heights, and elevated landforms. In terms of the American positions, the Putnam map illustrates the approximate placement of defensive fortifications, the American floating bridge, as well as

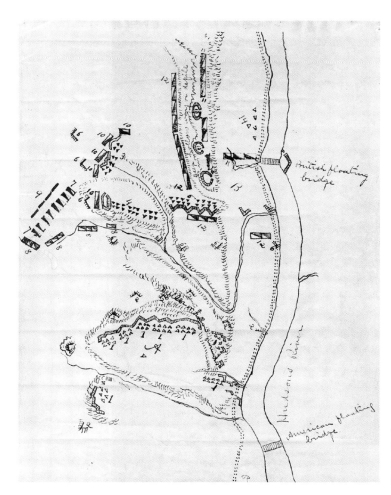

FIGURE 4.2. Tracing of the Putnam map after Snell (Unknown date). Unknown author; likely Charles Snell.

the north-south River Road. The road paralleled the Hudson River for much of its path, deviating from it near the very bottom of the map where the area is swampy and the road followed higher ground.

The British positions are also recorded with considerable detail and include the location of the troops, the British floating bridge, and the fortified earthen features. The British troop locations are highly stylized as was customary during this period, depicting the regiments with different hatching patterns. Like the Varick map, the original Putnam map is believed to be fairly accurate in its depiction of the American troop positions and the location of American fortifications.

A third source for the River Overlook fortifications comes from a letter written by Feldprediger (Military Chaplain) Milius to his father on November 20, 1777.[28] The German chaplain visited the area after the battles of Saratoga had been won, reporting:

> We were surprised [*erstaunten*] at the strength and appearance of the camp, about which we were permitted to walk in company with a young German-speaking lieutenant and a sergeant. Strong batteries were situated both on the river bank and along the lines. Trenches were thrown up from the river along the crest of hills and ravines. In some places, these were earthen, strengthened by tree—in other places, where there was insufficient earth or too many trees, they were of logs [*Klötze*]. There was a strong outwork on a ridge north of a tavern, and other outposts, which I did not see, were in front. The trenches ran up to the top of Baemus Hill and around its north slope. It then turned southward along the western and northwestern side of a hill and past the farm buildings [*die Schuene*] where the hospital was toward a woods.[29]

Another source for understanding the fortifications comes from General James Wilkinson, who in the first volume of his book *Memoirs of My Own Time* describes the fortifications as they appeared about October 4, 1777.

> General Gates's right occupied the brow of the hill near the river, with which it was connected by a deep intrenchment; his camp, in the form of a segment of a great circle, the convex toward the enemy, extending rather obliquely to his rear, about three-fourths of a mile to a knoll occupied by his left; his front was covered from the right to the left of center, by a sharp ravine running parallel with his line and closely wooded. . . . The extremities of this camp were defended by stoney batteries, and the interval was strengthened by a breastwork without intrenchments, constructed of the bodies of felled trees, logs and rails with an additional battery at an opening left of the center. The right was almost impracticable; the left difficult of approach.[30]

As might be expected, the British sources on the American fortifications are not nearly as illuminating as those provided by American and German observers. A series of British maps of the Saratoga battles is contained in the Wilkinson Collection in the Library of Congress (Washington, DC). These maps, drawn by Lieutenant William Wilkinson, an officer of the 62nd Regiment assigned to assist the British Corp of Engineers in 1777, were later engraved by William Faden for publication in Burgoyne's *A State of the Expedition from Canada, as Laid before the House of Commons*. This volume formed the core of Burgoyne's defense of conduct to Parliament following the surrender at Saratoga.[31]

Most pertinent to the discussion of the River Overlook fortifications is a map by Wilkinson dated 1777. Although the Wilkinson maps are visually beautiful, it is clear that the Americans knew much more about the British camps than the British did about the American camps, resulting in large areas of the American

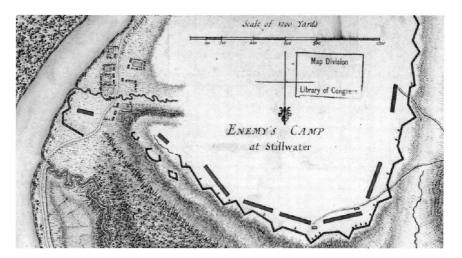

FIGURE 4.3. Detail of a portion of a map drawn by engraver William Faden in London circa 1780 after Wilkinson's original manuscript map showing the American fortifications on the floodplain and the heights. North is at the bottom of the image. Most of the fortifications drawn by Faden were contrived in London, and apparently based upon vague eyewitness accounts from British officers. Nevertheless, the general nature of the fortifications, being primarily contiguous with a refused western flank, was correctly depicted. William Faden Map Collection in the Library of Congress, G3803.S353 1777. W5 Faden 69.

camps either not being depicted at all or not properly depicted. In terms of the American River Overlook positions, Wilkinson illustrates the Hudson River, Bemis Heights, Mill Creek and other tributary watercourses, the breastworks on the floodplain, the north-south road to Albany, houses and outbuildings, and the three fortifications on top of the heights. Each of the redoubts on top of the heights was illustrated with different shapes, although it is not certain how much Wilkinson could see from the British position. The one shown furthest to the north is diamond shaped, the middle one is larger and crescent shaped, and the one furthest to the south is smaller, but still crescent shaped. Wilkinson simply labels much of the American-held land as "Ground of the Enemy"; he could only depict as much as he could see and he could not see the American positions well from his vantage point. Even Burgoyne commented on September 20, 1777, that "on the day following [September 20], it was known from prisoners and deserters, that the enemy were in a post strongly fortified; but from the thickness of the wood, it was impossible to catch a view of any part of their position."[32]

Figure 4.3 is a later map drawn by William Faden but based on Wilkinson's maps. It is not clear exactly how Faden got the information to depict the American fortifications and the accuracy of the renderings are unknown. Regardless of how he obtained the information, Faden's map provides interesting information about the arrangement of the American fortifications, although much of it may be speculative. The map, however, does seem to be in accordance with much of what is known about the fortifications.

It is quite challenging to render a coherent picture of the River Overlook fortifications solely based on the primary and the secondary historical accounts. However, even given the ambiguous and sometimes contradictory nature of these sources, a general scheme of the fortifications can be outlined. A battery was located at the river and a ditch and breastwork ran from the river to the heights. Three to four strong works were erected on the ridgeline, while ditches and breastworks continued from the ridgeline on the river overlook to the west following the line of a ravine. These fortification elements were strengthened at times, or completed in some cases, using logs and/or abatis. Undoubtedly, Kosciuszko would have used all methods at his disposal to create an impenetrable and defendable position.

The Archaeological Excavations

The twentieth century brought several new campaigns to the American fortifications at Saratoga, but this time the strategic goal was archaeology (figure 4.4). The earliest recorded professional excavations, done on behalf of the National Park Service, were conducted by archaeologist Robert Ehrich in 1941. Ehrich's objectives were fivefold: (1) to provide a rough check on surface topographical features based on historical maps; (2) to locate fortification elements where all surface traces of their earlier existence has vanished; (3) to gain knowledge about the fortification features and the technical problems associated with their excavation; (4) to gain information to develop a comprehensive archaeological program, and; (5) to gain insight into the possibilities for restoration and reconstruction for future park planning.[33]

NPS was hopeful that Ehrich's efforts would lead to additional research-oriented excavations on the battlefield as well as restoration of newly discovered features. Ehrich's excavations were not only an early example of historical archaeology, but also a very early use of historical archaeology by the National Park Service in the young Saratoga National Historical Park. Ehrich's broad objectives led him to conduct excavations not only on the east flank of the American fortifications, but also on the west flank, the east flank of the British lines, and on the Balcarres and Breymann Redoubts. Using earlier historical maps, Ehrich identified the most likely spot for the American fortifications on Bemis Heights as lying on the south edge of a deep and wide "ravine that starts some 700 feet east of the slope below Fort Neilson and runs down toward the river."[34] Ehrich excavated four trenches to profile this feature, noting that he could identify what he termed "conclusive results" only in trench 3. In this trench, he identified yellow compacted earth that he believed to be part of the earthworks.

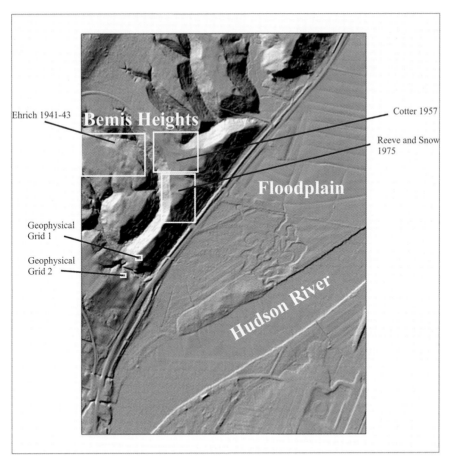

FIGURE 4.4. LiDAR image of Bemis Heights with the areas of archaeological and geophysical work labeled. White lines indicate approximate locations of the excavation campaigns. Illustration by the author.

One problem with Ehrich's work is his belief that the yellow soil he noted during excavation was fortification related, having been washed into the open trenches following heavy rains. While he suspected that the yellow soil cleaved from the other soils, his "cleavage planes" along the yellow soils were called into question by Snow's 1973–74 excavations (mentioned later in this chapter). In these later excavations, typical fortification profiles were identified, not simply Ehrich's yellow soils and cleavage planes.

Before World War II interrupted his endeavors, Ehrich found numerous battlefield-related features in other areas of the park. Ehrich ultimately wrote two annual reports (1941 and 1943) as well as progress reports documenting his excavations.[35] Based on his reports, Ehrich never excavated on the River Overlook, but concentrated his excavations on areas to the west of these fortifications.

Following Ehrich's work, a hiatus ensued on archaeological investigations at the park that was not broken until John Cotter excavated there in the 1950s. Like Ehrich before him, Cotter conducted excavations at many sites within the park, including two locations along the American lines, the Neilson House and at stop 3 on the tour road, within the American Overlook fortifications on Bemis Heights.[36] Cotter's study, conducted in reaction to a proposed tour road of the battlefield and in the area of the circular loop of tour stop 3, provides detailed maps and sections of the discoveries on Bemis Heights.

In trench A, southwest of the present parking loop, Cotter felt that he had found a ditch and related breastwork feature. In trench E, approximately twenty feet long and to the north of the present parking loop, Cotter discovered soils approximating fill within a ditch. While devoid of artifacts, Cotter nevertheless identified this as a fortification feature; it was approximately six feet deep in profile. He created a hypothetical reconstruction of the original dimensions of this fortification element, likely part of what is now interpreted as the North Redan. Cotter also reported finding part of the fortification breastworks in trench F, approximately 300 feet to the northwest of trench E. However, the profile that he illustrates for this feature is not as clear and well defined as that in trench E.

The next series of excavations on the American River fortifications were carried out by Dean Snow in the 1970s, as part of a longer excavation program utilizing a field school conducted with the State University of New York–Albany. Snow's approach was very methodical and utilized techniques that had not been previously employed, including aerial photographs to identify fortification features based on vegetation growth, coring along transects rather than large-scale trenching, and geophysical prospecting to identify features such as ditches, earthen mounds and ramps, and so on. Like Cotter, Snow conducted excavations at numerous locations within the park, including the American River fortifications. The goal of Snow's 1974 work was to establish the accuracy of the 1777 Putnam map and to assess the impact of additional roadwork on the American River overlook resources.[37] The work by Snow and Stuart Reeve located numerous elements of the American fortifications, and demonstrated the accuracy of the Putnam map.

At the River Overlook, Reeve and Snow's research examined six knolls for fortification elements that had been mentioned in primary and secondary accounts.[38] NPS historian Charles Snell subscribed to Chastellux's 1780 account that there were "three entrenched redoubts" at the River Overlook and the Varick letter to General Schuyler that noted that the North Redoubt would command the others.[39] Reeve and Snow recognized that the Putnam map had been overlooked in this discussion. Whereas the Wilkinson map only illustrates three entrenchments, in keeping with the primary and secondary accounts, the Putnam map shows four fortification structures on the bluff. Reeve and Snow note that the Wilkinson map denotes that the second entrenchment to the south is the largest, not the North Redoubt as Snell and others had speculated. This also agrees with the Putnam map, which illustrates the second redoubt as the largest of the bluff fortifications.[40] Therefore, the 1974 archaeological work was designed to intercept the second fortification and assess the accuracy of the Putnam map.

Aerial photographs taken in 1973 revealed a dark streak across a zone of lush grass in the project area. Using soil cores, Reeve and Snow identified the dark streak as backfill in fortification trenches. Coring along transects and a series of backhoe trenches allowed them to trace a ditch that had been excavated and subsequently backfilled. Using coring, Snow eventually exposed contiguous trenches that were part of the Revolutionary fortifications.

In addition to examining the six knolls, Reeve and Snow investigated an area to the south in search of the remains of the South Redan. A second baseline was established in this area and four soil-core transects were sampled for stratigraphic disturbance that would reveal possible fortification elements, but none were found in this location. In keeping with the Putnam map, the location of the South Redan is now thought to be approximately 600 feet southwest of the location investigated by Reeve and Snow. Snow also examined the central core of the American fortifications, those running west across the ravine where the River Overlook fortifications had been located toward the Neilson house.[41] This same area had been examined by Ehrich in the 1940s, but both the Ehrich excavations and the 1973 work by Snow were hampered by US Army maneuvers that had taken place in this sector of the park in 1936. These maneuvers included the excavation of trenches that further confused the archaeological record. Snow located several of Ehrich's excavation trenches and excavated new ones that accurately identified the battle-related trenches connecting the River Overlook and the Neilson house. The excavations and documentation by Snow accurately located the American fortifications on the heights (figure 4.4).[42]

Recent Geophysical Investigations

As an investigative tool, geophysics is gaining momentum among archaeologists. Although the instruments have been around for years, recent refinements have drastically increased their usefulness and accuracy. The instruments currently used for geophysical prospecting are providing spectacular imagery for features and deposits beneath the earth's surface. These nondestructive instruments can be used to quickly assess large areas, such as battlefields or skirmish sites, so archaeologists can focus their research. The field of geophysics is constantly improving the instruments so as to cover larger areas more quickly and provide ever better resolution in their imagery.

Based on the Putnam map, a limited geophysical survey was undertaken in 2010 at the presumed location of the South Redan, an area approximately 600 feet south of the area investigated by Reeve and Snow in 1974. The project was conducted to reconcile several questions about the fortifications constructed in this area during the time of the Saratoga battles: (1) Could geophysical methods be quickly employed to identify remains associated with the battle? (2) Could the various geophysical methods identify the shape of the various fortification elements? (3) How accurate is the 1777 Putnam map for this area of the park and can it be used to identify the location of other archaeological resources on the Saratoga battlefield? (4) How accurate is the Wilkinson (or later Faden) maps in depicting elements of the American positions and fortifications? If geophysics can be successfully used to identify the location of Revolutionary War fortifications, the story and locations of the defenses created for the battle may dramatically unfold based on the archaeological elements yet to be discovered.

Geophysical instruments are now routinely used by archaeologists to locate geophysical anomalies below the surface. Some of the geophysical instruments used today are relatively new technologies (ground-penetrating radar, resistivity meters, conductivity meters). Other technologies, such as magnetometers, are simply advanced versions of the ones used by Snow. All of these instruments are used to locate soil anomalies by detecting contrasting soil types or metals. Two of the foremost scholars on geophysics, Rinita Dalan and Bruce Bevan, have succinctly summarized the use of geophysics for archaeological applications:

> In the process of earthen construction, soils and sediments are moved, sometimes mixed, and redeposited. As a result of these activities, intrinsic characteristics of the materials are altered; these properties include porosity, consistence (the degree and kind of cohesion and adhesion), and structure. The culturally emplaced earthen materials forming the earthwork may have quite different properties from surrounding undisturbed and unmixed soils and sediment.[43]

Furthermore, Dalan and Bevan explain that:

> changes in density, porosity, and permeability result when the soil has been crushed and broken, destroying the structure and consistence (i.e., cohesion and adhesion) of the natural soil. Changes in density will affect seismic velocities. These changes may also affect electrical properties. Perhaps the addition of organic compounds and ash will decrease soil resistivity: carbon may increase the resistivity of the soil. The addition of sand to finer-grained soil in earthen construction will result in less conductive earthworks compared to surrounding fine-grained soil.[44]

Numerous geophysical instruments are used by archaeologists to detect changes in the soils, including ground-penetrating radar (GPR), resistivity meters, conductivity meters, and magnetometers, and each of these instruments detects different types of anomalies. Subsurface irregularities are identified as anomalies until they are confirmed as archaeological features by excavation or coring, because not all anomalies turn out to be archaeological features. Some are natural soil discontinuities, while others are made by natural activities like rodent burrows, tree roots, or tree falls.

GPR and a resistivity meter were used for the geophysical investigation of the likely South Redan area, and two grids were established to collect data using these instruments. One twenty-by-thirty-meter grid was laid out across the area that is currently identified as the site of the South Redan.[45] Additional geophysical data were collected slightly beyond the boundaries of the formal grid on the plateau until the wood line was encountered. The second grid was a twenty-by-twenty-meter grid laid out south of the first across a large ravine. The landform in this area was flat and out of character for the surrounding topography. These two areas match up well with locations identified on the Putnam map as containing possible fortification elements.

Geophysical data were collected using two different but complementary instruments, a SIR-3000 ground-penetrating radar with a 400 MHz antenna and an RM-15 resistance meter. These geophysical instruments gather different types of data based on the constituents of the soils. On its own, each instrument can identify particular types of soil anomalies. However, when used in combination, these instruments provide a much more accurate representation of buried features than could any single instrument.

Resistance meters measure the electrical resistance of the soil using a four-probe array, two of which are moved across the grid, while two remain stationary. The A-spacing (distance between the probes on the frame) on the meter was one meter, providing readings to approximately one meter of depth. Theoretically, resistance readings will be higher as one passes over a feature like a stone or brick wall where more resistance is encountered and lower when one passes over an in-filled trench or pit where less resistance is encountered.

GPR units introduce an electromagnetic radar signal through an antenna into the earth. These signals are reflected back, based on soil interfaces or buried features, and recorded in electronic files using a control panel attached to the antenna. Different antenna frequencies provide information from different depths. The 400 MHz antenna provides good information for archaeological studies because it usually penetrates the top two to three meters of soil. When one looks at the radar imagery, it is as if the ground were sliced open and one was looking at a vertical cross section or profile of the soil. All of these images are saved as files that can be examined separately or later assembled to create a three-dimensional block; the block can then be dissected based on signal depth. These time slices can illustrate anomalies across the grid at various depths.[46]

Grid 1 Results

Resistivity and the GPR results provide some help in understanding the River Overlook fortifications (figure 4.5). On the resistivity map, the light-gray areas illustrate low resistance and the areas in dark gray to black illustrate the areas of high resistivity. The GPR scan shown in figure 4.5 provides a west-to-east radar profile down the center of the grid (along line A–B). This GPR profile indicates an area that appears to be dug out in the middle of the profile that corresponds to the light-gray anomaly recorded in the resistivity data. The GPR profile also appears to show areas where the soil may have been piled on the edges of the excavated areas. One additional smaller rectilinear low-resistance anomaly can also be seen in figure 4.5, just east of the larger low-resistance anomaly.

Grid 2 Results

A resistivity survey was conducted in grid 2, south of grid 1 and across the ravine at a much lower elevation. GPR was not used in this grid because the extremely high clay content of the soil attenuated the radar signal, providing poor-quality data. The resistivity data from this project identified only one anomaly, which appeared as a north-south linear signal of high intensity to the extreme east of the grid (not illustrated).

Soil Coring

To verify the accuracy of the information collected by the geophysical instruments, soil coring was conducted in November 2013. This method of investigation, using a one-inch soil probe, is the same technique used by Snow during his work on the heights in the 1970s. Cores were collected to a depth of approximately 0.8 meters across grid 1 and at various depths in grid 2, and focused on the evaluation of anomalies as well as areas believed to contain intact soil profiles.

In grid 1, coring verified that the light-gray areas contained disturbed deposits, while the dark-gray and black areas contained intact soils. A natural soil profile, consisting of a brown (10YR 4/3) silty topsoil over a lighter (10YR 5/6) yellowish-brown silty subsoil, was observed in the soil cores in the dark-gray to black areas. All of the soils (both the light-gray and dark-gray to black areas) within grid 1 were composed of fine silt and the soil core easily penetrated the soils so that a full eighty centimeters of soil could be extracted with every core.

In grid 2, soil coring was done every two meters along a west-to-east transect down the middle of the grid. Unfortunately, coring in grid 2 was not as conclusive as that for grid 1. Soil cores indicated disturbance across much of the grid,

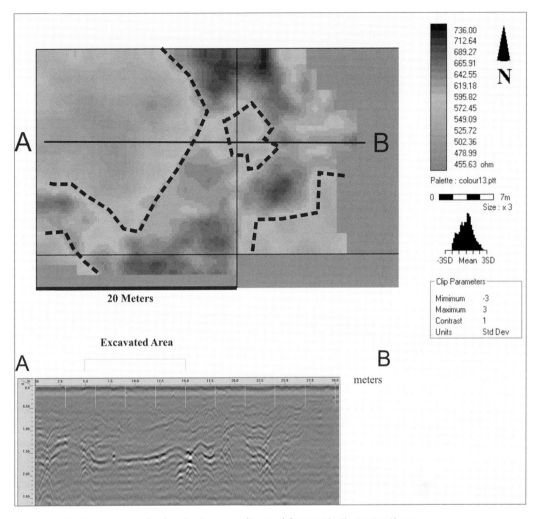

FIGURE 4.5. Resistance image (*top*) and radar image (*bottom*) from grid 1 illustrating the remains of a probable redan. The location on the radargram is identified on the resistivity image. Both images are displayed at approximately the same scale for comparative purposes. Illustration by the author.

except at the eastern end where the profiles appeared to be natural. The problem with the coring in grid 2 was that the soils in all of the cores were extremely high in clay content, so much so that the core only penetrated approximately forty centimeters in the west and only twenty-five centimeters in what appeared to be undisturbed soils in the eastern portion of the grid. It is difficult to assess the geophysical data based on coring where a full extraction of materials could not be obtained. Additional excavation, either by hand or by mechanical means, will be required for this area, but could not be undertaken in November 2013 when the coring was conducted.

Coring was enlightening for several reasons. First, it provided a quick and efficient method for examining the soils without completely disturbing the area. Second, it provided a data set comparable to trenching or excavation (at least for grid 1), although in grid 2, additional work is needed. Third, it provided enough information to interpret the geophysical data.

A likely scenario for interpreting the resistivity and GPR data from grid 1 is that soldiers excavated soils from the light-gray areas identified in figure 4.5 and piled them on top of the natural soils, the dark-gray to black areas, to create an earthen fortification or partially earthen fortification. Trees were, no doubt, used in the fortification construction to consolidate and harden the defenses. However, elements such as trees and wood that have completely decayed since the battle (unless they were burned) were not detected by the geophysical instruments used. Following the battles, the mounded fortification features were torn down and the earth replaced by farmers for agricultural use. This scenario would explain the geophysical anomalies and the lack of visible traces on the surface. This scenario would also indicate a fortification feature developed to command the floodplain and the river at this pinch point and would also serve to guard the rear of the American army from an invasion traveling up the ravine.

Another rather dramatic difference observed in the coring data from grids 1 and 2 was the type of soil found in each grid. The soils on the top of the plateau overlooking the river were composed of silt of various colors. The USDA Natural Resources Conservation Service Web Soil Survey identifies the primary soil type in grid 1 as Hudson silt loam, hilly (HuD), a moderately well-drained silt loam.[47] However, grid 2 contained soils composed primarily of clay, which were so dense that they prevented a complete sampling with a soil core.

The difference in soil types between grids 1 and 2 is interesting because it may have affected the types of construction that could have taken place within each area. In grid 1, the ease of sampling and the consistency of the soils demonstrate that it would have been easy to excavate the soil to build fortifications. These fortifications could have been hardened by the incorporation of timbers into their construction. Fortification of the river overlook would have been a relatively quick and easy process for the American army. The ease of excavation would mean that rather imposing fortifications could be quickly constructed. While probably not a primary factor in site selection, the ease of fortification construction using earthen materials was likely a latent benefit of this well-chosen site. The softness of the soils on the plateau area is in direct contrast to the clay deposits found to the south across the ravine in grid 2. In this area, which was at a lower elevation, dense clay deposits were identified. Areas of the floodplain also exhibit similar dense clay deposits. These areas would have challenged soldiers trying to construct earthen fortifications and may indicate areas where more timber was used. The shape of the landform where grid 2 was located was not in keeping with the natural topography of the area, so additional research is recommended for this area.

It is clear from the historical accounts that multiple measures were used to construct the American fortifications, including entrenchments, redoubts, redans, abatis, and so on. Undoubtedly, the commanders in charge of construction and the soldiers doing the work would use the natural environment to their advantage. High points on the landscape would have been fortified, logs from trees would have been used to harden fortifications or used as abatis to slow an approaching enemy, and passage on roads and rivers would have been restricted.

Conclusion

This chapter illustrates the brilliance behind Kosciuszko's selection of the heights as the place where the Americans made their stand against the advancing British army. Commanding the river, road, and floodplain, the almost unassailable selection of the River Overlook on Bemis Heights caused the advancing British to go west. Both of the battles fought at Saratoga (Freeman's Farm and Bemis Heights) were fought west of the River Overlook because the route to Albany along the river was judged by the British to be impassible. By choosing to fortify this area, General Gates could dictate the direction of the battle.

Scholars in numerous disciplines are working to create as accurate a picture as is possible of the fortifications erected on Bemis Heights and at the River Overlook. Historians have gleaned most of the available information concerning the fortifications constructed on the heights, including those on the ridgeline and to the east (the river) and the west (Neilson house), from primary and secondary sources. These historical sources provide a wealth of information about what was built before the battle. Archaeological surveys provide another complementary source of information about the defenses on the heights. Excavations by Ehrich, Cotter, and Snow have uncovered the location of several of the fortifications that would have existed on the heights (not to mention other areas of the park). Archaeological excavations also provide the physical location for the fortifications and other details about their construction not available in the historic record. No doubt future archaeological excavations and historical discoveries will augment the current data set.

Geophysics adds another layer of data to the examination of the fortification elements, one that has the ability to enrich the historical and archaeological data sets. The small geophysical and archaeological sampling investigation confirmed the use of the furthest extent of the plateau as part of the Revolutionary fortifications engineered by Thaddeus Kosciusko. The resistivity data documents the size and shape of the fortification that would have existed, and the GPR data illustrate a profile view of how the redan was created. The easily dug soils contained in this area would have allowed for quick construction of large fortifications and entrenchments in a relatively short time.

Probably the biggest advantage to using geophysics in a battlefield context is that the instruments allow the documentation of subsurface anomalies over fairly large areas of a battlefield. As time permits, these anomalies can then be ground-truthed—that is, physically verified—using a minimally invasive approach such as soil coring. Large-scale studies can lead to a more complete picture of the size of the fortifications, direction of defense, organization of fortification elements, amount of labor required for construction, and so on. In other words, the geophysical data, gathered across large segments of a battlefield, can open up avenues of research that more restrictive and invasive archaeological excavation alone cannot.

A multidisciplinary exploration of the fortifications at Saratoga is currently under way. This is happening not only on the American fortifications, but on resources all over the park as well. It is only by using all of the available information from numerous disciplines that a more accurate picture of the fortifications on Bemis Heights and a deeper understanding of the battles will emerge.

NOTES

1. Alex Storozynski, *The Peasant Prince: Thaddeus Kosciuszko and the Age of Revolution* (New York: St. Martin's Press, 2009), 39.
2. A fortification element, usually V-shaped, with the point projecting toward the area of the impending attack.
3. Storozynski, *Peasant Prince*, 10.
4. Ibid., 12.
5. Ibid.
6. Ibid., 12–13.
7. Ibid., 14–18.
8. Ibid., 20; James S. Pula, *Thaddeus Kościuszko: The Purest Son of Liberty* (New York: Hippocrene Books, 1999), 38.
9. Storozynski, *Peasant Prince*, 20–21.
10. Ibid., 21–24; Pula, *Thaddeus Kościuszko*, 50–51.
11. Storozynski, *Peasant Prince*, 27.
12. Francis Casimir Kajencki, *Thaddeus Kosciuszko: Military Engineer of the American Revolution* (El Paso, TX: Southwest Polonia Press, 1998), 14.
13. Storozynski, *Peasant Prince*, 30.
14. Ibid.
15. Ibid., 32–33.
16. Ibid.
17. John F. Luzader, "Historic Structures Report, Bemis Heights, September 12 to October 8, 1777 (Neilson Farm)," report on file at Saratoga National Historical Park (NHP), 1973, 4.
18. Ibid., 5.
19. Ibid., 24.

20. Ibid.

21. W. J. Wood, *Battles of the Revolutionary War 1775–1781* (Cambridge, MA: De Capo Press, 1990 [2003 edition]), 151.

22. Ibid., 151–52.

23. Charles W. Snell, "A Report on the American Fortified Camp at Bemis Heights September 12 to October 8, 1777," report on file at Saratoga NHP, 1950; J. Y. Shimoda, "The North Redan and Redan near Stop #7 on the American River Fortifications, Site Trail Development," report on file at Saratoga NHP, 1962; Luzader, "Historic Structures Report, Bemis Heights."

24. Additional historical information on these fortifications can be found in Snell, "Report on the American Fortified Camp at Bemis Heights"; Shimoda, "North Redan and Redan near Stop #7"; and Luzader, "Historic Structures Report, Bemis Heights."

25. Colonel Richard Varick to General Philip Schuyler, September 16, 1777, Philip Schuyler Papers, Manuscript Division, New York Public Library, New York (hereafter Schuyler Papers).

26. Varick to Schuyler, September 17, 1777, Schuyler Papers.

27. The location of the original Putnam Map is currently unknown. Nineteenth-century copies of the map are known to exist (NPS historian Schnitzer; personal communication) but could not be located to be reproduced for this book. The traced version of the map that is reproduced here is believed to be from a photostat of a copy of the document in the New York Historical Society.

28. Wolfenbüttel Urkunden, as translated in Luzader, "Historic Structures Report, Bemis Heights," 33.

29. Translation by Luzader, "Historic Structures Report, Bemis Heights," 33.

30. James Wilkinson, *Memoirs of My Own Times*, 3 vols. (Philadelphia: Abraham Small, 1816), 1:235–36.

31. See "Captain-Lieutenant William Cumberland Wilkinson, 62nd Regiment of Foot, ca. 1785," www.62ndregiment.org/William_Wilkinson.htm, accessed September 3, 2013.

32. "A state of the expedition from Canada: as laid before the House of Commons, by Lieutenant-General Burgoyne, . . . With a collection of authentic documents, . . . Written and collected by himself, . . ." University of Oxford Text Archive, http://ota.ahds.ac.uk/text/5017.html, 16, accessed June 21, 2014.

33. Robert W. Ehrich, "Progress Report on the Archeological Program of Saratoga National Historical Park," report on file at Saratoga NHP, 1941, 1.

34. Ibid., 9.

35. Ibid.; Robert W. Ehrich, "Proposed Archeological Program for Saratoga National Historical Park," report on file at Saratoga NHP, 1943.

36. John L. Cotter, "Results of Archeological Tests, Saratoga National Historical Park: 2. The American River Lines," report on file at Saratoga NHP, 1957.

37. Stuart A. Reeve and Dean R. Snow, "Report on Archaeological Investigations and Excavations of Revolutionary Sites, Saratoga National Historical Park, New York, 1974–1975," State University of New York–Albany, report on file Saratoga at NHP, 1975.

38. Ibid., 17.

39. Ibid.

40. Ibid., 19.

41. Dean R. Snow, "Report on Archaeological Investigations of the American Line, the Great Redoubt, and the Taylor House, Saratoga National Historical Park, 1973–1974," report on file at Saratoga NHP, Stillwater, NY, 1974.

42. Snow, "Report on Archaeological Investigations, 1973–1974"; Dean R. Snow, "Archaeological Atlas of the Saratoga Battlefield," Department of Anthropology, State University of New York–Albany, 1977.

43. Rinita A. Dalan and Bruce Bevan, "Geophysical Indicators of Culturally Emplaced Soils and Sediments," *Geoarchaeology* 17, no. 8 (2002): 779.

44. Ibid., 781.

45. Plastic surveying flags were inserted into the ground every two meters across the grid to guide the data collection. A Trimble GeoXT GPS recorder was brought into the field to record the positions of the corners of the grid. Following the completion of the data collection, nine-inch iron nails were driven into the corners of the grid so that the grid could be relocated for ground-truthing at a later time using a metal detector. Geophysical projects must always be ground-truthed by excavation or coring because, as mentioned earlier, the anomalies identified by the geophysical instruments cannot always be confirmed.

46. For this particular study, GPR data was collected using a normal (unidirectional) collection path with transects separated by one meter.

47. "Web Soil Survey," Natural Resources Conservation Service, US Department of Agriculture, http://websoilsurvey.sc.egov.usda.gov, accessed November 29, 2013.

CHAPTER FIVE | DAVID R. STARBUCK

The American Fortifications

Introduction

THE AMERICAN fortifications at Bemis Heights were located within farming areas that were vacated by their residents as military forces arrived. Farmhouses were subsequently occupied by American officers, while soldiers established tent sites across the open fields. Most of these farms were quickly reoccupied by their owners after the battles were over, leaving a landscape of earthworks and campsites on which the traces of military occupation represented no more than several weeks, sandwiched in between a great many years of farming activity.

Over the years, archaeologists have examined the American occupations at the Neilson house, the Woodworth farm (site of the American headquarters of General Horatio Gates, as well as the American field hospital), and the so-called river fortifications. Together these discoveries may be used to better understand the conditions under which officers and soldiers served as they camped at these locations both before and during the battles.

Based on historical sources, we know that General Horatio Gates occupied a farmhouse during the two battles, and the house was believed to have stood on what was referred to in the 1980s as the Price farm. This farm was purchased by the National Park Service (NPS) in 1984, and the park was eager to use archaeology to learn more about this latest acquisition. With a request from the NPS to locate and excavate the American headquarters, I began the search in 1985.[1]

This was by no means the first time that archaeologists had sought evidence for fortifications or encampments from the American side of the conflict. Robert Ehrich had already conducted extensive archaeology in the park in 1940 and 1941 using laborers from the Civilian Conservation Corps. Ehrich, as well as later archaeologists, relied heavily on a later print of the circa 1778 map by British Lieutenant William Wilkinson, 62nd Regiment of Foot. Based on his analysis of the map, Ehrich dug numerous trenches in what he termed the "Western Sector," the "Central Section," and the "Eastern Section" of the American lines.² Some of these trenches were located in the vicinity of the Neilson house site, named after John Neilson, a farmer who had joined with the American army to oppose Burgoyne. During the interval between the two battles, American officers occupied the Neilson farmhouse on Bemis Heights; John Cotter subsequently excavated at the Neilson farm.³ The carefully restored Neilson farmhouse is now a popular stop on the modern tour road that runs through the park.

More recently, Dean Snow conducted a mapping project at the battlefield between 1972 and 1975, locating numerous American and British sites.⁴ His base maps and accompanying fieldwork helped to locate many of the roads, earthworks, foundations, and walls that stood at the time of the battles, and these included many points on the American lines.

A short distance east-northeast of the American headquarters and Fort Neilson are the American river fortifications, positioned on high ground overlooking the Hudson River. It was at this location that Polish engineer Colonel Thaddeus Kosciuszko created a strong American position that was intended to prevent the British army from proceeding south on the Hudson toward Albany. A modest amount of archaeology has taken place over the years between this high ground and the fields that abut the river, but this is work that is largely unpublished (see chapter 4).

Each of these projects has produced essential information about the positions held by American forces in 1777, but none of these efforts had access to the farming fields that contained the American headquarters. Thus, when approached in the 1980s, I knew this was a once-in-a-lifetime opportunity to explore a key part of the American lines, the location of General Gates's headquarters and hospital. After all, this was where ranking officers successfully directed the winning strategy for the American side. What follows is a presentation of our work, stressing the foundations and artifacts that were uncovered.

The American Headquarters: History

In the 1770s, weaver Ephraim Woodworth leased fields within lots 13 and 14 of the Saratoga Patent, a tract of land on the Hudson River that had been purchased from the Mohawks about 1684. He then constructed a house, barn, and outbuildings. Woodworth was a captain in the Albany County Militia, and the farm lay close to the road to Bemis Heights and to the Bemus Tavern, which lay just to the east (today these fields lie near Routes 32 and 423). Little is known about their farming activities, and the Woodworth family departed when American troops arrived in 1777.

It was the Woodworth house where Gates and General Benedict Arnold quarreled after the first Battle of Saratoga on September 19. Arnold believed that he had not received sufficient credit for their efforts, and after the argument, Arnold left the Woodworth farmhouse and was essentially relieved of command until October 7, when he led American troops in heroic charges on British and German redoubts.

Most of the local farmers, including the Woodworth family, returned to their houses and fields after the surrender on October 17. The site of the American headquarters became a popular destination for visitors in the early nineteenth century, but we do not know exactly when the Woodworths departed their farm for the last time. The house was finally razed in 1829,[5] and there are few references to the barn after about 1820. The farm subsequently passed through a series of owners, notably William Denison in the late 1800s, and it was the William Price family that was the final private-property owner before acquisition by the NPS.

When Benjamin Silliman visited the American fortifications in 1819, he wrote of the Woodworth farmhouse that

> I am afraid that the traveler may not long find this memorable house, for it was much dilapidated—a part of the roof had fallen in, and the wind whistled through the naked timbers. One room was, however, tenantable, and was occupied by a cooper and his family. From the style of the panel-work and finishing of this room, the house appears to have been in its day one of the better sort—the panels were large and handsome and the door was still ornamented with brass handles.[6]

Next to the Woodworth farmhouse was the American field hospital, situated within the Woodworth barn. One account states that

> in the field was Gates's headquarters, and up to the right of it was the hospital. Here Gates stayed during the second day's battle, and here he had the heated argument with Sir Francis Clerke [sic], a wounded prisoner, over the merits of the questions at issue between the Americans and British.[7]

An account by General Epaphras Hoyt, who visited the site in 1825, notes that the farmhouse was painted red and "now fast going to decay." Hoyt went on to describe the presence of mass burials nearby:

> A small distance east of the [Woodworth] house, ast [sic] the time of the battles, stood a barn in which many of the wounded were deposited; but the foundation only remains to mark the spot. [In the] fields adjacent . . . here the bones of many a patriot who died of wounds received in the two actions of the 19th of September and 7th of October, rest in obscurity. My companion pointed out the spot where twenty-eight of these heroes were interred in one grave; and near this spot the veteran Col. Breyman [sic] and

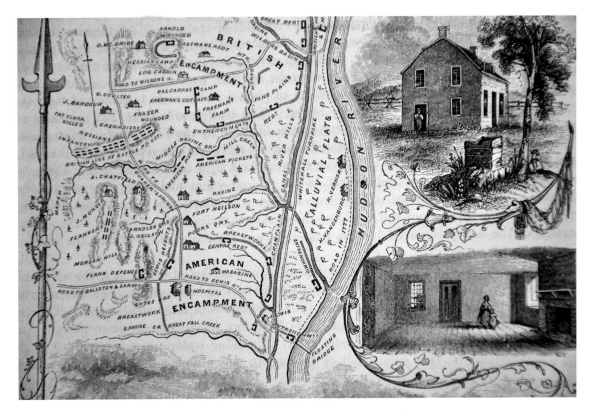

FIGURE 5.1. Plan of the American headquarters (*left*) and views of the Woodworth farmhouse (*right*). From Benson J. Lossing, 1851, *The Pictorial Field-Book of the Revolution* (New York: Harper Brothers), 46.

Sir Francis Clark [*sic*], Burgoyne's aide-de-camp, mortally wounded and taken prisoners in the second action mixed their remains with their brave conquerors.[8]

Hoyt's account suggests that the remains of Americans, Germans, and British soldiers were all intermixed in mass graves, having been carried from the Woodworth barn to the surrounding fields for burial.

Prominent Revolutionary War historian Benson Lossing visited the Woodworth farm site in 1848 and published sketches and a map that included the house and barn side by side (figure 5.1). Lossing's drawings, based on "a sketch furnished by Mr. Neilson," portray the headquarters as having two stories, with doors on the east and south, and a well just outside the southern door. "This house stood about one hundred and fifty rods south of Fort Neilson, and the traces of the cellar may now be seen a few yards to the left of the Ballston road."[9]

A map drawn by Edward West for the New York State Conservation Commission in 1926 shows a foundation that is labeled "Remains of Foundation of

Gen. Gates Headquarters." This was the last time that traces of the house were observed and documented prior to the 1985 excavations.

The American Headquarters: Archaeology

Archaeological fieldwork has been conducted at a great many Revolutionary War–era sites, including Fort Stanwix, the New Windsor Cantonment, Fort Montgomery, and the Bennington Battlefield, all in New York State;[10] Valley Forge in Pennsylvania;[11] Mount Independence in Vermont;[12] Morristown, Pluckemin, and the Monmouth Battlefield, all in New Jersey;[13] Camp Redding in Connecticut;[14] Fort Laurens in Ohio;[15] and Fort Donnally in West Virginia.[16] One of the most distinctive of these sites is Mount Independence on Lake Champlain, partially because it has the most intact American fortifications along the route that General Burgoyne's army took while traveling to Saratoga,[17] but also because everything at that site is "real" and not a twenty-first-century monument to the past.[18]

In recent years there has even been forensic archaeology that is pertinent to the American victory in Saratoga. This research focused on Jane McCrea, a young woman who was seized by Indians attached to Burgoyne's army as she waited for the arrival of her fiancé David Jones, a loyalist officer who was traveling with Burgoyne. The role that women played in the American victory was traditionally an untold story, with this one exception. Jane McCrea was murdered and scalped in Fort Edward, New York, and her death prompted outrage that was used by Gates as propaganda to encourage Americans to fight against the British and their Indian allies at Saratoga. When her body was exhumed from Union Cemetery at Fort Edward in 2004 (and again in 2006 for further study), her skeleton was systematically analyzed to understand better her appearance. A petite woman, perhaps five foot four and only twenty-three or twenty-four years of age, her scalp and even her skull were missing from the grave, making it difficult to precisely determine her cause of death.[19]

The Saratoga Battlefield is one of the most revealing of the American Revolutionary War sites just mentioned because it contains a great variety of military features within its borders, ranging from earthworks to farmhouses to encampments to battlefield areas. Artifacts from the two battlefields were surface-collected soon after the fighting was over, but the setting for the American headquarters was some distance away from the fighting, leaving it relatively undisturbed until our work in the 1980s. The Woodworth farm was sited more than a mile from either the September 19 or October 7 battle, and this distance traditionally raised the question of whether Gates chose this farm setting because it was in an easily defensible position or because it was as far as possible from the actual conflict (or both). It was this caution, and his distance from the actual fighting, that caused some nineteenth-century historians to give him the nickname of "Granny Gates." Gates was protected by American units on the north, west, and east, and to the south by a deep ravine on Great Fall Creek. His position could not be easily outflanked, but neither could he retreat.

The National Park Service desired to know the location of the farm buildings that Gates had occupied, and in discussions with Saratoga National Historical Park it was decided that the archaeological fieldwork to be conducted in 1985–86 would have as its primary objective the location of foundations from the Woodworth farmhouse and barn, as well as any associated burials. The Woodworth farmhouse had been occupied for ten to twenty years before the battle and for fifty-two years afterward, and so we did not expect to find many "military" artifacts inside or surrounding a cellar hole that had been filled in 1829 or shortly thereafter. The barn appeared to be a better candidate because of its use as a military hospital and because the structure had been removed prior to the house. At the same time, barns often have insubstantial foundations, making them somewhat more difficult to locate.

The search for the Woodworth farm complex started with a magnetometer survey that was conducted at five-meter intervals atop the highest rise in the field south of Routes 32 and 423. The results of this initial survey proved disappointing because the high iron content in the soil produced virtually identical magnetometer readings across the field. Archaeologist Dennis Howe explained that

> after three days and approximately 1,000 readings using both high and low resolution survey modes, it became apparent that magnetic anomalies could not be detected with the apparatus and methods we were using. . . . We concluded that either the soil or underlying bedrock contained ferromagnetic material in a sufficient mass to prevent the magnetic field in the vicinity from being influenced by certain finite amounts of culturally deposited stone, brick or iron. All of the survey measurements were within the range of the standard readings at that site so that no contours or profiles could be plotted.[20]

Subsequent attempts to dig shovel test pits at regular intervals proved fruitless because the field consisted of clay hardpan that shovels could not penetrate. Ultimately, park staff used a tractor-mounted power auger to excavate some 119 holes at five-meter intervals along a systematic grid; the presence/absence of artifacts was used to establish where human occupation had been most intensive. This was a more successful technique, and it revealed scatters of ceramics and bricks in the same area where woodchuck holes were already exposing stones.[21] Ironically, peering inside the woodchuck holes was our most successful, low-tech approach to locating the American headquarters.

Based on the auger holes, which revealed the general farmstead location,

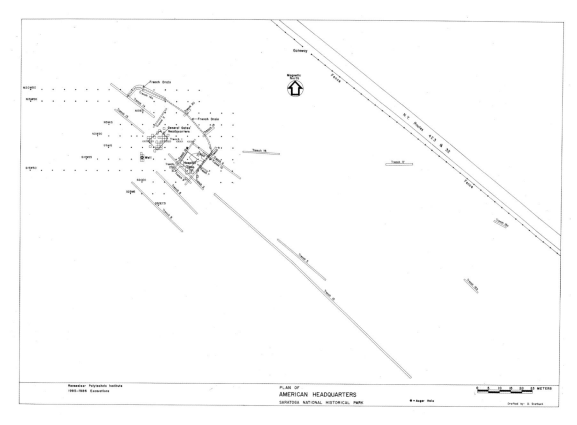

Figure 5.2. Site map showing the American headquarters, the American hospital, the well, and the distribution of the backhoe trenches and shovel test pits that were excavated in 1985 and 1986. Courtesy of David Starbuck.

we began digging backhoe trenches to locate the foundation walls (figure 5.2). Trench 1 successfully located two stone foundation walls from a single structure, and these walls were both substantial enough (at least one-foot thick) to suggest the remains of a house rather than a barn or other outbuilding. One-meter-square test pits were then used to expose larger portions of the building and to clarify its stratigraphy. Seven meters south of the house, additional woodchuck holes revealed more rocks and artifacts, and we quickly realized that we also had located the original Woodworth well.

As the 1985 field season ended, we still needed to locate the foundation of the barn that had served as the field hospital. To do this, we excavated twenty-four backhoe trenches across the northern part of the field in 1986. Most of these trenches were placed in close proximity to the foundation that had already been located, relying on the tendency of farm buildings to be tightly nucleated. Multiple trenches were placed just east of the first foundation because drawings by Lossing and others indicated that this was where the barn or hospital should have stood. Trenches were also used to examine all other high ground in the field.[22] In spite of the backhoe trenching, no evidence was found for mass burials (or even solitary burials) that might be expected in the vicinity of a hospital.

During the last week of the 1986 season, the backhoe trenches revealed small clusters of stones some eleven to sixteen meters (thirty-six to fifty-two feet) east of the first foundation. In trenches 21–23, we identified a structure supported on four corner piers. Artifacts were found inside the outline created by the rough "corners" of the building and ended abruptly outside of this outline.

The placement of the two foundations correlated very well with the two buildings shown in Lossing's drawing.[23] Because the more westerly site has a substantial foundation and cellar, while the easterly one does not, we are convinced that these two foundations represent the headquarters and the hospital, respectively.

The Woodworth Farmhouse: The American Headquarters

To delineate the American headquarters structure, we excavated thirty test pits and one backhoe trench (figure 5.3), but only eighteen of the test pits were dug within the cellar hole itself. The tops of the foundation stones were found at the base of the plow zone, approximately thirty centimeters (twelve inches) below the surface of the field. Test pits inside the cellar hole revealed a homogeneous gray clay, and at a depth of approximately forty to forty-five centimeters (sixteen to eighteen inches), this changed to a layer of brick fragments and foundation stones. Still deeper, we found a rich layer of artifacts that ranged in depth from sixty-five to eighty centimeters (twenty-five to thirty-two inches). This layer contained large quantities of animal bones, clamshells, pottery sherds, tobacco pipes, and much architectural debris. The artifacts thinned out at a depth of one meter, at which point wooden boards and smaller bits of wood and charcoal were scattered over the sterile clay hardpan that lay underneath.

All of the artifacts in the bottom of the cellar hole dated prior to 1829, and most were much earlier. Most of the debris in the cellar appears to have been thrown in before the abandonment of the house, perhaps during the years of its final decay when only a single room was occupied by a cooper and his family.[24]

The northern foundation wall measured approximately 5.6 meters (18 feet 3 inches), the southern wall 6.6 meters (21 feet 8 inches), the western wall 7.2 meters (23 feet 8 inches), and the eastern wall 5.6 meters (18 feet 3 inches). Allowing for some degree of slumpage, this suggests that the house originally measured approximately 20 feet on a side, or about 400 square feet (37.2 square meters) on the ground floor. Although Lossing's print published in 1851 showed a two-story house with doorways on the eastern and northern sides and two chimneys (figure 5.1), we could not confirm these details with archaeology. Relatively few

FIGURE 5.3. Excavations in the foundation of the American headquarters (Woodworth farmhouse) in 1986. Courtesy of David Starbuck.

bricks were found within the cellar hole, so most likely the complete bricks had been salvaged and taken elsewhere at the time the house was razed. Still, there were slightly higher numbers of bricks just inside the center of the western wall (chiefly in pit S1E5), suggesting that a fireplace/chimney may have stood there.

In order to preserve as much of the foundation as possible, while establishing its outline, we exposed all four corners, planning to remove only a moderate sample of what lay inside. However, given the small size of the building and the severe collapse that had occurred to foundation stones along the eastern wall, we ended up excavating nearly one-half of the interior.

The Woodworth Barn: The Field Hospital

The search for the American hospital was more difficult because early barns were often constructed with minimal stone foundations, and some may have been built directly upon the surface of the ground. This meant that traces could be so slight that we might not recognize the remains of a barn even if we were digging through it. Several auger holes (pit S5E20) turned up building debris, but it did not appear to have any particular orientation. However, in combination with available historical maps, this location seemed promising as the hospital site. Extremely thorough backhoe trenching in 1986, virtually blanketing the area between five and thirty-five meters east of the headquarters foundation, eventually identified small clusters of stones that appeared to be the corners of a building.

Trenches 21, 22, and 23 exposed these stones and contained a moderate quantity of artifacts, chiefly ceramics and animal bones. This artifact scatter covers an area measuring approximately six meters (twenty feet) north-south by five meters (sixteen feet) east-west, downslope and directly east of the headquarters foundation. There is no evidence for walls, but the clay matrix of the field does not contain stones except for ones that have been deliberately placed. This would appear to indicate a rather impermanent structure, with its weight carried on stone corner piers. Only a small area was excavated, and no artifacts were found that specifically suggested either a barn or a hospital. However, this area was nearly as large as the house foundation we had just exposed, and this is exactly where Neilson and Lossing placed the barn. The absence of artifacts pertaining to surgical operations is disappointing, but if the barn stood for perhaps twenty or thirty years after the battles, then there is no reason to expect that either doctors' implements or amputated body parts would be left inside the building.[25]

The Well behind the American Headquarters

In 1985, we discovered a well behind the American headquarters because a woodchuck hole had exposed some of the stones on its eastern side. We excavated seven shallow test pits around the well to establish its outline and then began excavating the interior. The 1985 dig revealed that the uppermost 1.83 meters (6 feet) of the shaft was completely filled with stones, while the next 0.61 meters (2 feet) contained a mixture of earth and stones. We halted the dig at a depth of 2.44 meters (8 feet) for safety reasons and because we had reached the water table. At that depth, boards were also beginning to appear. We installed a five-foot-high section of culvert within the shaft at the end of 1985 as a safety measure, and then in 1986 we continued to dig the well until we reached bedrock at about thirteen feet below the surface.

Below the eight-foot level, we wet-screened virtually all of the contents of the well, and preservation of organic material proved to be excellent in this oxygen-free, peat-like environment. Although much clay and numerous stones were found below 2.43 meters (8 feet), most of the matrix consisted of matted grass with only pockets of gray clay. Below 1.52 meters (5 feet), the walls of the well flared out slightly, but the diameter of the well measured 0.86 meters (34 inches) along most of its descent. Bedrock was encountered at a depth of 3.99

FIGURE 5.4. Some of the contents of the well. Top row (*left to right*): a red earthenware bottle neck, a whetstone fragment, and a fragment of an eyeglass frame. Bottom row (*left to right*): cherry pits, squash seeds, and hickory nuts. Courtesy of David Starbuck.

meters (13 feet 1 inch), at which point the bottom was slightly basin shaped where it cut some 38–46 centimeters (15–18 inches) into the bedrock. Inside the well we found small sherds of whiteware and redware, but it principally contained thousands of bones from small mammals (skunk, squirrel, and woodchuck) that must have fallen in. The well also contained great numbers of cherry pits and squash seeds, and smaller numbers of shells from hickory nuts; it even contained a single fragment of peanut shell.

Although we had hoped that quite a bit of garbage might have been thrown into the well upon abandonment of the farmstead, such was not the case. Some of the more distinctive artifacts from the lowermost part of the well included pieces of a wooden bucket, part of a red earthenware bottle, a whetstone fragment, part of the frame of a pair of eyeglasses, cherry pits, squash seeds, and hickory nuts. (Examples of some of these artifacts and ecofacts appear in figure 5.4.) Instead of rapid dumping, this assemblage had the appearance of debris that accumulated naturally from the surface of the field, with grass, stones, and

FIGURE 5.5. The French drain that diverted water away from the farmhouse (facing south). Courtesy of David Starbuck.

small animals occasionally falling in, until the top several feet were filled in with stones all at once to make it easier to plow the field. We placed all of the boards recovered from the well in a solution of polyethylene glycol (PEG) to stabilize them, and then we processed nearly all of the dirt from the bottom several feet of the well with water separation (flotation) in order to remove wood, charcoal, seeds, and bones from the matrix.

The French Drain

Perhaps the most distinctive feature exposed at the American headquarters was a lengthy, stone-lined drain that curved around the two foundations, collecting water that was running downslope from the north, west, or east (figure 5.5). The drain was first identified in our backhoe trenches (trenches 4, 7, 9, 14, 14a, 19, and 20), revealing what looks like a very large horseshoe, curving over a distance in excess of 61.7 meters (200 feet). Stones had been laid into a ditch, two to three stones deep and two to six stones wide, with individual stones measuring 10–20 centimeters (4–8 inches) in diameter. The top of these stones varied between 30 and 50 centimeters (12–20 inches) below the ground surface. While rather crude, this "French" style of drain, through which water is allowed to percolate

FIGURE 5.6. Evidence for firearms. Top row (*left to right*): a butt plate and a trigger guard. Bottom row (*left to right*): musket balls, canister shot, a worm, a musket tool, and gunflints. Courtesy of David Starbuck.

between stones, was massive and ambitious. The ceramics found within the surrounding ditch were all nineteenth century in date, and the drain no doubt postdates the military occupation of the site.

Artifacts

Most of the artifacts recovered during the 1985 and 1986 excavations were found inside the cellar hole of the headquarters building, and only a very few were found in the hospital area or around the well or drain. There do not appear to be significant chronological differences among the artifacts found at these three sites, and "military" artifacts at the Woodworth farm were extremely rare. The artifacts that pertained to firearms included just six musket balls, two pieces of canister shot, one butt plate, one trigger guard, a possible "worm" and a possible musket tool (both badly rusted), and three gunflints (figure 5.6). One of these is a French-style gunflint, whereas the others were cruder gun spalls. The canister shot is definitely of military issue, but everything else may have had a civilian origin. Most likely these sites had numerous military artifacts just after the two battles, but artifact collecting that continues to the present day would have removed most of what was once in these locations.

The most abundant types of ceramics excavated from the headquarters cellar hole were creamware and pearlware (most of which was undecorated), followed by redware, white salt-glazed stoneware, porcelain, delft, and very small amounts of Jackfield and whiteware. These include wares that would be expected on a rural farm site of this time period, but some of the ceramics (the pearlware and the whiteware) were postbattle and were left by the final occupants of the house early in the nineteenth century. X-ray fluorescence analysis was conducted on some of the "local" stoneware sherds excavated from the headquarters site in 1985. Based upon the small sample that was examined, it was demonstrated that the clays for many of the unrefined stoneware sherds derived from sources in New Jersey.[26]

In addition, the cellar hole contained a few hundred fragments of tobacco pipe stems, most of which were late eighteenth century in date (with a bore diameter of $4/64$ inch). Curiously, there also was a unique ceramic cube (approximately 1⅛ inch on a side) with small projections on three out of the nine surfaces. This appears to have been a child's toy or a gaming piece.

Given the dampness inside the headquarters foundation, the preservation of metal artifacts was extremely poor. Much of the metal found in the cellar was building hardware (many hundreds of handwrought nails, smaller numbers of cut nails, and nearly a dozen hinges), but nonarchitectural items, both utilitarian and personal, were also abundant. These included sixty-five whole or fragmentary metal buttons, manufactured chiefly of white metal (twenty-nine), brass (twenty-seven), and bronze (seven); one set of cuff links, octagonally shaped and made of cast bronze; and fourteen buckles or buckle fragments, consisting of brass and copper-alloy shoe buckles and iron harness buckles.[27]

Metal tools and kitchen implements were quite common in the cellar, including numerous bone-handled table knives and two-tined forks, a complete spoon, a spoon bowl, and several fragments from cast-iron cooking pots or kettles. Many artifacts were rusted beyond recognition, but some of the more interesting pieces included a thimble and a brass furniture escutcheon plate, the spigot from a barrel, and the complete blade (7¼ by 11½ inches) from a large iron spade.

Eight coins were found in or around the cellar hole at the headquarters site, and the earliest coins in the assemblage were two British half-pennies (both undated), followed by a New Jersey copper (1787), a Massachusetts copper (either 1787 or 1788), and four large cents (1798, 1800, 1800, and 1809). All of these dates accord well with a cellar that predated 1829.

Zooarchaeologist Barry Gray identified 6,262 animal bones that had been found in the house, barn, and drain. Bones were especially rich within the headquarters cellar, and we excavated most of these from the center and southeastern corner of the cellar. Limb extremities and teeth were so common that Gray has argued that "the Woodworth cellar hole was used as a garbage dump for butchering waste rather than the remains of food consumption."[28] Nevertheless, there were plenty of meaty parts, with many butchering marks from sawing and chopping. There is no definitive evidence that any of these bones represented meat that was consumed by the American army; some may have been, but it is more likely that they represent waste thrown into the cellar either just before or just after the house was taken down in 1829.

Pig, cow, and sheep bones were easily the most abundant, with pigs predominating; we found the bones from a minimum of thirteen pigs. Deer, turkey, chicken, and fish were also represented, and there were bones from mouse, rat, muskrat, woodchuck, cat, and dog; however, these last were most likely intrusive and do not represent food consumption. It appears that the hunting of wild animals did not form a significant addition to the diet, but a great many, probably a clear majority, of all bones were from immature animals. This suggests that most of the animals had been slaughtered just as soon as they neared full growth, probably in the fall so that they would not have to be fed through the winter.

Utilized bones were also common, including the many bone-handled knives and forks already mentioned, a single five-holed bone button, a bone gouge, and other nondiagnostic bone handle fragments. We also recovered a total of six wood buttons from the headquarters cellar hole, together with several boards that we found at a depth of approximately one meter in both the northeastern and southwestern corners of the foundation. These lay directly atop the sterile clay underlying the site, and their placement beneath all of the trash deposits strongly suggests that they were floorboards within the original Woodworth farmhouse. Other structural evidence inside the cellar appeared in the form of bricks, a great many plaster fragments, and numerous windowpanes. Interestingly, fragments of bottle glass or tablewares were practically nonexistent.

Summary and Conclusions

The excavations at the American headquarters (the Woodworth farm) were the most intensive archaeology that has been conducted anywhere on the American lines in Saratoga. This work identified the sites of a house, a well, and most likely a barn, all of which played an integral role in shaping the American victory in 1777. The military occupation was brief, so the vast majority of the artifacts pertain to the years of farm occupation both before and after the battles. Given the brevity of the military occupation in the farmhouse and barn, it is probably not surprising that we did not find direct, physical evidence for the officers who were stationed there. Still, we successfully located several of the key features of an upland farm that flourished in the late eighteenth century and that then declined and was abandoned in the early nineteenth century. Once Burgoyne's army had surrendered, local residents were able to resume their normal activities, and many of the fields surrounding the park have been farmed to the present day. There currently is a roadside monument on the southern side of Routes 32 and 423 that identifies the "Headquarters of General Horatio Gates."

We do not know how many soldiers and officers from both sides died in the American hospital and were buried within these fields. Clearly, further testing, and possibly the use of ground-penetrating radar, is warranted in order to locate these burials and any associated amputation pits that would contain evidence of surgical procedures conducted in field situations in the late eighteenth century. We used backhoes to test most points of high elevation close to the headquarters, but more distant fields still need to be checked for burials. More thorough testing should also be done in the hospital location in order to establish whether surgery was being practiced and to determine exactly when the barn was taken down. Finally, further testing is warranted on the west and the south of the headquarters foundation in order to learn whether additional Woodworth outbuildings extend in these directions. Because the French drain curves far to the west, this easily could mean that it flanked and protected an additional building or activity area on the western side of the farmhouse. This would have been an unusual farm site if there had not been some lesser sheds or workshops nearby.

This farmhouse and others like it were occupied by American officers for a very brief period, but the early farms of what is now Saratoga County were central to the story of the Battles of Saratoga. It was especially important that archaeology be used to locate the remains of the Woodworth farmhouse because the American commander, General Horatio Gates, was stationed at this location. That critical discovery was made in 1985 and 1986, and today visitors to the park are able to view the field where this historic farmhouse once stood.

NOTES

1. In 1985, I was a professor at Rensselaer Polytechnic Institute (RPI) when I was asked by Dick Ping Hsu, archaeologist for the Northeast Region of the National Park Service (NPS), whether I would like to find and excavate the American headquarters for the Battle of Saratoga.

2. Robert Ehrich, "Progress Report on the Archeological Program of Saratoga National Historical Park," Saratoga National Historical Park, 1942.

3. John L. Cotter, "Archeological Data, Neilson House," Saratoga National Historical Park, 1957.

4. Dean R. Snow, *Archaeological Atlas of the Saratoga Battlefield* (Albany, NY: Department of Anthropology, State University of New York at Albany, 1977); Dean R. Snow, "Battlefield Archeology," *Early Man* 3, no. 1 (1981): 18–21.

5. Jared Sparks, *Journal* (Cambridge, MA: Houghton Library, Harvard University, n.d.); John Luzader, "Historic Structure Report, Bemis Heights, September 12 to October 8, 1777" (Neilson Farm), National Park Service, Denver Service Center, 1973, 22.

6. William L. Stone, *Visits to the Saratoga Battle-Grounds 1780–1880* (Port Washington, NY: Kennikat Press, 1895), 117.

7. John Henry Brandow, *The Story of Old Saratoga and History of Schuylerville* (Saratoga Springs, NY: Robson and Adee, 1900), 501.

8. Stone, *Visits to the Saratoga Battle-Grounds*, 185.

9. Benson J. Lossing, *The Pictorial Field-Book of the Revolution*, vol. 1 (New York: Harper Brothers, 1851), 46–47.

10. Lee H. Hanson and Dick Ping Hsu, *Casements and Cannonballs, Archeological Investigations at Fort Stanwix, Rome, New York*. Publications in Archeology 14 (Washington, DC: National Park Service, 1975); Charles L. Fisher, "Archaeology at New Windsor Cantonment: Construction and Social Reproduction at a Revolutionary War Encampment," *Northeast Historical Archaeology* 12 (1983): 15–23; Charles L. Fisher, "Archaeological Survey and Historic Preservation at the Site of a Revolutionary War Cantonment in New Windsor, New York," *North American Archaeologist* 6, no. 1 (1984–85): 25–39; Charles L. Fisher, *Material Objects, Ideology, and Everyday Life: Archaeology of the Continental Soldier at the New Windsor Cantonment* (Waterford, NY: New York State Office of Parks, Recreation and Historic Preservation, Bureau of Historic Sites, Peebles Island, 1986); Charles L. Fisher, ed., *"The Most Advantageous Situation in the Highlands": An Archaeological Study of Fort Montgomery State Historic Site*. Cultural Resources Survey Program Series No. 2 (Albany, NY: New York State Museum, 2004); Philip Lord Jr., *War over Walloomscoick*. New York State Museum Bulletin No. 473 (Albany, NY: State Education Department, 1989).

11. Michael Parrington, "Geophysical and Aerial Prospecting Techniques at Valley Forge National Historical Park, Pennsylvania," *Journal of Field Archaeology* 6, no. 2 (1979): 193–201; Michael Parrington, "Revolutionary War Archaeology at Valley Forge, Pennsylvania," *North American Archaeologist* 1, no. 2 (1979–80): 161–75.

12. David R. Starbuck, "The General Hospital at Mount Independence," *Northeast Historical Archaeology* 19 (1990): 50–68; David R. Starbuck, "Building Independence on Lake Champlain," *Archaeology* 46, no. 5 (1993): 60–63; David R. Starbuck, "Archaeology at Mount Independence," *Journal of Vermont Archaeology* 1 (1994): 115–26.

13. Edward S. Rutsch and Kim M. Peters, "Forty Years of Archaeological Research at Morristown National Historical Park, Morristown, New Jersey," *Historical Archaeology* 11 (1977): 15–38; John L. Seidel, "The Archaeology of the American Revolution: A Reappraisal and Case Study at the Continental Artillery Cantonment of 1778–1779, Pluckemin, NJ," PhD diss., Department of Anthropology, University of Pennsylvania, 1987; Daniel M. Sivilich, "Analyzing Musket Balls to Interpret a Revolutionary War Site," *Historical Archaeology* 30, no. 2 (1996): 101–9.

14. Daniel Cruson and Kathleen von Jena, "The Different Lives of Officers and Enlisted Men at the Redding Winter Encampment of 1778–79," *Bulletin of the Archaeological Society of Connecticut* 64 (2002): 55–68.

15. Michael Gramly, *Fort Laurens 1778–9: The Archaeological Record* (Richmond, VA: William Byrd Press, 1978).

16. Kim McBride, "The Frontier Forts Project," *Council for Northeast Historical Archaeology Newsletter* 65 (2006): 17.

17. David R. Starbuck, *The Great Warpath: British Military Sites from Albany to Crown Point* (Hanover, NH: University Press of New England, 1999).

18. David R. Starbuck, *The Archaeology of Forts and Battlefields* (Gainesville: University Press of Florida, 2011), 68.

19. David R. Starbuck, "Fort Edward Martyr Mystery," *Adirondack Life* 37, no. 8 (2006): 48–52.

20. Dennis E. Howe, "Magnetometer Survey at Saratoga National Historical Park," Saratoga National Historical Park, 1985, 3.

21. David R. Starbuck, "Saratoga National Historical Park Archeology Progress Report—1985," Saratoga National Historical Park, 1986.

22. David R. Starbuck, "The American Headquarters for the Battle of Saratoga, 1985–1986 Excavations," Saratoga National Historical Park, 1987.

23. Lossing, *Pictorial Field-Book of the Revolution*, 46.

24. Stone, *Visits to the Saratoga Battle-Grounds*, 117.

25. The location of burials deriving from the hospital still needs to be established, primarily to ensure their protection from plowing or other earth-moving activities. Throughout our excavations we heard unverified stories about local contractors grinding up skeletons in the past with power machinery, and the park occasionally received long telephone calls from a woman in Albany who insisted that "we must not desecrate the dead!"

26. Allyson Brooks, "The Feasibility of X-Ray Fluorescence as an Analytical Tool in Historical Archaeology Using the Stoneware Ceramics from the Saratoga Battlefield," Saratoga National Historical Park, 1987.

27. Deborah L. Suciu, "Buttons, Buckles and Coins: The Analysis of Three Types of Everyday Artifacts Recovered from the Woodworth Farm Site," Saratoga National Historical Park, 1987.

28. Barry Gray, "Faunal Analysis: The Woodworth Farmhouse/American Headquarters for the Battle of Saratoga," Saratoga National Historical Park, 1988, 19.

CHAPTER SIX | MATTHEW KIRK AND JUSTIN DIVIRGILIO

The Retreat to Victory Woods

Introduction

EVOKING THE ROMAN goddess of fate, General John Burgoyne exclaimed to his counterpart at his surrender that the "fortune of war, General Horatio Gates, has made me your prisoner," to which Gates retorted, "It was not brought about by any fault of your Excellency."[1] While downplayed by Gates, Burgoyne's loss resulted in part from poor decision making and strategic planning. The British army had been for weeks cut off from its extended supply lines and local farms could not support the large number of troops and numerous horses and chattel, a situation worsened by battles at Saratoga. Thus, on October 17, 1777, Burgoyne traveled about a mile south of Victory Woods into the heart of the American lines and offered his sword to Horatio Gates in a formal act of surrender.

This chapter focuses on the landscape of Victory Woods and its environs, where a large contingent of Burgoyne's army set up its final defensive encampment, and examines how the landscape contributed to the dispirited condition of the British army and the general's eventual decision to surrender. On the day of the surrender, the British army marched from its stronghold in the hills of Saratoga down to the river plain and grounded their arms near the remains of Fort Hardy, a remnant of the French and Indian War, just east of Victory Woods.

Although the archaeology at Victory Woods unearthed both precontact Native American and British military deposits and features, this chapter focuses on the physical evidence related to the Revolutionary War battle on this landscape. For example, the archaeological excavation of the British earthworks revealed important details about their construction and the difficulties posed by the local conditions for the British. In addition, the lack of extensive historic archaeological deposits along the front of the British fortifications suggests that a "no-man's-land" developed as a result of the continual fire from the Americans. This work also speaks to the desperate state of Burgoyne's troops in the final days of their encampment, and to the deleterious effects of later relic collecting.

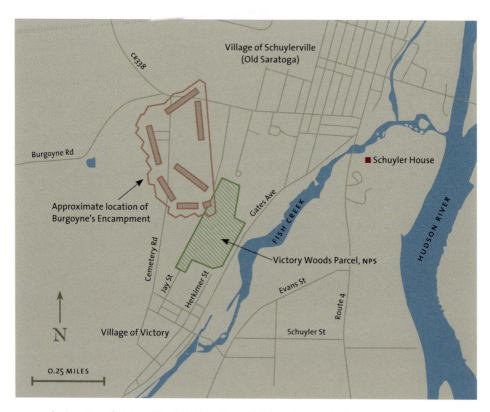

FIGURE 6.1. Location of Victory Woods in the village of Victory, New York. The approximate location of Burgoyne's final encampment is shown based on the William Faden map (c. 1780). Library of Congress Geography and Map Division.

Victory Woods is a twenty-two-acre parcel located south of County Route 338 and west of New York Route 32 that contains some of the ground to which British troops, under the command of General Burgoyne, retreated following their defeat at the Battles of Saratoga (figure 6.1).[2] An archaeological identification study focusing on Victory Woods was completed in 2007, while the National Park Service (NPS) simultaneously finished a cultural landscape report and archaeological sensitivity assessment of the property.[3] Based on data from these studies, the NPS selected twenty-two twenty-by-twenty-meter study areas for further investigation. This part of the project involved two phases: a geophysical investigation and an archaeological field reconnaissance. The project was undertaken in anticipation of opening the site for public visitation, which entailed the development of walking paths, the installation of monuments and/or interpretive signs, and the clearing of vistas. The geophysical study employed three techniques: ground-penetrating radar (GPR), magnetometry, and electrical resistivity. Based on the results of the geophysical investigations, the NPS selected eight study areas for additional archaeological field investigation.[4] The goal of this work was the identification of archaeological features pertaining to the encampment of British soldiers prior to their surrender.

The archaeology at Victory Woods focused primarily on exploring features readily visible at the surface in order to determine if they were cultural or natural in origin. The work also sought to identify anomalies discovered during the geophysical investigation, some at very shallow depths and others quite deep (one to two meters). In many instances there was agreement across the three geophysical techniques, meaning that the data from each instrument supported the interpretations for clear disturbance, soil movement, large objects, or the location of buried modern features such as a water pipeline. In other instances, the data from the instruments did not agree about the location of buried artifacts or features. For example, the magnetometer often located small metal objects not apparent in the other data sets. Based on experience from other studies, surface evidence, and the historical background of the site, the archaeologists concluded that approximately eighty anomalies were cultural in origin and required further investigation.

The NPS subsequently selected areas of archaeological interest for the excavation of units and trenches. Ultimately, nine of the anomalies in eight of the study grids were subject to archaeological verification. While the goals of the archaeology were to confirm the interpretations assigned to the geophysical data, the results were ultimately mixed. Some features interpreted as cultural were determined to be natural after the reconnaissance excavations, whereas others were identified as cultural but not from the Revolutionary War period. In addition to several precontact period deposits and features, three features likely related to the final encampment of Burgoyne's forces were identified.

The Landscape Prior to the Battles

The area that would later become known as Victory Woods was part of a large land transaction known as the Saratoga Patent. A small group of investors led by Pieter Philip Schuyler purchased the land about 1683 from a group of Native Americans. The Schuyler family had a guiding hand in the development and settlement of this area over the next hundred years. In 1702, the family undertook an earnest effort to increase settlement in the area by constructing a brick farmhouse, gristmill,[5] and later a sawmill.[6] This settlement, named Saratoga and later Schuylerville, was located on the Fish Creek near its confluence with the Hudson.[7]

In 1757, Fort Hardy was built on the floodplain directly below Victory Woods. A map of the fort and its environs depicts the Schuyler sawmill just below the hill of Victory Woods.[8] The map suggests the land may have been timbered for several of the nearby mills, despite the fact that the Schuyler mill was not operational during the construction of the fort. The Schuyler family increased their landholding in 1768 by purchasing more than 4,000 acres along the Fish Creek from the heirs of Robert Livingston. Within the next few years, the British decommissioned Fort Hardy and dismantled the buildings and barracks, although apparently much of the defensive earthworks were still extant during the Revolutionary War (see chapter 7).[9]

According to General Philip Schuyler, the Schuyler family leased their farmland, likely including all of the fertile floodplains along Fish Creek and the Hudson, to tenants.[10] Exactly when, or if, the woods along the heights west of the creek were cleared is not known. It is likely these woods above the creek were harvested at least once before General Burgoyne and his men first arrived at the site in September 1777.[11]

Victory Woods is situated along the eastern escarpment of a large terrace that overlooks Fish Creek below. The creek tumbles through a series of falls near Victory Woods that would later power many of the manufactories in Victory Mills. The heights command a view of the extensive floodplains and agricultural fields along the west side of the Hudson River south of its confluence with the creek. The eastern portion of the archaeological survey area is particularly steep, as the upper portions of the terrace lie at about 260 feet above mean sea level (AMSL), and about 500 feet away the creek is at an elevation of only 140 feet above MSL. Fish Creek forms an oxbow to the south creating a large V shape that afforded the heights an added measure of security (figure 6.2). The sandy terraces of Victory Woods also featured several small springs and wetlands that were later exploited by a nineteenth-century waterworks.

The Coming of the British

Burgoyne's army, consisting of a diverse collection of British regulars, loyalist American volunteers, French Canadian draftees, German Braunschweig and Hessen-Hanau regulars, and Native Americans, mostly Iroquois, occupied Victory Woods twice, bookending the two major battles. In September 1777, his army crossed over the Hudson and followed the road on the west side of the river in their push toward Albany, and then again as his flagging and faltering troops attempted to retreat north following the bruising days of intense fighting at the Battles of Saratoga.

The oblong hill containing Victory Woods was a strategic location from which artillery could command Fish Creek and its confluence with the Hudson River. The hill also provided a key observation point to survey both sides of the Hudson River, an important consideration as Burgoyne's floating bridge to bring supplies to the west side of the river was located in the vicinity. Exposed to

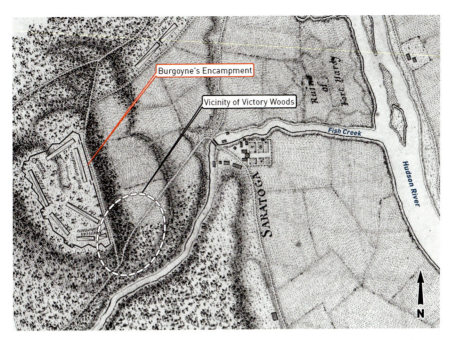

FIGURE 6.2. A schematic of the disposition of the American and British forces on October 8, 1777, attributed to William Faden, ca. 1780. Library of Congress Geography and Map Division.

enemy fire at the crest of the hill, the erection of earthworks and entrenchments were necessary for protection and concealment. The area of Victory Woods was periodically occupied by advance and expeditionary forces of both the British and American armies in the early part of September. According to *The Specht Journal*, on September 13, Brigadier-General Fraser "crossed the bateaux bridge over the Hudson with his corps and moved into a camp on the height by the Fishkill [Fish Creek] and facing it."[12] During the next two days, the British constructed earthworks to strengthen their positions in light of an unknown disposition of rebel forces. Once all of Burgoyne's troops crossed the river, it was expected by the soldiers that the various regiments would dig in. However, "instead of our corps moving into new camps at Saratoga today, the entire army received orders to move closer to the enemy" and the British positions at Victory Woods were hastily abandoned.

The British army returned to Saratoga nearly a month later, following the stinging losses at Freeman's farm. By October 9, a portion of Burgoyne's army crossed Fish Creek, but not without many difficulties because American troops had destroyed the bridges. Major-General von Riedesel's troops forded the creek and along with Lord Balcarres (53rd Foot) and Brigadier-General Hamilton (21st Foot) and the remnants of Fraser's brigade (24th Foot) "crowned and thus dominated the heights on which they stood."[13] The Americans, however, were

THE RETREAT TO VICTORY WOODS | 149

quickly closing in on the beleaguered British and German regiments. American Major Ebenezer Stevens brought his corps of cannons to bear and destroyed the bateaux that were busily shuttling supplies to Burgoyne's encampment.[14] Although the British supply lines were taxed, the troops themselves commanded a defensive posture that was stout, especially the main body in and around Victory Woods. The heights were quickly strengthened with field pieces and protected by supporting encampments by the grenadiers, loyalist militia, and other smaller detachments. The position was so strongly held that after General Burgoyne burned Philip Schuyler's house, he took refuge on the flats immediately below, but eventually he moved his headquarters within the safety of the growing earthworks on the heights. By this time, Burgoyne's army had dwindled to less than 6,000 soldiers,[15] while the American forces were growing with an influx of reinforcements and were now triple that of their enemy.

According to *The Specht Journal,* on the evening of October 10, 1777, calm settled over the area,

> but the army had to remain under arms during the night. All the regts. were ordered to dig in place as much as possible and to establish lines in the most advantageous places for that and the work succeeded very well during the night. . . . The terrain on the right wing, however, was so rocky that it was not possible to work the stony ground without separating it with hoes and axes before using shovel and spades. The German corps, therefore, could dig their entrenchments not much more than a foot deep.[16]

The next day was similar to the previous because "the troops had continued the whole day to dig themselves in and the left wing became so strong that the enemy would have fared rather badly if he attacked us in this position."[17] Lieutenant William Digby of the 53rd Regiment of Foot noted of the developing siege: "Their cannon and ours begin to play on each other. They took many of our Batows on the river, as our cannons could not protect them. We were obliged to bring our oxen and horses into our lines, where they had the wretched prospect of living but a few days as our grass was gone, and nothing after but leaves of trees for them."[18]

Once Burgoyne's army had become stationary, the Americans moved with greater assurance and surrounded his position. Despite their advantage, General Gates nearly blundered by advancing a large detachment against the British positions on the floodplain, thinking the main body was advancing to Fort Edward and that only a rear guard remained at Saratoga. The confusion was brought about by faulty intelligence and a persistent fog that concealed the British lines. Once the disposition of the enemy was understood by his commanding officers, the attack was aborted and disaster averted. Gates could now confidently extend a cordon around Burgoyne's army, slowly encircling his tiring troops.

Despite his strong tactical position, Burgoyne stumbled into a strategic nightmare. The only hope for escape was a brazen march through enemy lines, either south to Albany or north to Fort George. By this point in the campaign, the morale of his army was at its lowest and "every soldier and officer in the entrenchments feared that nothing could save them from defeat and surrender."[19] Although Burgoyne still held out hope that General Clinton and his army would push northward through the Hudson Valley to provide support, his perilous position forced him to concede defeat. Following a cease-fire on October 13, a convention was drafted two days later that allowed for an honorable end to the fighting. After several days of some negotiations, the British handed their weapons over to the Americans at what would become known as the Field of Grounded Arms near Fort Hardy.

Unfortunately, various developments during the nineteenth and twentieth centuries destroyed much (but not all) of the British encampment in and around Victory Woods. Builders of the Prospect Hill Cemetery leveled entrenchments along the western portion of the camp about 1870.[20] Construction of the Saratoga Monument within the bounds of the British camp began in 1877 to commemorate the centennial of the Battles of Saratoga.[21] Waterworks supplying the Village of Victory (about 1920) were constructed in the southern half of the encampment and included a water tower, several spring-fed pumping stations, an underground reservoir, and pipes; an icehouse was built in the same area about 1930.[22] Later residents of the area recalled the destruction of some of the earthworks outside of Victory Woods in the late 1800s, indicating the entrenchments were made of "pine logs and earth."[23] Eminent local historian John Brandow wrote in 1900 that "in the Victory Woods, south of the monument, there are hundreds of feet of the British breastworks in an excellent state of preservation. The ground never having been permanently cleared or plowed, these earthworks remain as the British left them, except that the logs, which may have entered into their construction, are rotted away."[24]

The Victory Woods parcel of the Saratoga National Historical Park was largely protected from development by past industrial owners, eventually being transferred to the NPS in 1974 for permanent preservation. The mixed hardwood forest of the parcel today is dominated by oak and maple trees, many dating between 50 and 150 years. Vistas that would have been open in October 1777 are now largely blocked by vegetation, the Victory Mills apartment complex, and neighboring houses.[25]

Ultimately, the historic record is not clear as to the exact nature of the landscape at Victory Woods prior to and during the closing days of the Saratoga campaign. It is likely that the area was not farm fields, as there is no archaeological evidence of plowing. At the time of the Revolutionary War, it seems that it was partially wooded, but may also have been a woodlot, pasturelands,

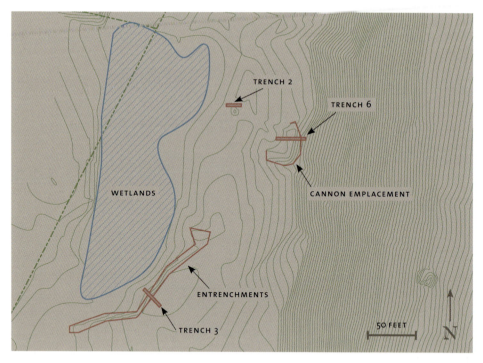

FIGURE 6.3. A plan of the northern extent of archaeological excavations at Victory Woods. Three potential defensive features (cannon emplacement, entrenchments, and possible magazine) were investigated with trench excavations (trenches 2, 3, and 6). Image courtesy of Hartgen.

or selectively forested for the nearby mills. The few trees that remained were no doubt quickly felled by the British to create defensive breastworks and to use for cooking and heating. Afterward, the area was largely controlled by the nearby mills, eventually reverting to a mature stand of trees, when it likely developed the moniker *Victory Woods*.

Archaeology of the Earthworks at Victory Woods

Victory Woods contains evidence of a scatter of potential earthworks constructed by either the Americans or British when they controlled the heights over Saratoga. Utilizing geophysical instruments including GPR, a magnetometer, and a resistivity meter, several areas of potential archaeological interest were selected for further investigation. The excavation of relatively narrow slit trenches provided important stratigraphic information concerning potential earthworks, while largely preserving and protecting the aboveground evidence that remained. Based on preservation concerns, excavation was limited in extent and scope.

Of the eleven trenches excavated, two crosscut potential military earthworks.

FIGURE 6.4. A trench excavation of a surface feature interpreted as a cannon emplacement along the steep eastern slope of Victory Woods. The emplacement features piled sand over a steep escarp, and recent downwashed sediments. Image courtesy of Hartgen.

The first (trench 6), located near the edge of the hillside in the northeast portion of the Victory Woods parcel, may have been a gun emplacement, and the second (trench 3), located to the south, a defensive outwork (figure 6.3).

Trench 6 was placed to investigate a crescent-shaped earthen berm located at the top of a steep slope and traditionally interpreted as a cannon emplacement (figure 6.4). The ten-meter long trench was oriented perpendicular to the berm and extended from the interior to the exterior slope. Although excavation was generally stopped when the surface of the earthwork was exposed, a small section at the base of the feature was removed to determine whether there was a ditch around the perimeter of the battery. There was no evidence of a ditch at the lower portion of the feature, suggesting that the material used to create the earthwork came from above. No Revolutionary War artifacts were recovered from the trench, but orange plastic in the topsoil suggests the area may have been subject to looting in the past.

Trench 2 was excavated to explore a depression that was interpreted as the possible location of a magazine because of its proximity to the cannon emplacement just described. Coincidentally, the feature was also the source of a magnetic

FIGURE 6.5. A profile of the archaeological excavations of the British earthworks at Victory Woods. The excavations evidenced a natural rise with an interior and exterior ditch to create a breastwork or parapet to protect the encamped soldiers. The entrenchments were built directly over a precontact roasting platform (or cooking surface), likely created thousands of years before the battles. Image courtesy of Hartgen.

anomaly identified during the geophysical survey. The four-meter-long trench was placed across the northern end of the depression to explore both the feature and the anomaly.

The excavations revealed evidence of a basin-shaped pit feature filled with redeposited topsoil. The pit was bisected, removing half the fill, to reveal its original shape in profile. The only early historic item was a wrought nail recovered from redeposited subsoil outside the edge of the pit. The remainder of the artifacts was twentieth century in origin. The results of the excavation provide little evidence to either support or contradict the interpretation of the feature as a magazine. Although the presence of modern artifacts in the feature indicate that recent disturbance has occurred, this does not preclude the possibility that the pit was initially excavated to serve as a small magazine.

Trench 3 cut across a long linear earthwork feature, interpreted as a defensive entrenchment, running in a northwest-southeast orientation (figure 6.5). This V-shaped outwork was likely part of a more extensive feature. Approximately 175 feet of this feature remains, angled southeast toward Fish Creek. Although it appears to connect to the cannon emplacement, it is not certain these works were ever joined. As a result, it is unclear if the cannon emplacement was part of a redan (joined earthworks) or ravelin (detached earthworks).[26]

The archaeology suggests that soldiers constructed the earthwork by excavating two ditches, one along the interior (west side) and the other along the exterior (east side). The interior ditch provided a platform or banquette from which soldiers could fire onto the enemy from within the earthwork. The earthwork was situated along a natural rise that was accentuated by piling the spoil material from the ditches on top. Three strata were excavated in the trench. The first stratum appears to represent the redeposited material excavated from the two ditches along front and back of the earthwork, forming the parapet itself. The ditches partially truncated a large precontact roasting platform that was part of the original ground surface and the second stratum.[27] Finally, the last stratum was formed as the parapet eroded over the years, creating slope wash on the front and back of the raised earthwork (figure 6.5).

The possible cannon emplacement did not contain a distinct opening or embrasure from which to fire. Rather, it was likely the cannons fired over the short embankment, or *en barbette*.[28] This would have left the field piece exposed to enemy fire.

The defensive outworks constructed by the British during the final days of their campaign down the Hudson were likely a mixture of wood, stone, and rammed earth, depending on the local conditions. According to the standards of the day as prescribed by military engineers, an earthwork or parapet is the bank of earth surrounding the post to be defended, and serves to cover the troops and artillery.[29] A ditch was often incorporated into the parapet to help raise the face and provide better protection. The width of the parapet depended on the circumstances and varied from three to eighteen feet. The earthworks at Victory Woods were likely at the smaller end, probably no more than four feet wide at the top. Within the parapet could be a framework of wooden timbers, fascines, gabions (woven baskets of dirt), or hurdles (vertical woven mats), all of which were fixed to the ground with stakes (see figure 6.6). In some cases, dirt was simply piled up and tamped down, as appears to be the case at Victory Woods.[30] The breastworks evidenced in the archaeological excavations likely represent only the inner core of the original construction. Tree falls, animal burrows, and erosion from wind and water all likely contributed to the slow eradication of these features following the surrender.

Even with prior investigations of potential British earthworks in the Saratoga campaign, there is little comparative archaeological information to assess the earthworks at Victory Woods.[31] The historical records indicate that the earthworks built by Burgoyne's men in the closing days of the fight were constructed under extreme duress. Major-General von Riedesel recalled: "The soldiers could

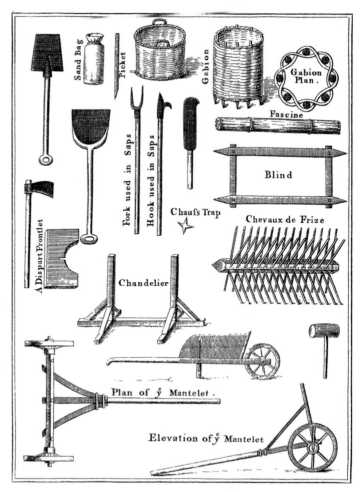

FIGURE 6.6. The typical eighteenth-century tools and weapons associated with entrenchments and siege warfare from John Muller's treatise *The Attac and Defence of Fortified Places* (1757). By the time Burgoyne had reoccupied the heights of Saratoga, it is doubtful that many of these tools would have been available to the soldiers because many of the army's supplies had been abandoned, captured, or destroyed by this time. Image courtesy of David Manthey.

not lay down his arms day or night, except to exchange his gun for the spade when new entrenchments were thrown up."[32] As a result, these hastily erected fortifications were not constructed according to strict military procedures, nor did they necessarily meet strict military construction guidelines. The archaeology suggests that the earthworks reflect the realities of the local topography, soil conditions, availability of wood and timber, the exhaustion of the men constructing the works, and overall lack of tools and supplies (figure 6.6).

Dwindling Supplies

Supply issues had clearly plagued Burgoyne's army since July 1777. As Burgoyne and his troops were slowly pushing southward, they increasingly stretched their supply lines as they moved. Supplies were sent primarily from Saint-Jean,

Quebec, and then up Lake Champlain, over a grueling portage near Fort Ticonderoga, up to Lake George, overland to Fort Edward, and eventually to Fort Miller and the forward positions of the army. By this time, "his supply line was tenuous at best and there were hints it was beginning to unravel."[33] Adding to the complications for Burgoyne was the lack of farms and settlements in the Saratoga area from which to buy or take provisions. The few resources that were available were destroyed by the "scorched-earth policy" of the American army, who desperately tried to slow the British approach until reinforcements arrived.[34] In August 1777, Burgoyne sent troops into Vermont, en route to the Connecticut Valley, in a desperate bid to obtain horses, cattle, and other provisions from loyalist supporters and through plunder to assist his beleaguered army.[35] They were stymied in their quest in what has become known as the Battle of Bennington.

Despite the fact that the army suddenly moved out of the dense wilderness and into an emerging agricultural community, the landscape along this part of the Hudson River could not adequately augment their supplies. Finding fresh vegetables on a nearby farm provided fleeting joy to the British troops as they moved through Saratoga in the middle of September. During the days at Victory Woods when the British were surrounded, finding food and forage or purchasing food through sutlers became increasingly difficult. Archaeological evidence from Governor's Island near New York City[36] and Carleton Island[37] along the St. Lawrence documents the extent to which British troops relied on local resources to augment their issued provisions, even near supply hubs at Montreal and New York City.[38]

As the Americans closed in on Burgoyne's army, his troops' ability to find their own food through hunting (although forbidden), fishing, trading, coercion, or outright theft diminished. Once entrenched at Victory Woods and under constant harassing fire from the Americans, Burgoyne's army had no ability to obtain local provisions. While these conditions were particularly difficult for the common solider, it appears that the officers were also affected. Major-General von Riedesel's wife, who followed her husband's campaign, documented her experiences and the plight of the army at Saratoga in a memoir. For October 10, she reminisced, "the greatest misery and utmost disorder prevailed in the army. The commissaries had forgotten to distribute provisions among the troops. There were cattle enough but not one had been slaughtered. More than thirty officers came to me, who could not endure the hunger."[39]

Ironically, the day before Burgoyne's surrender, Riedesel recalled that his officers were provided "a large amount of fresh meat . . . who, up to this time, had received only salted provisions, which had exceedingly aggravated the wounds of the men."[40] Lady Riedesel's account bespeaks of the problems providing supplies to the troops and officers in the waning days of the campaign. As for herself and her family, she remembered that "we had a cook, although an arrant knave, was smart in all expedients, and often in the night crossed small rivers, in order to steal from the country people, poultry and pigs."[41]

On October 13, Specht's chronicler could clearly see the end for the army, declaring that "all things in the camp became sadder and sadder for us . . . the horses began to die for lack of forage or they became living skeletons . . . all such things indispensable for the soldier as brandy, tobacco, etc. were now entirely lacking . . . want, misery, and hunger would therefore soon gain ground and a lot of people, not able to endure, such kind of difficulties, would be lost without any recourse."[42]

The journalist concludes by noting that "finally, in the position we were in, we could last 5 days with the present supplies but once that period was over, our situation would be the same, nay, in view of the want, much worse."[43] Major-General von Riedesel also recorded the deteriorating conditions of the encampment: "the ground was covered with dead horses that had either been killed by the enemy's bullets or by exhaustion, as there had been no forage for several days."[44]

In addition to declining provisions, the British army continually lost other necessary supplies and equipment as they advanced, fought, and then retreated to their final encampment. Braunschweig officer Schuler von Senden wrote on October 10, just before digging in, that "we have burned our tents and all encumbrances, because the troops can no longer carry them."[45] In typical circumstances, the British army would have a full complement of tools with which to construct and maintain defensive outworks and entrenchments (figure 6.6). However, by the time they reached Victory Woods, they would have few of these items to assist them in constructing protective earthworks. This may have contributed to selecting areas of sandy soils for breastworks, since they may have been easier to excavate and shape.

By the time they reoccupied the heights of Saratoga and Victory Woods, the British army was exhausted from its engagement with the enemy, suffering as a result of declining weather conditions, fighting sickness, disease, and injuries,[46] and in want of food and supplies. The bedraggled army and its leaders capitulated on October 17, apparently without any hint of remorse. "But as it was, will it be said, my Lord," Burgoyne wrote to Lord George Germain in London, "that in the exhausted condition described, and in the jaws of famine, and invested by quadruple numbers, a treaty which saves the army to the state . . . was not more than could have been expected?"[47]

Interpretations

The archaeological evidence of the British occupation of Victory Woods is as scant as their stay was brief. Evidence is limited to the partially eroded remains of two earthworks and a depression that may have served as a magazine. In spite of the large number of soldiers at the British encampment, no artifacts associated with the period were recovered. Given that the earthworks were visible at the surface, the most surprising result of the fieldwork is the absence of related cultural material. Three potential theories may help to explain this absence: (1) looters have already collected the Revolutionary War–era artifacts at the site; (2) the soldiers were concentrated in parts of the encampment not yet excavated, where artifacts are more likely to be found, or in previously destroyed areas; and (3) the British left few artifacts during their brief stay as many of their supplies were abandoned following the battles in expectation of a full-fledged retreat. It seems likely all three of these hypotheses have merit and the effects of each of the three contributed in some respect to the overall pattern witnessed at the site. Archaeologists at similar British encampments in New Jersey have struggled with the same lack of artifacts and utilized similar sets of explanations as to the exact cause.[48]

In the areas covered by the archaeological study, the landscape evidenced few distinct disturbances from looting pits. Yet it is known that looting has been a perennial problem at the Victory Woods site.[49] In fact, artifacts recovered from "near" the Saratoga battlefield are regularly advertised for sale on eBay. The principal tool employed by looters is the metal detector, thus musket balls, buckles, and buttons have likely been removed from much of the site. However, the absence of all other cultural material from the period, including ceramic sherds, pipe stems, and vessel glass, is curious. As suggested at other military sites, the use of metal detectors in a formal archaeological study may be much more productive in terms of artifact recovery than the trenching excavations utilized for the present study.[50]

Based on the size of the British encampment as reported on late eighteenth-century historic maps, the troops may simply have been concentrated elsewhere. If they spent little time defending the hastily built earthworks in the archaeological study area, one would expect to find few artifacts. Figure 6.1 presents the approximate location and size of the defensive earthworks in relation to Victory Woods in the modern context. Considering that the archaeological study covered only a small portion of the encampment, it is plausible that artifact deposits exist in other areas.

Another explanation for the absence of artifacts in the archaeological study area points to the nature of the occupation. Under military threat from the Americans, the exhausted British troops fell back to Victory Woods and hastily erected the defensive works. Short on food and other supplies, the British waited for reinforcements that never arrived. In the immediate aftermath of the Battles of Saratoga, many within the British army envisioned a full-fledged retreat to the safety of Fort Edward and eventually Fort Ticonderoga. Whether on their own, or as directed by their commanding officers, many British troops left or destroyed their equipment as they fled northward—completely unaware that Burgoyne would later halt the march and order the army to erect a defensive position at what became Victory Woods.

Too weak to mount a fight against the numerically superior American forces, the British negotiated their surrender eight days later. Given the haste with which the earthworks were built, it is understandable that they contained no artifacts. Stated succinctly: little food and supplies equals little garbage for archaeologists to later recover. With the exception of the earthen defensive features, the archaeological footprint left behind by the troops was very light.

Conclusions

At Victory Woods, the archaeology revealed three defensive features within Burgoyne's final encampment but a dearth of artifacts from his army. Victory Woods and the heights over the confluence of the Fish Creek and Hudson were selected by the British as a strong tactical position that commanded the surrounding areas. The earthworks were built around natural springs that likely provided water for the troops as well as for their horses and cattle. Given the hurried nature of the construction, the earthworks were likely sited in areas that followed along natural high ground and could be easily excavated with the few tools left available to the struggling British army.

The stronghold at Victory Woods belied the perils that Burgoyne and his army faced after the battles. The Saratoga countryside at this time was dotted with small farms, yet it could not support a large standing army during the course of a month with adequate fresh food for the troops and forage for the animals. Once constrained within the cantonment and surrounded by American forces, the deteriorating situation of dwindling supplies, provisions, and forage was exacerbated. The few resources provided by the Saratoga hillside were steadily exhausted, and Americans quickly surrounded the British in a siege that could not be broken. The archaeological studies highlight the role of the environment and landscape, and how these variables contributed to Burgoyne's agonizing decision to save his army and capitulate to the enemy.

NOTES

1. W. A. Roberts, *Place in History: Albany in the Age of Revolution* (Albany: State University of New York Press, 2010), 65. Although the quote is thought to be apocryphal and of nineteenth-century origin, it captures the emotions of the moment.

2. Hartgen Archeological Associates (Hartgen) was retained by the National Park Service (NPS) to conduct an archaeological identification study at Victory Woods, and the geophysical investigation was conducted by Radar Solutions International (RSI). Hartgen,

"Archeological Identification Study (Vol. 2), Victory Woods, Village of Victory, Saratoga County, New York," manuscript on file, Office of Parks, Recreation and Historic Preservation, Waterford, NY, 2007.

3. C. Stevens, L. White, W. A. Griswold, and M. C. Brown, *Cultural Landscape Report and Archeological Assessment for Victory Woods, Saratoga National Historical Park, Saratoga, New York* (Boston: US Department of the Interior, National Park Service, 2007).

4. The geophysical surveys occurred in October through December 2005, and again in February 2006. The subsequent archaeological fieldwork was undertaken in April 2006.

5. T. Holmes and L. Smith-Holmes, *Saratoga: America's Battlefield* (Charleston, SC: History Press, 2010), 20.

6. Stevens et al., *Cultural Landscape Report and Archeological Assessment*, 39.

7. Holmes and Smith-Holmes, *Saratoga: America's Battlefield*, 20–21.

8. Stevens et al., *Cultural Landscape Report and Archeological Assessment*, 31.

9. Ibid., 31–32.

10. R. M. Ketchum, *Saratoga: Turning Point of America's Revolutionary War* (New York: Henry Holt, 1997).

11. Stevens et al., *Cultural Landscape Report and Archeological Assessment*, 32–33.

12. *The Specht Journal* chronicles the activities of Colonel Johann Friedrich Specht, commander of the 1st German Brigade, who served during the entire Burgoyne campaign. The journal has been attributed to a close subordinate who has yet to be identified. J. F. Specht, *The Specht Journal: A Military Journal of the Burgoyne Campaign*, trans. Helga Doblin, ed. M. C. Lynn (Westport, CT: Greenwood Press, 1995), 75.

13. Specht, *Specht Journal*, 110.

14. J. F. Luzader, *Saratoga: A Military History of the Decisive Campaign of the American Revolution* (New York: Savas Beatie, 2008), 306.

15. Stevens et al., *Cultural Landscape Report and Archeological Assessment*, 64.

16. Specht, *Specht Journal*, 94–95.

17. Ibid.

18. Luzader, *Saratoga*, 304–5.

19. Ibid., 311.

20. Stevens et al., *Cultural Landscape Report and Archeological Assessment*, 84–85.

21. Ibid., 85.

22. Ibid., 88–89.

23. Ibid.

24. J. H. Brandow, *The Story of Old Saratoga and History of Schuylerville* (Albany, NY: Fort Orange Press, 1900), 368.

25. Stevens et al., *Cultural Landscape Report and Archeological Assessment*, 132, 135.

26. J. Muller, *The Attac and Defence of Fortified Places*, 2nd ed., ed. D. Manthey (1757; repr., Arlington, VA: Flower-de-Luce Books, Invisible College Press, 2004), 300–301.

27. Hartgen, "Archeological Identification Study," 2007.

28. Muller, *Attac and Defence of Fortified Places*, 278, 288.

29. L. Lochee, *Elements of Field Fortification* (London: T. Cadwell and T. Egerton, 1783), 10.

30. D. R. Cubbison, *Historic Structures Report: The Redoubts of West Point* (West Point, NY: Directorate of Housing and Public Works, US Military Academy, 2004), 8.

31. D. R. Snow, *Archaeological Atlas of the Saratoga Battlefield* (Albany: State University of New York at Albany, 1977), 24; G. K. Kelso and D. P. Hsu, "Battlefield Palynology: Reinterpretation of British Earthworks, Saratoga National Historical Park, Stillwater, New York," *Northeast Historical Archaeology* 24, no. 1 (1995): 87–96.

32. Ketchum, *Saratoga: Turning Point*, 417.

33. Ibid., 241.

34. Ibid., 242.

35. T. Corbett, *No Turning Point: The Saratoga Campaign in Perspective* (Norman: University of Oklahoma Press, 2012), 183–84; Luzader, *Saratoga*, 94–95; Ketchum, *Saratoga: Turning Point*, 293.

36. W. A. Griswold and T. B. Largy, "A Tale of Two Middens," in *Soldiers, Cities, and Landscapes: Papers in Honor of Charles L. Fisher*, ed. P. B. Drooker and J. P. Hart (Albany: New York State Education Department, 2010), 57–66.

37. D. J. Pippin, "Distressed for the Want of Provisions: Supplying the British Soldier on Carleton Island (1778–1784)," in *Soldiers, Cities, and Landscapes: Papers in Honor of Charles L. Fisher*, ed. P. B. Drooker and J. P. Hart (Albany: New York State Education Department, 2010), 67–86.

38. In the best of circumstances, the daily rations provided by the British army to its soldiers in North America included: "1.5 pounds of flour or bread; 1 pound of beef or .5 pound of pork [likely salted]; a quarter pint of peas; an ounce of butter; and an ounce of rice"; Pippin, "Distressed for the Want of Provisions," 76.

39. F. C. Riedesel, *Diary of Lady Riedesel: Letters and Journals Relating to the War of American Independence and the Capture of German Troops at Saratoga* (Scarborough, ON: German-Canadian Museum of Applied History, n.d.), 109.

40. Ibid., 116.

41. Ibid., 109.

42. Specht, *Specht Journal*, 96–97.

43. Ibid.

44. Ketchum, *Saratoga: Turning Point*, 417.

45. Luzader, *Saratoga*, 303.

46. P. Kopperman, "The Numbers Game: Health Issues in the Army That Burgoyne Led to Saratoga," *New York History* 88, no. 3 (2007): 255–86.

47. Luzader, *Saratoga*, 337.

48. R. F. Veit, R. G. Wieneck, and J. W. Martin, "Route 18 Extension, Section 2A: Phase II Archaeological Investigation and Data Recovery, British Revolutionary War Encampment (28-Mi-212), Piscataway Township, Middlesex County, New Jersey," manuscript on file, State Historic Preservation Office, Trenton, NJ, 2008.

49. Stevens et al., *Cultural Landscape Report and Archeological Assessment*.

50. W. F. Hanna, "Geophysics, Some Recommendations and Applications," in *The Historical Archaeology of Military Sites: Method and Topic*, ed. C. R. Geier, L. E. Babits, D. D. Scott, and D. G. Orr (College Station: Texas A&M University Press, 2010), 11–20; D. D. Scott, R. A. Fox Jr., M. A. Connor, and D. Harmon, *Archaeological Perspectives on the Battle of the Little Bighorn* (Norman: University of Oklahoma Press, 1989); D. M. Sivilich, "Analyzing Musket Balls to Interpret a Revolutionary War Site," *Historical Archaeology* 30, no. 2 (1996): 101–9.

CHAPTER SEVEN | SCOTT STULL, MICHAEL ROGERS, AND LEN TANTILLO

The Surrender and Aftermath of the Battles

FOLLOWING THE Battles of Saratoga, Burgoyne and his army retreated northward, intending to return to Canada. Burgoyne's grand strategy of dividing the colonies had failed because of fierce and sustained opposition from the army led by Gates. Lieutenant-Colonel St. Leger, commander of the western British force, had been unable to pass Fort Stanwix in August to come to Burgoyne's aid from the west, as the fort had been reinforced by American forces, including local militia and troops moving from the east. Likewise, General Clinton's plans to reinforce Burgoyne from the south amounted to little more than raids reaching only as far as Peekskill on October 5. Ultimately, Clinton was unable to penetrate the fortified Hudson Highlands and reach Burgoyne's army.

This chapter examines the aftermath of the Saratoga battles, including Burgoyne's surrender and his army's grounding of arms near Fort Hardy, a French and Indian War supply fort in Saratoga that had fallen into disrepair by the time of the American Revolution. The land containing Fort Hardy and the Field of Grounded Arms has undergone archaeological and geophysical examination culminating in the artistic reconstruction of the landscape at the time of the surrender. This chapter draws on historical and archaeological information generated by these studies to examine what the reconstructed landscape would have looked like at the time of the surrender.

The Retreat and Surrender

Although his situation was increasingly dire, Burgoyne's retreat was anything but disorganized. When the army reached the village of Saratoga, now Schuylerville, the British forces established defensive positions north and west of the village. A significant force was located on the high ground west of the village and north of the Fishkill (also referred to as Fish Creek), an area now known as Victory Woods. The British force here included five British battalions, a company of British Rangers, and most of the army's American loyalist corps, all utilizing a position commanding the road along the Fishkill to the west, one established during their advance to Stillwater (see chapter 6). Further north, Burgoyne's main forces deployed along the ridge and commandeered rebel barracks. To protect their position from attack along the Hudson River, they placed an artillery unit overlooking the farm fields between Saratoga and the river. From this position, Burgoyne dispatched a unit to Fort Edward to prepare to move the army further north on its journey back to Canada. Burgoyne was aware of the American forces coming north, referring to them as a large column of troops. Located along the road south of the Fishkill, General Schuyler's house blocked the field of fire from Burgoyne's artillery, so he ordered Schuyler's house and outbuildings burned.[1]

October 11, 1777

The American forces did not know how Burgoyne had deployed his forces. When the working party left for Fort Edward, General Gates believed that the bulk of the British army had moved north, leaving only limited protection for their baggage. After reaching the Fishkill on the afternoon of October 10, Gates set up camp. The next morning, light infantry under Colonel Daniel Morgan advanced to the north and west and encountered a British picket line, losing three soldiers in the ensuing skirmish. Gates sent two brigades commanded by Brigadier Generals John Nixon and John Glover under cover of fog to cross the creek and attack the British camp, intending to capture the baggage with little opposition. The bulk of the American army waited on the south bank of the Fishkill while Nixon crossed to the north side close to where it emptied into the Hudson, the site of the French and Indian War Fort Hardy. Upon crossing, Nixon captured a unit of sixty men and several bateaux. A "deserter" informed them that the full army was still present. A British reconnoitering party of thirty-five men was subsequently captured, confirming that intelligence. By this point, the morning fog had burned off, revealing the enemy artillery stationed above the fields and a British army prepared to face the advancing Americans. Heavy fire by both musketry and cannon met the Americans, forcing Nixon's advance guard to retreat in disarray back across the Fishkill. The clearest account of the battle action in the vicinity of Fort Hardy and the Field of Grounded Arms comes from Stone:

> Meanwhile, General Gates, who had begun the pursuit at noon of the 10th with his main army, reached the high ground south of Fish creek, at four

the same afternoon. The departure of Burgoyne's working party for Fort Edward led him to believe that the entire British army was in full retreat having left only a small guard to protect their baggage. Acting upon this impression, he ordered Nixon and Glover, with their brigades, to cross the creek early next morning, under cover of the fog which at this time of year usually prevails till after sunrise, and attack the British camp. The English general had notice of this plan, and placing a battery in position, he posted his troops in ambush behind the thickets along the banks of the creek; and concealed also by the fog, waited the attack confident of victory. At early daylight, Morgan, who had again been selected to begin the action, crossed the creek with his men, on a raft of floating logs, and falling in with a British picket, was fired upon, losing a lieutenant, and two privates [this action was outside the Fort Hardy area]. This led him to believe that the main body of the enemy had not moved, in which case, with the creek in his rear, enveloped by a dense fog and unacquainted with the ground, he felt his position to be most critical. Meanwhile, the whole army advanced as far as the south bank of the creek and halted. Nixon, however, who was in advance, had already crossed the stream near its confluence with the Hudson, and captured a picket of sixty men, and a number of bateaux, and Glover was preparing to follow him, when a "deserter" from the enemy confirmed the suspicions of Morgan. This was corroborated a few moments afterward, by the capture of a reconnoitering party of thirty-five men by the advanced guard under Captain Goodale of Putnam's regiment, who, discerning them through the fog just as he neared the opposite bank, charged and took them without firing a gun. Gates was at this time at his headquarters a mile and a half in the rear and before intelligence could be sent to him, the fog cleared up, and exposed the entire British army under arms. A heavy fire of artillery and musketry was immediately opened upon Nixon's brigade, and they retreated in considerable disorder across the creek.[2]

After the retreat by Nixon, the American and British forces settled into a stalemate. The American forces could not dislodge the British, and the British could not force their way out and back to Ticonderoga. The positions remained as they were for the next week, until the British surrender.

Landscape

The Hudson River effectively served as the eastern boundary of the conflict. The Americans were established on the southern side of Fish Creek while the British were on the north. The western boundary of the battle area was the high ground of the river terrace approximately three-quarters of a mile to the west. At the time of the battle, the main road between Albany and Fort Edward, River Road, passed along the base of this terrace, and a second road paralleled Fish Creek from the main road to the west. The village of Saratoga was divided by Fish Creek, with settlement primarily on the south side of the creek. The American position on the south side of Fish Creek included the just-burned residence and ancillary structures of General Schuyler. The lands on the north side of Fish Creek were farm fields, divided by what appear to be ditches and fence lines. These fields also contained the remains of Fort Hardy, illustrated and labeled as ruins on contemporary maps. A second, small tributary of the Hudson River was located north of Fish Creek, curving to the north and west as it crossed through the farmlands. North of that tributary was a rise, located between the river terrace and the Hudson River. West of River Road and on the terrace there were woodlands, either forest or orchards, with four lesser roadways going west from River Road, giving access to the terrace and woodlands.

The American army was at a distinct disadvantage entering into the battle area on October 11, 1777. While heavy morning fog concealed their actions for a period of time, when the fog lifted they were exposed to the British forces situated in a vastly superior position. The "Artillery of the Park" are noted by Faden to have been located on the rise to the north of the battle area in earthworks or other fortifications. Northwest of the battle area, four battalions of the British army were located on the river terrace, at least partially concealed in the woodland according to the 1780 Faden map (figure 7.1), but with easy access to the battle area by roadways. Additional British units were located to the north and west, which prevented American flanking forces from engaging in the battle area. Nixon's brigade, the lead American forces in the battle area, was outpositioned on the landscape, with the British occupying the advantageous terrain, leading to the hasty American retreat across Fish Creek. Supporting American artillery was located across the Hudson River and thus outside the range to be effective. The woodland west of the October 11 battlefield served as a place to provide cover for the British forces.[3] Although the ruins of Fort Hardy were noted on the landscape, they did not serve as an important part of the military terrain. Instead, they served to mark the location, providing a specific context to both sides in the conflict.

The Surrender

As noted previously, the British were in a strong strategic position, but unable to move. Colonel Morgan's forces blocked them to the west, the bulk of the American army to the south, and even presuming the logistics of crossing the Hudson could have been managed, American artillery and infantry forces were

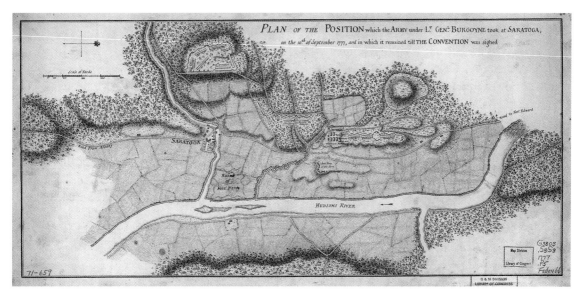

FIGURE 7.1. The 1780 William Faden map of the position of the British army at Saratoga in October. The site of Fort Hardy is in the center left of the map. River Road passes along the base of the slope at this time. Library of Congress Maps of North America, 1750–1789, no. 1178.

located on the east bank to prevent that avenue of escape. After nearly a week, Burgoyne decided to surrender, but on his own conditions. The terms of surrender were called a convention, allowing Burgoyne to save some small measure of his reputation. The formal act of surrender took place about a mile south of the village of Saratoga on October 17, 1777. General Burgoyne gave up his sword to General Gates, a scene made famous by the 1821 *Surrender of General Burgoyne* by John Trumbull, now displayed in the US Capitol. This location was close to where Gates had his field headquarters, described as one-and-a-half miles south of Saratoga. Burgoyne saw the surrender and convention as a calamitous but honorable event, as it preserved the lives of the survivors of the battles.[4] The first article of the convention stated: "The troops under General Burgoyne are to march out of their camp with the honours of war, and the artillery of the entrenchments, to the verge of the river, where the old fort stood, where the arms and artillery are to be left. The arms to be piled by word of command of their own officers."[5]

The Field of Grounded Arms, as it came to be called, was in the same location as the October 11 skirmish between Nixon's troops and the British. The Americans obtained much-needed supplies, including a train of brass artillery consisting of thirty pieces of artillery, 4,647 muskets, 190 sets of harness, and a large supply of ammunition. The British and allied prisoners numbered 5,804.[6]

Fort Hardy and the Field of Grounded Arms Today

A visitor to the site of Fort Hardy and the Field of Grounded Arms today will find a scene completely different from the one Burgoyne's men encountered in 1777. The area contains a community park, marina, and houses, and no visible remains of the fort exist above ground; no artifacts of the encounter have been reported from the site.

With no aboveground remains visible, the exact location of the Field of Grounded Arms remained unclear. How could its location be identified when all traces of it and Fort Hardy had vanished? The field was reported to lay between the old fort and the colonial-era road, now the alignment of the Champlain Canal.[7] Thus, locating the "old fort" was key to identifying the precise location of the field. The "Plan of Saratogha" shows the extent of the earthworks around Fort Hardy and, based on the scale, it suggests an area of approximately ten to fifteen acres (figure 7.2). Locating the earthworks around Fort Hardy, the "low mounds" of the Revolutionary era, would help pinpoint the eastern boundary of the Field of Grounded Arms.

A French and Indian War supply base, Fort Hardy was constructed in stages from 1755 to 1757 by the British as part of the campaign in the northern Hudson Valley and Lake Champlain.[8] Located on the Hudson River at the mouth of Fish Creek, it guarded a ferry crossing on the Hudson. The fort was named for Sir Charles Hardy, royal governor of New York.[9] The first fortified structure at the mouth of the Fishkill was a blockhouse or similar temporary fort, built in 1755 by Colonel Phineas Lyman.[10] The Bouquet and Haldimand map (not pictured) suggests that the earthworks had been planned from the outset, and shows the location of the blockhouse at the mouth of the Fishkill where it enters the Hudson River. Fort Hardy's earthworks were completed in 1756 to provide defensible camping grounds, which were used for the 48th Regiment. The main fort structure was built in 1757 under Colonel James Montressor, and the earlier 1755 structure was demolished at this time. The Montressor fort is documented both in his journal and with drawings. Montressor's drawing served as the basis of the widely used Rocque map, which only shows the central portion of the fortification that Montressor constructed and not the larger outlying earthworks.[11] Fort Hardy was never attacked during the French and Indian War, and was abandoned after peace returned in 1763. Five barracks buildings that remained standing were used as late as 1771 as homes by local residents.[12]

While a fortified center, Fort Hardy was not intended to be a major battle fort. The "Plan of Saratogha" (figure 7.2) shows that the fort is surrounded by high ground, including a rise with the words "Ground commanded" north of the fort. Because Fort Hardy was designed to control and defend the road between Albany and Fort Edward (figure 7.3), as well as protect British forces from raids

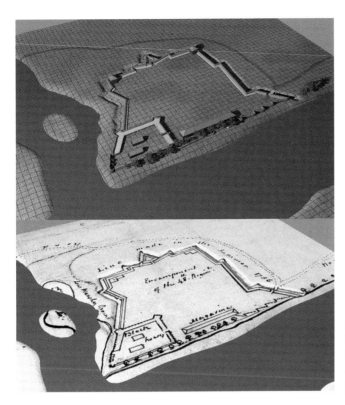

FIGURE 7.2. Digital reconstruction of Fort Hardy as it would have looked in 1757 (*above*); digital reconstruction overlaid on the "Plan of Saratogha" (*below*). L. F. Tantillo, 2012.

that typified the early phases of the French and Indian War, the defenses of the fort needed to be effective and expedient, especially the earthworks. One common form of construction was to reinforce the exposed earthen faces of the ditches and ramparts using a fascine, a bundle of saplings or branches (figure 7.4), or *saucissons*, made with larger branches.[13] These wall liners were then anchored in the ground with stakes to prevent the earthen faces from slumping. Earthworks built in this fashion do not generally survive lengthy exposure to the elements, and this construction technique contributed to the ruined condition of Fort Hardy; that is, the low mounds as described in the Revolutionary War–period documents.[14]

Archaeogeophysical and Archaeological Investigations

As part of an archaeological study for new water and electrical line installations in present-day Schuylerville, Black Drake Consulting (a local archaeological and cultural resources consulting firm) conducted shovel testing and backhoe trenching in the vicinity of Fort Hardy in 2003. One of the backhoe trenches uncovered a ditch-like feature in the eastern portion of the park near the Hudson

FIGURE 7.3. Reconstructed Fort Hardy (*above*), compared to the "Prospect of Saratogha, 1757" (*below*). Library of Congress LC-DIG-ds-02053; L. F. Tantillo, 2012.

River that was suspected to be part of Fort Hardy. Black Drake Consulting used ground-penetrating radar (GPR) to investigate the ditch feature. Later investigations to identify the remains of Fort Hardy, including shovel test pits excavated along two transects, recovered material from the late nineteenth and early twentieth centuries, but failed to identify additional evidence of Fort Hardy.[15]

The shovel testing was followed by more intensive archaeogeophysical surveys.[16] A cesium magnetometer[17] and GPR[18] were used in areas likely to bisect the earthwork defenses of the fort (figure 7.5). The GPR located a buried, fourteen-meter-wide (approximately forty-five feet) mound-trench-mound feature consistent with the earthwork defenses of Fort Hardy (figure 7.4). GPR data were gathered along transects spaced fifty centimeters apart. The mound-trench-mound feature appears in seventy contiguous GPR profiles, making it thirty-five meters (approximately 115 feet) long before it disappears beneath a modern basketball court.

Based on the GPR results, Stull and Rogers created a model of the buried remains to identify the most promising locations to excavate to uncover earthwork defense features such as post molds. Excavation was limited to prevent

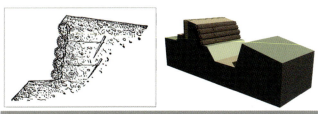

FIGURE 7.4. *Upper left*, fascines and anchoring system (Sebastien Le Prestre de Vauban, *Traite des Sieges et L'Attaque des Places*, 1704); *upper right*, reconstruction of fascine bundles at Fort Hardy; *lower*, reconstruction of western earthworks. L. F. Tantillo, 2012.

disruption to the park, and a single 1.0 meter by 0.5 meter excavation unit was targeted to confirm the mound-trench-mound structure located in the GPR signature. The excavation unit revealed soils that slope off as expected from the GPR, and also uncovered three small post molds at the top of the rise, precisely where a fascine bundle would have been anchored on an earthwork embankment.[19] This provides strong evidence that the buried ruins of Fort Hardy have been located, marking the boundary of the Field of Grounded Arms in the area of Reds Road and the Visitor's Center.

Reconstructing Fort Hardy

Recreating aspects of archaeologically and historically known sites has a long history,[20] and can provide new insight about these sites that other forms of study cannot provide. There are numerous examples of reconstructed colonial-era forts in America. Fort Stanwix National Monument in Rome, New York, is a comparable site, being a mainly earthen fortification in the same region. While valuable from both an experimental and interpretive perspective, such reconstructions are expensive and require major investments in land, time, money, and maintenance. For these reasons, digital reconstructions are being used to provide similar insights into the form and use of historic sites with far less expense. This type of digital investigation was used at Fort Hardy in an effort to

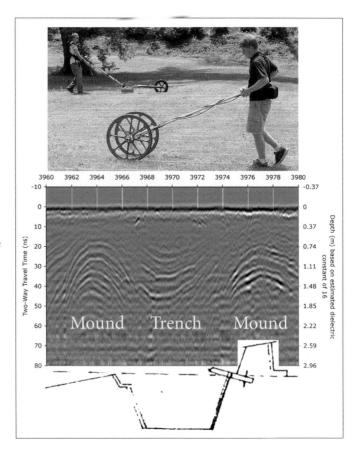

FIGURE 7.5. *Upper*, photograph of the archaeogeophysical instruments used at Fort Hardy Park to locate below-ground evidence of Fort Hardy. A Geometrics G-858 dual cesium magnetometer (Geometrics, 1995) is in the foreground and a Geophysical Survey System (GSSI) SIR-3000 with a 400 MHz antenna (GSSI, 2003) is in the background; *center*, radargram showing evidence for the buried earthwork defenses of Fort Hardy; *lower*, detail from the 1757 "Plan of Fort Hardy" by Colonel James Montressor showing the section through the earthworks, which matches the results of the archaeological investigation. British Museum Crown Collection, cxxi: 97.

understand the nature of the fort and how the site would have been used in the French and Indian War.

While the "Plan of Saratogha" (figure 7.2) served as the main source for the reconstruction, a second source, the "Prospect of Saratogha, 1757" (figure 7.3), provided corroborating evidence. The digital reconstruction was created using these two sources and the documentary evidence from the construction of the fort. The first step in creating the reconstruction was establishing the landforms and landscape, including the earthworks of the rampart and ditch. This was followed by the addition of the structures visible on the map and prospect (figures 7.2 and 7.3).

Fort Hardy possessed some unique features according to the "Plan of Saratogha" and the "Prospect of Saratogha." One distinctive feature was the line of trees along the bank of the Hudson River, visible in figure 7.2. Another section of the fort along the river bank had a sawtooth palisade adjacent to the gate, an unusual aspect to Fort Hardy, also visible in figure 7.2. Precisely why this section was constructed in this fashion is uncertain. Other features include the blockhouses on the western portion of the fort and the defended portion at the southeast illustrated on the Montressor 1757 plan. This is often considered by modern researchers to be the "core" of the fort, but the reconstruction and the 1757 prospect and map reveal that the earthworks were an integral part of the fort, particularly as a safe camping ground for troops in transit to and from the active campaign areas to the north. The accuracy of the reconstruction was compared to the image of the fort in the 1757 prospect. Although there are slight differences between the map and the prospect, the overall similarities are strong. The earthworks, rampart, and ditch are present, as are the structures within the fort, such as the magazine, gate, blockhouses, and other buildings. The prospect also shows the huts built to house the troops camping within the fort, such as those of the 48th Regiment who were there in 1756.

Another aspect of the fort reconstruction was to understand the use of fascines, evidence for which was found in the archaeological excavations. These bundles were anchored into the earth with spikes through the fascine bundles themselves and additional anchors buried in the rampart, as illustrated in a 1704 military manual.[21] The postholes for these anchors were found in the excavation in 2007.[22] Although these details are not visible in the finished reconstruction or the 1757 prospect, they are an important part of the evidence for the construction of Fort Hardy. Because these bundles were fairly small and held in place by buried ropes and posts, the structural stability of the fort was limited to the period that these elements were intact, prior to their decay. Once the cords and bundles rotted away, the earthworks would slump and the ditches would fill with earth from the eroding ramparts. Fortunately, the structure was still there and could be detected by subsurface investigation. The overall reconstruction (figure 7.2) provides us with the needed evidence to understand the fort as it was built, and the nature of that construction allows us to understand how it would have decayed after abandonment.

Fort Hardy was not simply the "core" area of barracks and fortifications illustrated in the 1765 Roque map but included the larger system of earthworks. The Fadden map revealed the pattern of fields and the ruined fort in 1777, and the Articles of Convention stated that the Field of Grounded Arms was located by the old fort, which is best interpreted as the fields west of the earthworks. Finding the earthworks meant the boundary of the Field of Grounded Arms had been found (figure 7.6).

After the Surrender

After the surrender, the American forces held nearly 6,000 prisoners, thirty pieces of artillery, and more than 4,500 muskets and accompanying ammunition. The weapons were distributed to the American military forces, and the prisoners

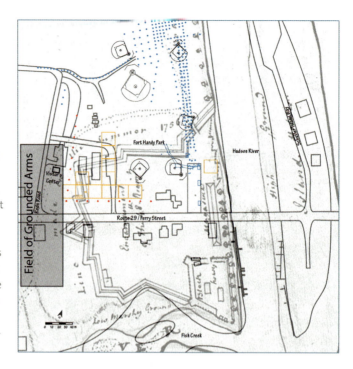

FIGURE 7.6. Drawing showing archaeological investigations at Fort Hardy Park. The eastern and northern dots and rectangles are Black Drake Consulting shovel test pits and mechanical test pits. The small squares and lines are Black Drake Consulting GPR results. Southern and western dots are the best approximation of the shovel test pits excavated by D. Klinge. Larger squares are Stull and Rogers archaeogeophysics survey units. Units 5 and 11 contain the GPR mound-trench-mound feature. The small rectangle in unit 5 is the location of the Stull and Rogers test excavation that uncovered post molds. British Museum Crown Collection, cxxi: 96.

were marched to Cambridge, Massachusetts, just outside Boston, for intended return to England. Terms of the convention required that the soldiers were not to return to fight in the war again, and Congress demanded a list of names of the soldiers to confirm British compliance with the convention. When this was refused, Congress declined to honor the return article, leading to great consternation in England, and especially in Parliament.[23] Some of the captured troops were sent to England, including Burgoyne and some of his officers, while others were kept confined and eventually marched to the Albemarle Barracks outside Charlottesville, Virginia. According to Burgoyne, five or six hundred deserted as individuals, and not as complete regiments or military units. Most had left the military service, becoming day laborers or tradesmen, with a few attempting to rejoin the British army under Generals Howe or Clinton.[24]

General John Burgoyne was not well received in England after the loss at Saratoga, as the blame for the loss was placed solely at his hands. He sought an audience with the King to clear his name, but was denied. Burgoyne suggests it was Lord George Germain, secretary of state for the colonies, who blocked this audience. Burgoyne thought that the state of affairs in America was quite different from what it was believed to be in the King's council, and contrary to the position promoted by Lord Germain. Thus, Burgoyne was never given the opportunity to clear himself in person.[25] In 1778, Burgoyne addressed Parliament to answer questions about the events at Saratoga and the broader execution of the conflict, where he reiterated his charges against Lord Germain and associated ministers, but rarely by name. There was an attempt to remove Burgoyne from his seat in Parliament, but that effort failed. In 1779, Burgoyne offered the resignation of his military commission, which was accepted.[26]

After his resignation from the army, Burgoyne returned to being a playwright. Prior to joining the British army in 1775, Burgoyne had written a comic play, *The Maid in the Oaks,* in 1774. His play *The Lord of the Manor* was later published in 1780 and *The Heiress* in 1786. These comedies and other plays were performed in London at the Theatre-Royal in Drury Lane.[27] Burgoyne returned to active military service in 1782 after he was appointed commander in chief in Ireland. John Burgoyne died in 1792 at his home in Mayfair, London.

As for General Horatio Gates, he was moved to the Highlands Department of the American army in 1778, then on to the Eastern Department. In June of 1780, Gates was given command of the Southern Department. Gates commanded every region of the war except the Western Department, the only general to serve so widely, in part due to his successes at Saratoga and in part due to his apparent effectiveness at leading citizen-soldier militias rather than a standing regular army. Just over one month after taking command of the Southern Department, Gates suffered a humiliating defeat at the Battle of Camden in South Carolina. In October, Gates was replaced as commander of the Southern Department, and the supporters of a citizen militia lost their most promising advocate.[28] Gates rejoined the main army in October 1782. In 1783, Gates was part of a group that was prepared to use the military strength of the army to force Congress on issues of pension and pay, as Congress considered dismantling the Continental army to reduce expenditures. Although Gates may have been in favor of militias to avoid the use of a professional army against the citizens of the country, he apparently did not have qualms about using that army against the elected representatives of the people. George Washington did not support the use of force, and in March the issue was resolved peaceably. The peace treaty was signed with Great Britain in 1783, eight years after the beginning of the conflict at Lexington and Concord.[29] Horatio Gates returned to his estate in Virginia after the war. Gates moved to New York City in 1790, served a term in the Twenty-Fourth New York Assembly in 1800–1801,[30] and died in 1806.

Conclusion

The surrender of Burgoyne's army at Saratoga was, in Burgoyne's own words, calamitous for the British campaign.[31] From the acquisition of the cannons and armaments to the eventual entry of the French into the conflict, the consequences of Burgoyne's defeat changed the course of the war from a series of minor victories and substantial defeats to a pitched conflict between forces of more and more equal standing. The location of the Field of Grounded Arms is a small but important piece of that transformation, and its identification is thus significant. A combination of documentary research and careful, low-impact fieldwork has provided conclusive evidence of the field's location without destroying the archaeological record in the process. The Field of Grounded Arms was bordered by the ruins of a French and Indian War fort, and that distinctive place proved to be the key to locating the landscape where the British gave up their arms. This field, now a public park where children and adults play in peace, was central to the event, which led to the peace and independence of our nation. Often it is the battles that get the most attention when examining the history and archaeology of war, but it is the peace that comes afterward that is the most important.

NOTES

1. John Burgoyne, *The Substance of General Burgoyne's Speeches, on Mr. Vyner's Motion, on the 26th of May* (London: J. Almon, 1778), 9.

2. William L. Stone, *The Campaign of Lieut. Gen. John Burgoyne, and the Expedition of Lieut. Col. Barry St. Leger* (Albany, NY: Joel Munsell, 1877), chap. 11.

3. John Carman and Patricia Carman, "Mustering Landscapes: What Historic Battlefields Share in Common," in *Fields of Conflict: Battlefield Archaeology from the Roman Empire to the Korean War*, 2 vols., ed. D. Scott, L. Babits and C. Haecker (Westport, CT: Praeger, 2007), 43.

4. Burgoyne, *Substance of General Burgoyne's Speeches*, 30–32.

5. *Articles of Convention between Lieutenant General Burgoyne and Major General Gates*, October 16, 1777, Avalon Project at Yale Law School, available at http://avalon.law.yale.edu/18th_century/burgoyne_gates.asp, accessed January 4, 2007.

6. Stone, *Campaign of Lieut. Gen John Burgoyne*, chap. 12; National Archives and Records Administration, Numbered Record Books Concerning Military Operations and Service, Pay and Settlement of Accounts, and Supplies in the War Department Collection of Revolutionary War Records, vol. 129, roll 39, 1777.

7. "[T]o the verge of the river, where the old fort stood, where the arms and artillery are to be left," *Articles of Convention*; Stone, *Campaign of Lieut. Gen John Burgoyne*, appendix 5.

8. David Starbuck, *The Great Warpath: British Military Sites from Albany to Crown Point* (Hanover, NH: University Press of New England, 1999).

9. New York Military Museum, 2006.

10. A nearly identical blockhouse is shown for Still-Water, including the linear storehouse seen later at Fort Hardy parallel to the Hudson River; see Archer B. Hulbert, "Plan of Still-Water with Its Block House etc.," *The Crown Collection of Photographs of American Maps*, ser. 1, vol. 3 (Cleveland: Arthur H. Clark, 1907), cxxi: 104, plate 16.

11. Robert Rogers, *The Annotated and Illustrated Journals of Major Robert Rogers*, annotated and with an introduction by Timothy J. Todish (Fleischmanns, NY: Purple Mountain Press, 2002); John Brandow, *The Story of Old Saratoga* (Albany, NY: Brandow, 1901); Mary Ann Rocque, "A Plan of the Fort at Saratoga," published in *A Set of Plans and Forts in America* (London: Mary Ann Rocque, 1763).

12. Stephen Strach, *The Saratoga Estate of General Phillip Schuyler 1745–1839: An Interpretive*

and Historic Grounds Report (Philadelphia: Eastern National Park and Monument Association, 1986).

13. John Newbery, *The News-Readers Pocket-Book; or, A Military Dictionary* (London: Bible and Sun, 1759), 51.

14. Richard Ketchum, *Saratoga: Turning Point of America's Revolutionary War* (New York: Henry Holt, 1997).

15. The Town of Saratoga contracted Hartgen Archeology Associates (HAA) in 2004 after being awarded a National Park Service American Battlefield Protection Program grant.

16. Chris Gaffney and John Gater, *Revealing the Buried Past: Geophysics for Archaeologists* (Stroud, UK: Tempus, 2003); Michael Rogers, "Archaeological Geophysics: Seeing Deeper with Technology to Complement Digging," in *Archaeology in 3D: Deciphering Buried Sites in the Western US*, ed. Matthew Seddon, Heidi Roberts, and Richard V. N. Ahlstrom (Washington, DC: SAA Press, 2011), 114–37; Scott Stull, Michael Rogers, and Kevin Hurley, "Colonial Houses and Cultural Identity in New York State's Mohawk River Valley," *Archaeological Discovery* 2, no. 2 (2014): 13–25.

17. Arnold Aspinall, Chris F. Gaffney, and Armin Schmidt, *Magnetometry for Archaeologists*, vol. 2 (Lanham, MD: Rowman AltaMira, 2009).

18. Lawrence B. Conyers, *Ground-Penetrating Radar for Archaeology* (Walnut Creek, CA: AltaMira Press, 2004).

19. Scott Stull, Michael Rogers, and Nik Batruch, "Finding Fort Hardy: Combining Documentary Research, Archaeogeophysics, and Excavation to Locate a French and Indian War Fort," *Northeast Historical Archaeology* 79–80 (2014): 125–43.

20. For examples see Stephen Saraydar, *Replicating the Past: The Art and Science of the Archaeological Experiment* (Long Grove, IL: Waveland Press, 2008).

21. Sebastien Le Prestre de Vauban, *Traite des Sieges et L'Attaque des Places* (1704, repr., Paris: Libraire pour l'art Militaire, 1828).

22. Stull, Rogers, and Batruch, "Finding Fort Hardy."

23. Burgoyne, *Substance of General Burgoyne's Speeches*, 1–2, 31–32.

24. Ibid., 14–15.

25. John Burgoyne, *A Letter from Lieut. Gen. Burgoyne to His Constituents, upon His Late Resignation* (London: J. Almon, 1779), 7–10.

26. Burgoyne, *Substance of General Burgoyne's Speeches,* 21–23, 36, 41–42, 49–51; Burgoyne, *Letter.*

27. John Burgoyne, *Airs, Duets, Trios, &c. in the Lord of the Manor, a Comic Opera* (London: T. Evans, 1780); John Burgoyne, *The Heiress: A Comedy in Five Acts* (London: J. Debrett, 1786).

28. Robert K. Wright Jr., *The Continental Army* (Washington, DC: Center of Military History, United States Army, 1983), 153–54, 163, 431–32; Paul David Nelson, "Citizen Soldiers or Regulars: The Views of American General Officers on the Military Establishment, 1775–1781," *Military Affairs* 43, no. 3 (1979): 131.

29. Wright, *Continental Army*, 178–79.

30. Franklin B. Hough, *The New York Civil List* (Albany, NY: Weed, Parsons, 1858), 173.

31. Burgoyne, *Substance of General Burgoyne's Speeches*, 30–31.

CHAPTER EIGHT | DAVID R. STARBUCK

The Schuyler House

Introduction

OF DUTCH DESCENT, the Schuylers were one of the most distinguished families in early America, and their expansion north from the Albany area resulted in the creation of one of the largest estates in Saratoga County. The community they founded in what is now Schuylerville, New York, was bounded by Fish Creek on the north and the Hudson River on the east. Three Schuyler houses were constructed here and the second house, built in 1767, was one of the largest and most significant mansions in the colonies. Along with the mansion, General Schuyler's grand estate was the setting for at least twenty buildings, including sawmills. Its owner, Major General Philip Schuyler (1733–1804), was a delegate to the Continental Congress, a senator, Indian commissioner, the first commander of the Northern army (June 1775 to August 1777), and one of the wealthiest landowners in the region. Above all, he was a great patriot at the time of the American Revolution.[1]

As British troops retreated north after the second battle of Saratoga, on October 10, 1777, Schuyler's second house stood in their way. Schuyler's fields of grain were cut down by General Burgoyne's soldiers, his buildings were vandalized, and then the British burned down the house, mills, and outbuildings, ostensibly so that American forces could not use the buildings for cover. The only buildings that were spared were Schuyler's upper sawmill and a privy house. Undeterred, Schuyler rapidly rebuilt many of the structures, and the third Schuyler house, constructed in late 1777, is the one that stands today.

The National Park Service (NPS) acquired the Philip Schuyler estate in 1950. Located on what is now Route 4, the third Schuyler house is a magnificent structure, open seasonally to the public and surrounded by extensive lawns (figure 8.1). Numerous archaeological excavations have been conducted in the yards since its acquisition, often with the objective of locating traces of the elegant house that was destroyed by the British. These excavations throughout

FIGURE 8.1. 1777 Schuyler house as it appears today (facing northeast). Courtesy of David Starbuck.

the Schuyler yards have discovered burned building foundations, rich artifact concentrations, and very sizeable prehistoric occupations from the Late Archaic and Middle Woodland periods. Throughout the work, a primary goal of the archaeologists and other scholars has been to locate the footprint of each building and thus to bring this estate back to life.

History of the Schuyler Property

In the Paleo-Indian period (ca. 10,000–8000 BC), Native Americans were already traveling along the Hudson River, just east of the Schuyler property,[2] and prehistoric remains are extremely dense in the Schuyler yards and along Fish Creek (the "Fishkill").[3] These finds chiefly date from the Late Archaic period through the Middle Woodland period (ca. 3000 BC to AD 1000), although evidence from other periods has also been identified.

Moving into the early historic period, Captain Johannes Schuyler (1668–1747) arrived and built a garrison house in the early 1700s. By 1745, his son, Philip Schuyler (uncle of General Philip Schuyler), had constructed approximately twenty buildings, most of them on the southern side of Fish Creek. The first

Schuyler house was constructed of brick and contained a cellar; nearby they erected a sawmill, a blacksmith's house, and an unknown number of barns and stables. There were perhaps 200 people in this initial community.

A party of French and Indians, led by Paul Marin de la Malgue, attacked the fledgling settlement on November 28, 1745, and most of the buildings, including the original Schuyler house and Fort Saratoga (located about three-quarters of a mile to the south), were burned to the ground. Philip Schuyler and twelve to fifteen settlers who had taken refuge in the cellar of the house were burned to death, and 109 people were taken prisoner; the rest escaped the attack. It has been claimed by John Brandow that the cellar was rediscovered when the Champlain Canal was widened in 1855. The cellar fill was excavated in 1895, and the foundations and the fireplace inside were totally removed.[4]

From 1745 until 1763 it appears that no buildings stood on the Schuyler grounds, but the British built Fort Hardy to the north, at the mouth of Fish Creek, in August 1757. While the fort fell into disrepair after the Treaty of Paris in 1763, life on the frontier became much safer, and larger numbers of settlers began to move to the Saratoga area; the population rapidly increased from about 200 to 300 people in 1763 to 1,200 people by 1767.[5]

Young Philip Schuyler, who had inherited his uncle's lands (1,900 acres), came to the area to live about 1763 and built two sawmills on Fish Creek between 1763 and 1765. He subsequently constructed a home, the second Schuyler house, in 1767, and a flax mill in about 1768. Schuyler employed hundreds of tenants in his various businesses. Lumber became the chief product of this community, and products of Schuyler's estate were sent to Albany and New York City. By 1775, the American army had become Schuyler's chief customer, and he sold them supplies and lumber. At this time his estate included about twenty-four buildings, including seven barracks buildings north of Fish Creek and seventeen structures on the south side of the creek (figure 8.2). Even his Albany mansion (the "Schuyler Mansion") was built with lumber sawn by his mills in Schuylerville.

During the first year of the Revolution, Philip Schuyler was promoted to the rank of major general and one of his first actions was to fortify Mount Independence on Lake Champlain with the goal of blocking any invasion of British forces from Canada. However, this effort proved unsuccessful, and when the British arrived in Schuylerville ("Old Saratoga") in September 1777, Schuyler's estate stood in the way of Burgoyne's army. Burgoyne's soldiers found extensive fields of wheat and corn that they cut down and also used Schuyler's grist- and sawmills, which helped in provisioning the British army. In the following weeks, the British were responsible for considerable vandalism to Schuyler's home. On October 10, 1777, Burgoyne issued orders that led to the burning of Schuyler's house, mills, and other outbuildings. Schuyler reported afterward that the only

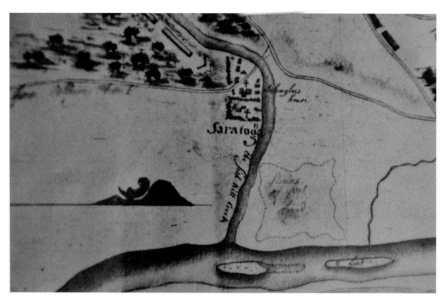

FIGURE 8.2. "Plan of the Position Which the Army under Lieutenant Gel. Burgoine took at Saratoga on the 10th of September 1777 and in Which It Remained till the Convention Was Signed." From the archives of Saratoga National Historical Park.

building not destroyed was his upper sawmill, although a "necessary," or privy, associated with the main house also survived the fire. Historian Benson Lossing later stated that this property had a value of $20,000,[6] a huge sum of money at that time.

General Schuyler's frame house had been the centerpiece of the estate, and it consisted of a large, rectangular main (or central) block, with two enormous rectangular wings extending from either side. Although no contemporary paintings exist of the house prior to its destruction, a 1791 sketch by John Trumbull shows three chimneys rising from the ruins. Much later, John Brandow depicted the center of the house with three stories and the wings with two stories. His conjectural view includes Grecian columns on the front of the house.[7]

East of the house, stretching toward the Hudson River, was a large formal garden that was portrayed on contemporary maps. Years later, this appeared on a circa 1837 map as "an oblong garden, fenced or walled, with twelve garden beds separated by walks. One of the beds, near the center of the garden, has a circular walk."[8] This garden would have been comparable to the great gardens of Europe with decorative walkways, shrubbery, and trees.

After the surrender of the British army on October 17, General Schuyler immediately began to rebuild his country estate by putting his upper sawmill back into operation, turning out planks. A third main house, much smaller than the second, was constructed on the property in November 1777. This house

182 | DAVID R. STARBUCK

was built atop an already-existing foundation, which may have been that of the second house, but scholars are in considerable disagreement on this point. For example, one source states that the second "house stood about twelve rods southeast of the present one."[9] In 1819, Professor Benjamin Silliman described passing "the ruins of General Schuyler's house, which are still conspicuous,"[10] and this would have been impossible if the third house had been built atop the ruins of the second. General Epaphras Hoyt, visiting the battle sites in 1825, mentioned observing the third Schuyler house "standing nearly on the site of General Schuyler's, burnt by Burgoyne."[11] The *Standard Daily* of October 17, 1877, reported that the existing Schuyler house is "northwest of the site of the burned building of 1777."

A kitchen wing was added onto the third Schuyler house about 1780. General Philip Schuyler spent the later years of his life residing at his mansion in Albany, treating his Schuylerville property as a summer residence that he only occasionally visited. His son, John B. Schuyler, managed the estate from 1787 until 1795 but added no new buildings. Philip Schuyler died in Albany in 1804, and his grandson, Philip Schuyler II (son of John B. Schuyler), lived in the Saratoga house from 1811 to 1837. During that time, he erected a cotton mill on Fish Creek, plus a carriage barn east of the main house. Schuyler also promoted construction of the Champlain Canal, which reached the Saratoga area in 1821 to 1822. In 1831, the houses north of Fish Creek were officially given the name of "Schuylerville." The estate subsequently passed out of the Schuyler family's hands when the Panic of 1837 forced Philip Schuyler II to sell. In 1839, the Schuyler house and grounds were purchased by George Strover of Schuylerville, and he lived there until his death in 1886. Strover's descendants lived in the house until 1946, and the property has subsequently been owned and interpreted by the National Park Service.

Archaeology at the Schuyler House

By 1985, the National Park Service had already conducted numerous excavations in the yards around the third Schuyler house. John Cotter had excavated the site in 1958, 1959, and 1964; Jackson Moore in 1959; and Edward Larrabee in 1959 and 1960.[12] Each of these efforts had discovered foundations from small structures, as well as much sheet refuse, but none of the excavations located any remains related to Philip Schuyler's burned mansion.

During the 1958 and 1960 work, Cotter and Larrabee successfully exposed a "burned structure," located about ninety feet southeast of the present Schuyler house. This foundation measured twenty-two feet wide by about forty feet long.[13] Larrabee believed that it dated to about 1788 or 1798, but the presence of Dutch tiles and pottery suggests that it was actually earlier, from the time of either the first or second Schuyler house. Larrabee also noted the presence of a buried foundation and artifacts just north of the present (third) Schuyler house, inside the modern-day service road. Brandow identified a large wood house and slave quarters in this same location,[14] and Larrabee discovered that buildings appeared here on maps dating to 1777, 1820, and 1837.[15]

In addition to these sizeable structures, Larrabee and Cotter excavated a privy and dry well just northwest of the current privy house, two possible root or vegetable cellars, a well, and scattered traces of stone walls or foundations some 80 to 140 feet northeast of the present Schuyler house. These indications of occupation throughout the Schuyler yards suggested a very intensive eighteenth- to nineteenth-century utilization of the property, but the number of features still falls far short of the two dozen structures estimated for the time of General Schuyler's occupation. In fact, if known historic structures were to be counted from both the French and Indian War and postcolonial periods, this two dozen structures would probably rise to forty or more.

In 1985, an extensive magnetometer survey was conducted over much of the Schuyler property in advance of excavations in the yards surrounding the 1777 Schuyler house.[16] During six weeks of excavation, the foundations of the buildings burned by the British in 1777 were sought, in hopes of interpreting and preserving the estate layout from the late eighteenth century. Locating General Schuyler's burned mansion was of paramount importance because it had been the focus of daily life on the estate during Schuyler's period of residence. That said, locating the other two dozen "burned" buildings was of comparable importance because they might be able to shed light on the host of other activities being performed in this frontier community.

The choice of an excavation strategy was shaped by the considerable size of the surviving estate, the potentially small size of typical outbuildings, and the rather inconclusive results from the 1985 survey in the yard north of the present Schuyler house, but it too produced little useful information. We also considered digging rows of shovel test pits but concluded that although they might produce some information about the limits of sheet refuse, they were not well suited to locating foundations, trash pits, or privies (unless an extremely small sampling interval were used).

In the end, we employed backhoe trenches to locate foundations, after which we used one-meter-square test pits to expose individual features and artifact concentrations. Lengthy trenches ensured that foundations would be hit (and not inadvertently "jumped over"), and we closely examined the stratigraphic profiles of the trench walls as we looked for cultural features.

Accordingly, some twenty-eight backhoe trenches were placed throughout the yards of the Schuyler house with care being taken to avoid modern utility lines as well as the root systems of the locust trees that blanket the yard on the

TABLE 8.1 Schuyler Yards, Excavation Trenches

TRENCH	LENGTH (FT.)	DEPTH (FT.)	FEATURES ENCOUNTERED
1	50	4'3"	
2	40	4'	
3	60	3'9"	
4	50	3'4"	
5	?	?	
6	35	2'	much building rubble
7	15	1'6"	rich in Indian artifacts
8	43	2'	
9	25	2'	
10	19	0–15"	foundation of tenant house
11	29	2'6"	modern telephone cable
12	32	1'6"	scatter of bricks in mid-trench
13	89	24"–31"	stone rubble
14	90	1'6"	
15	82	35"–47"	foundation wall at west end
16	40	39"–43"	foundation wall in mid-trench
17a	61	2'4"	
17b	47	2'4"	
18	101	2'7"	
19	96	2'4"	
20	74	2'4"	
21	59	2'7"	
22	—	—	foundation wall in mid-trench
23	—	—	
24	—	—	foundation wall and corner
25	—	—	foundation wall
26	—	—	foundation wall and possible corner
27	—	—	foundation wall and burned wood
28	—	—	foundation wall and burned wood

western (front) side of the house. We also deliberately avoided all areas of the southern yard that were in close proximity to the house. This zone had been heavily trenched by Edward Larrabee and appeared too disturbed to warrant further testing.

Many of the backhoe trenches revealed foundation remains, or the rubble from buildings, and dense artifact concentrations that run north from the

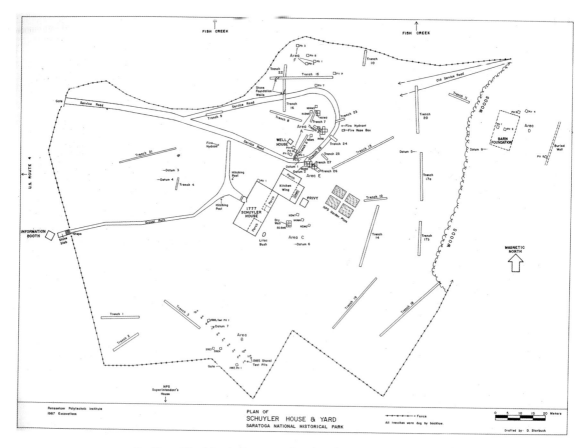

FIGURE 8.3. Plan of the Schuyler houses and yards, 1987 excavation. Courtesy of David Starbuck.

current Schuyler house to the fence abutting Fish Creek (table 8.1; figure 8.3). This prompted the decision to place test pits adjacent to the edges of trenches where features had been located and to expand outward with "block excavations" as additional evidence warranted.

In the north yard, the zones that were more intensively tested were termed areas A, E, and F. In the east yard, just south of the privy house, all pits were designated as area C; in the south yard, the zone was designated area B; and in the woods on the east, atop a nineteenth-century barn foundation, the pits were designated area D. These zones are discussed in sequence, and pit coordinates are listed in table 8.2.

Area A

Backhoe trenches and test pits excavated north of the current Schuyler house revealed the foundation remains of three structures as well as a very sizeable prehistoric occupation. In all cases, the stratigraphy showed a thorough mixing

TABLE 8.2 Schuyler Yards, Excavation Areas

AREA A	Pit 1, Pit 2, Pit 3, Pit 4, Pit 5, Pit 6, Pit 7, Pit 8, Pit 9, N3W5, N3E2, N3E3, N4W1, N4E0, N4E1, N4E3, N5W1, N5E0, N5E1, N6W2, N6E0, N11W2.5, N11W2, N12W5, N12W2.5, N12W2, N14W3
AREA B	(1987): S9E1, S9E4, Pit 1; (1985): Shovel Test Pits 1–12, Pit 1
AREA C	S1W8 (1/2 pit), S1W7 (1/2 pit), N0W8, N0W7, N1W8, N1W7, N2W2, N4W4, N5W7
AREA D	Pit 1, Pit 2, Pit 3, Pit 4, Pit 5
AREA E	S1E0 (1/2 pit), S1E1, N0W2, N0W1, N0E0, N0E1, N0E2, N1W2, N1W1, N1E0
AREA F	Pit 1, Pit 2, Pit 3

of prehistoric with eighteenth- through twentieth-century artifacts, although deeper soil levels tended to have exclusively prehistoric materials. Historical artifacts (of all periods) tended to be densest within building foundations, and also in close proximity to the Schuyler house.

Prehistoric artifacts occurred at all depths from the ground surface down to 70–80 centimeters (27–31 inches), with the greatest frequency in the northern part of the yard, closest to Fish Creek. A single prehistoric hearth was found in pits N11W2.5, N11W2, N12W2.5, and N12W2, and the surface of the hearth was at a depth of about 45 centimeters (18 inches). Associated with this hearth were a Greene projectile point, a chert scraper, and numerous sherds of Middle Woodland pottery. While insufficient charcoal was obtained for radiocarbon dating, the artifacts would suggest that this feature dates to about AD 400–800.

Thousands of chert flakes were excavated from the northern yard, where there had been intensive prehistoric occupations, and projectile point types include Otter Creek, Susquehanna Broad, Normanskill, Jack's Reef Corner-Notched, and Levanna, thus ranging from the Late Archaic period until just before European contact. Almost all diagnostic artifacts were made of chert, with only a few of quartz and quartzite; a single point base was made of Ohio chalcedony. Hundreds of pottery sherds were also recovered, most of which were Middle Woodland in age, although a few rim sherds with incised decoration were clearly Late Woodland. The quantities of pottery and the predominance of Levanna points suggest that people were utilizing the terraces of the Fish Creek chiefly during the Middle and Late Woodland periods, although with sporadic occupations extending back to 3000 to 4000 BC (as indicated by the single Otter Creek point).

Similar artifact types were excavated by Hetty Jo Brumbach and Susan Bender at the nearby Winney's Rift site, a few miles further west on Fish Creek.[17] In reporting prehistoric sites along Fish Creek, Robert Funk also described "12 Levanna points, three Jack's Reef Corner-Notched points, three celts, Vinette Dentate and Point Peninsula Rocker-stamped pottery . . . and

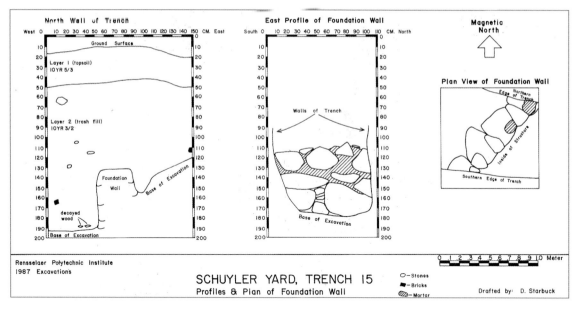

FIGURE 8.4. Trench 15, profiles and plan view of the foundation wall. Courtesy of David Starbuck.

one Adena point."[18] These types, and Funk's assessment that there was a late Middle Woodland occupation here, accord well with our own findings in 1987.

Historic foundation debris was found in two locations within area A, as well as a third location that has been termed area E. The first structure was found within the loop formed by the NPS service road and consists of extremely scattered stone rubble with very large quantities of nineteenth- and twentieth-century artifacts. This was the structure identified by Larrabee as site 8 on his "Master Plan of Archeological Excavations,"[19] and it is also the location where Brandow identified a large wood house and slave quarters.[20] However, it was impossible to determine an outline for this building, and no evidence was found to prove that this had ever been a "slave quarters." Only in one location was intact stonework found, and this appears to have been the base of a fireplace. Consequently, it is impossible to assign either a construction date or a function to this building.

In the northwestern corner of this yard, we dug several backhoe trenches (trenches 15, 16, and 22) that located a second set of foundations, and these walls were in exceptionally good condition (figure 8.4). Although this building's function is unclear, its foundation was buried so deeply (under more than one meter of overburden) that fill must have been placed over the top when it was demolished. The artifacts inside the cellar hole span from the eighteenth to the twentieth centuries, and the well-mortared stone walls suggest that this building probably was not demolished until the twentieth century.

A single one meter by one meter pit (pit 1) was also placed against the northwest corner of the current Schuyler house, in an attempt to learn whether the 1777 house had been constructed atop an earlier foundation. No evidence was found for a wing of the 1767 house coming out from the foundation, although soil deposits were extremely disturbed.

Area B

A dozen shovel test pits were excavated in 1985, some forty meters south of the current Schuyler house and along the boundary of the property, because of the possibility that a comfort station might be erected in this area. In 1987, we dug three additional test pits in this area to obtain a larger artifact sample. These pits identified a thin scatter of sheet refuse, but failed to locate any foundation debris. Artifacts were predominantly nineteenth century in origin.

Area C

Several test pits were placed just east of the current Schuyler house, looking for evidence of earlier privy holes adjacent to the existing privy. Interestingly, some of the artifacts recovered here (including delft tiles) were the oldest found in any of the Schuyler yard areas, but the only feature to be found was the surface of a dry well. This was discovered because there was a very slight depression on the ground surface, and it was not until after all stonework had been exposed that it was learned that it had been installed by park staff in 1952.

Archaeological trenching was also done in late 1987 around the base of the existing privy house; this work was necessitated by the planned reconstruction of the privy's foundations by NPS staff. The NPS asked that we excavate around the privy using the English system of measurement, and the average width of this trench was sixteen inches, with an average depth of fifteen inches. The only feature encountered was an ash lens on the north side that was four feet in length and began approximately six inches north of the privy wall; this feature ranged in depth from ten inches to seventeen inches. An excavation unit that measured three feet by three feet was also placed some three feet from the south wall of the privy (aligned with the privy door); this was excavated to a depth of eighteen inches but revealed no features. The artifacts surrounding the privy (chiefly pottery and window glass) were recent in origin, and the ceramic assemblage was dominated by whiteware, which did not come into production until the 1810s.

Area D

Four one meter by one meter test pits were placed in and around the rectangular barn foundation that was visible in the woods on the eastern side of the site. This had been identified by Larrabee as a nineteenth-century barn,[21] but no excavation had been conducted, and it was unknown whether there might be earlier material here.

While admittedly limited in extent, these excavations revealed twentieth-century bottles and pottery and no evidence for a 1777 occupation. However, we found prehistoric artifacts, including two scrapers, lying on the ground surface next to the barn, a reminder that the rich prehistoric deposits in the Schuyler yards continue along the entire length of Fish Creek. A buried wall was partially uncovered approximately fifteen meters east of the barn, and a single test pit (pit 5) was placed alongside it; however, we found no artifacts with which to date this feature.

Area E

Just before the conclusion of excavations in 1987, we decided to resume trenching with a backhoe in a final effort to locate the perimeter of the foundation inside the loop of the service road. Accordingly, we excavated a series of very short trenches along the eastern and southeastern side of the road (trenches 23–28). We then discovered the foundation of a burned building that was just five meters northeast of the kitchen wing on the current Schuyler house. In the remaining days of the 1987 field season, ten and ½ test pits were used to expose one side of this foundation, revealing the many small stones of a French drain that ran along the southern side of the building (figure 8.5). This drain was surrounded by a matrix of charcoal, burned earth, and burned (or melted) artifacts, including many burned kaolin pipe stem fragments, much melted glass and warped pottery sherds, and a scatter of animal bones. This material was totally unlike any of the other artifact concentrations we had encountered in the Schuyler yards, and many of the artifacts, while shallow, were clearly of eighteenth-century origin. There is a very high probability that this structure was one of General Schuyler's buildings that had been burned by the British in 1777.

Area F

In the fall of 1988, we dug a small cluster of three one-meter-square pits between trench 15 and the fence bordering Fish Creek. We recovered a great deal of prehistoric material (chert debitage, pottery, and projectile points), but there were no structural remains.

We also excavated other backhoe trenches across portions of the Schuyler yards that do not fall within any of the previously named areas. Only one, trench 10, produced significant structural debris, and this consisted of rubble from the so-called tenant house that had been taken down in 1963. Elsewhere, trenches were excavated across a large depression at the southwest corner of the property (trenches 1–2), but we did not even find "sheet refuse," a thin scatter of artifacts. We dug trenches west of the Schuyler house (trenches 4 and 21), and found

FIGURE 8.5. The 1987 excavation of the French drain in area E. Courtesy of David Starbuck.

FIGURE 8.6. Examples of artifacts excavated from the yards of the Schuyler house. (The broken utensil on the far right is the handle from a candle snuffer.) Courtesy of David Starbuck.

only a few prehistoric artifacts. We also blanketed the entire eastern side of the property with trenches (trenches 11–14 and 17–20), and once again we found only prehistoric artifacts. The only areas we did *not* examine were those where Edward Larrabee and John Cotter had already tested or where locust trees made trenching impossible.

Artifacts Discovered at the Schuyler House

The historic artifacts recovered during the 1987 excavations included buttons, pottery, buckles, a pewter spoon, a fragment of a cast-iron pot, forks, a knife, gun sights, a gunflint, musket balls, a hammer head, as well as numerous butchered animal bones (figure 8.6). All of these artifacts are quite appropriate for the yards surrounding the remains of multiple houses and outbuildings that have stood in this location from the early 1700s until the present. Still, nothing is Dutch, nothing would have been in use while the first Schuyler house was standing, and only one artifact convincingly dates to the battles of 1777. That artifact is an exploded fragment of a cast-iron mortar bomb found in area A, trench 6.

We discovered that porcelain is quite abundant in the yards of the Schuyler house, much more so than at local farm sites. This was a high-status residence by frontier standards, and the artifacts left behind by the Schuylers demonstrate a greater access to elite goods than might be found at the Woodworth farm (chapter 5) or any other contemporary residence in Saratoga County.

Summary and Conclusions

It is often suggested locally that the Schuyler house that stands on the property today was probably constructed atop the cellar hole of the burned second Schuyler house. This runs counter to several of the historical accounts that place the ruins elsewhere on the property. Still, that may be the only possible explanation for why years of excavation have not located the 1767–77 Schuyler house. Larrabee and Cotter, by focusing closely upon the eastern and southern perimeter of the house, were successful in locating several minor features (wells and root cellars), but even the broad horizontal expanses that were excavated identified only one actual building, the "burned structure" southeast of the current Schuyler house.

The 1987 excavations revealed an exceptional assemblage of Native American material in the northern yards of the current Schuyler house, as well as evidence for three additional outbuildings. However, this is a minimal number of buildings when compared to the twenty that reportedly existed at the time. It would appear that one of these buildings, within area E, dates to the Revolutionary War period and was probably burned at that time; another, within the loop of the service road, may have been the wood house and slave quarters mentioned by Brandow; that structure was removed sometime prior to 1857. The third outbuilding (exposed in trenches 15 and 16) is definitely of the postcolonial period and may have been standing into the twentieth century. All of these structures lie to the north of the existing house.

Part of our inability to find better evidence for outbuildings from both the French and Indian War and the Revolutionary War may be because of a lack of substantial foundations. Salvaging of building materials may also have occurred after the British burned the buildings. In the future, exhibits and tours need to incorporate the locations of already-discovered outbuildings; the positions of the burned structures, wells, root cellars, and other features should all be displayed and interpreted for visitors on the surface of the yard as well.

The Schuyler house as it appears today is totally isolated as a stately centerpiece in the middle of extensive, open lawns. However, when the estate was fully operative in the eighteenth century, all three Schuyler houses were surrounded by other buildings. Thus, it is important to locate and outline (on the ground surface) the footprints of the other Schuyler buildings because only then will this very special estate be fully revealed in all of its complexities and grandeur.

NOTES

1. Don R. Gerlach, *Philip Schuyler and the American Revolution in New York, 1733–1777* (Lincoln: University of Nebraska Press, 1964); Don R. Gerlach, *Proud Patriot: Philip Schuyler and the War of Independence, 1755–1783* (Syracuse, NY: Syracuse University Press, 1987).
2. Robert E. Funk, *Recent Contributions to Hudson Valley Prehistory*, Memoir 22 (Albany: New York State Museum, 1976).
3. Hetty Jo Brumbach and Susan J. Bender, "Winney's Rift: A Late Woodland Village Site in the Upper Hudson River Valley," *Bulletin and Journal of Archaeology for New York State* 92 (1986): 1–8.
4. John Henry Brandow, *The Story of Old Saratoga and History of Schuylerville* (Saratoga Springs, NY: Robson and Adee, 1900).
5. Ibid.
6. Benson J. Lossing, *The Pictorial Field-Book of the Revolution*, vol. 1 (New York: Harper Brothers, 1851), 73.
7. Brandow, *Story of Old Saratoga*.
8. Edward M. Larrabee, "Report of Archeological Excavations Conducted at Schuyler House, Saratoga National Historical Park, Schuylerville, New York, from June 8 through June 29, 1959," Saratoga National Historical Park, 1960, 65.
9. Brandow, *Story of Old Saratoga*.
10. William L. Stone, *Visits to the Saratoga Battle-Grounds 1780–1880* (Port Washington, NY: Kennikat Press, 1895), 134.
11. Stone, *Visits to the Saratoga Battle-Grounds*, 203.
12. John L. Cotter, "Report of Schuyler House Archeological Investigations, July 23–27, 1958," Saratoga National Historical Park, 1958; Jackson W. Moore, "Archeological Investigation of the Schuyler House Parking Lot Area," Saratoga National Historical Park, 1960; Larrabee, "Report of Archeological Excavations Conducted at Schuyler House."
13. Larrabee, "Report of Archeological Excavations Conducted at Schuyler House," 43.
14. Brandow, *Story of Old Saratoga*, 288.
15. Larrabee, "Report of Archeological Excavations Conducted at Schuyler House," 40.
16. We collected approximately 10,000 magnetometer readings on the Schuyler house grounds; see Dennis E. Howe, "Magnetometer Survey at Saratoga National Historical Park," Saratoga National Historical Park, 1985, 4.
17. Brumbach and Bender, "Winney's Rift," 1–8.
18. Funk, *Recent Contributions to Hudson Valley Prehistory*, 27.
19. Larrabee, "Report of Archeological Excavations Conducted at Schuyler House."
20. Brandow, *Story of Old Saratoga*.
21. Larrabee, "Report of Archeological Excavations Conducted at Schuyler House," 40.

CHAPTER NINE | CHRISTINE VALOSIN

The Saratoga Battles in Fifty Artifacts

Introduction

Although many traditional histories, gathered from letters, official reports, and eyewitness accounts, have been written about the Saratoga battles, much less has been done to tell stories about the participants and events of this conflict using artifacts from museum collections. This chapter endeavors to address whether important stories of the Saratoga battlefield can be told through surviving objects. Ultimately, can we glean new insights into battlefield history using artifacts in the Saratoga National Historical Park (NHP) museum collection? Artifacts have immense power to tell unique stories about the people who created and/or used them. As such, they connect us to the past in unique ways, providing physical and tangible links to specific events, activities, and individuals.

In this chapter, fifty different artifacts were selected to highlight the different stories that can be told through the park's museum collections. Because the Saratoga collection is predominantly from archaeological investigations, there is a special focus on artifacts uncovered from excavations. However, several of the original manuscripts and documents from the park's museum collection are also included in this chapter. Other items within the collection, including donated items like furniture and cannons, also communicate lively stories and are included in the discussion. The analysis of the selected artifacts and objects from the Saratoga National Historical Park provide an opportunity to better understand the people who lived here, the people who fought here, and the people who remembered the conflict in the years before there was a national park.

After a brief discussion of the history of the collection, this chapter examines artifacts from the context of the battlefield farms, the settings of the Battles of Saratoga. Next, collections are grouped together for the Schuyler estate, a unique property and separate unit of the park. Artifacts from the battlefield and areas where soldiers were encamped between the first and second battles are likewise grouped. Manuscripts, surrendered arms, and American plunder from British camps highlight the story of the British army's surrender to the Army of the United States, providing another thematic grouping of objects. Farm families who lived on the battlefield in the nineteenth century and visitors who came to see the site gathered souvenirs of the conflict, and these also provide insight into the battles and the subsequent memory and commemoration of the site.

The Creation of a Collection at Saratoga

In all, more than 90 percent of the museum collections at Saratoga National Historical Park (excluding archival documents) are archaeological artifacts from more than twenty-five different projects conducted at the park's battlefield and Old Saratoga units. These collections consist largely of ceramics, glass, and metals, including military hardware and remnants of artillery and musket balls. Saratoga National Historical Park also curates a small collection of items from the Northern Campaign of 1777 that come from lands outside the park boundary.

The park's museum collections are divided into subcategories including archives, archaeology, and history. The history collection consists of about 5,200 objects, such as furniture, fireplace and cooking equipment, battlefield relics that were collected as surface artifacts by local families prior to 1927, cannons, eighteenth-century military equipage, and other items. The approximately 235,000-piece archival and manuscript collection includes park administrative and resource management records, historical documents, rare books, prints, maps, and photographs. About 250,000 artifacts from domestic sites, campsites, and fortifications on the battlefield make up the park's archaeology collections.[1]

Collections of artifacts and manuscripts were begun under the direction of the site's first superintendent, George O. Slingerland; the park was first administered by the New York State Conservation Department, Division of Lands and Forests. In 1927, as the 150th anniversary of the Battles of Saratoga were commemorated, Slingerland assembled a formal museum collection through the acquisition of furnishings, battlefield relics, maps, books, and other related materials. Between 1927 and his untimely death in 1932, Slingerland acquired artifacts for exhibit at the battlefield and documents and images used for research and planning. Most of the collection that Slingerland amassed for New York State between 1927 and 1932 was transferred to the National Park Service on July 8, 1942, becoming the first accession (*SARA 1*) of Saratoga National Historical Park.

Beginning in 1940, the National Park Service began a vigorous program of archival and archaeological research at Saratoga. The reconnaissance archaeology, led by Robert Ehrich in the 1940s, was intended to verify key military locations of combat and the position of fortifications on the battlefield. The collections from Ehrich's investigations include documentation of burials at the Balcarres Redoubt, sections through various redoubts, and numerous artifacts including musket balls, shells, military accoutrements, and personal items. Archaeological research in the late 1950s yielded additional information, most notably about the Schuyler house and the Neilson farmhouse and barn complex. While locations within the park slated for development and interpretation were being investigated through archaeology, thousands of artifacts were recovered and added to the museum collections. In the 1970s, archaeological investigations led by Dean Snow resulted in additional collections, as did David Starbuck's 1985–87 projects at the Woodworth farm/American hospital, Schuyler house, and Taylor house. The nature of most of the archaeological investigations at Saratoga National Historical Park has been to locate, or verify the location of, structures (including fortifications) and not to investigate the battles themselves; that is, "battlefield archaeology." This focus has led to the recovery of a preponderance of nonmilitary artifacts from the battlefield (table 9.1).

Battlefield Farms/House Sites

By the summer of 1777, the battlefield area was made up of a number of small farms leased from lot holders of the Saratoga Patent. The Saratoga Patent was an approximately 170,000-acre colonial land grant dating to 1684 that extended along both sides of the Hudson River in modern-day Saratoga and Washington Counties, north of the city of Albany, New York. The lands in the Saratoga Patent were divided into lots, and farms within the lots were leased to tenant farmers by the landowners, who included several members of the influential Schuyler and Livingston families. After 1750, the land was further subdivided into smaller lots. The end of the French and Indian War in 1763 brought an influx of settlers to the area, and by the summer of 1777, the battlefield area was made up of a number of small farms of about 100 to 150 acres each, many of which were long-term leases from the larger landowners. At the time of the battles in 1777, about 35 percent of the area that would make up the battlefield was cleared land in agriculture (figure 9.1).[2]

The Neilson Farm (American Divisional Headquarters)

Since military occupation of the Neilson farm was ephemeral and it was not the scene of combat or extensive encampment, most of the artifacts in the museum collection relate to the occupation by multiple generations of the Neilson family,

TABLE 9.1 Saratoga Battles in Fifty Artifacts

OBJECT NAME	DATE	PROJECT REFERENCE / COLLECTION	CATALOG NUMBER
Bemus warrant	1777	Neilson Papers, Museum Collection	SARA-557-3
Receipt, Bemus goods sale	1777	Neilson Papers, Museum Collection	SARA-557-6
McCarty warrant	1777	Neilson Papers, Museum Collection	SARA-557-8
Tea bowl, creamware	ca. 1765–75	Neilson Farm/American Fortified Lines (1940)	SARA-931
Ox shoe	ca. 1775–1800	Neilson Farm (1957)	SARA-2348
Teapot lid, scratch blue	ca. 1750–75	Taylor House Site (1973)	SARA-1083
Saucer sherds, scratch blue	ca. 1750–75	Woodworth House Site (1985–86)	SARA-6218, 8144
Harness buckle	ca. 1775–1800	Taylor House Site (1973)	SARA-1149
Sleeve buttons	ca. 1750	Woodworth House Site/American HQ (1986)	SARA-13,866
Dinner plate, pearlware	ca. 1790–1810	Woodworth House Site (1985)	SARA-7437
Case bottle fragment	ca. 1770–90	Woodworth House Site/American HQ (1986)	SARA-13,024
Child's commode basin, creamware	ca. 1765–80	Schuyler House (1958)	SARA-29,271
Milk pan, redware	ca. 1765–95	Schuyler House (1958–59)	SARA-30,850
Fireplace crane	ca. 1720	Schuyler House Field Collection	SARA-4611
Tobacco pipe fragment	ca. 1690–1750	Schuyler House (1959)	SARA-30,463
Delft tiles	ca. 1760–70	Schuyler House (1958–59)	SARA-30,866, 5171
Watch fob seal	ca. 1775–1800	Schuyler House (1958)	SARA-2831
Case shot	1777	Balcarres Redoubt (1940)	SARA-813
Waistcoat buttons, pewter	1777	Balcarres Redoubt (1940)	SARA-823
Tobacco pipe fragments	1777	Balcarres Redoubt (1940)	SARA-818, 820
Iron shell fragment	1777	Balcarres Redoubt (1940)	SARA-806
Square poll hatchet	ca. 1750–63	Breymann Fortified Camp (1972)	SARA-1680
Iron kettle fragments	ca. 1760–75	Breymann Fortified Camp (1972)	SARA-1477, 1531, 1534
Haversack buckles	ca. 1775	Breymann Fortified Camp (1972)	SARA-1529, 1533
Razor blade	ca. 1775	Breymann Fortified Camp (1972)	SARA-1433
Musket lock	ca. 1770	Breymann Fortified Camp (1972)	SARA-1681
Shoe buckle	ca. 1770	Breymann Fortified Camp (1972)	SARA-1434
Cartridge box plate	ca. 1776	Breymann Fortified Camp (1972)	SARA-686
Ordnance insignia	ca. 1776	Wheat Field Area (1940)	SARA-650
Cut musket ball	1777	21st Regiment Encampment (1975)	SARA-1735
Sewing thimble, brass	ca. 1750–75	21st Regiment Encampment (1975)	SARA-1720
Spoon handle, pewter	ca. 1765–75	21st Regiment Encampment (1975)	SARA-1791
Coat button, "21"	ca. 1776	21st Regiment Encampment (1975)	SARA-1798
Barrel hoop broiler	1777	21st Regiment Encampment (1975)	SARA-1770
Combination musket tool	ca. 1776	21st Regiment Encampment (1975)	SARA-1827
Musket worm	ca. 1776	Encampment Area (1975)	SARA-1950
Shoe buckle	ca. 1760–75	Encampment Area (1975)	SARA-2023
Cartridge box plate, crown	ca. 1776	Encampment Area (1975)	SARA-1982

OBJECT NAME	DATE	PROJECT REFERENCE / COLLECTION	CATALOG NUMBER
Combination musket tool	ca. 1776	Encampment Area (1975)	SARA-1710
Convention of Saratoga, draft	1777	Museum Collection	SARA-683
Elihu Ely letter	1777	Museum Collection	SARA-648
Convention Army List of Married Men	ca. 1781	Museum Collection	SARA-19,642
Six-pounder cannon	1756	Loan	SARA-28,731
Twelve-pounder cannon	1760	Museum Collection	SARA-373
Musket balls	1777	Freeman Farm Site, Field Collection	SARA-269, 274
Cannonball	ca. 1776	Victory Woods Site, Field Collection	SARA-181
Sleeve buttons	ca. 1770–75	Museum Collection	SARA-3769, 3770
Brazier	ca. 1770–75	Museum Collection	SARA-3768
Camp table	ca. 1775	Museum Collection	SARA-3767
Camp bed	ca. 1775	Museum Collection	SARA-3766

who lived on the site from around 1775 until 1926. The Neilson house is the only eighteenth-century structure left standing on the battlefield; all other farms and structures from that period are archaeological sites.

John Neilson was one of many settlers to the Saratoga District of Albany County following the French and Indian War. Neilson may have been in Stillwater as early as 1769, according to an affidavit he submitted for another man's pension. In 1769, Neilson would have been a teenager of fifteen or sixteen.[3] An ambitious man, John Neilson was involved in land acquisition and leasing and other enterprises such as timber harvesting. While John and his wife Lydia were considered a farming family of middling means in 1777, by the second decade of the nineteenth century, Neilson was considered moderately wealthy. The Neilsons' dwelling, a small, one-and-a-half-story house and barn, along with a few outbuildings, was located on the summit of Bemis Heights.

During the battles, their farm was occupied for strategic reasons by American officers for a three-week period from September to October 1777. Located behind the fortified lines, the farm was never the scene of combat, but the encamped American army caused enough damage that Neilson submitted an appraisal of damages to his property in March 1778. Among his losses, he claimed two tons of standing grass used as pasture and forty bushels of potatoes taken by the soldiers. Because Neilson did not claim damage or loss to any livestock or movables (household furnishings), it is assumed that he had enough time to remove them from the premises prior to the American army occupation.

John Cotter's archaeological investigations at the Neilson house and barn sites in the late 1950s were intended to provide information about the original

FIGURE 9.1. Saratoga Battlefield in 1777 showing the Saratoga Patent lot lines, road networks, and clearings. Farms occupied by John Taylor, John Freeman, John Neilson, and Ephraim Woodworth; Jotham Bemus's tavern, and the area where the 21st Regiment was encamped between the battles are noted. Courtesy of Saratoga National Historical Park.

location of the structures so that the National Park Service could relocate the house to its original setting. The small house, built about 1775, had been moved and reoriented to face west by New York State in 1927 when the administrative complex for the Saratoga Battlefield was being constructed at the Neilson farm. The state removed the nineteenth-century farm structures and added three new conjectural buildings, including a stone powder magazine east of the Neilson house; a house called the "Period House," which was referred to as "Arnold's Headquarters"; and a two-story blockhouse, to serve administrative and visitor needs. These buildings provided administrative offices and visitor contact and museum space until the Mission 66–funded tour road and new visitor center at Fraser Hill were completed in the early 1960s by the National Park Service.[4] Through archaeology, Cotter was able to locate the original Neilson house foundation and the building was returned to its earliest location.

In 1954, a Neilson descendant donated a collection of family papers to Saratoga National Historical Park. Many of the papers were nineteenth-century receipts, but a small portion was directly related to John Neilson's activities during the American War for Independence. They include the Bemus and McCarty warrants.

During the early part of the Revolutionary War, John Neilson served as a sergeant in the 4th Company, 13th Regiment, Albany County Militia, and his neighbor, Ephraim Woodworth, was captain of the company. Six individual documents in the Neilson Papers in the Saratoga NHP museum collections illustrate the consequences for local men who failed to show up for duty when they were called, or who left their military posts without permission. Jotham Bemus, a tavern keeper in the Stillwater district, suffered numerous arrests, imprisonments, and assessments of fines during the course of the war for his ambiguous political stance and absence from military duty. Ironically, his property would become incorporated in the American defensive lines at Bemus Heights in the fall of 1777.

In February 1777, Bemus failed to show up at Fort Edward to the north in answer to a general alarm calling the militia to assemble. Captain Ephraim Woodworth, who resided on the Woodworth farm, the site of General Gates's headquarters, just to the south of Neilson's, issued an order to Sergeant John Neilson to assess a fine of twenty pounds for the "second offense" by Bemus. Neilson and Woodworth lived on the hill just west of Bemus's tavern; the tavern sat at the base of the hill known as "Bemus Heights." Neilson was to seize from Bemus "goods and chattels" equivalent to twenty pounds in value, and to sell it at a public auction. If the sale price was more than twenty pounds, Neilson was ordered to pay the overage back to Bemus. If the auction failed to make enough money to cover the amount of the fine, or if Bemus did not have goods that could be seized and sold for the amount, then Neilson was ordered to take Bemus into custody and commit him to the common jail. Neilson seized two yoke of oxen, and these were sold at public auction to Dr. Ebenezer Marvin, a resident of the village of Stillwater and chairman of the Saratoga Committee, Albany County Committee of Correspondence. Marvin questioned Jotham Bemus regarding the charges, and he also posted bail for him. Just before the battles of Saratoga in September 1777, Bemus was arrested on suspicion of giving information to the enemy and confined in the "fleet prison" on the Esopus Creek near Kingston, New York. Freed from this prison at some point, Bemus continued to raise enough suspicion about his political loyalties that he was brought to Albany for questioning in October 1778 and again in 1779 and 1780. In November 1780, he was confined to the City Hall in Albany. Bemus had enough support from his neighbors that they signed a petition in December 1780 requesting his release from jail. It appears that he continually raised the alarm of others, in that he was brought in for questioning, confined to jail, and forced to pay fines at least five times between 1777 and 1781.[5]

John McCarty was farming land in Stillwater by the mid-1760s.[6] McCarty leased Farm no. 2 in Great Lot 16 of the Saratoga Patent from Philip Schuyler in 1765. His farm was just east of John Freeman's, where the majority of the fighting occurred on September 19 and October 7. In February 1777, McCarty went absent without leave from his post at Fort Edward. Like Jotham Bemus, his neighbor to the south, McCarty was also fined and goods were seized. Unlike Bemus, John McCarty weathered the political storms and maintained his residence in Stillwater after the war ended in 1783. Jotham Bemus moved away from Stillwater in the 1780s, never to return.

Although the archaeology did not uncover a large number of eighteenth-century artifacts at the Neilson house site, one creamware tea bowl (figure 9.2) was found in the earthen fill of the western end of the American fortification line north of the Neilson house investigated by archaeologist Robert Ehrich in 1941. During the eighteenth century, English potters were emulating the style of porcelain tea bowls without handles being made in China. This tea bowl has a small foot ring and a delicate beaded band impressed around the top outer rim. The bowl could have been used by an American officer on the property in the fall of 1777, although it could have belonged to the Neilson family. Around 1760, English potters began producing the white-bodied refined earthenware called *creamware* that became widely popular in England and America. The ceramic assemblage from all of the excavated eighteenth-century domestic sites on the battlefield indicates that English-made creamware (1760–1800) and pearlware (1780–1820) predominate in terms of quantity. The ceramics from the Woodworth site, just to the south of the Neilson farm, include large numbers of creamware and pearlware sherds, but also included redware, white salt-glazed stoneware, porcelain, English delft, and small amounts of Jackfield earthenware and whiteware.[7]

As another reminder of the story of John Neilson seizing his neighbor Jotham Bemus's oxen in 1777, an iron ox shoe was found by archaeologist John Cotter near the Neilson house in 1957. It speaks to the hard work of farming in the eighteenth century. Teams of oxen were used to pull wagons and farm equipment; thus, a good team of oxen was highly prized by its owners. The seizure and sale

FIGURE 9.2. *Upper left*, eighteenth-century English shield-shaped cast metal harness buckle with tin plating, Taylor house site, SARA-1149; *upper right,* partial teapot lid, English white salt-glazed stoneware with scratch blue decoration, found at the Taylor house site in 1973, SARA-1083; *lower left,* sleeve buttons, circa 1750, found at the site of the Ephraim Woodworth house, SARA-13,866; *lower right,* tea bowl, English creamware, found during an excavation of the western portion of the American fortified lines on the Neilson farm in 1940, SARA-931. Courtesy of Saratoga National Historical Park.

of teams of oxen to satisfy fines levied against delinquent soldiers in the 13th Regiment, Albany County Militia is illustrative of the economic value of these draft animals to the farmers who settled in the Stillwater and Saratoga regions in the mid- to late eighteenth century.

The Taylor House Site

The Taylor house, located on the river flats north of the park's entrance road, was traditionally recognized as the site where British General Simon Fraser was brought, mortally wounded, on the evening of October 7, although modern research disputes that claim. In September and early October 1777, the area immediately south of the Taylor house site was used by the British army. Burgoyne's forces, including six companies of the 47th Regiment of Foot, the general hospital, the Royal Regiment of Artillery Park, Hessen-Hanau Regiment Erbprinz,

American volunteers (Peters's, Jessup's and McAlpin's corps), the Mohawk and Seven Nations of Canada warriors and families, Royal Navy, commissary department, and artificers, provisions, and baggage, encamped in this area.[8] The site of the Taylor house would have been at the northernmost limits of the encampment, just west of the area where the Native Americans were posted. Given its possible connection with General Fraser and his funeral and interment nearby, the Taylor house site was investigated twice by archaeologists: the first time in 1973 by Dean Snow and again in 1987 by David Starbuck. Both investigations sought to locate the original site of the Taylor house, which had been moved from its foundation between 1815 and 1820 (around the time the Champlain Canal was constructed) and situated closer to the bank of the Hudson River.

On September 10, 1772, almost exactly five years before the Battles of Saratoga, John Taylor (sometimes spelled *Tayler*) purchased Farm no. 1 in Lot 17 of the Saratoga Patent from Judith Bruce, who was related by marriage to Philip Schuyler's wife, Catherine.[9] John Taylor was a merchant and a politician in Albany, his main residence, thirty miles south of his Stillwater farm. In addition to Taylor's Albany home and Stillwater farm, he also held property in the town of Ballston, west of the battlefield. On his Stillwater land, Taylor grew hemp and flax, raised cattle and produced smoked meat, and sold lumber, potash, and rope.[10] Taylor retained ownership of the Stillwater farm for about eleven years. In 1783, he sold 200 acres of Farm no. 1, Lot 17, and a mill to Ezekiel Ensign, a tavern keeper who resided north of Taylor during the war.[11] Even though the Taylor family did not occupy the site for the entire time period, the Taylor name has been associated with the site and the archaeological collections through their connection with the stories from the Revolutionary War. Many questions remain as to who exactly lived on the site during the battles and for how long.

Following his archaeological excavations at the site in the 1970s, Dean Snow concluded that the major occupation of the site took place between 1760 and 1820 based on the large quantity of various types of ceramics and other tablewares. Both the Snow and Starbuck archaeological collections (SARA 200 and SARA 257) are incredibly rich, with more than 2,500 sherds of different ceramic types dating between 1740 and 1820.

As seen at the Neilson house, the predominant ceramic type at the Taylor House site is creamware. There are more than 1,550 sherds of creamware, making this one ceramic type the most common tableware (62 percent) used by the families living on the site. About 16 percent of the total collection of ceramics from the Taylor house site is pearlware, which is found on American sites after 1783. Although the bulk of the ceramic types are of English origin, a small percentage of redware and stoneware utility vessels could have been manufactured in America.

Several different types of ceramic teapot sherds were found at the Taylor house site, including Jackfield type, with its distinctive glossy black glaze over a red earthenware body, and a type of white salt-glazed stoneware with incised decorations known as *scratch blue*. Both of these ceramic tea wares date from the 1740–60 time period, making their presence on Taylor's property either older pieces that the family brought with them or evidence that someone else was living on the site prior to 1772 when John Taylor purchased the property. Tea wares were very popular in America in the eighteenth century, and tea drinking followed English fashions and customs at the time. Ceramic tea services were commonly sold in sets, which would have included cups, saucers, sugar and cream pots, a slop bowl for depositing the used tea leaves, and the teapot.[12] A teapot lid (figure 9.2) from an English-made white salt-glazed scratch blue stoneware teapot made between 1750 and 1770 was found at the Taylor house site. Similar scratch blue tea wares (saucers) were found at the Woodworth house site. Most scratch blue tea wares of this quality were popular in America prior to the American Revolution. The Taylor house teapot lid and the Woodworth house saucers have hand-incised floral designs filled with cobalt-blue oxide pigment.[13]

Although the Taylor house was close to the British army encampment during the fall of 1777, very few artifacts were recovered from the site that can be definitively called "military" in origin. An eighteenth-century English shield-shaped cast metal harness buckle with tin plating (figure 9.2) may represent military activity in the vicinity of the property in 1777. Such a harness buckle would have been found in conjunction with the use of horses to pull wagons to transport provisions and stores. It is also possible, however, that the buckle might have been used in a nonmilitary context.

Like the Woodworth and Neilson farms on the south end of the battlefield, evidence of the Taylor site's use by the British during their occupation of the river flats area in the fall of 1777 is impossible to pin down definitively through the artifacts. The actual value of the artifacts from the Taylor house assemblage lies in their potential to explore the range of eighteenth-century ceramic types in use on an upper Hudson Valley house site, and to ponder their role as props in elaborate social rituals that extended into the settlements of the upper Hudson north of Albany.

The Woodworth House (Gates's Headquarters)

The Woodworth family likely arrived in Stillwater in the mid- to late 1760s, and built their home and outbuildings south of the Neilson farm on a hilltop west of the Bemus tavern. According to family tradition, Ephraim Woodworth was a weaver. By 1777, Woodworth was serving as captain of the 4th company, 13th Regiment, Albany County Militia, and his house was used as headquarters by General Gates and his staff in September and early October

1777. Published accounts written as early as 1819 note that Gates's headquarters (Woodworth's house) was dilapidated; by 1830, the house and outbuildings had been demolished.

The Woodworth farm was also the site of a barn that had served as a hospital for sick and wounded American soldiers during the army's occupation at Bemis Heights. Because of their role during the Battles of Saratoga, the Woodworth house and barn site was investigated in 1986 by David Starbuck. Like other eighteenth-century house sites on the battlefield, artifacts related to military occupation in 1777 are minimal, but the collections are rich in material culture remains of family occupation from the 1760s into the early nineteenth century. Most of the artifacts recovered from the site came from the cellar hole of the Woodworth dwelling house.[14]

Much like the Taylor house, the ceramic collection from the Woodworth site consisted mostly of creamware (ca. 1765–1800) and pearlware (ca. 1780–1820). Several hundred clay tobacco pipe fragments, dating to the late eighteenth century, were also recovered. The large number of butchered animal bones, mostly cow and pig, indicate a predominance of beef and pork in the family's diet. Personal artifacts from domestic sites like the Woodworth farm often indicate the economic status of the occupants. Excavating the Woodworth farm cellar, Starbuck found several eighteenth-century men's sleeve buttons (figure 9.2). These buttons include one faceted clear glass (paste) sleeve button set in a pewter mount with a beaded edge; a single sleeve button of cast pewter with an embossed pattern of a crown over two hearts on a stippled background, and a pair of brass sleeve buttons with stylized tulips dating to about 1750. Although these men's sleeve buttons might have been worn by an officer who occupied the house in 1777, it is more likely that Ephraim Woodworth (1732–1825) or a family visitor wore them. Not made of gold or set with real gemstones, these sleeve buttons are common, yet they also display a sense of taste and style, and were meant to be noticed.

Very common to many American domestic sites in the late eighteenth to early nineteenth century was the English-made tableware known today as *pearlware*. Fragments of pearlware plates found at the Woodworth farm site with blue glazed impressed shell edges probably date to the early nineteenth century. Likely manufactured after the end of the Revolutionary War, the presence of pearlware at this location indicates the resurgence in popularity of English-made ceramics following the war.

Table glass was not found in any great quantity at the Woodworth house site, but a case bottle fragment might be associated with the Woodworth house occupation during the fall of 1777. Made in the last quarter of the eighteenth century, the green glass bottle was blown in a mold. Case bottles were square-shaped liquor bottles made in various sizes. They were made square so that they could be stored in a rectangular wood case that usually held between four and sixteen bottles.[15] The square bottle sides made it an efficient way to store a number of liquor bottles along with other drinking equipment in one portable chest. Case bottles such as the one found at the Woodworth house site have been found at military sites, and it is possible that this fragment is associated with the occupation of General Gates and his staff in 1777. It is equally possible that the bottle was part of the Woodworth family's eighteenth-century possessions.

The Schuyler Estate

Two sizeable collections of archaeological materials from the Schuyler house and grounds, totaling approximately 15,000 artifacts, are the result of two extensive research projects focusing on the house, grounds, and outbuildings of the estate. This work was completed principally by John Cotter and Edward Larrabee in the 1950s and David Starbuck in the 1980s. Archaeological investigations began on the Schuyler house grounds in 1958 (John Cotter) and 1959 (Edward Larrabee/John Cotter). The architectural restoration of the house, led by historic architect Henry Judd, was also in progress at this time. This resulted in the simultaneous collection of some architectural objects along with archaeological collections.[16] David Starbuck continued research on the Schuyler house site between 1985 and 1987 (see chapter 8).

The Schuyler family occupation of the site extends from the 1690s to 1837. The estate supported timber harvesting, flax and hemp cultivation and linen milling, fishing enterprises, agriculture, and the business of tenant farming. Enslaved African Americans are known to have worked in all of these enterprises as well as in domestic duties for the Schuyler family. While the focus of interpretation at the Schuyler house is General Philip Schuyler (1734–1804) and his immediate family, the Schuyler estate encompasses the rich, complex history of the multi-generation Schuyler family, based in Albany, from the late seventeenth century to 1837. The Schuylers were an elite Anglo-Dutch family immersed in commerce and politics in New York.

Because the focus of archaeology at the Schuyler estate has been locating and confirming structures on the estate, especially the 1760s house and outbuildings burned by the British in October 1777, the artifacts have received less attention. Serious study of the material culture—looking at the relationships between the people at the Schuyler estate and the objects they left behind—has languished up to this point, and the lack of research on these collections has had the unfortunate consequence of isolating the Schuyler estate's rich material culture history from its connections with related family collections in Albany and the upper Hudson River valley.

A broad consensus exists that the artifacts excavated from the Schuyler estate principally reflect the nineteenth-century occupation of the property. That said,

FIGURE 9.3. *Upper left,* creamware child's commode basin, found at the Schuyler estate in 1958, SARA-29,271; *upper right,* portion of a clay tobacco pipe, ⁵⁄₆₄-inch-bore diameter, retaining part of the stem with a small pointed heel (spur) at the base, found at the "burned structure" site, east of the 1777 Schuyler house, by Edward Larrabee in 1959, SARA-30,463; *lower,* redware milk pan found during archaeological investigations at the Schuyler estate in 1958 or 1959, SARA-30,850. Courtesy of Saratoga National Historical Park.

there are some artifacts that clearly date to the Schuyler family's occupancy during the war years. The presence of young children in the Schuyler house at Saratoga during the late 1760s into the 1780s is evident in a creamware child's commode basin (figure 9.3) recovered from the site. Also known as a "close stool pan," this conical-shaped flat-bottomed ceramic basin has a broad flat rim that would allow it to hang suspended on the rim of a commode chair (today's "potty chair"). It is small in size, measuring only 4½ inches high. The chair in which this pot once fit is no longer extant.[17]

Archaeological evidence of agricultural work on Schuyler's estate is also found in the ceramics collection. The 1958–59 archaeological investigation uncovered six plain redware milk pans (figure 9.3). Milk pans were used in the eighteenth century to process raw milk. The fresh milk would be poured into these broad and shallow milk pans to speed cooling. Cream would rise to the top and be skimmed from the broad, flat surface of the pan. The existence of these milk pans is evidence that there was a dairy operation (cheese and butter making) at the Schuyler estate, perhaps large enough to support the family's needs; dairying was a typical enterprise for women to oversee.[18]

The construction of the Champlain Canal in the 1820s and subsequent widening of the canal in the area behind the Schuyler house affected the remains of at least one earlier structure on the Schuyler estate. This discovery was confirmed in the *Schuylerville Standard* on July 10, 1895: in the process of removing gravel from a section along the canal in back of the Schuyler (George Strover) house, "they came upon the remains of this old cellar wall of the Schuyler House . . . already hundreds of people have visited this spot [and] many valuable relics have been found."[19] The article identified the cellar as the house burned during a French raid in November 1745 (this would have been the first Schuyler house; see chapter 8). Of the artifacts taken from the exposed foundation, two remain in public collections today: the large iron fireplace crane from the kitchen and a lock mechanism from a door on the dwelling (today in the collection of the Saratoga Springs History Museum). The exposed cellar and foundation is not far from another feature found during the 1958–59 archaeological investigation on the Schuyler estate grounds. Called the "burned structure," this site yielded artifacts that date to the eighteenth century and was one of the structures that was possibly burned by Burgoyne in 1777.

The "burned structure" is a shallow foundation measuring twenty-two feet wide by about forty-three feet long with a stone platform along the west wall. It was discovered southeast of the current house in 1958 by John Cotter and excavated in 1959 by Edward Larrabee. Although it was interpreted by the archaeologists as a stand-alone structure, it could have been a detached kitchen or kitchen wing, associated with a house predating the Revolution, especially when looked at in the context of other nearby features; a well is located to the south and another smaller foundation, interpreted in the 1950s as a vegetable cellar, just to the west. The stone feature at the westernmost end of the foundation appears to be a hearth, and the dimensions of the structure would suggest a detached kitchen having no basement.[20] The artifacts from the "burned structure" include a collection of architectural remains: bricks, window glass, a piece of lead window came, some wood fragments, and nails. The bulk of the artifacts are ceramics, and the ceramics found at this site are English-made wares dating between 1740 and 1770. Like the Taylor house and Woodworth house sites at the battlefield, sherds found at the Schuyler estate indicate the use of Jackfield-type and scratch blue tea wares.[21] If this space was, in fact, a kitchen, that might account for the discovery of mammal bones with butcher marks.

Clay tobacco pipes (figure 9.3) with bore diameters of $5/64$ inches found in the "burned structure" fit with the mid-eighteenth-century ceramic context. Clay pipes with a $5/64$-inch-bore diameter are generally dated between 1720 and 1750, although they have been found in Revolutionary War contexts.[22] Two $6/64$-inch-bore diameter pipe fragments, dating between 1680 and 1710, were found in the area of Schuyler's extensive garden to the east of the house.

Although the complete analysis of the ceramic collection at the Schuyler estate is ongoing, the predominance of creamware tablewares (1762–1800) throughout the excavations illustrates the same pattern of ceramic use at both Schuyler properties in Albany and Saratoga.[23] While their Albany home was the public face of the Philip Schuyler family to the world, the Saratoga estate, with its house, mills, farm structures, store, and other supporting buildings, was the heart of the family's economic enterprise prior to the Revolutionary War.

Dutch culture in the form of religious practice, social traditions, and even the use of the Dutch language remained vibrant in the upper Hudson Valley for more than a hundred years after the British takeover of New Netherland in 1664. Therefore, it is not surprising that sherds of Dutch delft tiles have been found at the Schuyler estate. In 1958 and 1959, archaeologists found seven sherds of cobalt-blue-decorated delft tiles that were likely manufactured in Utrecht between 1725 and 1775. They appear to be scripture (bible) tiles with double-roundel borders and ox-head corners. The blue decorated delft tiles were found at the site of the "burned structure" and at another small foundation labeled the "vegetable cellar."[24] During the eighteenth century, these tiles would have been used as facings for the area around the firebox in an English-style fireplace.[25] The use of scripture tiles based on print sources from biblical texts was very popular among families of Dutch descent in the Albany area throughout the eighteenth century. Tiles similar to these have been found at other Albany County sites.[26] Ten scripture tile fragments decorated in manganese (purple) have also been uncovered: two at the "burned structure" location; four from locations closer to the 1777 house; and four that are unfortunately unprovenienced. One of the manganese tiles has a distinctive carnation ornament in the corner, rather than the ox-head motif found on the blue tiles and at least one other purple tile. The different color tiles suggest that at least two different fireplace installations using the delft tiles existed on the property in the eighteenth century.

A paste seal from a man's watch fob, circa 1770–1850, was found near the Schuyler house kitchen in 1958. It is made of a glass-based substance known as "paste" that was made to imitate a gemstone—in this case, amethyst. Paste was used widely in the eighteenth century and throughout the nineteenth century as well. The incised decoration on the flat surface of the seal is known as *intaglio*. At the center is a pelican feeding its young in the nest. This symbol is seen in European heraldry, and it symbolizes self-sacrifice and charity. A motto surrounds the pelican that reads: "Live & Die for Those We Love."[27] Originally set into a metal mount and attached by a chain to a man's pocket watch, this emblem was both a symbol of family status and likely a personal memento. The fob seal was probably worn by a visitor to the Schuyler estate in the eighteenth century, since the imagery or motto does not appear in the Schuyler family crest.

Combat and Encampment Sites

Freeman's Farm

Freeman's farm, the site of the Balcarres Redoubt, is the most investigated archaeological location in the park. The site of fighting on both September 19 and October 7, 1777, the farm had been occupied by John Freeman, his wife, and their children, who had a long-term lease for the property from Philip Schuyler. The Freemans abandoned the farm and fled to Canada, where all but three family members died during a smallpox outbreak in early 1778. The farm site was occupied for most of the nineteenth century by the Leggett and Esmond families. The Esmonds lost the property in foreclosure in 1918.[28] By 1923, the Saratoga Battlefield Association purchased the farm, holding it until funding allowed New York State to acquire the properties that became the Saratoga Battlefield, a public park, in 1927. Extensive artifact collections have been created as archaeologists have sought to understand the location, extent, and composition of fortifications, as well as the remains of farm structures that stood on the site at the time of the battles.

As discussed in chapter 3, Robert Ehrich's excavations in 1940 discovered the skeletal remains of four soldiers buried in two separate locations in the fortification ditch. These would have been casualties of the October 7 battle, since the fortification structure did not exist during the September engagement. In each location, the remains of a double burial was found. Burials 1 and 4 occurred as a double burial in the western fortification ditch, and their bodies appeared to have been carefully placed side by side on their backs. The arms of both were bent as though the hands had been folded across the chest or abdomen. These soldiers died on the field, probably not too far from where they were buried.

Ehrich left the human remains in situ, but collected some of the artifacts associated with them, including a piece of iron case shot found in the pelvic cavity of burial 1 (figure 9.4), which was the likely cause of death for this man. The case shot came from a British six-pounder cannon being fired from the Balcarres Redoubt. While it is not known if this soldier was injured in any other way, the presence of the iron ball lodged in his pelvis indicates that he suffered a terrible wound in his abdomen. In the eighteenth century, such a wound would be fatal. If the soldier was not instantly killed, he surely suffered on the field before he died. Ten pewter buttons, probably from the soldier's waistcoat, came from the grave associated with burial 3 (figure 9.4). Clay tobacco pipe fragments lay near both burial 1 and burial 2. The fragments are very small. These tobacco pipes can

FIGURE 9.4. *Upper left,* pewter buttons, probably from a soldier's waistcoat, which came from one of the four soldier burials found in 1940, SARA-823; *upper right,* fragment of an exploded iron shell discovered during the archaeological investigation of the Balcarres Redoubt in 1940, SARA-806; *lower left,* iron case shot from a British six-pounder cannon found in the pelvic cavity of skeletal remains during the Balcarres Redoubt archaeological investigations in 1940, SARA-813; *lower right,* musket balls collected from the site of Freeman's farm between 1883 and 1910 by the William W. Esmond family, who lived on the site, SARA-269, 274. Courtesy of Saratoga National Historical Park.

be considered the personal effects of both of these men; they may have been in the soldiers' pockets at the time they died. In the course of the battle, or during the process of burial, the pipes were smashed. It is likely that all four of these burials were of American soldiers mortally wounded or killed on October 7. They were buried after the redoubt had been abandoned. The remains had been laid carefully, and evidently with respect, in the ditch and covered with wood from the fortification wall. Near the bodies of burials 1 and 4, Ehrich also uncovered a fragment of an exploded iron shell (figure 9.4).

Breymann Fortified Camp

In the 1970s, Dean Snow had the opportunity to investigate the loyalist encampment site in the area north of the Breymann fortified camp. The use of metal detector reconnaissance proved valuable in identifying and collecting clusters of

FIGURE 9.5. *Top*, lock from a Brown Bess musket, found in the loyalist encampment area at the Breymann fortified camp in 1972 by Dean Snow, SARA-1681; *lower left*, cast brass cartridge box plate, probably worn by a soldier in MacKay's Loyal Volunteers, SARA-686; *lower right*, haversack buckles, iron frame, found in an encampment area located at the Breymann fortified camp, SARA-1529 and SARA-1533. Courtesy of Saratoga National Historical Park.

artifacts.[29] In 1972, Snow uncovered a hearth, camp refuse, and part of a fortification line. Some of the artifacts related to the encampment area included a square poll hatchet that probably dates between 1750 and 1763. Since the German troops at the Breymann fortified camp would not have been carrying this type of weapon, it was likely carried by a loyalist in MacKay's company. The small-size hatchet, carried on a soldier's belt, was intended to be used as a weapon.

When the camp of the loyalist troops was overrun and abandoned during the October 7 battle, several iron kettle fragments were left behind. They had been part of the camp equipment used by these soldiers. Knapsack or cartridge pouch buckles found at the site (figure 9.5) were common iron-frame buckles that secured the solders' knapsacks, which contained personal goods, such as clothing, shaving gear, eating utensils, and other personal equipment.[30] An iron razor blade was just such a personal artifact that would have been carried in a knapsack by a soldier in the loyalist encampment area. It would have folded into a handle that was covered with bone or wood. A cluster of musket parts, including a Brown Bess musket lock in excellent condition, were found in the center of the loyalist encampment (figure 9.5).

Two years later, Snow returned to continue investigating this area with the goal of better understanding the layout of the camp and camp life.[31] Artifact collection was minimal, but included some battle-related artifacts, including brass shoe buckles and an oval cast brass cartridge box plate (figure 9.5). The plate, engraved "GR," was a piece commonly issued to loyalist American troops during the war. These plates were attached to belts or cartridge pouches. The "GR" stands for "Georgius Rex," Latin for *King George*. This piece was probably worn by a soldier in Captain Samuel MacKay's Corps of Loyal Volunteers, encamped at Breymann's fortified camp.

Western Portion of the October 7 Battlefield

A cast brass flaming grenade ordnance insignia (figure 9.6), with two mounting lugs on the back, was found in the area near the wheat field in 1940. Discovered by archaeologist Robert Ehrich during a reconnaissance of the battlefield, the insignia measures about 41.3 millimeters and might have come off a British or German grenadier's pouch flap.[32] Ehrich's reconnaissance efforts on this part of the battlefield were minimal, and very few artifacts exist in the museum collection to document this part of the October 7 battle.

Military Encampment Sites on the Battlefield

Encampment areas have great potential for deposits of artifacts related to the daily life of soldiers, including what they wore and carried and how they lived in camp. Although there has never been a complete archaeological investigation of soldier encampment areas at the Saratoga Battlefield, there have been two projects that focused on portions of the British encampment areas on land above the river flats.[33] The first of the encampment sites was investigated by Dean Snow in 1974, and the artifacts recovered, combined with information from historic maps, confirmed the location of a portion of the British center column encampment area. The companies of the 21st Regiment of Foot, or Royal North British Fusiliers commanded by Major George Forster, encamped on that ground from about September 20 until October 8, 1777, or about two and a half weeks. Based on the position of the fortification wall, Snow probably located a portion of the area at the front of the encampment. The layout for a standard British regiment camp at this time included, from front to back, a fortification wall, parade ground, bell tents for the soldiers' firearms, tents for soldiers, tents for officers, camp kitchens, and an area for sutlers. At this site, the camp was laid out from south to north. With the location of the fortification wall verified, the artifacts provide a picture of the encampment layout. The predominance of soldiers', rather than officers', artifacts, along with the gun parts that were recovered,

FIGURE 9.6. *Upper left*, musket worm, found in an encampment area to the east of the Balcarres Redoubt, SARA-1950; *upper right*, cast brass cartridge box plate in the form of a crown, which would have been affixed to a cartridge box used by a soldier of the 24th Regiment of Foot, SARA-1982; *lower left*, cast brass flaming grenade ordnance insignia, found in 1940 by Robert Ehrich during his archaeological reconnaissance of the battlefield, SARA-650; *lower right*, combination tool, 21st Royal North British Fusiliers encampment area on the Saratoga Battlefield, SARA-1710. Courtesy of Saratoga National Historical Park.

suggests that part of the parade ground, perhaps the area for the bell tents for arms and a portion of the area where the soldiers camped, was uncovered.

The artifact collection from the 21st Royal North British Fusilier's encampment site (*SARA-202*) contains 102 musket balls. Approximately half of these musket balls were unfired. Five of the unfired balls were deliberately cut or otherwise altered. These musket balls were deliberately altered in such a way that had they been fired, they would have inflicted more damage. One cut musket ball (figure 9.7) was incised along the surface, cutting it into four quarters. Musket balls were cut partially through so that when fired, the ball would fragment and spray out, making it a more lethal projectile. There is evidence that both sides used such tactics, even though British General Sir William Howe wrote to George Washington in 1777 complaining about this "unwarrantable and malicious practice." Washington's response called the practice of mutilating musket

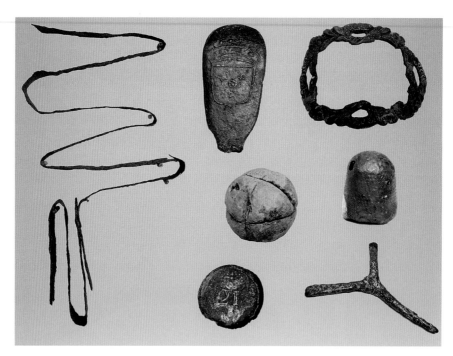

FIGURE 9.7. *Left*, iron broiler made from a barrel hoop, from the encampment area of the 21st Regiment, SARA-1770; *upper middle*, cast pewter spoon handle fragment with a family crest, ca. 1765–75, found in the 21st Regiment encampment area, SARA-1791; *upper right*, cast brass man's shoe buckle frame, ca. 1760–75, found to the east of the Balcarres Redoubt, SARA-2023; *middle left*, cut musket ball, found in the encampment area of the 21st Regiment, Royal North British Fusiliers, on the Saratoga Battlefield, occupied between the battles. The soldier who scored this musket ball into quarters had already witnessed the bloody fighting of September 19, SARA-1735; *middle right*, thimble, brass, ca. 1750–75, found in the encampment area of the 21st Regiment, SARA-1720; *lower middle*, cast pewter coat button, 21st Regiment, Royal North British Fusiliers, SARA-1798; *lower right*, combination tool, 21st Regiment encampment area. The combination musket tool had two arms with flat blades on the end of each arm that were used as screwdrivers. The third arm of these tools had a round treaded end that may have been used to store the threaded musket worm, SARA-1827. Courtesy of Saratoga National Historical Park.

balls so that they would produce greater casualties "highly abhorred by me." The altered musket balls found in the 21st Regiment camp demonstrate that, even though officially frowned upon, the practice was clearly being used on the battlefield at Saratoga.[34]

In addition to military items, domestic materials were also uncovered in this encampment area. For example, a small brass thimble documents domestic activities behind the front lines of the army (figure 9.7). Camp followers did laundry and mending for the soldiers, and this thimble points to the presence of women in the camp of the 21st Regiment. One of the most intriguing artifacts

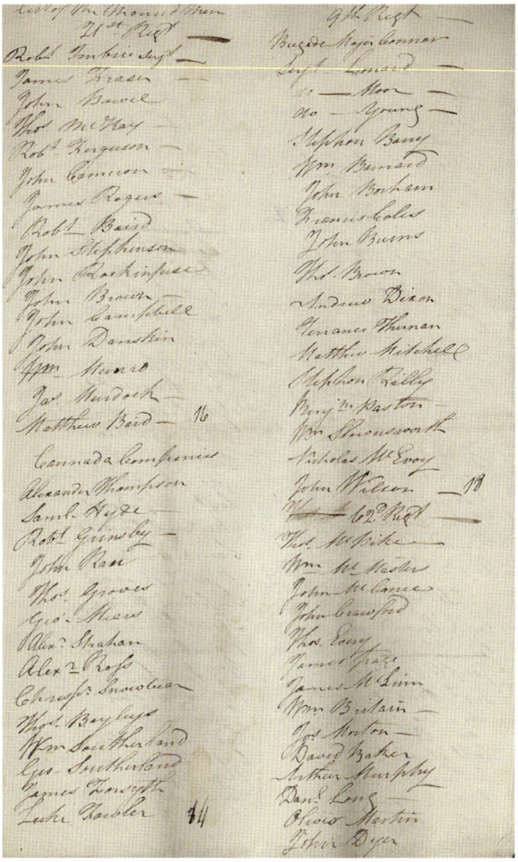

FIGURE 9.8. Convention Army List of Married Men, a handwritten list of nearly 200 soldiers of the (British) Convention army who were married and had families. Although it is not dated and no location is given, it is assumed that the document dates from about 1781, since the Army of the United States separated Convention prisoners who were married from those who were single and "unattached" during the latter part of the War, SARA-19,642. Courtesy of Saratoga National Historical Park.

from the encampment area is a pewter spoon, broken into pieces and missing its bowl (figure 9.7). The shape of the end of the handle indicates that it was made between 1765 and 1775. Made of pewter, the spoon has a family crest impressed on the tip of the handle. Although no maker's mark is present, the owner of the spoon, a soldier in the 21st Regiment, scratched his initials, "I. R.," just below the crest. In the eighteenth century, the initial "J" was commonly inscribed as an "I," so this soldier's initials were "J. R." Based on muster rolls taken from St. Pierre, Canada, on February 24, 1777, eleven possible soldiers in the 21st Regiment had the initials "J. R."[35] Soldiers in flank companies encamping at Freeman's farm and not the area investigated were eliminated, leaving six names, and these were then researched for the possibility that their families had heraldic crests. The crest on the spoon is distinctive, although the emblems in the field are worn. Preliminary research points to James Rogers of William Thomas Tayler's company as the spoon's owner. If that is the case, then it is of special interest, since James Rogers was listed on the Convention Army List of Married Men from the 21st Regiment, a list made about 1781 (figure 9.8). Rogers's wife and probably his children were in the encampment area on the battlefield, and remained prisoners in the Convention army. A Convention army document in a private collection lists eighteen women and twenty-nine children in the 21st Regiment camp in Maryland in April 1781. It is not known whether Rogers and his family survived the war and captivity or where they might have lived following the conflict.

Other personal items found in the encampment area included 21st Regiment coat buttons, a barrel hoop broiler, combination musket tools, and a musket worm. Of the twenty-three buttons found within this encampment location, seventeen are cast pewter coat buttons from the 21st Regiment of Foot, Royal North British Fusiliers (figure 9.7). These buttons were found scattered in different locations across the encampment area.

The barrel hoop broiler was used for cooking meat over a fire (figure 9.7). This iron broiler was handmade by bending a hoop from a barrel into the shape of a grill so that it could be placed over a fire for cooking meat. This broiler was found in the 21st Regiment encampment site, and may have been in a soldier's personal equipment to be used in his mess.

The combination musket tool had two arms with flat blades on the end of each arm that were used as screwdrivers (figures 9.6 and 9.7). Different-size screws were used to affix the metal components of a musket to the stock. The third arm of these tools had a round threaded end that may have been used to store the threaded musket worm. The musket worm was a tool used by a soldier to clean the inside of the barrel of a musket (figure 9.6). Its twisted tines held a patch of tow, which was pushed into the barrel to remove gunpowder residue. Found to the east of the Balcarres Redoubt in another likely encampment area, the frame of a man's cast brass shoe buckle is decorated with a foliate design that appears to be laurel leaves (figure 9.7). Its overall rococo design with rounded corners and curved leafy forms date the buckle between 1760 and 1775. Found nearby, a cartridge box plate (figure 9.6) in the form of a cast brass crown would have been affixed to a cartridge box used by a soldier of the 24th Regiment of Foot.

Siege and Surrender

Draft of the Convention of Saratoga

In addition to the thousands of archaeological artifacts, Saratoga National Historical Park has numerous manuscripts in its collection that document the surrender at Saratoga. The surrender of the British army, then the mightiest army in the world, to the Army of the United States, the world's newest military force, was a profound shock to many. The effect of the surrender was to bring new allies, like France, with their supplies and funds to the American cause. The Articles of Convention were signed the evening of October 16, one day before the British surrendered their arms, stacking them and marching southward as captives from Saratoga toward Albany. A handwritten draft of the convention, dated October 16, 1777, was prepared by Lieutenant Colonel Giles Jackson of Massachusetts. Lieutenant Colonel Jackson saved the document, and after his death in Monterey, Massachusetts, in 1810, it was passed down in his family. At some point in the late 1920s, the document was sold in an estate sale in western New York State and acquired by Dr. William Otis Sawtelle, a physics professor as well as a collector of historical documents and objects. Dr. Sawtelle developed the Islesford Historical Museum, now part of Acadia National Park, and the document was transferred from Acadia National Park to Saratoga National Historical Park in October 1974.

On the same day the convention document was signed and the British army surrendered to the Americans at Saratoga, an officer from Colonel Jonathan Latimer's Regiment of Connecticut Militia, encamped at Saratoga, wrote home to his family in Colchester. Although hastily penned, this letter documents the momentous event of the British surrender from the perspective of a common soldier. It was preserved by generations of the family of Hepzibah Ely Pratt (1745–1815), the soldier's sister, until it was donated to Saratoga National Historical Park in 1967. Elihu Ely, born in 1737, died in Lyme, Connecticut, on June 25, 1815, and is buried in the Ely Family Cemetery. He served in Captain Jonathan Calking's company, Colonel Jonathan Latimer's Regiment of Connecticut Militia, from August 23 through October 30, 1777. The following is a transcription of the letter.

> Camp Saritoga October 16th 1777
>
> Loving Brother & Sister These with my Love to you and yr Children may inform that through Divine goodness I enjoy a comfortable state of Health and hope that you Enjoy the same Blessing. There has been a sessation of arms hear it took Place the Day before yesterday and I understand that this Day Mr. Burgoin and his army are to resign themselves Prisoners of War and be conducted through Albany and so on to Boston the Tuesday before Last there was a smart Engagement Between the troops of Genel. Gates and General Burgoyn when the former came of Victorious and the Latter retreated about 8 miles to this Place as fast as their surcumstances would admit of our troops followed them and so surrounded their Camp that they were oblig'd to comply as above mentioned as is reported and Depended on in Camp tho the particulars of the Capitulation has not yet made Publick. I have no time to write but subscribe my self yr
>
> Loving Brother
> Elihu Ely

Burgoyne's army, known as the "Convention army," surrendered at Saratoga to General Gates on October 17, 1777. The Convention army, originally numbering about 6,000 officers and men, remained prisoners of war through the rest of the war, and were marched and quartered in Massachusetts, Virginia, Maryland, Pennsylvania, and Connecticut at various times. By the end of the war in 1783, desertions and deaths had cut their number to about 600 men. A handwritten list of nearly 200 soldiers of the (British) Convention army who were married and had families (figure 9.8) details men by regiment, including the 21st, "Canada Companies" (flank companies of the 29th, 31st, 34th, and 53rd Regiments), 9th, 62nd, Royal Artillery, 24th, 20th, and a detachment of the 33rd Regiment. This single manuscript is from a larger body of the Saratoga Convention Army Papers, now split up. No date or location is listed on the manuscript, but it can be assumed that it dates from about 1781, since the Army of the United States separated Convention prisoners who were married from those who were single and "unattached" during the latter part of the War. It is particularly interesting to read the names of the married men of the 21st Regiment, Royal North British Fusiliers, whose encampment on the Saratoga Battlefield was investigated by Dean Snow in 1974.

Surrendered Weapons

American forces captured eight cannons during the battle on October 7: two twelve-pounders and six six-pounders. Ten days later, on October 17, 1777, the British army surrendered all government-owned weapons and ammunition to the Army of the United States at Saratoga. Among the items surrendered were muskets, artillery pieces, case shot and musket balls, wagons, and equipment. Of the thirty-eight captured and surrendered pieces of ordnance, eight are now in the museum collection of Saratoga National Historical Park. Although the legal title of all trophy cannons remains with the US Army, the park has custody of two howitzers, one three-pounder, four twelve-pounders, and one twenty-four-pounder. In addition, a rare and important six-pounder cannon is on loan to the park from the US Army.

Trophy cannons have many tales to tell, but the most notable story of the cannon in figure 9.9 comes not from the eighteenth century, but from the twentieth century. Captured by the Americans, or surrendered in October 1777, the cannon was one of eighteen six-pounders in Burgoyne's artillery train. Of those eighteen, only three are known to survive today. The cannon's whereabouts after the war are not known, but it likely was used in coastal defense of New York Harbor in the War of 1812. By the late nineteenth century, it had been transferred from the armory in Central Park to Prospect Park in Brooklyn, the site of the 1776 Battle of Long Island. In 1934, Town of Saratoga historian Thomas Hanrahan discovered its whereabouts, and was able to secure the loan of the cannon from New York City to Schuylerville/Town of Saratoga in October of that year. For unknown

FIGURE 9.9. Medium twelve-pounder cannon, William Bowen, 1760, cast at the Woolwich Arsenal in England. Surrendered by the Convention of Saratoga in 1777, by the early 1940s, this cannon was displayed outside of the US Department of State, War, and Navy Building in Washington, DC. As plans for a scrap-metal drive took place during World War II, the Saratoga Trophy cannons were retrieved from various places and sent to Saratoga National Historical Park by order of President Franklin D. Roosevelt in 1943, SARA-373. Courtesy of Saratoga National Historical Park.

reasons, the cannon was never put on public display as it had been originally intended. It sat in storage until 1961, when it was removed from the Saratoga town historian's barn without permission. From there, it began a fifty-four-year odyssey through five states in possession of seven different individuals, none of whom had legal title. Although the provenance, the title of the cannon, was never clear, it was sold and resold until it ended up in a private museum in Tuscaloosa, Alabama. Finally located by National Park Service staff in 2009, after more than forty years of uncertainty, custody of the cannon was sought by the US Army, the holder of the legal title, in 2011. After negotiation, the cannon was returned to the US Army in May 2013 and was brought to Saratoga National Historical Park on loan. Today, it occupies a prominent place in the park's visitor center.

Burgoyne had four twelve-pounder bronze cannons in his artillery train. On October 7, two of the twelve-pounders were brought onto the field from the artillery park. In the bloody fighting that took place in the wheat field, both twelve-pounders were captured by American forces. The other two twelve-pounder cannons were surrendered at Saratoga on October 17. All four of the twelve-pounders are today in the museum collection at Saratoga NHP, although it is unknown which two were brought into battle on October 7 (figure 9.9). All four were engraved in 1783 with identical trophy honors: "Surrendered by the Convention of Saratoga, October 17, 1777."

After the Battle: Battlefield Souvenirs

Collecting battlefield artifacts began soon after the conflict ended in 1777 and continued into the nineteenth century, with local residents and battlefield tourists collecting souvenirs. Musket balls were picked up over the years, many times after spring plowing exposed the distinctive white coating on the lead musket balls still in the ground. Beginning in the late 1920s, some of these private collections were donated to the Saratoga Battlefield's museum collections. Today, the museum collections contain more than fifty examples of shot and shell that people picked up on the battlefield over the years. While the private collections of the nineteenth century are not pinpointed rigorously to specific locations, they retain a special place as evidence of early interest in preserving the stories of what happened on the land that quickly reverted to farm fields in the generations after the conflict. For example, a collection of musket balls from the Freeman's farm/Balcarres Redoubt site was donated to the park in 1952 by Lewis J. Ellsworth, a local farmer who lived near the battlefield all his life (figure 9.4). Ellsworth married (Phoebe) Annie Esmond in 1886. She was the daughter of William W. Esmond, who purchased the Freeman farm property on the Saratoga battlefield in 1883. William Esmond died in his home on the battlefield in 1913. It is likely that these musket balls were collected in the late nineteenth to early twentieth century by Mr. Esmond or his daughter, Annie Esmond Ellsworth, from their land.[36] A six-pound English cannonball was also unearthed around 1940 in Schuylerville and donated to the park in 1947. The impressed "broad arrow" on the iron cannonball indicates it was a British-owned piece. It may have been found in the vicinity of the British encampment at Victory Woods.

Soldier's Loot and Auctioned Furnishings

The museum collection also contains four unique objects that have intriguing ties to the American victory at Saratoga. Aside from the cache of the arms and supplies surrendered to the Army of the United States on October 17, 1777, there is evidence that some American soldiers were helping themselves to objects left behind by British soldiers, both at the battlefield and nine miles north at the Saratoga surrender site. In 1988, Saratoga National Historical Park received a brass brazier and a pair of eighteenth-century sleeve buttons (cuff links) from the New Hampshire Historical Society. The two objects had been donated to the society in 1956 along with a family history that they had come from Burgoyne's tent at Saratoga. A family descendant affixed a handwritten tag to the brazier that read: "Taken from Burgoyne's tent at Saratoga by a descendant of Christian Remick." It is ironic that the soldier's ancestor, the progenitor of the Remick

FIGURE 9.10. Brass brazier, known as a "smoker's brazier." Missing its wooden handle, this brazier would have held hot coals used to light tobacco pipes for smoking. It was allegedly acquired from a British camp at Saratoga by Private James Remick (1760–1836) of Haverhill, Massachusetts, of Captain Joseph Eaton's company, Colonel Samuel Johnson's Regiment of Massachusetts Militia. Remick arrived at the battlefield on October 6 and fought in the October 7 battle, then marched north to Saratoga, SARA-3768. Courtesy of Saratoga National Historical Park.

family in America, was named, but the soldier, himself, was not. Through pension documents and other archival records, the name of the American soldier who took these things at Saratoga was identified. He was James Remick (1760–1836) of Haverhill, Massachusetts, a seventeen-year-old private in Captain Joseph Eaton's company, Colonel Samuel Johnson's Regiment of Massachusetts Militia. He had enlisted for a three-month term from the middle of August to the middle of October 1777. Remick ended up at the battlefield on October 6 and fought in the October 7 battle, then marched north to Saratoga.[37] The brazier and sleeve buttons were mentioned in Remick's great-grandson Daniel Clark Remick's February 1898 application for membership in the Sons of the American Revolution:

> He [James Remick] was at the surrender of Saratoga, and I have in my possession Burgoyne's Sleeve Buttons and Brass Chafing Dish, which were taken from his tent by said James Remick, they having descended to me by will from David Remick, late of Kennebunk, Maine.[38]

Upon his death in 1917, the brazier and sleeve buttons went to Daniel Clark Remick's brother, James, whose daughter, Gladys Remick (Mrs. Jesse Wilson), donated them to the New Hampshire Historical Society in 1956.

The brazier has a round bowl on a hollow circular foot, with a socket for a wood handle (not extant), and three brass supports fastened to the rim with copper rivets (figure 9.10). The brazier's vented sides allowed air to move through hot coals placed in the bowl. The top brackets were intended to support a kettle or pan. While braziers were typically used to heat tea kettles or pots, this one would have been known as a "smoker's brazier." It would have held hot coals used to light tobacco pipes for smoking. Fragments of similar brass smoker's braziers have been found in archaeological investigations at Colonial Williamsburg, including at the Wetherburn's Tavern site in the mid-1960s, and a nearly identical intact smoker's brazier (1952-106) is in the museum collection of Colonial Williamsburg.[39] The bottom of the bowl is pierced with heart-shaped openings, and the foot is pierced with heart, oval, diamond, and crescent shapes.

In addition to the brass brazier, Remick also brought home a pair of sleeve buttons. They have a silver setting with quartz crystal over a twisted-wire design backed with red foil. Although cyphers, or sets of initials, were sometimes woven in wire under the crystal, these sleeve buttons do not appear to have a cypher, but rather a simple twisted decorative design under the crystal.

Once collected, these items were treasured possessions for five generations of the Remick family. Today, they are evidence not only of what British officers had on campaign in 1777, but also what was taken as a trophy and treasured by a family as an ancestral connection to a pivotal moment in the war for American independence.

Two other intriguing objects, an English eighteenth-century folding camp bed and half of a folding dining table, were donated to the park's museum collection in 1987. Used by an English officer, this folding bed with a canopy top, sometimes known as a "camp bed," a "field bed," or a "tent bed," was made in England around 1775. A functional piece of furniture made of hardwood with brass hardware, the bed was designed to provide some of the comforts of home while on campaign. The hinged top, tapering posts, turned legs, and rails are hinged so that the bed can be folded. Once folded, it could be stored and carried from camp to camp. It would have been used with a mattress on top of a sacking bottom, which is no longer extant. Bed curtains would have hung over the canopy top.

According to the donor, this bed, along with a two-piece folding table and a set of chairs, was taken from Burgoyne's camp equipment, and could have belonged to General John Burgoyne. The donor claimed that the furnishings were taken by Major General Benjamin Lincoln, but recent research has determined that the furnishings descended in another branch of the Lincoln family. Because General Lincoln had suffered a wound following the October 7 battle and was taken to a hospital, it is not known who might have taken them from an officer's tent at Saratoga, if that is how the furnishings started on their journey. It is possible that these furnishings, taken from a camp at Saratoga, were acquired at auction by one of the Lincolns in the Worcester, Massachusetts, branch of the family.

The mahogany table with brass hardware also folds for portability, and is actually one-half of a larger dining table. After Saratoga, the history of this table is not documented until thirty-five years later, when it was mentioned as having been used by John W. Lincoln (1787–1852) during the War of 1812. John W. Lincoln was the son of Levi Lincoln, who settled in Worcester, Massachusetts, in

1775. Levi was a lieutenant governor of the commonwealth of Massachusetts and he was President Thomas Jefferson's attorney general. Both Levi Lincoln and his father, Enoch, would have been of an appropriate age to have been soldiers during the American Revolution, but records show that neither man served in a capacity that took them to the battlefield. Therefore, it is not known from whom John W. Lincoln got the table.

At John W. Lincoln's death, it appears the two halves of the table, six chairs, and presumably the bed, went to his younger brother, Levi Lincoln Jr., also of Worcester. Levi Lincoln Jr.'s son, (Civil War General) William Sever Lincoln (1811–89) apparently left his estate to his wife, Elizabeth T. Lincoln, and her 1898 will specifies that her son, Winslow S. Lincoln (1848–1902), was to get "one of the tables formerly General Burgoynes [sic], and used by his uncle, John W. Lincoln during the War of 1812."[40] Winslow's five children each got one of the chairs from what must have been a set of six, and one of Winslow's daughters, Margaret, got "the bedstead belonging to the camp outfit of General Burgoyne, which is now in my Homestead House, known as the General Winslow S. Lincoln farm."[41] Another son, Levi, got "one of the chairs and one of the tables formerly belonging to General Burgoyne."[42] By 1987, when the donation was made to the park, only the bed and half of the table were available. Despite the inability to authenticate the donor's claim that General Benjamin Lincoln had acquired these pieces at Saratoga, the bed and the dining table are wonderful examples of late eighteenth-century English camp furniture that would have been used by an officer.

Conclusion

The artifacts and manuscripts used to tell the stories of the soldiers and civilians at Saratoga in this chapter are preserved in a collection storage facility at the park along with thousands of others. Some are on exhibit in the park's visitor center, while others related to the Schuyler family are occasionally exhibited at the General Philip Schuyler House in Schuylerville, open to the public seasonally. Many more await further research and all have the potential to bring greater understanding to the conflict and the characters that shaped the nation's future at Saratoga.

NOTES

1. Data is from the 2014 Collections Management Report for Saratoga National Historical Park. The archives collection also includes the Saratoga Battlefield Papers (1927–38), an important group of records on the early administration of the park under New York State; the Park Administration Papers from 1938 to 1948; the Neilson Papers; the George Strover

Papers (1821–1938) (the Strover/Lowber family owned the Schuyler house from 1839 to 1948); and the Edwin Hoyt Papers, a research collection of rare primary-source material on the Northern Campaign of 1777 and the Battles of Saratoga. There is also a small collection of Saratoga Battlefield–related manuscripts, including letters and receipts. The museum collection also holds a draft of the October 1777 Convention of Saratoga document.

2. Stephen Olausen, Kristen Heitert, Laura Kline, and Carey Jones, *National Register of Historic Places Nomination Form*, Saratoga National Historical Park, 2011, 5.

3. Ezra Buel's pension application, *Executive Documents of the 22nd Congress, December 7, 1831*, vol. 2 (Washington, DC: US Government Printing Office, 1831), 285–86.

4. Olausen et al., *National Register of Historic Places Nomination Form*, 64.

5. Victor Hugo Paltsits, ed., *Minutes of the Commissioners for Detecting and Defeating Conspiracies in the State of New York, Albany County Sessions, 1778–1781*, 3 vols. (Albany: State of New York, 1909).

6. His name also appeared in public documents as "Carthy," "McCarthy," or "McCarty."

7. David R. Starbuck, "The American Headquarters for the Battle of Saratoga: 1985–1986 Excavations," manuscript, Saratoga National Historical Park archives, 1987, 31.

8. Eric Schnitzer, "Alteration and Devastation: The Upper Hudson River Valley during the Latter Phase of the Northern Campaign of 1777," unpublished manuscript, 2014, 11.

9. Albany County Deed Book 19, Albany County Hall of Records, Albany, New York, 230.

10. Tricia A. Barbagallo, "John Tayler," New York State Museum, Colonial Albany Social History Project, available at http://www.nysm.nysed.gov/albany/bios/t/jotayler.html, accessed August 2014.

11. Albany County Deed Book 10, Albany County Hall of Records, Albany, New York, 320.

12. Rodris Roth, "Tea Drinking in 18th-Century America: Its Etiquette and Equipage," United States Museum Bulletin no. 225 (Washington, DC: Smithsonian Institution, 1961), 79.

13. Ivor Noel Hume, *A Guide to Artifacts of Colonial America* (Philadelphia: University of Pennsylvania Press, 1969).

14. Eric S. Johnson, "Archeological Overview and Assessment of the Saratoga National Historical Park, New York" (draft), National Park Service manuscript, 1997, 116.

15. Arlene Palmer, *Glass in Early America* (Wilmington, DE: Henry Francis Du Pont Winterthur Museum, 1993), 357.

16. Jennifer McCann, "Completion Report: Archaeology Backlog Cataloging, Fiscal Years 2011/2012, Saratoga National Historical Park, New York," manuscript, Northeast Museum Services Center, National Park Service, 2013, 7.

17. Janine E. Skerry and Suzanne Findlen Hood, *Salt-Glazed Stoneware in Early America* (Williamsburg, VA: Colonial Williamsburg Foundation, 2009), 160.

18. See references to Catherine Schuyler's concern over the "milch cows" in Susan May Haswell, "Catherine Schuyler" monograph, Schuyler Mansion State Historic Site. See also "On the Score of Hospitality: Selected Receipts of a Van Rensselaer Family," Albany, New York, 1785–1835, Historic Cherry Hill, 1986, 85–90.

19. "The Talk of the Town," *Schuylerville Standard*, July 10, 1895, available at http://www.fultonhistory.com/Fulton.html (Schuylerville_NY_Standard_1895-0242.pdf), accessed September 26, 2014.

20. I am grateful to Walter Richard Wheeler of Hartgen Associates for his ideas on this and other nearby features discovered in 1958 and 1959. The original report is Edward McMillan Larrabee, "Report of Archeological Excavations Conducted at Schuyler House, Saratoga

National Historical Park, Schuylerville, New York, from June 8 through June 29, 1959," manuscript, 1960, 43–60.

21. The amount of eating utensils located by both Cotter/Larrabee and Starbuck was relatively small, but the spoons, forks, and dinner knives located all date to the eighteenth century. Two pewter spoon bowls (*SARA-30,612* and *SARA-30,081*), two two-tine forks (*SARA-30,702* and *SARA-30,772*), and two dinner knives (*SARA-30,208* and *SARA-30,294*) are in the Cotter/Larrabee collection. An intact pewter "wavy-end type" spoon (Starbuck #956), forks (#879, #975), and an eighteenth-century table knife (#879) were found by Starbuck.

22. Larrabee, "Report of Archeological Excavations Conducted at Schuyler House," 298. The very narrow spur or heel on the pipe fragment matches figure 19 on page 303 in Ivor Noel Hume's *A Guide to Artifacts of Colonial America* (Philadelphia: University of Pennsylvania Press, 1969). Hume dates this English-made clay tobacco pipe form to between 1690 and 1750. Considering the history of the Schuyler estate site, the pipe fragment may date to the 1740s, when a French-led raid destroyed the first Schuyler house, possibly in this vicinity.

23. Archaeological excavations were also undertaken at the Schuyler mansion in Albany by Lois Feister in the 1990s. Lois M. Feister, "A Synthesis of Archaeology at Schuyler Mansion State Historic Site, Albany, New York, prior to the 1994 Visitor Center Addition Project" (Waterford, NY: New York State Office of Parks, Recreation and Historic Preservation, Archaeology Unit, Bureau of Historic Sites, 1995).

24. The approximately eight foot by eleven foot foundation, excavated and measured in 1958 and 1959, was interpreted as a "vegetable cellar" by Cotter and Larrabee. This attribution of use was tentative, however, and as more is learned about the layout of structures on the Schuyler estate, a better identification of this building might be made. See Eric S. Johnson, "Archeological Overview and Assessment of the Saratoga National Historical Park, New York" (draft), National Park Service manuscript, 1997, 136–37.

25. Walter Richard Wheeler, "'Once Adorned with Quaint Dutch Tiles': A Preliminary Analysis of Delft Tiles Found in Archaeological Contexts and Historical Collections in the Upper Hudson Valley," in *Soldiers, Cities, and Landscapes: Papers in Honor of Charles L. Fisher*, ed. Penelope Ballard Drooker and John P. Hart, New York State Museum Bulletin 513 (Albany: New York State Education Department, 2010). See also Leslie E. Gerhauser, "Hart Tyles and Histories: Dutch Bible Tiles in Eighteenth-Century New York," in *Soldiers, Cities, and Landscapes: Papers in Honor of Charles L. Fisher,* ed. Penelope Ballard Drooker and John P. Hart, New York State Museum Bulletin 513 (Albany: New York State Education Department, 2010).

26. Wheeler, "'Once Adorned with Quaint Dutch Tiles,'" 110.

27. Alicia Paresi, "What's Love Got to Do with It?," *Northeast Museum Services Center Archeology and Museum Blog*, available at http://nmscarcheologylab.wordpress.com/2013/02/14/whats-love-got-to-do-with-it, accessed February 14, 2013.

28. "Historic Freeman Farm Sold," *Saratogian*, August 14, 1918.

29. Dean Snow, "Report on Archaeological Investigations and Excavations of Revolutionary Sites, Saratoga National Historical Park, New York, 1974–1975," manuscript, 5.

30. John U. Rees, "'This Napsack I carryd through the war of the Revolution': Knapsacks of the American War, 1775–1783" (part 2 of 3), *Brigade Dispatch*, Autumn 2014, 4.

31. Snow, "Report on Archaeological Investigations and Excavations of Revolutionary Sites," 62.

32. Don Troiani and James L. Kochan, *Insignia of Independence* (Gettysburg, PA: Thomas, 2012), 157. Figure BGPL18 is most similar in style and size, and it was "found near Saratoga," according to the authors.

33. The American encampment areas on the south end of the battlefield have not been investigated archaeologically.

34. Daniel M. Sivilich, "Revolutionary War Musket Ball Typology: An Analysis of Lead Artifacts Excavated at Monmouth Battlefield State Park," *Southern Campaigns of the American Revolution* 2, no. 1 (January 2005): 15–16, available at http://southerncampaign.org/newsletter/v2n1.pdf.

35. "21st Foot, 1st Battalion General Muster Books and Pay Lists, 1769–1783," National Archives UK, Kew WO/12/3778–2, copy from files at Saratoga NHP.

36. William W. Esmond death notice, *Saratogian*, February 3, 1913, 1.

37. Pension application, James Remick of Barrington, New Hampshire, September 1832, accessed on Fold3.com.

38. Daniel C. Remick, Sons of the American Revolution membership application, February 19, 1898, accessed on Ancestry.com.

39. Audrey Noel Hume, *Wetherburn's Tavern Archaeological Report, Block 9 Building 00 Lot 20 & 21* (originally titled: *The Wetherburn Site Volume II Part 4A Small Finds and Iron Objects*), Colonial Williamsburg Foundation Library Research Report Series 1182, Williamsburg, Virginia, 1971, 1990.

40. Copy of will of Elizabeth T. Lincoln, in *SARA-248* accession file, Saratoga National Historical Park Museum Collections Files.

41. Ibid.

42. Ibid.

CHAPTER TEN | DONALD W. LINEBAUGH

Commemorating and Preserving an Embattled Landscape

Introduction

THE COMMEMORATION OF the people, places, and events of the Revolutionary War actually began before the fighting stopped. In fact, some events were deemed worthy of memorialization by Congress within days of their occurrence. Unlike battles that only revealed their true significance with the benefit of hindsight and reflection, the American victory at Saratoga was immediately recognized as a profoundly important event. Commemoration of battles like Saratoga occurred in a variety of ways, from published histories and lectures, to battlefield tours and tourism, to monuments and markers, and finally to anniversary celebrations. With the passage of time, the nature of commemoration at Revolutionary War battlefields evolved to reflect current social and political trends. Because of its prominence in the American psyche, commemoration at Saratoga has been sustained over time and reflects different concepts of and approaches to memory and commemoration.

Commemorative efforts at Saratoga have taken place for well over two centuries. While monuments and memorial markers initially took center stage, the importance of place and space, including landscape and military features, was acknowledged as critical to memory from early in the commemorative period. Major monuments like the enormous obelisk begun at Saratoga in 1877 established the Revolutionary War as a fundamental moment in our national experience; early monuments helped to unify an otherwise fractious and disparate republic, and the post–Civil War monuments to the Revolution again provided tangible symbols of a common national history and purpose. With the dawn of the twentieth century, these symbols of fighting for freedom and independence were again called on to unite a nation at war. By mid-century, the country's Revolutionary pursuit of freedom was singled out in the fight against Communism.

In fact, the New York State Regents sought to strengthen their curriculum to enhance the "teaching of American history and heritage . . . in the ideological war against communism."[1] With a much broader cross section of the population visiting historic sites, the mid-twentieth century also witnessed the growing importance of experiencing history on the "spot" where it happened, making space and place matter and driving new interpretive programs like living history and reenactments at battlefields. This chapter traces the evolution of commemorative efforts at Saratoga over time and examines changing relationships between memory, commemoration, and preservation.

From their beginning, commemorative expressions were undertaken first by private citizens and organizations and only later by local, state, or federal government agencies. For battlefields like Saratoga, ultimately deemed worthy of the highest degree of attention, the role played by the federal government in their commemorative efforts has been paramount. However, involvement of the federal government in the commemoration of Revolutionary War battlefields was a gradual and incremental matter and, thus, not always apparent. As at Saratoga, it was the efforts of private individuals first accepting the challenge to commemorate the battlefields and then these groups' subsequent funding challenges that finally brought the federal government into the effort. These interventions first took the form of monument building and memorialization and only later did the federal government embrace the protection of entire battlefield landscapes. The story of commemoration at Saratoga chronicles the development of a nascent preservation practice at the local, state, and regional levels, and marks an early foray of the federal government into the realm of historic preservation.

Celebrating Place: Early Visits and Memorials

"By commemorating the Revolutionary War in sermons, newspapers, monuments, parades, songs, and material culture," writes historian Sarah Purcell, "Americans created a set of stories that sought to give meaning to the real violence of war."[2] One of the earliest recorded narratives to celebrate the American victory at Saratoga occurred as a "stirring sermon" read "immediately after the capitulation" of the British at Yorktown in 1781. On the invitation of General Washington to offer divine services, the Reverend Israel Evans delivered a "most patriotic discourse in praise of the glorious victory which had virtually brought to an end the English cause in this country."[3] Summarizing the course of the war, Evans noted that following the victories at Trenton and Princeton, "an American army again took the field, and the enemy found they had the war to begin anew. Near the close of this year, the Almighty, 'who had not given us as a prey to their teeth,' remarkably helped us, and gave Burgoyne and all his army into the hands of the United States."[4] Drawing on the wisdom of the psalmist, Evans plainly viewed the victory at Saratoga as an example of God's support of the American cause, casting the Almighty as the deliverer of American victory and freedom.[5]

Visits to the Saratoga Battlefield began within years of the American capture of Burgoyne's army. These sojourners provide the earliest descriptions of the battle and battlefield, memorializing Saratoga in the pantheon of Revolutionary War battles by committing their observations to print. These early visits were broadly in the tradition of the grand tour of the continent, "integral to the life of the gentry in both Europe and the United States."[6] Among the early travelers to Saratoga was the Marquis de Chastellux, who accompanied Rochambeau to America in 1780, served as a major general, and, following the capture of Cornwallis, traveled across the United States. These travels formed the narrative of his book "Voyage dans l'Amerique Septentrionale dans les années, 1780–2," published in Paris in 1786.[7]

While at Albany in 1780, Chastellux accepted an invitation from General Philip Schuyler to visit the Saratoga battlefield and surrender grounds. Chastellux and Schuyler traveled up the Hudson to Stillwater, where Chastellux transferred to a sledge to reach "Bream's Heights" [Bemis Heights]. Describing "the spot chosen by General Gates for his position," Chastellux noted the clear remains of several redoubts and large entrenchments on the heights. From there, the group visited Freeman's farm, and then "the spot where Arnold . . . leaped his horse over the entrenchment of the enemy."[8] "After surveying Burgoyne's lines," wrote Chastellux, "I passed through a field where he had established his hospital." From there, he traveled to General Schuyler's country estate in Saratoga, where the following morning they visited the surrender grounds. Chastellux was clearly moved by his visit to this sacred ground: "I confess that when I was conducted to the spot where the English laid down their arms . . . I could not but partake of the triumph of the Americans."[9]

In 1795, another European traveler, the Duc de la Rochefoucauld-Liancourt, visited the surrender grounds at Saratoga as part of his extensive travels through the United States. In his account of the visit, the Duc writes that "I have seen this truly memorable place, which may be considered as the spot where the independence of America was sealed."[10] Speaking of the spot at which General Burgoyne surrendered his army, Rochefoucauld-Liancourt explains that "it remains exactly as it then was. . . . Not the least alteration has taken place since that time. The entrenchments still exist; nay, the footpath is still seen on which the adjutant of General Gates proceeded to the English general with the ultimatum of the American commander."[11] Stopping at the home of John Schuyler, the son of General Philip Schuyler, the Duc observed that the tract held the encampments of both armies. "How happy," he exclaimed, "must an American feel in the possession of such property."[12] Sensing the great importance of the place and noting the lack of formal recognition, Rochefoucauld-Liancourt was astonished "that neither Congress nor the Legislature of New York should have erected a monument on this spot reciting in plain terms this glorious event and calling it to the recollection of all men who should pass this way."[13]

Another sojourner to the battlefields was the Reverend Timothy Dwight, who published an emotional account of one of several visits he made to Saratoga while traveling across New England. Speaking in 1799 of his stops on the "heights of Stillwater" and "Plains of Saratoga," Dwight recounted: "These scenes I have examined—the former with solemnity and awe, the latter with ardor and admiration . . . here it was impossible not to remember that on this very spot a controversy was decided upon which hung the liberty and happiness of a nation."[14] Dwight, president of Yale College since 1795, explained that "future travelers will resort to this spot with the same emotions which we experience, and recall with enthusiasm the glorious events of which it is the perpetual memorial." In so doing, he established the landscape of the battlefield area as a lasting memorial to the event, and that memory was perpetuated with each visitor to the site.[15]

Benjamin Silliman, a professor of science at Yale College, commented on the Saratoga battlefields after a visit in 1819. Silliman's detailed account highlights the value of his tour guide, Ezra "Major" Buel, a local resident who participated in the conflict.[16] Asserting the importance of place in historical memory, Silliman movingly records that he was "writing in the very house, and my table stands on the very spot in the room where General Fraser breathed his last."[17] Further emphasizing the importance of tangible links to the event, he reports that "before me lies one of the bullets shot on that occasion; they are often found in plowing the battle field."[18] Later in the narrative, Silliman reported that his guide led him from the American camp along the heights, where he "had the satisfaction of treading the same ground which they trod."[19] Silliman also noted that they came across a vernacular memorial to the conflict in a barn near Freeman's farm, "one of the beams of which contains a six-pound ball. It was imbedded in the tree out of which the timber was cut; and the builder considerately left the ball in as a memento."[20] Silliman further explained that "people often find, even now, gun-barrels and bayonets, cannon-balls, grape shot, bullets, and human bones." From one of the local farmers, he writes, he took some "painful specimens" of grape shot, bullets, and human bones; "some of the bullets were battered and misshaped, evincing that they had come into collision with opposing obstacles."[21] Linking the importance of Saratoga's legacy to famous battlefields of old, Silliman writes that "thousands and thousands yet unborn will visit Saratoga with feelings of the deepest interest, and it will not be forgotten till Thermopylae and Marathon and Bannockburn and Waterloo shall cease to be remembered."[22]

By labeling the Saratoga Battlefield as a place of "solemnity and awe," "ardor and admiration," and a sacred spot, these early visitors helped to "transform the bloodshed, division, and violence of war into beautiful symbols of unity and national cohesion."[23] In this way, a highly contested and divided landscape became the tangible and physical symbol of a common sacrifice that bound together the often fractious young nation. The foreign and domestic visitors alike describe a veneration of the event, one incumbent on experiencing the "sacred" battlefield landscape with its remaining earthen military features, surviving structures, and prosaic artifacts. The sense of a place-based engagement and memory of the critical battle is evident in these accounts, and this notion of place was further reinforced as the site became a regular part of the increasingly popular northern tour. As Silliman foresaw, "thousands and thousands yet unborn will visit Saratoga."[24]

Tourism Reaches Saratoga: The Fashionable or Northern Tour

By the 1820s, the "fashionable" or northern tour was all the rage and bringing increasing numbers of tourists to the Saratoga area. The tour included a "string of attractions" that stretched from New York City to Albany via the Hudson River. From Albany, travelers could take a stage or boat to "the Springs" for several days, return to Albany, and continue on to Niagara Falls via the Erie Canal.[25] During this period, the "fashionable" tour became a part of the growing commercialization of tourism in terms of accommodations, souvenirs, and a "booming market for guidebooks and travel literature."[26] A host of authors produced guidebooks and pocket guides that provided details on where to stay, what to see, and how to travel, along with recommendations for visiting sites of scenic beauty and historical importance. For visitors to Saratoga Springs's intense social scene, a day trip to the Saratoga Battlefield became a welcome break to reflect on the past glories of the Revolution and take in the "sublime" or "picturesque" Hudson River valley scenery.

One of the many visitors to Saratoga in the 1820s was the Honorable William Wirt, influential statesman, attorney, and author. Wirt's tour of the battlefield area exposes an early antiquarian interest in artifacts as battle souvenirs. "On returning from Lake George," Wirt wrote to his brother in Washington, "we came to old Fort Edward," where I "procured a Revolutionary bullet or two which had been got out of the wall of the fort."[27] They subsequently arrived at the village of Saratoga for dinner, and Wirt commented that they looked out upon "the field on which Burgoyne laid down his arms," noting that "I have some relics also from this field." Wirt went on to explain that relics were available at each house they visited, including "Freeman's farm," where "bullets and bones were offered—even the little children handling and offering the human bones."[28] Interestingly, Wirt ends by telling his brother that the relics "have no value, except from the associated sentiments you will give them."[29]

Another interesting tourist of the early 1820s was Philip Stansbury, who took a pedestrian tour across New York, New England, and Canada, publishing his observations in 1822.[30] Arriving at Bemis Heights, Stansbury was filled with emotion, reporting that "with a sensation of awe I slowly paced the road to the spot where our forefathers fought and conquered."[31] Accompanied by a battlefield guide—the son of the innkeeper where he spent the night—Stansbury set out the next day to see the "fields of battle." He remarked on the impact of agriculture on the various earthen fortifications, noting that "few vestiges are to be seen; the plough has strove with invidious zeal to destroy even these few remaining evidences of Revolutionary heroism."[32] For example, he reported that "the line of Burgoyne's camp . . . is visible and daily washing away and exposing rotten logs." Likewise, a visit to the house that had served as General Gates's headquarters found a structure that was "untenanted and ready to fall."[33] At Saratoga, he reflected, evidence of the final encampments and surrender ground were "scarcely perceptible." Stansbury's observations indicate the extent of damage to military features on the battlefield and the rapidly decreasing visibility of these important tangible elements of the battle's history.

Perhaps the most famous tourist of the period to visit Saratoga was General Lafayette, whose tour of the country in 1824 and 1825 took the nation by storm. After a huge and successful celebration in Boston in 1825, Lafayette headed north to tour New Hampshire and Vermont; while returning south along the Champlain-Hudson corridor, he stopped in Saratoga after dark on the evening of June 30. According to Lafayette's secretary Auguste Levasseur, they "stopped some minutes at the house of Mr. Schuyler, which is built on the precise spot where General Burgoyne delivered his sword to General Gates."[34] The group expressed disappointment at not getting to "visit this theatre of one of the most glorious events of the revolution," explaining that "the night was too far advanced."[35] To accommodate Lafayette and his entourage, Philip Schuyler II, grandson of General Philip Schuyler, who lived at the Schuyler house from 1811 until 1837, had "the goodness to give us a very detailed account of the battle of Saratoga." Somewhat contrary to Stansbury's earlier observations, Schuyler explained that "'the ground has not undergone any change; the entrenchments, though considerably effaced by time, are nevertheless easy to be recognized.'"[36] While it was noted that "old patriots of that period can still show their children the path which the aide of General Gates took," Levasseur cautions that "these traces will one day disappear."[37] "Why not erect in the midst of them," Levasseur continues, "a more durable monument, which shall remind future generations of the courage and patriotism of this glorious generation, which time will soon render extinct?"[38] This durable monument to commemorate Saratoga would take another sixty years to be fully realized.

By the time of the semicentennial or jubilee in 1827, the Revolutionary War landscape of the Saratoga battlefields remained partially discernible amid the cultivated fields but was fading quickly from weather and plowing. The rise in tourism to the area, combined with Lafayette's triumphant tour and the coming jubilee of the Saratoga battles, created increased interest in the landscape and sites of Gates's victory and Burgoyne's humiliation. This was particularly true for those who fought at Saratoga and who were entering their senior years. One such visitor during the jubilee year was Samuel Woodruff, Esq., of Windsor, Connecticut, a sixty-seven-year-old veteran of the battle. On his first day at Saratoga, October 17, the fiftieth anniversary of the surrender of Burgoyne, Woodruff visited the "ruins of the British fortifications and headquarters of Gen. Burgoyne."[39] From there, he hiked to the surrender grounds, noting the remains of Fort Hardy. While little evidence of the surrender ground could be seen through the thick brush, he reported with interest that "human bones, fragments of fire-arms, swords, balls, tools, implements, broken crockery, etc., etc., are frequently picked up on this ground."[40] For veterans like Woodruff, who had last been at Saratoga as a seventeen-year-old militiaman, the fiftieth anniversary was an opportunity to reflect on and reconsider their part in the victory. With a distance of fifty years, the artifacts of war that Woodruff discovered on the ground provided him a tangible link to the battles that he fought, helping to recall and validate the fleeting moments he spent on this ground.

Objects of Remembrance: Revolutionary War Battle Monuments

Along with the heightened touristic interest in visiting Revolutionary War battlefields like Saratoga, the 1820s also witnessed the beginnings of a public movement to commemorate the war. As the semicentennial approached and factional tensions between Republicans and Federalists declined, the nation found itself in an "Era of Good Feelings."[41] With adoration and worship of George Washington escalating following his death in 1799, the country experienced mounting interest in its short history and its Revolutionary founding, resulting in intensifying patriotic and nationalistic fervor.[42] The passing of the Revolutionary generation, both its leaders and the militiamen and soldiers, created a common reverence and unity that achieved almost mythic quality with the passing of Jefferson and Adams on July 4, 1826. As historian Sarah Purcell explains, "the generation that was losing its direct link to the Revolution felt increasing nostalgia for the past, and monument building offered the chance for the current generation to mark its own public gratitude."[43] As noted earlier, the triumphant visit of General Lafayette further stoked the patriotic fires of the period.

In *Remaking America*, John Bodnar argues that the period's growing class of entrepreneurs and professionals also played a role in the heightened desire to commemorate the Revolutionary era, seeking "to associate themselves with the heroic makers of the new nation."[44] The material progress and entrepreneurial activity that these leaders sought was, they contended, a natural outgrowth of the Revolutionary spirit and the nation's very origins. Thus, these men could both honor and "improve upon the past by working toward material advancement." As Daniel Webster noted in a speech for the groundbreaking of the Bunker Hill monument in 1825, "our proper business is improvement."[45] As seen at Bunker Hill, one way of honoring and preserving the past and establishing that the country's entrepreneurial zeal and expansionist plans were natural heirs to the Revolutionary spirit was to celebrate the war's important battles by erecting commemorative monuments. These massive structures were not only symbols to a very real patriotic impulse of the period but also offered the perfect physical manifestation of Webster's business of "internal improvements." This commemorative movement acknowledged the disappearance of both the war's leaders and participants and, as tourists were discovering, the physical remains of the conflict on the landscape of battlefields like Saratoga. The loss of first-person recollection and the battlefield features, like Saratoga's earthen fortifications and redoubts, heightened the need for permanent reminders of the importance of the war as a unifying national story and memory.

One of the earliest monuments to the war was the Revolutionary Monument erected in 1799 on the green in the town of Lexington, Massachusetts. Built by the town and funded by the Massachusetts General Court, the monument is "the nation's oldest surviving war memorial," commemorating the eight soldiers killed during the war's first engagement.[46] In 1809, residents of Baltimore began planning their monument to George Washington, completing construction of this first major monument to the former president in 1829. Given uncertain funding from lotteries, this project and the many subsequent monuments to Revolutionary War battles often took decades to finish. Following completion of the Groton and Bunker Hill monuments in the 1830s and 1840s, battle monuments were planned and constructed from Vermont to Georgia (table 10.1). Most of these monuments were the work of private "monument associations": state-chartered, nonprofit entities.[47]

The decade before the Civil War saw the formation of organizations to shepherd the construction of major monument projects in both the north and south, including the chartering of the Saratoga Monument Association in 1856 (see

TABLE 10.1 Early Monuments to the American Revolution

MONUMENT	EVENT/PERSON	LOCATION	PLANNING	CORNERSTONE LAID/ CONSTRUCTION BEGUN	COMPLETION/ DEDICATION	FUNDING SOURCES
Revolutionary Monument	Battle of Lexington	MA	1799?	1799	1799	Town of Lexington, MA General Court
Washington Monument, Baltimore	George Washington	MD	1809	1815	1829	Private (lotteries)
Paoli Massacre Monument	Paoli Massacre	PA	1817	1817	1817	Private
Bunker Hill Monument	Battle of Bunker Hill	MA	1823	1825	1842	Private
Groton Monument	Battle of Groton Heights	CT	1824	1826	1830	Private (lotteries)
Washington Monument	George Washington	DC	1833	1848	1885	Congress
Mecklenburg Monument	Mecklenburg Declaration of Independence	NC	1842	1890–98	1898	Private
Trenton Monument	Battle of Trenton	NJ	1844	1891	1893	Private, NJ, Congress
Pulaski Monument	General Casimir Pulaski	GA	1850s	1853	1856	Private
Bennington Monument	Battle of Bennington	VT	1854	1887	1891	Private, VT, Congress
Yorktown Monument	Battle of Yorktown	VA	1781	1881	1884	Congress
Saratoga Monument	Battle of Saratoga	NY	1856	1877/1881	1887/1912	Private, NY, Congress

table 10.1). Most of these organizations struggled with fund-raising to support the major costs of constructing a large monument. A principal funding impediment was the antilottery movement of the early nineteenth century; while Baltimore's Washington Monument and the Groton Battle Monument were funded largely from lottery proceeds, by the mid-nineteenth century many states had outlawed this fund-raising scheme following massive financial scandals and an antilottery campaign by evangelical reformers.[48] Further complicating the financial picture was the fact that although the federal government had stepped forward with money for the Washington Monument in the 1840s, any prospect of federal funding for other projects "evaporated as the politics of the antebellum period became more fractious."[49] Relying solely on private donations, many monument associations found themselves unable to even purchase land for the monument let alone begin construction; others, like Saratoga, found that even after a well-attended groundbreaking and cornerstone ceremony, public support for the project waned and their finances deteriorated.

The idea for a Saratoga Battle Monument is thought to have begun at a meeting in the old Schuyler estate in Schuylerville on October 17, 1856, the seventy-ninth anniversary of Burgoyne's surrender to Gates. Antiquarian William Leete Stone reported that George Strover, John A. Corey, and "other patriotic gentlemen" gathered for a "small scale" celebration, including the recitation of a poem by Alfred B. Street and a banquet, and it was here that plans for a monument were first discussed.[50] Three years later, on the eve of the next major American war, the Saratoga Monument Association (SMA) was formally organized under a State of New York charter. The goal of the group, which included Hamilton Fish, Horatio Seymour, John A. Corey, Peter Gansevoort, and others, was "the erection of a fitting memorial on the site of Burgoyne's surrender."[51] The group's trustees and membership included New York governors, such as Fish and Seymour; US congressmen; state legislators; local mayors, like Corey; local businessmen, such as Strover; historians; military men; newspaper editors; and ancestors of battle participants, like Gansevoort. Even with a membership that provided an "array of political, financial, and social connections," the organization struggled with fund-raising throughout its early years.[52] While Stone recalls that the trustees met several times and also selected a spot for the monument, the start of "the civil war in 1861 cast such a gloom over the whole country . . . that the movement to build the monument was suspended" until 1872.[53]

Like many of the other monument associations around the country, the SMA was revived following the war and renewed its push to raise money and create plans to build a "fitting memorial." With an amended charter, the association reorganized its committee structure, and by the later 1870s had broadened the geographical scope of its trustees and members, expanding to "garner national support for the monument."⁵⁴ The revived group hired a largely unknown architect, Jared C. Markham, to design the monument, and his plans called for "the erection of a massive 230-ft.-tall obelisk, 80 ft. square at the bottom and 10 ft. at the top."⁵⁵ The facts behind Markham's selection remain unclear, although he may have been known to William L. Stone, the chairman of SMA's Committee on Design. His willingness to work without immediate compensation could also have influenced his selection by the poorly funded organization. While the obelisk form, with its roots in ancient Egypt, was used for several major Revolutionary War monuments constructed prior to the Civil War, including the Groton Battle Monument, Bunker Hill, and the Washington Monument, the Saratoga Monument was the only major monument constructed after the war that used the obelisk form.⁵⁶ Designed with unique Gothic-style ornamentation and niches for statues of Schuyler, Gates, and Morgan—a niche labeled Arnold would be left empty—the huge, eight-sided obelisk was estimated to cost $300,000.⁵⁷

With a plan in hand, the trustees redoubled their fund-raising efforts; however, private donations were scarce due to the lingering economic depression that followed the Panic of 1873. At the state level, the organization was successful in obtaining a $50,000 appropriation from the New York legislature in 1874, but, after petitioning the original thirteen states asking each to contribute $5,000, received only a single pledge from Rhode Island. The trustees also submitted a petition to Congress to financially support the project, arguing that "Lexington and Bunker Hill have their imposing memorials . . . and, in our own day . . . , Antietam and Gettysburg are made enduring in granite records for the admiration of generations yet to be."⁵⁸ These monuments and the proposed Saratoga Monument, the group explained, stand "as an educator to gratitude and patriotism."⁵⁹ Neither this federal appeal, nor the earlier state appropriation, which required that the association raise matching funds, was successful. With the centennial rapidly approaching, the group again petitioned the state legislature for funding, hoping to construct the foundation and set the cornerstone by the centennial anniversary. The result of this lobbying was passage of legislation to provide $10,000 to the association, but the bill was subsequently vetoed by the governor.⁶⁰ The SMA took stock of its anemic treasury and directed architect Markham to scale back the project. In so doing, he decreased the height to 150 feet and the size of the base from eighty to forty square feet, saving money in both time and materials.⁶¹ Having no prospect of federal or state funding, the group pressed private "patriotic" sources and was eventually able to raise enough cash and material donations to proceed with laying "the foundation of the monument and the corner-stone, together with one-fourth of the plinth, or base."⁶² Booth Brothers, a New York City granite supply and construction firm who eventually served as contractor for the project, generously donated the cornerstone and materials. With these commitments in hand, and absent a clear strategy to finish the monument, the anniversary celebration could move forward.

Centennial Night Fever: 1876 and 1877

While the Panic of 1873 certainly dampened the preparation for the national centennial in 1876 and the centennial for the Saratoga battles in 1877, the upcoming anniversaries were catalysts that generated intense interest at the local, state, and national level to honor and remember the events and participants of the Revolutionary era.[63] As noted earlier, the swelling fervor of the Declaration of Independence's one-hundredth birthday helped to reinvigorate many monument associations, and along with the end of Reconstruction provided the perfect opportunity for national unification and healing. Celebrations were held in virtually every city, town, and village, and the keynote event was the Philadelphia Centennial Exhibition of 1876, which attracted close to ten million visitors. In addition, almost every major battlefield was feted with parades, pageants, speeches, and reenactments, all performed to crowds numbering in the tens of thousands. If the earlier work of monument associations began the process of connecting the spirit of the Revolution to the sense of a country destined for progress and improvement, then the Centennial Exhibition helped to cement this notion. Ironically, at the very moment that the monument movement was gaining steam toward the goal of commemorating and remembering important Revolutionary War battles, a new invention, known as dry-plate photography, was being touted at the Centennial Exhibition, one that would shortly revolutionize and democratize the memory business.[64] In keeping with the festive mood across the country, the citizens of the Saratoga area held small events in 1876, while making plans for the "main event" in the fall of 1877; Saratoga Springs and Ballston Spa both organized events during which local historians delivered a historical address and a town father offered a centennial oration.[65]

The cornerstone ceremony held on October 17, 1877, the one-hundredth anniversary of Burgoyne's surrender, launched the centennial festivities. As Stone described it, "a procession, two miles in length, and forming the most splendid civic, masonic and military pageant ever witnessed in northern New York, marched to the site of the monument."[66] The cornerstone was officially laid by J. J. Couch, grand master of the Grand Lodge of New York, in "due and ancient [Masonic] form." After a short address by Couch, the grand secretary of the event read a list of the cornerstone's contents, which included various histories and addresses, Mrs. Walworth's visitor's guide to the battlefield, a coin dated 1777, a commemorative song, a photograph of the architect's drawing and his statement on the progress of construction, a bundle of newspapers from the day, along with many other items.⁶⁷ The remainder of the day, reportedly witnessed by an estimated 40,000 people, consisted of exercises "of a high order of literary excellence," including many addresses and speeches punctuated by musical numbers and readings, including Fritz Green Halleck's "stirring" poem "Field of Grounded Arms."⁶⁸ Horatio Seymour, former governor and president of the Saratoga Monument Association, gave the keynote address reminding the audience of the central importance of the monument given the country's lack of clear historical memory:

> We meet . . . to lay the corner stone of a monument which will commemorate not only that event [Burgoyne's surrender], but every fact which led to that result. The reproach rests upon the United States, that while they stand in the front ranks of the power of the earth . . . they give no proof to the eyes of the world that they honor their fathers or those whose sacrifices laid the foundations of their prosperity and greatness. We hope that a suitable structure here will tell all who look upon it that this was the scene of an occurrence unsurpassed in importance in military annals.⁶⁹

As these words make clear, monuments like Saratoga were, for men like Seymour, important symbols of national history and the nation's commitment to the past, particularly in the "eyes of the world." The failure of the young nation to properly honor and celebrate the Revolutionary generation brought to light a lingering contradiction in its republican ideology, "the fascination with military heroes and the simultaneous suspicion of actual military power."⁷⁰ In this context, the Saratoga Monument celebrated the battles' many citizen-soldiers, literally writing the idea of individual service and sacrifice to the nation in stone.

Saratoga Monument Association: 1878 to 1900 — The Obelisk Rises

Even with the extraordinary attendance at the centennial event, the Saratoga Monument Association found itself in 1878 without funds to proceed with construction, having "not one dollar in the Treasury."⁷¹ In 1880, US congressman and SMA trustee John H. Starin crafted a bill to provide $30,000 in appropriations for the monument's completion. Although he held off introducing the bill in that session, Starin felt certain that it would pass in the next. With pursuit of federal funding on hold, the organization approached the New York legislature and was successful in acquiring an appropriation of $10,000. The year also saw adoption of Markham's final design, creation of a Building Committee to shepherd the construction process, and the election of two new trustees, C. M. Bliss, secretary of the Bennington Monument Association, and Ellen Hardin Walworth, one of the few women to serve on a monument association board.

Walworth, who was one of the founding members of the national chapter of the Daughters of the American Revolution (DAR), quickly became involved, heading up the Committee on Tablets to "mark the battlefield with appropriate small-scale monuments."[72]

At the 1881 meeting of the trustees, it was announced that Starin's bill had been passed by Congress on March 3, appropriating "$30,000 in Treasury funds to erect the granite obelisk shaft of the monument." The bill required that the SMA would raise any additional funds necessary to complete the monument, and after some internal debates between the trustees and architect Markham, the Building Committee awarded the contract to Booth Brothers in August 1881.[73] It seemed that all that stood in the way of resuming construction on the obelisk was settling a small matter regarding title to the property. As the monument rose in late 1881, the organization realized that they would need more funds to complete all of the exterior decorative stonework, and requested another $15,000 appropriation from New York State. Receiving this additional funding in 1882, work to finish the monument progressed rapidly and on November 3, 1882, the capstone was set in place (figure 10.1).[74] Although the main structure was complete, there remained interior finish work to be done as well as completion of various artistic elements, such as the sculptures for the niches. Using another federal appropriation of $40,000, the artwork and interior was completed in 1884, but the SMA continued to incur unexpected expenses that "threw it into debt."[75] With no funds to support a dedication ceremony, the SMA decided to quietly transfer the monument to the State of New York in 1895, and then disbanded.[76]

At the same time that the SMA was attempting to finish the Saratoga Monument, they initiated an effort to mark important locations and points of interest on the Saratoga Battlefield using small-scale tablets. Saratoga Springs resident Ellen Walworth, who had published a tour guide to the battlefield in 1877, led the Committee on Tablets.[77] Representing the first formal attention given to the entire battlefield landscape, the plan would, noted member Horatio Seymour, "give additional interest to the numerous drives around Saratoga—thus enhancing the already numerous attractions of the place."[78] The committee also struggled with funding the markers so as not to compete with the already feeble fund-raising campaign for the monument, arriving at a plan to ask individuals to give a "tablet of some kind for a particular spot."[79] In the end, the group selected twenty places of "especial interest" where monuments were to be erected (table 10.2). For example, in 1887, SMA trustee General John Watts de Peyster donated money to erect the famous Arnold boot monument. The marble monument, sculpted by George Bissell, featured a relief of Arnold's left boot, the spot where he was wounded, draped over a howitzer (figure 10.2).[80] By the time that the SMA disbanded in 1895, ten markers had been placed on the battlefield.

FIGURE 10.1. Saratoga Monument. Photograph by author.

With the Saratoga Monument complete and the SMA defunct, the direction of activity continued to build on the work of Ellen Walworth's committee, focusing broadly on preservation of the site of the battles and associated property.

Battlefield Preservation Begins: 1895 to 1933

By the time that the SMA disbanded in 1895, a national crusade was under way to preserve battlefields on American soil. This effort had its roots in the Civil War battlefield movement of the late nineteenth century, and the precedents set by the establishment of scenic and natural national parks beginning in the 1870s.[81] As with the large natural parks in the western United States, federal government

TABLE 10.2 List of places of "especial interest" on the Saratoga battlefield marked to receive a monument by the Saratoga Monument Association's Committee on Tablets, 1882

STAKE NUMBER	EVENT OR SITE COMMEMORATED
1	Freeman's Farm
2	Balcarres Redoubt
3	Fraser's Camp
4	Arnold Wounded—Breymann's Redoubt
5	Fraser Fell
6	British Line of Battle, October 7
7	Morgan's Hill
8	Fort Neilson, northwest angle of American breastworks at Bemis Heights
9	General Gates Headquarters
10	Site of Bemus Tavern
11	Dirck Swart's House
12	American Entrenchments near Mill Creek
13	Place of Lady Acland's Embarkation
14	Site of Swords's House
15	Tayler's House
16	Fraser Buried
17	Position of American Artillery, October 8
18	Burgoyne's Headquarters
19	British Redoubt
20	Old Battle Well, Freeman's Farm

Ellen Hardin Walworth, *Battles of Saratoga, 1777: The Saratoga Monument Association, 1856–1891* (Albany, NY: Joel Munsell's Sons, 1891), 68–69.

support was necessary to preserve the major Civil War battlefields. With the creation of Chickamauga and Chattanooga (1890), Shiloh (1894), Gettysburg (1895), and Vicksburg (1899) as national military parks, the precedent was established for "setting aside land" and using "federal funds to acquire nationally significant historic sites for permanent preservation."[82]

By the turn of the twentieth century, "Congress was deluged with petitions to create additional national military parks" at both Civil War and Revolutionary War battlefields.[83] Although a major battlefield preservation bill failed to gain support, various special acts and appropriations were passed, establishing the first battlefield preservation at a Revolutionary War site by creating the Guilford Court House National Military Park in 1917. After a lull during World War I, bills for new military battlefields grew in the early 1920s. With more requests

FIGURE 10.2. Arnold Monument. Photograph by author.

than money, Congress authorized a study of battlefields in 1925 to include the creation of a system for classifying battles according to their importance and for making future preservation decisions.[84] Saratoga Battlefield was eventually evaluated as a Class I site within the four-tiered system, one of only five designated battlefields of "exceptional political and military importance."[85]

Although the federal government increased its support for battlefield protection during the first several decades of the twentieth century, much of the initial effort remained local and was spurred by various threats to the landscape.[86] In the case of Saratoga, agriculture continued to affect the battlefield, particularly its expansion into formerly forested parcels. Road systems expanded and a trolley line connected the area to Albany, fueling concern that the area might be "developed as a residential suburb of the capital city."[87] Organizations like the Saratoga chapter of the DAR and the New York Historical Association became concerned about the potential for development impacts to the battlefield area. These organizations had worked with the state legislature to expand the newly created state park system to include historical sites. As early as 1914, a bill was introduced to establish the Saratoga Battlefield as a state park, but this effort ultimately failed.[88] With the onset of World War I, priorities shifted and no further action was taken until the war ended.

With the revival of the national battlefield protection movement following World War I and the rapidly approaching sesquicentennial of the Battles of Saratoga, interest in preserving the battlefield received new urgency in the early 1920s. While the initial effort was focused on creating a national military park at Saratoga, Congress refused to act, returning the responsibility to local and state leaders. With support from the national Sons of the American Revolution, the Rochester chapter of the Empire State Society of the Sons of the American Revolution, and local Rotary clubs and interested residents, the New York legislature chartered the Saratoga Battlefield Association (SBA) in 1923. In addition to planning the sesquicentennial celebration, the group was established to purchase and hold land "for the purpose of preserving the battlefield in public trust."[89] The group immediately began negotiations for the purchase of several farms on the battlefield, acquiring the Wright (former Freeman), Sarle, Neilson, and Gannon farms, a total of 655 acres.[90]

As the SBA acquired land, support for the creation of a state park increased from both local and state entities, including patriotic organizations, historical societies, and the regional business community. Several significant leaders emerged during this period, including George O. Slingerland, mayor of Mechanicsville and Rotary club president; Adolph Ochs, editor of the *New York Times*; state historian Alexander Flick, and state assemblyman Burton Esmond.[91] After a gathering on the 1925 anniversary of the first battle of Saratoga, leaders vowed to increase pressure for the creation of a state park. Emphasizing the need for preservation and restoration, Ochs's *New York Times* described the battlefield area as the "weed-grown and deserted acres where one of the fifteen decisive battles of history was fought."[92] The effort paid off in 1926, when the legislature passed a bill to provide money for land purchase and restoration activities at several battlefields; the State of New York acquired title to the battlefield lands purchased by the SBA in 1926. With the appointment of Mayor George Slingerland to the state board created to oversee the restoration and development of the state's battlefields, the Saratoga Battlefield gained an important and lifelong advocate.[93]

Sesquicentennial Celebration: 1927

Slingerland's first task was to prepare for the formal dedication of the battlefield scheduled on October 8, 1927, the day after the sesquicentennial of the second battle. In addition to constructing temporary stages, bleachers, communication stations, and a parking area for the anticipated crowds, the state undertook the renovation of the Neilson farm as the focal point of the visitor experience.[94] Along with removing farm buildings that dated after the battle and relocating the Neilson farmhouse, the state added three new buildings on the site; unfortunately, "no documentation existed to suggest that any such buildings were present at the time of the battles."[95] These structures included a stone powder magazine, a dwelling referred to as "Arnold's Headquarters," and a two-story blockhouse, which became the visitor center and museum. Finally, Slingerland began work on what he called his memorial landscape, "creating a symbolic American Cemetery."[96] Slingerland's idea was to memorialize fallen American soldiers thought to be buried near Fort Neilson. The result was a "square shaped planting of evergreens" in 1927, inside of which was the symbolic cemetery.[97]

The daylong sesquicentennial festivities were considered a great success, attracting upward of 160,000 visitors (figure 10.3). Following a 150-gun salute at 9:00 a.m., the crowd was led on a "historical pilgrimage over the Saratoga Battlefield" by "guides in Continental uniform." At ten o'clock, the State of New Hampshire monument was unveiled and dedicated with music and addresses by members of the New Hampshire Monument Commission. At eleven o'clock, the assembled masses gathered at the "Pageant Field" for the sesquicentennial address and dedication of the battlefield park. After introductory remarks by *New York Times* publisher Adolph Ochs, honorary president of the Celebration Committee, New York governor Alfred E. Smith gave a welcome address, followed by remarks from the governors of Vermont, New Hampshire, and Connecticut. The formal ceremony to dedicate the battlefield was highlighted by a speech titled "Acquisition and Rehabilitation of Saratoga Battlefield as a Public Park" by Mechanicsville mayor George Slingerland.[98]

The afternoon was set aside for a "gigantic historical pageant" with thousands of costumed participants (figure 10.4). A spectacle extraordinaire, the pageant boasted a cast of 6,000, including 1,000 musicians and 3,000 soldiers, along with "dancers, Indians, farmers, women, and children."[99] After a successful dress rehearsal, the visitors were treated to a series of performances culminating in the "Battle of Saratoga reenacted in [the] Great Ravine where it actually occurred 150 years ago."[100] The following day's *New York Times* reported that "colonials and foes of 150 years ago thrill 100,000 visitors on historic battleground." The paper explained that even with the difficulties of condensing the original fourteen-hour event into twenty minutes and restricting it to an area that could be viewed from the bleachers, the crowd watched the reenactment with rapt attention. When the enemy reenactors retreated, the reporter explained, the "audience of 100 per cent Colonial sympathies cheered heartily as the British and Brunswickers followed by the Indian and Canadian allies, were swept back into the ravine under a terrific fire." Although there were several "strategic

FIGURE 10.3. Poster for the sesquicentennial celebration. SARA Archives.

problems" during the battle, these were, the report continued, "skillfully met" and the "battle flowed on at a smart pace and without a serious hitch."[101] With the Americans once again victorious, state and local officials turned their attention to preserving more battlefield acreage and adding "new commemorative and interpretive elements" to the park.[102]

Following the successful sesquicentennial celebration, Slingerland lost little time in enhancing his "memorial landscape." Working with state architect Stanton P. Lee in 1927, Slingerland designed a classical revival "Memorial Pavilion," completed in 1928, to mark the entryway to the "American Cemetery."[103] Following a 1927 study on "future land acquisition priorities," Slingerland also began negotiations with landowners and worked with state legislators in 1928 on an "appropriation of $192,000 for the purchase of an additional 2,084 acres" of battlefield land.[104] After a heated battle, the bill was reduced to $100,000, and,

FIGURE 10.4. "Panorama of the Vast Throng at the Sesquicentennial Celebration of the Battle of Saratoga." SARA Archives.

once approved, used to purchase 564 acres. By 1930, the park contained almost 1,430 acres of the original battlefield area.[105]

At the same time that the state was acquiring additional land for the park, Slingerland was cautiously following the increasing interest in establishing the battlefield as a national military park. This effort was apparently supported by the secretary of war, who reported to President Calvin Coolidge in 1928 that the battlefield was one of only two Class I battlefields not yet designated as a national park. The following year, New York governor Franklin D. Roosevelt proclaimed an interest in the preservation of the battlefield and its federal acquisition.[106] The headline of the *New York Times* article on Roosevelt's 1929 speech at Saratoga announced that he "Proposes Saratoga as National Shrine" (figure 10.5).[107] Roosevelt also embraced the importance of preserving the place and space of history, explaining that on a battlefield like Saratoga, "we should be able to visualize the history which took place here."[108] Of course, timing is everything, and Roosevelt's speech occurred just twelve days before the stock market crash and subsequent economic depression, relegating federal battlefield preservation to a low-priority issue.[109]

The idea of a national military park at Saratoga gained new momentum when several members of New York's congressional delegation "took up the cause" in 1930.[110] While successful in getting Congress and the president to approve a survey of the battlefield as a prelude to federal control, subsequent legislation for an outright purchase died in committee in 1930.[111] During this period of continued advocacy for a federal takeover, Slingerland also continued to work on his memorial area. In 1931, the Daughters of the American Revolution added their "Monument to the Unknown American Dead" to the "American Cemetery" memorial area, and Slingerland planted a grove of memorial trees as part of the national program to commemorate the bicentennial of Washington's birth.[112]

FIGURE 10.5. *Left to right:* Mayor George O. Slingerland, Governor Franklin D. Roosevelt, *New York Times* owner Adolph Ochs, and Judge Dow Beekman, September 19, 1929. SARA Archives.

Sadly, Slingerland's own memorial was soon to appear on the landscape with his sudden death in 1932. Following Slingerland's departure from the scene, the battlefield languished under state managers who made it widely known that they fully supported the site's federal acquisition, and would "deliver its holdings to the government free of charge."[113]

Creating a National Park: 1933 to 1938

With the addition of a new category of national historical parks in the early 1930s and the transfer of national military parks to National Park Service (NPS) control in 1933, the stage was set to revisit federal acquisition of the Saratoga battlefield.[114] In a conversation between Park Service director Horace Albright and President Roosevelt, during which Albright proposed the transfer of the military parks to the Park Service, Roosevelt "simply said that it should be done." The president then quickly turned his attention to Saratoga, asking Albright, "How about Saratoga Battlefield in New York?" After explaining the current status to Roosevelt, Albright recollects that "he told me—really ordered me—to get busy and have Saratoga Battlefield made a national park or monument. Just a moment or two later, with a grin, he said, 'Suppose you do something tomorrow about this.'"[115] Although the transfer of military parks was accomplished by executive order in 1933, it was another five years before Roosevelt signed Public Law 576, "An Act to provide for the creation of Saratoga National Historical Park in the State of New York."[116] The NPS worked with the New York State Parks in an advisory role until the formal transfer of the land in 1941.[117]

The transfer of the battlefield to the National Park Service quickly reenergized the preservation initiative at Saratoga. With the State of New York continuing to manage the site until 1941, the Park Service's initial activities focused on land acquisition and planning for interpretation and visitor's services. A 1938 report identified 2,450 acres for future acquisition, but Park Service officials moved slowly because they thought additional land would further burden the small park staff.[118] In 1939, work began on a master planning process for the site; regional supervisor Roy Appleman explained the philosophy: "In planning the development of an historical area . . . do only that which will aid in presenting a simple clear picture of events."[119] Appleman recommended the removal of the historically inaccurate buildings constructed during state ownership, including the period house, powder magazine, and blockhouse, to create a more authentic experience.[120] He also felt strongly that the 1777 landscape should not be restored through reforestation, arguing that the open agricultural lands offered the visitor a better view of the battlefield.[121] Appleman also began planning for a tour road through the park with "pull-outs" at each monument and memorial marker and parking areas for important observation points along the route.[122]

The other major initiative of 1939 was the creation of a historical base map to provide a better sense of the landscape at the time of the battle and to guide planned and future park development.[123] Prepared largely by historian Francis Wilshin and archaeologist Robert Ehrich, this work included documentary research to identify maps, battle accounts, and any other sources that could assist in locating the sites of significant battle events, along with archaeological investigations to identify physical remains of the battles. Working with Civilian Conservation Corps crews for two years, Ehrich identified numerous segments of the British and American lines.[124] The finished map, completed in 1941, illustrated the "buildings, structures, roads, farm fields, and forest that existed at the time of the battles and noted with symbols the positions of the American and British encampment, along with the lines of fortifications."[125]

Working with Wilshin and Ehrich's battlefield data, planners drafted an interpretive tour and an accompanying roads and trails plan that eventually formed portions of the *General Development Plan for Saratoga* (1941). A surprise visit by President Roosevelt in 1940 helped cement Fraser's Hill as the location for the future administration and museum building. With the site of this building established, park planners set out to develop more detailed plans for the tour roads. However, before any of this planning work could be implemented, the

United States declared war on Japan and Germany, shifting the national focus to the war effort.[126]

Although the battlefield was formally established as the Saratoga National Historical Park in 1948, little else happened in the decade following the end of World War II. Most activity during this period involved planning for future park development and interpretation, although the Park Service did acquire the Schuyler house and twenty-five acres of land through a donation in 1950. They also continued to debate approaches to landscape reconstruction, with park historian Charles Snell arguing that retaining the cleared, open land created a false impression of the battlefield to the visitors.[127] He subsequently revised the historical base map to include large areas of forest that more closely resembled the battlefield of 1777, and this work was folded into a revised master plan completed in 1951. As in the past, implementation of these new plans would await additional funding, this time in the form of the Park Service's Mission 66 program.[128]

The Mission 66 program was an ambitious ten-year funding initiative to restore park infrastructure and enhance visitor services, both of which had suffered from deterioration during the previous decade or more. This commitment during the decade leading up to the Park Service's fiftieth anniversary in 1966 addressed the outdated facilities at most parks and acknowledged the huge increase in visitors to the park system, as Americans took to the road on vacations fueled by the economic prosperity of the 1950s. The Mission 66 program resulted in new roads, trails, visitor centers, museum exhibits, interpretive infrastructure, and employee housing. At Saratoga, the program funded the construction of the long-awaited battlefield tour road. Begun in 1958, the road's various sections and loops were completed in stages; as part of this construction, the Park Service finally removed the buildings added in the mid-1920s during state ownership, restored the Neilson house to its original location, and relocated several of the commemorative monuments placed by the SMA and other private groups. These ground-disturbing development projects on the battlefield also required additional archaeological investigation, resulting in several Mission 66–related archaeological projects. NPS regional archaeologist John Cotter initially focused on locating and examining the original Neilson house site and then investigating portions of the American fortifications on the bluffs above the Hudson River and several other locations in advance of tour road construction.[129]

The Mission 66 program also finally funded plans for a visitor center at Saratoga, first discussed in the master plan of 1941 but never built due to lack of funding. Begun in 1960 and completed in 1962, this mid-century modern building provided an essential orientation point for visitors, offering "extensive views over much of the battlefield." The building also provided interpretation of the battles to visitors prior to their engaging the landscape directly via the recently completed tour road.[130]

As another major anniversary and commemorative moment approached, the park was better prepared for a new invasion of visitors to its 2,432 acres. In the lead-up to the bicentennial of the nation and Saratoga battles, the Victory Woods parcel, a 22.7-acre tract that contained portions of the British encampment at the time of Burgoyne's surrender, was donated to the Park Service in 1974. The approaching bicentennial also reinvigorated archaeological research at the park (see chapter 3).

Saratoga 1977 Bicentennial Celebration and Beyond

As Park Service staff prepared for the bicentennial celebrations of 1976 and 1977, new approaches to and philosophies about history, memory, and commemoration at historic sites were evident. Rather than the elaborate and theatrical "pageant" of the site's sesquicentennial celebration, the Park Service sought to "provide a more stirring and meaningful 'park experience' for visitors."[131]

In place of the festival-type celebration, a 1970 report suggested more modest physical and interpretive interventions, including an expanded living history program, along with "construction of historical replica buildings, and restoration of the 1777 vegetation patterns."[132] These suggestions resulted in several tangible changes, including the "placement of post lines representing fortifications, construction of the Freeman cabin (no longer extant), and periodic living history demonstrations."[133] Although battle reenactments on park property were against Park Service policy, they were included in the 1977 celebration. Along with other living history demonstrations, various ceremonies were held to commemorate the anniversaries of the battles. New interpretive materials were also produced for the bicentennial, including enhanced waysides along the tour road and a visitor film, *Checkmate on the Hudson*.[134]

Although the National Park Service continued to acquire small parcels in the decades following the bicentennial, the last major addition to the park was the acquisition of the Saratoga Monument in 1980. Under ownership and control of the State of New York since 1895, the monument and its almost three-acre parcel was deeded to the federal government. With this final transfer, the state relinquished the last vestige of its earlier stewardship of the battlefield site.

Towering over Schuylerville, the monument stands as a lasting and obvious symbol of commemoration and preservation efforts at the park for more than a century and a half. As discussed previously, the type of commemoration represented by monument building had largely given way to an approach focused on preserving the actual sites and resources associated with the battle. With the use of advanced landscape and archaeological investigations that sought to provide accuracy and authenticity in terms of battlefield interpretation, monuments became impediments. For some, monuments like Saratoga did little to assist in the interpretation and celebration of a battlefield site to visitors. In fact, in many cases these objects were thought to hinder "authentic" viewsheds and settings, affecting a visitor's ability to fully engage in the site. To others, the host of monuments and memorial markers at a site like Saratoga were important material reminders of the history of commemoration. As such, they provided direct evidence of changing sensibilities about the past and the ways that it was valued in terms of evolving notions of patriotism, freedom, and independence, and within the context of changing social and cultural norms throughout the nation's first 200-plus years.

Commemoration and Preservation

Through participation in or exposure to commemorative efforts at Revolutionary or Civil War battlefields, Americans have come to appreciate and support the need for site preservation. As with efforts to commemorate battlefield sites, early individual efforts to preserve the Saratoga battlefield eventually required direct governmental support. From the late nineteenth through the early twentieth centuries, the private initiatives to preserve the Saratoga battlefield were slowly transferred to the State of New York. The rising political fortunes of Franklin Delano Roosevelt proved to be instrumental in ushering the Saratoga battlefield from state ownership into the expanding portfolio of battlefield sites held by the National Park Service. Roosevelt was uniquely positioned to carry forward the groundwork laid by numerous private individuals who, prior to his arrival, recognized and appreciated the battlefield's value and worked tirelessly to preserve it. With the ultimate national recognition for the significance of Saratoga to our nation's history expressed via the signing of a bill authorizing Saratoga National Historical Park on June 1, 1938, FDR conferred America's highest expression of commemoration upon the embattled landscape at Saratoga.

NOTES

1. Michael Kammen, *Mystic Chords of Memory: The Transformation of Tradition in American Culture* (New York: Alfred A. Knopf, 1991), 586–87.

2. Sarah J. Purcell, *Sealed with Blood: War, Sacrifice, and Memory in Revolutionary America* (Philadelphia: University of Pennsylvania Press, 2002), 1.

3. John Calvin Thorne, *A Monograph on the Rev. Israel Evans, A.M.* (1902; repr., New York: William Abbatt, 1907), 18.

4. Israel Evans, *A Discourse Delivered near York in Virginia, on the Memorable Occasion of the Surrender of the British Army to the Allied Forces of America and France* (Philadelphia: Francis Bailey, 1782), 26.

5. Psalms 124, King James Version.

6. Dona Brown, *Inventing New England: Regional Tourism in the Nineteenth Century* (Washington, DC: Smithsonian Institution Press, 1995), 22.

7. William L. Stone, *Visits to the Saratoga Battle-Grounds 1780–1880* (1895; reissued, Port Washington, NY: Kennikat Press, 1970), 63–64.

8. Ibid., 66–71.

9. Ibid., 72–80.

10. Ibid., 101.

11. Ibid., 102.

12. Ibid., 101.

13. Ibid.

14. Ibid., 106.

15. Ibid., 107–8.

16. Ibid., 110. Although Buel is colloquially known as "Major," his pension application indicates he never attained that rank.

17. Ibid.

18. Ibid., 111.

19. Ibid., 118.

20. Ibid.

21. Ibid., 129.

22. Ibid., 134.

23. Purcell, *Sealed with Blood*, 3.

24. Stone, *Visits to the Saratoga Battle-Grounds*, 134.

25. Brown, *Inventing New England*, 16.

26. Ibid., 28.

27. Stone, *Visits to the Saratoga Battle-Grounds*, 149.

28. Ibid., 154.

29. Ibid., 161.

30. Philip Stansbury, *A Pedestrian Tour of Two Thousand Three Hundred Miles, in North America* (New York: J. D. Myers and W. Smith, 1822), x.

31. Ibid.

32. Ibid.

33. Ibid.

34. Auguste Levasseur, *Lafayette in America in 1824 and 1825; or, Journal of a Voyage to the United States*, vol. 2 (Philadelphia: Carey and Lea, 1829), 216.

35. Ibid.

36. Ibid.

37. Ibid.

38. Ibid.

39. Stone, *Visits to the Saratoga Battle-Grounds*, 213.

40. Ibid., 215.

41. John Bodnar, *Remaking America: Public Memory, Commemoration, and Patriotism in the Twentieth Century* (Princeton, NJ: Princeton University Press, 1992), 23–24.

42. Andrew Burstein, *America's Jubilee* (New York: Alfred A. Knopf, 2001), 4.

43. Purcell, *Sealed with Blood*, 195.

44. Bodnar, *Remaking America*, 24.

45. Ibid., 24–25.

46. Stephen Olausen, Kristen Heitert, Laura Kline, and Carey Jones, Saratoga National

Historical Park, National Register of Historic Places Nomination Form, form prepared by the Public Archaeology Laboratory, Pawtucket, RI, 2011, 44.

47. Ibid., 44–45.

48. Ann-Marie E. Szymanski, *Pathways to Prohibition: Radicals, Moderates, and Social Movement Outcomes* (Durham, NC: Duke University Press, 2003), 95–96.

49. Olausen et al., Saratoga National Historical Park, National Register of Historic Places Nomination Form, 45–46.

50. William L. Stone, *History of the Saratoga Monument Association* (Albany, NY: Joel Munsell, 1879), 5.

51. Ibid.

52. Olausen et al., Saratoga National Historical Park, National Register of Historic Places Nomination Form, 48.

53. Stone, *History of the Saratoga Monument Association*, 6.

54. Olausen et al., Saratoga National Historical Park, National Register of Historic Places Nomination Form, 49.

55. Ibid.

56. Ibid., 79.

57. Ibid., 49.

58. Stone, *History of the Saratoga Monument Association*, 9.

59. Ibid.

60. Ibid., 10–11.

61. Olausen et al., Saratoga National Historical Park, National Register of Historic Places Nomination Form, 49.

62. Stone, *History of the Saratoga Monument Association*, 11.

63. Olausen et al., Saratoga National Historical Park, National Register of Historic Places Nomination Form, 46.

64. Kammen, *Mystic Chords of Memory*, 96. An even bigger impact came in 1884 with the introduction of rolled film.

65. Nathaniel Bartlett Sylvester, *History of Saratoga County, New York* (1878), available at www.rootsweb.ancestry.com/~nysarato/Sylvester/chap24.html.

66. Stone, *History of the Saratoga Monument Association*, 13.

67. Ibid., 13–14.

68. Ibid., 15–16.

69. Ibid., "Address of Hon. Horatio Seymour," 4.

70. Purcell, *Sealed with Blood*, 3.

71. Ellen Hardin Walworth, *Battles of Saratoga, 1777: The Saratoga Monument Association, 1856–1891* (Albany, NY: Joel Munsell's Sons, 1891), 53.

72. Ibid., 53–56; "Ellen Hardin Walworth," *National Historical Magazine* 74, no. 10 (October 1940): 15–16. For more on Mrs. Walworth's tragic life, see Geoffrey O'Brien, *The Fall of the House of Walworth: A Tale of Madness and Murder in Gilded Age America* (New York: St. Martin's Griffin, 2011).

73. Olausen et al., Saratoga National Historical Park, National Register of Historic Places Nomination Form, 51.

74. Ibid., 52.

75. Ibid., 52–53; Walworth, *Battles of Saratoga*, 70–110.

76. Olausen et al., Saratoga National Historical Park, National Register of Historic Places Nomination Form, 53.

77. Ellen Hardin Walworth, *Saratoga: The Battle-Battleground-Visitor's Guide* (New York: American News, 1877).

78. Olausen et al., Saratoga National Historical Park, National Register of Historic Places Nomination Form, 54–55.

79. Ibid., 55.

80. Ibid., 56.

81. Ibid., 60.

82. Ibid.

83. Ibid.

84. Ibid., 61.

85. Ibid.

86. Ibid., 62.

87. Ibid., 62–63.

88. Ibid., 63.

89. Ibid.

90. Ibid.

91. Ibid.

92. "Move to Restore Field at Saratoga: Patriotic Bodies and Rotarians Formulate Plan at Celebration on Battle Site," *New York Times*, September 20, 1925, special to the *New York Times*.

93. Olausen et al., Saratoga National Historical Park, National Register of Historic Places Nomination Form, 64.

94. Ibid.

95. Ibid.

96. Ibid.

97. Olmsted Center for Landscape Preservation, *Cultural Landscape Report: Saratoga Battlefield*, 118.

98. "The One Hundred and Fiftieth Anniversary, Battles of Saratoga and Surrender of Burgoyne. On the Battlefield, October 8th, 1927," official program, SARA Archives, B3, F4.

99. "1777 Saratoga 1927," advertising poster, J. D. Lyon Company, Albany, NY, SARA Archives, Slingerland Scrapbook, box 12 and 13.

100. "The One Hundred and Fiftieth Anniversary, Battles of Saratoga and Surrender of Burgoyne. On the Battlefield, October 8th, 1927," official program, SARA Archives, B3, F4.

101. "Burgoyne's Defeat Enacted in Pageant on Saratoga Field," *New York Times*, October 9, 1927, 1.

102. Olausen et al., Saratoga National Historical Park, National Register of Historic Places Nomination Form, 64.

103. Olmsted Center for Landscape Preservation, *Cultural Landscape Report: Saratoga Battlefield*, 118.

104. Olausen et al., Saratoga National Historical Park, National Register of Historic Places Nomination Form, 64–65.

105. Ibid., 65.

106. Ibid.

107. "Proposes Saratoga as National Shrine," *New York Times*, October 18, 1929, 3.

108. Ibid.

109. Olausen et al., Saratoga National Historical Park, National Register of Historic Places Nomination Form, 66.

110. Ibid.
111. Ibid.
112. Ibid., 65.
113. Ibid., 66.
114. Ibid.
115. Albright (1971), cited in ibid., 67.
116. Olausen et al., Saratoga National Historical Park, National Register of Historic Places Nomination Form, 67–68.
117. Ibid., 68.
118. Ibid., 69.
119. Ibid.
120. Ibid.
121. Ibid.
122. Ibid.
123. Ibid.
124. Ibid.; Robert W. Ehrich, "Progress Report on the Archeological Program of Saratoga National Historical Park," National Park Service, 1941.
125. Olausen et al., Saratoga National Historical Park, National Register of Historic Places Nomination Form, 69.
126. Ibid.
127. Charles W. Snell, "Historical Base Map, Part of the Master Plan," Saratoga National Historical Park, National Park Service, 1950.
128. Olausen et al., Saratoga National Historical Park, National Register of Historic Places Nomination Form, 70.
129. Ibid., 94–95.
130. Ibid., 70–71.
131. Olmsted Center for Landscape Preservation, *Cultural Landscape Report: Saratoga Battlefield, Saratoga National Historical Park*. Vol. 1, *Site History, Existing Conditions, and Analysis*, Saratoga National Historical Park, September 2002, 160.
132. Olmsted Center for Landscape Preservation, *Cultural Landscape Report: Saratoga Battlefield*, 160.
133. Ibid.
134. Ibid. Although these waysides are still in use, they are scheduled to be replaced over the next few years. The original film was replaced with a new film, *Something More at Stake*, in 2003.

About the Contributors

Justin DiVirgilio is the president and part owner of Hartgen Archeological Associates, a cultural resource management firm based in New York. A lifelong love of history and archaeology inspired him to make the change from engineering to anthropology. What started as a part-time field engagement with Hartgen unexpectedly became a career, during which he has been fortunate to learn from many wonderful people. Justin's proudest contributions to the field are his work on urban sites in Albany, New York, including a remarkably well-preserved rum distillery established during the French and Indian Wars; a group of row houses in an Irish American neighborhood in Sheridan Hollow, Albany's eighteenth-century waterfront; and comparative studies investigating health indicators and the medicinal use of heavy metals.

William Griswold, PhD, RPA, is the regional coordinator for the Archeological Resources Protection Act (ARPA) program in the Northeast Region of the National Park Service. Dr. Griswold has been with the National Park Service for twenty-two years and has conducted numerous archaeological and geophysical projects within national parks across the region during that time. He received his BA in anthropology from Missouri State University and his MA and PhD from Harvard University. Currently, he is archeological advisor for more than twenty parks within the Northeast Region, including Saratoga National Historical Park.

Matthew Kirk is an archaeologist with a BA in anthropology from Binghamton University and an MA from the University at Albany. He is a registered professional archaeologist (RPA) employed with Hartgen Archeological Associates, currently serving as the principal investigator. Mr. Kirk's scholarly work has been featured in popular publications and peer-reviewed journals. He regularly presents lectures at both professional conferences and public venues, often on his experiences with colonial sites in downtown Albany, New York.

Donald W. Linebaugh, PhD, RPA, is professor and area chair of the Historic Preservation Program in the University of Maryland's School of Architecture, Planning, and Preservation and associate dean for academic affairs. Dr. Linebaugh has published books on archaeologist Roland Robbins, *The Man Who Found Thoreau: Roland Wells Robbins and the Rise of Historical Archaeology in America* (University Press of New England, 2005); a historic ironworks, *Saugus Iron Works: The Roland W. Robbins Excavations 1948–1953* (edited volume with Dr. William Griswold, 2011); and, most recently, *The Springfield Gas Machine: Illuminating Industry and Leisure, 1860s to 1920s*, which focuses on historic lighting in the nineteenth century. In addition to these several books, he has completed numerous journal articles and book reviews, and has chapters in edited books on preservation, archaeology, history, and cultural resource management. Dr. Linebaugh is currently working on a new book about his several decades of research and excavation of the Kippax site in Virginia, a trading plantation belonging to the Bolling and Bland families.

John Luzader has served as historian with the Department of Defense; park historian and planning curator with the Branch of Museums; staff historian, colonial and Revolutionary periods, chief of historic preservation, and agency historian, all with the National Park Service. He has held lecturer appointments at the University of Virginia and the George Washington University. Mr. Luzader has written several books, including *Decision on the Hudson*, *Construction and Military History of Ft. Stanwix*, and *Saratoga: Military History of the Decisive Campaign of the American Revolution*. He is retired from the National Park Service.

Michael "Bodhi" Rogers is an associate professor in the Department of Physics and Astronomy at Ithaca College. He has PhD and MS degrees in physics and an MAIS in archaeology from Oregon State University. His archaeogeophysics and 3D laser-scanning research spans late Bronze Age cities in Cyprus, American Revolutionary War–era sites, and Haudenosaunee sites in central New York.

Eric H. Schnitzer has worked at Saratoga National Historical Park since 1997, becoming park ranger/historian in 2000. He has dedicated his life's study to the organization, personnel, and material culture of the British, German, and American armed forces of the American War for Independence, particularly the Northern Campaign of 1777. He lectures extensively on these subjects, has written articles for journals such as *The Hessians* and *The Brigade Dispatch*, and created illustrations for books such as *Philadelphia 1777*, *Wenches, Wives, and Servant Girls*, and *British Soldier, American War: Voices of the American Revolution*. He and his wife, Jenna, live in an eighteenth-century house in the White Creek historic district near Bennington Battlefield, New York, where they spend much of their time sewing reproduction eighteenth-century garments for living history and museum applications.

Dean R. Snow received his BA from the University of Minnesota and his PhD from the University of Oregon. He taught at the University of Maine for three years and at the University of Albany for twenty-six years, during which time he established and carried out archaeological research programs in highland Mexico, New England, New York, and the British Isles. He is known for his research into the paleodemography of prehistoric populations in all of these areas. His New York research included major projects on the Saratoga Battlefield, in the Lake George region, and in the Mohawk Valley. Snow moved to The Pennsylvania State University in 1995, where he served as head of the Department of Anthropology for the next ten years. In 2005, he was a fellow at Dumbarton Oaks in Washington, DC, before returning to Penn State as professor of anthropology. He served as president of the Society for American Archaeology from 2007 to 2009. In recent years, he has carried out research on human sexual dimorphism as expressed in hand stencils found in prehistoric art contexts in Europe and many other parts of the world. He has also been closely involved with the development of Digital Antiquity, a cyberinfrastructure program for the archiving of archaeological data initiated with funding from the Andrew Mellon Foundation.

David R. Starbuck is professor of anthropology at Plymouth State University in New Hampshire, and he has conducted research at eighteenth-century military sites in New York State since 1985. He has directed excavations at Saratoga National Historical Park, Mount Independence State Historic Site, Rogers Island, Fort Edward, Fort William Henry, and the Lake George Battlefield Park. His books on military topics include *The Great Warpath* (1999), *Massacre at Fort William Henry* (2002), *Rangers and Redcoats on the Hudson* (2004), *Excavating the Sutlers' House* (2010), *The Archaeology of Forts and Battlefields* (2011), and *The Legacy of Fort William Henry* (2014).

Scott Stull is a historic archaeologist with a focus on landscape and the built environment. He has more than fifteen years' experience in cultural resource management and has taught at Ithaca College, SUNY Cortland, and Cornell University. He has worked on colonial-era sites in New York, New Jersey, and Massachusetts, with a particular focus on New York's Mohawk and Hudson River valleys. He has an additional interest in the archaeology of medieval Western Europe, examining power relations and identity as expressed through the built environment. Dr. Stull received his PhD in anthropology from Binghamton University. He is currently a lecturer at SUNY Cortland and codirector of the Colonial Houses of the Mohawk Valley research project with Michael Rogers of Ithaca College.

Len Tantillo is a graduate of the Rhode Island School of Design and a licensed architect who left the field of architecture in 1986 to pursue a career in the fine art of historical and marine painting. Since that time, his work has appeared internationally in exhibitions, publications, and film documentaries. He is the author of four books and the recipient of two honorary degrees. He is a fellow of the American Society of Marine Artists. His work is included in the collections of the Fenimore Art Museum, the Minnesota Museum of Marine Art, numerous historical societies, and corporate and private collections in the United States and abroad. In 2004, he was commissioned by the Metropolitan Museum of Art to create a painting depicting the Daniel Winne house as it may have appeared in 1755. He has produced more than three hundred paintings and drawings of New York State history.

Christine Valosin is a graduate of Siena College with a degree in history, and studied for her MA in American history at the University at Albany, with an emphasis on community history in the nineteenth century. She is currently the museum curator at Saratoga National Historical Park (NHP), a position she has held since 2001. In this role, Ms. Valosin has overseen reorganizations of museum collection storage and numerous projects to catalog a variety of collections from archives to archaeology. She has researched topics on late eighteenth-century furnishings and the Schuyler family and has undertaken an effort to update furnishings and information at the Schuyler house, part of Saratoga NHP. She served as a regional representative for the formulation of strategic goals and objectives from 2011 to 2015 for the National Park Service Park Museum Management Program (PMMP). Prior to Saratoga, Ms. Valosin held the position of curator at the Saratoga Springs History Museum, and also worked at Brookside Museum (the Saratoga County Historical Society). She was also curator at Historic Cherry Hill in Albany, New York, a house museum with an intact family collection spanning five generations from the eighteenth to the twentieth centuries. She has presented on a variety of topics, including the Albany Army Relief Association, a local branch of the United States Sanitary Commission during the Civil War, and the Albany Army Relief Bazaar of 1864. Most recently she has given talks on the Schuyler family at Saratoga using the archaeology collections held by Saratoga NHP. Ms. Valosin's interest in community and family history led to a recently published article titled "'Where LaFleur Had Lived . . .': The Hidden History of a French Family in the Saratoga Patent, 1685–1708" in conjunction with ongoing research into the borderlands and conflict at Saratoga (Schuylerville).

Index

Page numbers in *italics* refer to tables or illustrations.

Albright, Horace, 250–51
Allen, Ethan, 14
American Cemetery, 247, 248, 249
American Divisional Headquarters, 127–28, *128–34*, 136–38, 141–42, 205–7
Amherst, Jeffrey, 10, 13
Appleman, Roy, 251
archaeological methods: aerial photography, xx, 86, 91–92, *93*; historical archaeology, x–xiii, 81, 114–17; LiDAR data sets, xx, *83*, 115; magnetometry, xx, 86, 91, *93*, 118, 132, 146–47, 170, 172, 184; soil coring, xx, 116, 117, 119, 120–24, 126n45; trench excavation, xxi, 114–17, 152–56, *153*, 189
Arnold, Benedict, 19, 22–23, 29–30, 45, 49–51, 53, 55, 66–67, 92–94, 128–129
Arnold Monument, xii, 94, 242, 244 (table), 245
artifacts: animal bones, 137, 140–41, 191; as battle souvenirs, 233–34; camp and combat artifacts, 211–18; ceramics/tableware, 137, 140, 141, 202, 204–5, 206–7, 209–10; class status and, 192, 206; clothing/buttons, 137, 141, 191, 206, 212; coins, 140; cookware, 140, 196, 218; farm equipment, 202–3; foodstuff, 137, 140–41, 160; glassware, 206–7; military artifacts, 139, 191, 205; Native American, xiii, xivn36, xxi, 145, 180, 187–88, 192; pocket watch, 210–11; prehistoric artifacts, 187–88; tobacco pipes, 134, 209–10, 211–12, 223–24

Balcarres Redoubt (Light Infantry Redoubt): archaeological evidence of, xi–xii, 84–87; burials, xii, 30, 85, *85*, 87–91, 197; construction of, xx, 58, 77n62; farm structures, 90–91; function of, 59–60, 83–84; geophysical survey of, 58, 59, 79n91, 84–87; historical reconstruction of, 81–83, 100–1; maps of, *82*, *83*, *85*; strategic placement of, 22, 24, 57–59, 83–84. *See also* Battle of Bemis Heights
Barber Wheat fields, 27, 60–61, 64, 68, 77nn69–70, 88, 198, 214, 221
Battle of Bemis Heights: American advance/response, 65–68, 109; Balcarres Redoubt, 64–65; battle reconstruction, 62–65; Breymann Redoubt, 65; British advance/response, 60–68, 109; Canadian involvement, 68n2; casualties, 64, 65, 66, 67, 75n53, 78n83, 78n87; combatants, 62–63, 64, 68n2, 68n7, 73n43, 76n58; commander effectiveness, 63–64, 65, 66–68, 75n56, 75n60, 79n93; German involvement, 43, 62–63, 64, 68n2, 78n87; maps of, *47*, *61*, 70n11; Marshall farm, 64–65; Native American involvement, 68n2, 69n5; natural landscape, 64–65, 69n10; tactical and strategic assessment of, 65–65, 75n49, 75n51, 79n95; weaponry/equipment, 62–63, 66, 69n3, 73n43, 74nn45–48, 79n95. *See also* Balcarres Redoubt; Breymann Redoubt
Battle of Bunker Hill, 44, 75n49, 75n51, 236, 237 (table), 239
Battle of Freeman's Farm: American advance/response, xx, 50–51, 53–57, 59–62; battle reconstruction, 45–51; British advance/response, xx, 45, 51, 53–57, 59–62; Canadian involvement, 68n2; casualties, 53, 55–56, 71n18; combatants, 40, 41–42, 44, 48, 51, 53–54, 68n2, 68n7, 69n5, 70n14, 70nn13–14, 72nn25–26; commander effectiveness, 53–55, 56, 70n14, 70n16, 71n18; Freeman farm, 211–12, 233–34, 246; German involvement, 43, 52–53, 56–57, 68n2; maps of, *47*, *61*, 70n11; Native American involvement, 68n2, 69n5;

Battle of Freeman's Farm (*continued*) natural landscape, 45–48, 52–53, 54–55, 60–61, 69n4, 69n10; tactical and strategic assessment of, 53–57, 70n14, 70n16, 71nn18–19, 72n23; weaponry/equipment, 50, 51, 54, 56, 71n19, 72nn24–25. *See also* Balcarres Redoubt; Breymann Redoubt

Battle of Valcour, 8, 55, 75n51

Bell, Thomas, 104n43

Bemis Heights: American fortifications, 20–22, 127–28; archaeological information, 114–17; Chastellux description of, 231; geophysical information, 24, 108–9, 117–24; historical information, 109–14; maps of, 110–14. *See also* American Divisional Headquarters; Battle of Bemis Heights; Fort Neilson; River Overlook fortifications

Bemus, Jotham, 106, 201–2

Bemus Tavern, 110, 128, 200, 201, 205, 244

Bender, Susan, 187

Bevan, Bruce, 118

Bissell, George, 242

Bliss, C. M., 241

Bodnar, John, 236

Bolton, Reginald Pelham, x–xi, xxiiin12

Booth Brothers, 239–40, 242

Brandow, John Henry, 151, 181, 182, 184, 188, 192

Breymann, Heinrich, 21, 24–25, 29, 41–43, 64–67, 78n87

Breymann Redoubt: archaeological research, 91–94, 212–14; burials, 94–95, 101; construction of, xx, 58–59, 77n63, 100–101; function of, 59–60; historical reconstruction of, 81–83, 100–101; maps of, 82, 83, 91–94; strategic placement of, xx, 22–24, 58–59

Brumbach, Hetty Jo, 187

Buel, Ezra "Major," 232, 256n16

Burgoyne, John: American/British fighting, 15–20; British forces and, 2–11, 14, 68; Burgoyne retreat, xxi, 148–51, 156–58; Canadian forces and, 58, 59–60; Champlain-Hudson corridor and, 6–7; Chastellux description of, 231; effectiveness of, 53–55, 56, 63–64, 65, 66–68; Germaine and, 1, 3–5, 11–12, 26, 174–75; military strategies of, 8–12; post-surrender, 173–75; retreat and surrender, xxi, 30–34, 68, 145, 148–51, 156–58, 163–65, 166–67; Schuyler estate and, xxii, 179, 181–82; Stansbury on, 234; strategic positions and tactics, 8, 35n26, 40–43

burials: Balcarres Redoubt, xii, 30, 85, 87–91, 197; Breymann Redoubt, 94–95; female casualties, 89–90; Fraser burial site, 97; Freeman's farm, 211–12; Great Redoubt, 97; Woodworth farm complex, 129–30, 132, 134, 142, 144n25

Calver, William F., x–xi, xxiiin12

Canadian camps, 95–96

Carleton, Guy, 2, 6–9, 11, 12, 17, 18

Champlain Canal, 97, 181, 183, 204, 209

Chastellux, Marquis de, 116, 231

Checkmate on the Hudson (1977), 253

Clinton, Henry, 1, 3, 7–8, 10, 24, 25, 31, 57

commemoration: bicentennial celebration, 253–54; centennial celebrations, 240–41; funding for, 238–40, 241–42, 252–53; government support for, 230, 239, 241–42, 244–46, 248–49, 252–253; impact of photography on, 240; memorials and monuments, 229, 235–40; patriotism and, 236; private citizen support and, 230, 237, 238, 246; public movements for, 235–36; Roosevelt and, 221, 249, 250–51, 254; Saratoga semicentennial/jubilee, 235; sermon narrative, 230; Sesquicentennial Celebration, 246–50; Slingerland and, 196, 246–50, 250; teaching curricula, 230

Corey, John A., 238

Cornwallis, Lord, 1, 5, 231

Cotter, John: Bemis Heights and, 116, 128; Neilson House and, 128, 199–201, 202, 207, 209, 227n21, 227n24, 252; NPS and, xii, 252; Schuyler house and, xxii, 183–91

Couch, J. J., 240

Dalan, Rinita, 118

de Fermoy, Alexis, 14

Denison, William, 129

de Peyster, John Watts, 239–40, 242

DiVirgilio, Justin, xxi, 145–62
Dwight, Timothy, 232

earthworks: at Balcarres Redoubt, xx, 24–25, 58, 86–87, 100–101; at Breymann Redoubt, 58–59, 93–94, 100, 101; fascines, xx, 169, 171, 173; at Fort Hardy, xix, 168–73; at River Overlook, 109–17, 118–23; at Victory Woods, 145, 148, 149–50, 151, 152–56, 158–60
Ehrich, Robert: Balcarres Redoubt and, xi–xii, 84–90, 197; Breymann Redoubt and, xii, 93, 94; Freeman's Farm, 211–12; Neilson house, 127–28, 197, 202; reconnaissance of Saratoga battlefields, xi–xii, 17–18, 83, 114–17, 197, 214, 215, 251
Ellsworth, (Phoebe) Annie Esmond, 222
Esmond, Burton, 246
Esmond, William W., 211, *212*, 222
European settlement, xvi, xviii–xix, 147, 157, 166, 181
Evans, Israel (Reverend), 230–31

Faden, William, 113–14
Faden map, 113–14, 118, 146, 166, 167
Field of Grounded Arms, 166–67, 168, 173, 176, 241. *See also* Fort Hardy
Fish, Hamilton, 238
Flick, Alexander, 246, 247, *250*
Fort Hardy: archaeological survey of, 169–71, 174; Burgoyne retreat to, 163–65, 166–67; contemporary use of, 168; documentary evidence of, 168–69; earthworks at, xix, 168–73; fascines at, 169, 171, 173; Field of Grounded Arms, 166–67, 168, 173, 176, 241; geophysical survey of, xxi, 168–73; landscape analysis, 165–66; maps of, 167; overview of, 168–69; public dissemination of discoveries, 171–72, 176; reconstruction of, 169–73, 174
Fort Neilson, 114, 128, 130, 244 (table), 247. *See also* Neilson House
Fort Saratoga (Fort Vrooman), xviii
Fort Ticonderoga, ix–x, 8, 13–20, 23, 33, 41, 55, 107, 157, 159, 165
Fraser, Simon: British advance, 14–16, 21–28, 41–42, 48, 50–51, 64–65, 149–50;

Fraser Hill, 201, 251; funeral procession, 104n44; shooting of, 78n83, 81–82, 98, 99, 101, 104n41. *See also* Taylor House
Fraser Hill, 201, 251
Freeman's Farm, 211–12, 233–34, 246. *See also* Battle of Freeman's Farm; Wright Farm
French drain, 138–39, 190, *191*
Funk, Robert E., xvii, xxivn36, 187–88

Gannon Farm, 246
Gansevoort, Peter, 17, 238
Gates, Horatio: background of, 13, 18–19; Burgoyne defeat, ix, 30–34, 65–68, 145, 163–67; post-surrender, 173–75; Price farm headquarters, 127, 234; Saratoga campaigns, 15–20, 20–30, 69n5; strategic analysis of, 13, 19–20, 43–44, 54–55, 57, 60–62, 65–68, 109; on value of fortifications, 105–7, 109, 112; Woodworth headquarters, 109, 128–32, 142, 201–2, 205–7. *See also* Woodworth farm complex
geophysical methods: advantage of using, 124; aerial photography, 86, 91–92, 93; anomaly detection, xxiiin7, 86, 118–20, 122, 124, 126n45, 147; as discipline, xxiiin7; ground penetrating radar, 118, 119, 123, 146, 170–71; impact of on commemoration, 240; soil coring, xx, 116, 117, 119, 120–24, 126n45
George, King, III, 9–10
Germaine, George, 1, 3–5, 11–12, 26, 174–75
Great Redoubt, 24, 88, 96–100, 101
Griswold, William A., ix–xxv, 105–26
Groton Battle Monument (CT), 236, 237, 238, 239
Gruber, Jacob W., x–xi, xxiiin12
Guilford Court House National Military Park, 244

Halleck, Fritz Green, 241
Hamilton, James, 21, 27–28, 42–43, 48, 50–51, 55–57, 70n13, 72n24, 76n60, 84, 149
Hancock, John, 13
Harrington, Jean C. "Pinky," xii–xiii
Harvey, Edward, 10, 12

Hesse-Hanau Artillery, 15, 39–40, 42, 61, 64, 148
hospital sites, 127, 129, 133–34, 135–36, 142, 206
Howe, Richard, 6
Howe, William, 1–7, 10–12
Hoyt, Epaphras 129–30, 183
Hsu, Dick Ping, 142n1

Johnson, Eric, xvii
Judd, Henry, 207

King William's War, xviii
Kirk, Matthew, xxi, 145–62
Kosciuszko, Thaddeus, xx–xxi, 63, 105–9, 114, 123–24, 128. *See also* River Overlook fortifications

Lafayette, General, 234–35, 236
Larrabee, Edward, xxii, 183–91, 192, 208, 209
Lavasseur, Auguste, 234–35
Lee, Stanton P., 248
Light Infantry Redoubt. *See* Balcarres Redoubt
Linebaugh, Donald W., ix–xxv, 229–58
Livingston, Henry Brockholst, 23
Livingston, Phillip, xviii
Livingston, Robert, xix, 148
Livingston, William, 5–6
Lossing, Benson, 97, 98, 99–100, 130, 133–34, 136, 182
Luzader, John, xix–xx, 1–38

Mackesy, Piers, 1, 33
maps: Balcarres Redoubt (Light Infantry Redoubt), 82, 83, 85; Battle of Bemis Heights, 47, 61, 70n11; Battle of Freeman's Farm, 47, 61, 70n11; battle reconstruction maps, 14, 21, 27, 47, 61; Bemis Heights, 110–14; Breymann Redoubt, 82, 83, 91–94; Faden map, 113–14, 118, 146, 166, 167; Fort Hardy, 167; Putnam map, 110–11, 116–18, 119, 125n27; of River Overlook, 110–14, 116–17, 118; Varick map, 110; Victory Woods, 146, 152; Wilkinson map, 112–13
Markham, Jared C., 239, 241, 242

McCarty, John, 201, 202
McCarty warrant, 201, 202
McCrea, Jane, 131
memorialization: American Cemetery, 247, 248, 249; Arnold Monument, xii, 94, 242, 244 (table), 245; battlefield preservation, 243–46, 254; battle monuments, 235–40, 241–44; historical memory and, 232; nostalgia for the past and, 235–36; patriotism and, 236; reenactments, 247–48; tourism, 233–35; travel narratives, 231–33; vernacular memorials, 232–33. *See also* commemoration
Miliius, Feldprediger, 111–12
military parks, 243–46, 254
Mission 66 program, 201, 252–53
Moore, Jackson, 183
Mount Independence (VT), 13, 14, 16, 55, 131, 181–82
Murphy, Timothy, 78n83, 81–82, 98, 99, 101, 104n41

National Park Service (NPS): battlefield preservation, 243–46, 249, 250–53, 254; Cotter and, xii; development of, 250–53; military parks, 243–46, 249, 250–53, 254. *See also* Saratoga National Historical Park
Native Americans: artifacts of, xiii, xivn36, xxi, 145, 180, 187–88, 192; Battle of Bemis Heights and, 68n2, 69n5; Battle of Freeman's Farm and, 68n2, 69n5; European settlement and, xviii, 128, 147; fish runs, xvi–xvii; Hudson Valley settlements, xv–xvi, xvi–xviii; Mahicans (Mohicans), xvii–xviii; Mohawks, xvii–xviii; Saratoga campaigns and, 7, 17, 19, 68n2, 148, 203–4
Neilson, John, 23, 128, 199–203
Neilson House, xii, 107, 110, 116–17, 127–28, 197–203, 204, 246, 247, 252. *See also* Bemis Heights; Fort Neilson; River Overlook fortifications

Ochs, Adolph, 246, 247, 250

Paoli Massacre, 237
Paterson, John, 14, 18–19
Päusch, Georg, 15, 24, 64, 82

Philadelphia Centennial Exhibition (1876), 240
Poor, Enoch, 14, 22, 28–29, 50, 51, 53, 54, 57, 61, 62, 63
Price, William, 127, 129
Purcell, Sarah, 230, 235–36
Putnam map, 110–11, 116–18, 119, 125n27

Queen Anne's War, xviii

Reeve, Stuart, 116–17
Revolutionary Monument (MA), 236, 237
Riedesel, Friedrich Adolph von, 16–17, 21, 25–29, 42–43, 51–57, 149, 155–58
River Overlook fortifications: archaeological excavations, 114–17, 123; as bottleneck, xx–xxi, 108–9, 123; design/building of, xx–xxi, 105–9, 123; geophysical methods and, xxi, 117–23, 123–24; historical accounts of, 109–14, 123; maps of, 110–14, 116–17, 118; North Redan, 116, 119; overview of, xx–xxi, 105; Putnam map, 110–11, 116–18, 119, 125n27; South Redan, xx, 105, 117–18, 119; Varick map, 110. *See also* Burgoyne, John; Neilson House
Rochefoucauld-Liancourt, Duc de la, 231–32
Rogers, James, 217–18
Rogers, Michael "Bodhi," xxi, 163–77

Saratoga Battlefield Association, 211, 246
Saratoga Campaign: American advance, 12–15; American/British engagement, 15–30; battle reconstruction, 14, 20–30, 47, 61; British advance, 2–11, 14, 57–62; Burgoyne's strategy, 40–43; Canadian involvement, 59; Fort Ticonderoga engagements, 15–20; Freeman farm fight, 22–23; Gates's strategy, 13, 19–20, 43–44, 54–55, 57, 60–62, 65–68, 109; historical context, xx–xxi; personnel composition, 39–40; political situation, xx–xxi; popular media and, 39–40, 81–83; retreat and surrender, 30–34; soldier formations, 39–40. *See also* Battle of Bemis Heights; Battle of Freeman's Farm; Burgoyne, John
Saratoga Massacre, xviii
Saratoga Monument Association, 151, 237 (table), 238, 241–44, 243–46, 253, 254

Saratoga National Historical Park: battlefield preservation, 243–46, 249, 250–53, 254; Breymann Fortified Camp, 212–14; camp and combat artifacts, 211–18, 220–22; collection development, 195–97; Convention of Saratoga draft, 218–20; Freeman's Farm, 211–12; furniture collection, 224–25; manuscript collections, 201, 217, 218–19, 218–20; memorabilia collection, 222; Mission 66 program, 201, 252–53; Nielson Farm, 197–203; overview of, xxi–xxii, 195–96; public dissemination of discoveries, 171–72, 176; Roosevelt and, *221*, 249, *250*, 250–51, 254; Schuyler Estate, 205–11; Slingerland and, 196, 246–50, *250*; soldier's loot, 222–24; Taylor House, 203–5; weapons collection, 220–21; Woodworth House, 205–7. *See also* Cotter, John; Larrabee, Edward; National Park Service
Saratoga Patent, xviii, 77n69, 128, 147, 197, 200, 202, 204
Saratoga region: environmental settings of, xiii–xvi; European settlement of, xvi, xviii–xix, 147, 157, 166, 181, 197; Native American settlement of, xvi–xviii; prehistory of, xvi–xviii; tourism and, ix–x, xxii, 222, 229–30, 233–35
Schnitzer, Eric, xx, 39–79
Schuyler, John, 231–32
Schuyler, Phillip: bio of, xxi–xxii, 179, 181–83; Kosciuszko and, 106; Marquis de Chastellux and, 231; Native Americans and, 147; Saratoga Patent and, 147–48; Varick and, 110–11
Schuyler estate: archaeological survey of, xxi–xxii, 179–80, 207–11; artifact collection, 207–11; British campaign and, xxii, 179, 181–82; Burgoyne's soldiers and, xxii; burned structure artifacts, 183–84, 192, 208, 209–10; destruction of, 181–82, 182–83; Fort Hardy and, xix; French and Indian War and, 180; Lafayette visit to, 234–35; mills, xxii, 179, 181; NPS acquisition of, xxii, 179–80, 183; overview of estate, xxi–xxii, 179–83, 192, 207; Schuyler mansion, 179, 182–86, 191–93
Sesquicentennial Celebration, 246–50, *248*

Seymour, Horatio, 238, 241, 242
Silliman, Benjamin, 129, 183, 232–33
Slingerland, George O., 196, 246–50, 250
Smith, Alfred E., 247
Snell, Charles W., 68n2, 81, 83, 110, *111*, 116–17, 252
Snow, Dean R., xx, 81–104; American headquarters excavation, 128; Breymann camp, 212–14; River Overlook excavation, 116–17; Taylor House and, 204
Something More at Stake (2003), 258n134
Southern Redan, xx, 105, 117–118, 119
Stansbury, Phillip, 234
Starbuck, David R., xxi, xxi–xxii, 127–44, 179–93, 197, 204, 206, 207, 227n21
Starin, John H., 241–42
State of New Hampshire Monument, 247
St. Clair, Arthur, 13–17
Stone, William Leete, 99, 164–65, 238, 239, 240–41
Storozynski, Alex, 106
Street, Alfred B., 238
Strover, George, 238
Stull, Scott, xxi, 163–77

Tantillo, Len, xxi, 163–77
Taylor, John, 204
Taylor House, 96, 97, 100, 101, 104n42, 198, 203–5
tourism, ix–x, xxii, 222, 229–30, 233–35

Uhlig, Heinrich Wilhelm, 77n66

Valosin, Christine, xxii, 195–228
Van Cortlandt, Phillip, 79n91
Varick, Richard, 22–23, 71n22, 75n52, 110–11, 116
Varick map, 110
Victory Woods: archaeological excavation, xxi, 146–47, 152–56, 160n2; British troops and, 148–52; Burgoyne retreat, xxi, 145, 148–51, 156–58; cultural artifacts, 156, 158–60; earthworks at, 145, 148, 149–50, 151, 152–56, 158–60; Fort Hardy, 147–48; geophysical survey of, xxi, 146–47, 160n2, 161n4; maps of, 146, 152; modern development of, 148, 151–52; Native American artifacts, 145; natural landscape, 147–48, 151–52; overview of, 145–48, 160; Saratoga Patent, 147–48. *See also* Fort Hardy
Vrooman, Bartel, xviii

Walworth, Ellen Hardin, 240, 241–43, 256n72
Warren, Benjamin, 29
Washington, George, 1, 5, 12–13, 175, 230, 235
Washington Monument (Baltimore, MD), 236, 237, 238
weaponry/equipment: Battle of Bemis Heights, 62–63, 66, 69n3, 73n43, 74nn45–48, 79n95; Battle of Freeman's Farm, 50, 51, 54, 56, 71n19, 72nn24–25; camp and combat artifacts, 211–18; military artifacts, 139, 191, 205; naval equipment, 75n51
Webster, Daniel, 236
Weisser House, 60–61, 64, 77n70
West, Edward, 130–31
Wilkinson, James, 13–17, 23, 28, 31, 62, 70n14, 70n16, 73n32, 82, 112
Wilkinson, William C., xi–xii, 70n11, 83–85, 90, 91, 93–97, 100, 102n5, 102n8, 112–13, 116–18, 127–28
Wilkinson map, 112–13
Williams, Griffith, 14
Wilshin, Frances, 251
Wirt, William, 233–34
Wood, W. J., 109
Woodruff, Samuel, 138–39, 235
Woodworth farm complex: archaeological fieldwork, 131–41, 197; artifacts from, 139–41, 192, 206; burial grounds, 132, 142; as Gates's headquarters, 109, 201–2, 205–7; NPS acquisition, 127; overview of, 127–30, 128–34, 141–42, 205–7; Woodworth field hospital, 127, 129, 135–36, 142, 144n25, 206; Woodworth House, 109, 134–35, 201–2, 205–7
Wright Farm, 246